PHP
A Beginner's Guide

About the Author

Vikram Vaswani is the founder and CEO of Melonfire (www.melonfire.com/), a consultancy firm with special expertise in open-source tools and technologies. He is a passionate proponent of the open-source movement and frequently contributes articles and tutorials on open-source technologies—including Perl, Python, PHP, MySQL, and Linux—to the community at large. His previous books include *MySQL: The Complete Reference* (www.mysql-tcr.com/), *How to Do Everything with PHP and MySQL* (www.everythingphpmysql.com/), and *PHP Programming Solutions* (www.php-programming-solutions.com/).

Vikram has over ten years of experience working with PHP and MySQL as an application developer. He is the author of Zend Technologies' *PHP 101* series for PHP beginners, and he has extensive experience deploying PHP in a variety of different environments (including corporate intranets, high-traffic Internet Web sites, and mission-critical thin client applications).

A Felix Scholar at the University of Oxford, England, Vikram combines his interest in Web application development with various other activities. When not dreaming up plans for world domination, he amuses himself by reading crime fiction, watching old movies, playing squash, blogging, and keeping an eye out for unfriendly Agents. Read more about him and *PHP: A Beginner's Guide* at www.php-beginners-guide.com.

About the Technical Editor

Chris Cornutt has been involved in the PHP community for more than eight years. Soon after discovering the language, he started up his news site, PHPDeveloper.org, to share the latest happenings and opinions from other PHPers around the world. Chris has written for PHP publications such as *php|architect* and the *International PHP Magazine* on topics ranging from geocoding to trackbacks. He is also a coauthor of *PHP String Handling* (Wrox Press, 2003). Chris lives in Dallas, Texas, with his wife and son, and works for a large natural gas distributor maintaining their Web site and developing PHP-based applications.

PHP
A Beginner's Guide

Vikram Vaswani

McGraw
Hill

New York Chicago San Francisco
Lisbon London Madrid Mexico City
Milan New Delhi San Juan
Seoul Singapore Sydney Toronto

The **McGraw·Hill** Companies

Library of Congress Cataloging-in-Publication Data

Vaswani, Vikram.
 PHP : a beginner's guide / Vikram Vaswani.
   p. cm.
 Includes index.
 ISBN 978-0-07-154901-1 (alk. paper)
 1. PHP (Computer program language) I. Title.
 QA76.73.P224V378 2007
 005.13'3—dc22

                          2008039041

McGraw-Hill books are available at special quantity discounts to use as premiums and sales
promotions, or for use in corporate training programs. To contact a special sales representative,
please visit the Contact Us page at www.mhprofessional.com.

PHP: A Beginner's Guide

1 2 3 4 5 6 7 8 9 0   FGR FGR   0 1 9 8

ISBN   978-0-07-154901-1
MHID   0-07-154901-3

Sponsoring Editor   Jane K. Brownlow

Editorial Supervisor   Janet Walden

Project Manager   Harleen Chopra, International Typesetting and Composition

Acquisitions Coordinator   Jennifer Housh

Technical Editor   Chris Cornutt

Copy Editor   Bob Campbell

Proofreader   Jean Butterfield

Indexer   Claire Splan

Production Supervisor   Jean Bodeaux

Composition   International Typesetting and Composition

Illustration   International Typesetting and Composition

Art Director, Cover   Jeff Weeks

For Gurgle and Tonka, my two babies

Contents at a Glance

Contents

Foreword

I have been programming computers for a long time. In that time, I have moved between more languages than I can count. With each new language, I have always said that once you learn how to program properly, everything else is just syntax. I still believe that's true for a lot of languages, but for PHP, that may be an oversimplification.

In PHP, there are usually several ways to accomplish any given task. Some of them are better than others, but a few of them—mainly, anything that requires the `globals` command—are outright wrong. This is always confusing to programmers new to PHP because if there are several correct ways to accomplish a task, how do you know which one is the best? "Best Practices" has been a theme in the PHP community for several years now as an attempt to answer this question.

Whenever a new member of the PHP community asks me where to learn the Best Practices of programming PHP, I invariably point them to Vikram's "PHP 101" series, posted in several places around the Web. His work on that 14-part series has earned him a name in the community as an authority not only on teaching new users how to program but teaching them how to program correctly.

I have had the pleasure of working with Vikram for two years now on DevZone. His articles are without a doubt some of the most popular we have published. I know as you read this book you will come to understand why.

—Cal Evans
Editor-in-chief, Zend's DevZone

Acknowledgments

This book was written across 2007 and 2008, when PHP 5.3 was still under development. Writing a book about a piece of software that is still under development is always a challenging task. Fortunately, I was aided immeasurably in the process by a diverse group of people, all of whom played an important role in getting this book into your hands.

First and foremost, I'd like to thank my wife, who helped keep me grounded throughout the process. Beauty and intelligence: I lack both, but fortunately she more than makes up for my failings. Thanks, babe!

The editorial and marketing team at McGraw-Hill Professional has been a pleasure to work with (as usual). This is my fourth book with them, and they seem to get better and better with each one. Acquisitions coordinator Jennifer Housh, technical editor Chris Cornutt, and executive editor Jane Brownlow all guided this book through the development process and played no small part in turning it from concept into reality. I'd like to thank them for their expertise, dedication, and efforts on my behalf.

Finally, for making the entire book-writing process more enjoyable than it usually is, thanks to: Patrick Quinlan, Ian Fleming, Bryan Adams, the Stones, Peter O'Donnell, *MAD Magazine*, Scott Adams, FHM, Gary Larson, VH1, George Michael, Kylie Minogue, *Buffy*, Farah Malegam, Adam and Anna, Stephen King, Shakira, Anahita Marker, Park End, John le Carre, Barry White, Gwen Stefani, Robert Crais, Robert B. Parker, Baz Luhrmann, Stefy, Anna Kournikova, John Connolly, Wasabi, Omega, Pidgin, Cal Evans,

Ling's Pavilion, Tonka and his evil twin Bonka, Din Tai Fung, HBO, Mark Twain, Tim Burton, Harish Kamath, Madonna, John Sandford, Iron Man, the Tube, Dido, Google.com, *The Matrix*, Lee Child, Michael Connelly, Quentin Tarantino, Alfred Hitchcock, Woody Allen, Percy Jackson, the St. Hugh's College bops, Booty Luv, Mambo's and Tito's, Easyjet, Humphrey Bogart, Thai Pavilion, Brix, Wikipedia, *24*, Amazon.com, U2, The Three Stooges, Pacha, Oscar Wilde, Hugh Grant, Punch, Kelly Clarkson, Scott Turow, Slackware Linux, Calvin and Hobbes, Blizzard Entertainment, Alfred Kropp, Otto, Pablo Picasso, Popeye and Olive Oyl, Dennis Lehane, Trattoria, Dire Straits, Bruce Springsteen, David Mitchell, *The West Wing*, Santana, Rod Stewart, and all my friends, at home and elsewhere.

Introduction

No matter which way you cut it, PHP is pretty amazing: a language strung together by volunteer programmers that today has the enviable distinction of being in use on more than *a third* of the planet's Web servers. Flexible, scalable, extensible, stable, open—PHP is all of these and more, which is why it's one of the most popular programming toolkits in the world.

Ask me why I like PHP, though, and my reason has nothing to do with any of the preceding buzzwords and everything to do with how friendly and nonthreatening the language is. There's no tortuous syntax or obfuscated code in the average PHP script: instead, it's clear, understandable, and easy to read, and this makes both programming and debugging with it a pleasure. This is no small achievement: a shorter learning curve makes it easier for novice programmers to quickly begin "doing something useful" with the language, and increases both user interest and adoption levels. This isn't just good design: it's smart marketing as well!

As an open-source project, PHP is completely free, and supported by a worldwide community of volunteers. This open-source, community-driven approach has produced a platform that is significantly more robust and error-free than many commercial alternatives. So using PHP is also good economics for organizations: it allows them to save on licensing fees and expensive server hardware, while simultaneously producing higher-quality products in shorter time frames.

If all these sound like good reasons to begin looking into PHP, well, you're in the right place. This book will guide you through the world of PHP, teaching you to write basic PHP programs and then enhance them with more advanced features such as database queries, XML input, and third-party extensions. In short, it has everything necessary to turn you into a PHP expert . . . and it might even make you crack a smile on occasion!

So come on in, and let's get started.

Who Should Read This Book

As you might have guessed from the title, *PHP: A Beginner's Guide* is intended for users who are new to the PHP programming language. Unlike many other books, *PHP: A Beginner's Guide* doesn't assume prior knowledge of Web programming or database fundamentals. Rather, it teaches by example, using in-chapter projects and examples to explain basic concepts and, thus, gradually increase the reader's familiarity with PHP concepts and programming tools. Therefore, it is most suitable for novice programmers who are familiar with HTML and CSS, and are interested in widening their skill set to also build dynamic, data-driven sites using PHP.

What This Book Covers

PHP: A Beginner's Guide contains information on the PHP 5.2 and 5.3-alpha programming toolkit and its most commonly used features: MySQL and SQLite database integration, XML processing capabilities, and third-party extensions. It provides one-stop coverage of software installation, language syntax and data structures, flow control routines, built-in functions, and best practices. Each chapter also includes numerous practical projects that the reader can "follow along with" to gain a practical understanding of the material being discussed.

The following outline describes the contents of the book and shows how the book is broken down into task-focused chapters.

Part I: Understanding PHP Basics

Chapter 1: Introducing PHP introduces the PHP programming language, explains why it's so popular for Web application development, and explains how the components of a typical PHP system interact.

Chapter 2: Using Variables and Operators explains PHP's data types, variables, and operators, and discusses one of PHP's most popular applications, form input processing.

Chapter 3: Controlling Program Flow demonstrates how to add intelligence to PHP scripts with conditional statements, automate repetitive tasks with loops, and make use of built-in functions for working with strings and numbers.

Chapter 4: Working with Arrays introduces PHP's array data type, explains how it can be used with loops and Web forms, and demonstrates some of PHP's built-in functions to sort, merge, add, modify, and split arrays.

Chapter 5: Using Functions and Classes provides a crash course in two of PHP's more complex features, functions and classes. Recursion, variable-length argument lists, visibility, extensibility, and reflection are just some of the topics covered in this chapter, which focuses on PHP's frameworks for turning frequently used code blocks into reusable components.

Part II: Working with Data from Other Sources

Chapter 6: Working with Files and Directories explains PHP's file system functions, demonstrating the PHP routines available to read and write files, create and modify directories, and work with file paths and attributes.

Chapter 7: Working with Databases and SQL explains databases and Structured Query Language (SQL), and then introduces the two databases most commonly used with PHP: MySQL and SQLite. It illustrates how PHP can be used to build Web applications that interact with a database to view, add, and edit data, and also discusses new database portability features.

Chapter 8: Working with XML explains basic XML concepts and technologies, and discusses how PHP can be used to process XML data using the SimpleXML extension.

Chapter 9: Working with Cookies, Sessions, and Headers explains PHP's built-in functions to create sessions and cookies, and demonstrates how these functions can be used to make Web applications more user-friendly.

Part III: Security and Troubleshooting

Chapter 10: Handling Errors focuses on PHP's error-handling framework. It explains the PHP error and exception model, and shows how to create customized error handling routines tailored to specific requirements.

Chapter 11: Securing PHP discusses security issues and common attacks, and suggests ways to increase the security of a PHP application. It discusses key application-hardening techniques of input validation, output escaping, and PHP security configuration.

Chapter 12: Extending PHP introduces you to two of the largest repositories of free PHP code on the Internet: PEAR, the PHP Extension and Application Repository, and PECL, the PHP Extension Community Library. It explains how freely available components from these repositories can be used to quickly add new capabilities and features to PHP, making application development faster and more effective.

Part IV: Appendixes

The appendixes include reference material for the information presented in the first three parts.

Appendix A: Installing and Configuring Required Software discusses the process of obtaining, installing, and configuring Apache, PHP, MySQL, and SQLite.

Appendix B: Answers to Self Test provides answers to the self-test questions that appear at the end of each chapter in this book.

Chapter Content

- **Try This**   Each chapter contains at least one self-contained, hands-on project that is relevant to the topic under discussed and that the reader can use to gain a practical understanding of the material.

- **Ask the Expert**   Each chapter contains one or two Ask the Expert sections that provide expert guidance and information on questions that might arise about the material presented in the chapter.

- **Self Test**   Each chapter ends with a Self Test, which is a set of questions that tests you on the information and skills you learned in that chapter. The answers to the Self Test are included in Appendix B, at the end of the book.

Part I

Understanding
PHP Basics

Chapter 1

Introducing PHP

Key Skills & Concepts

- Know PHP's history

- Learn PHP's unique capabilities for Web application development

- See how the components of a PHP system interact

- Understand the basic grammar and structure of a PHP script

- Create and run a simple PHP program

- Embed PHP in an HTML page

PHP. Three letters that together constitute the name of one of the world's most popular programming languages for Web development, the PHP Hypertext Preprocessor. And while you might chuckle at the geekiness of the recursive acronym, statistics indicate that PHP is not be taken lightly: the language is today in use on over *twenty million* Web sites and more than a third of the world's Web servers—no small feat, especially when you consider that the language has been developed entirely by a worldwide community of volunteers and is freely available on the Internet at no cost whatsoever!

Over the last few years, PHP has become the de facto choice for the development of data-driven Web applications, notably on account of its scalability, ease of use, and widespread support for different databases and data formats. This first chapter will gently introduce you to the world of PHP, by taking you on a whirlwind tour of PHP's history and features, and then guiding you through writing and executing your first PHP program. So flip the page, and let's get started!

History

The current version of PHP, PHP 5.3, has been more than fourteen years in the making; its lineage can be traced back to 1994, when a developer named Rasmus Lerdorf first created a set of CGI scripts to monitor page views for his online résumé. This early version of PHP, named PHP/FI, was fairly primitive; although it had support for form input and the mSQL database, it lacked many of the security features and add-ons found in modern PHP versions.

Lerdorf later improved PHP/F1 1.0 and released it as PHP/FI 2.0, but it was only in 1997, when the developers Andi Gutmans and Zeev Suraski rewrote the PHP parser and released it as PHP 3.0, that the PHP movement really began to pick up steam. Not only was PHP 3.0's syntax more powerful and consistent, but it also introduced a new, extensible architecture that encouraged independent developers to create their own enhancements and extensions to the language. Needless to say, this only encouraged adoption of the language, and it wasn't long before PHP 3.0 began appearing on many thousands of Web servers.

The next iteration of the code tree, PHP 4.0, was released in 2000. It offered a new engine, better performance and reliability, and built-in support for sessions and object-oriented features. A Nexen survey in July 2007 revealed that this version of PHP, PHP 4.x, was still the dominant version in use on the Internet's Web sites, accounting for almost 80 percent of the PHP-capable servers surveyed. However, in July 2007, the PHP development team announced that PHP 4.x would no longer be supported after December 2007, paving the way for more widespread adoption of newer versions.

PHP 5.0, released in 2004, was a radical redesign of PHP 4.0, boasting a completely rewritten engine, a much-improved object model, and various security and performance improvements. Of particular interest to developers was the new object model, which now included support for such stalwarts of the OOP paradigm as abstract classes, destructors, multiple interfaces, and class type hints. PHP 5.0 also introduced various new and important tools: a common database access layer; Java-style exception handling; and an integrated database engine.

PHP 5.3, the most recent version (and the version used throughout this book), was released in January 2008. It improves on the new features first shown in PHP 5.0, and also attempts to correct some of the shortcomings noted by users of earlier versions. Some of the most noticeable improvements in this version are: support for namespacs; a cleaner and more secure environment for managing the variable space; built-in support for SQLite 3; and a new native driver for MySQL. So far, all these changes have conspired to make PHP 5.3 the best PHP release in the language's fourteen-year history, a fact amply illustrated by the April 2008 Netcraft survey, which shows PHP in use on over thirty million Web sites.

Unique Features

If you're familiar with other server-side languages like ASP.NET or JSP, you might be wondering what makes PHP so special, or so different from these competing alternatives. Well, here are some reasons:

Performance   Scripts written in PHP execute faster than those written in other scripting languages, with numerous independent benchmarks putting the language ahead of competing alternatives like JSP, ASP.NET, and Perl. The PHP 5.0 engine was completely redesigned with an optimized memory manager to improve performance, and is noticeably faster than previous versions. In addition, third-party accelerators are available to further improve performance and response time.

Portability   PHP is available for UNIX, Microsoft Windows, Mac OS, and OS/2, and PHP programs are portable between platforms. As a result, a PHP application developed on, say, Windows will typically run on UNIX without any significant issues. This ability to easily undertake cross-platform development is a valuable one, especially when operating in a multiplatform corporate environment or when trying to address multiple market segments.

Ease of Use   "Simplicity is the ultimate sophistication," said Leonardo da Vinci, and by that measure, PHP is an extremely sophisticated programming language. Its syntax is clear and consistent, and it comes with exhaustive documentation for the 5000+ functions included with the core distributions. This significantly reduces the learning curve for both novice and experienced programmers, and it's one of the reasons that PHP is favored as a rapid prototyping tool for Web-based applications.

Open Source   PHP is an open-source project—the language is developed by a worldwide team of volunteers who make its source code freely available on the Web, and it may be used without payment of licensing fees or investments in expensive hardware or software. This reduces software development costs without affecting either flexibility or reliability. The open-source nature of the code further means that any developer, anywhere, can inspect the code tree, spot errors, and suggest possible fixes; this produces a stable, robust product wherein bugs, once discovered, are rapidly resolved—sometimes within a few hours of discovery!

Community Support   One of the nice things about a community-supported language like PHP is the access it offers to the creativity and imagination of hundreds of developers across the world. Within the PHP community, the fruits of this creativity may be found in PEAR, the PHP Extension and Application Repository (http://pear.php.net/), and PECL, the PHP Extension Community Library (http://pecl.php.net/), which contains hundreds of ready-made widgets and extensions that developers can use to painlessly add new functionality to PHP. Using these widgets is often a more time- and cost-efficient alternative to rolling your own code.

Third-Party Application Support   One of PHP's strengths has historically been its support for a wide range of different databases, including MySQL, PostgreSQL, Oracle, and Microsoft SQL Server. PHP 5.3 supports more than fifteen different database engines, and it includes a common API for database access. XML support makes it easy to read (and write) XML documents as though they were native PHP data structures, access XML node collections using XPath, and transform XML into other formats with XSLT style sheets.

It doesn't just stop there either. PHP's extensible architecture allows developers to write custom add-ons to the language, with the result that PHP developers can today read and write the GIF, JPEG, and PNG image formats; send and receive e-mail using the SMTP, IMAP, and POP3 protocols; interface with Web services using the SOAP and REST protocols; validate input using Perl regular expressions; and create and manipulate PDF documents. Heck, PHP can even access C libraries, Java classes, and COM objects and take advantage of program code written for these languages!

Ask the Expert

Q: Do I need to compile PHP programs before executing them, as in Java or C++?

A: No, because PHP is an interpreted language. One advantage of an interpreted language is that it allows you to make changes to your source code and immediately test these changes, without first needing to compile your source code into binary form. Skipping the compilation step makes the development process much faster, and PHP comes with built-in memory management and caching to negate the effect of the additional run-time load associated with using an interpreter.

Basic Development Concepts

When developing a PHP application for the Web, the typical approach is to embed PHP code into one or more standard HTML documents using special "tags," or delimiters. Here's an example:

```
<html>
 <head></head>
 <body>
  <div>
   <?php echo sqrt(49); ?>
  </div>
 </body>
</html>
```

When such an HTML document is requested by a user, a PHP-aware Web server can recognize and execute the PHP code blocks and interpolate the resulting output into the HTML document before returning it to the requesting user. The result: a Web page or application that almost seems alive, responding intelligently to user actions by virtue of the PHP program logic embedded within it. Figure 1-1 illustrates the process, showing the four elements of the LAMP framework, described later in this section.

Here's what's happening in Figure 1-1:

1. Joe pops open his Web browser at home and types in the URL to a Web site. After looking up the domain, Joe's browser (the client) sends an HTTP request to the corresponding server IP address.

2. The Web server handling HTTP requests for the domain receives the request and notes that the URL ends with a .php suffix. Because the server is programmed to automatically redirect all such requests to the PHP layer, it simply invokes the PHP interpreter and passes it the contents of the named file.

3. The PHP interpreter parses the file, executing the code in the special PHP tags. Within these tags, you can perform calculations, process user input, interact with a database, read and write files . . . the list goes on! Once the script interpreter has completed executing the PHP instructions, it returns the result to the browser, cleans up after itself, and goes back into hibernation.

4. The results returned by the interpreter are transmitted to Joe's browser by the Web server.

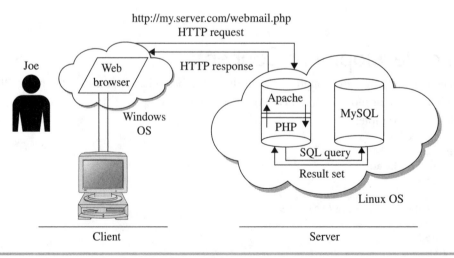

Figure 1-1 The LAMP development framework

From the preceding explanation, it should be clear that to get started building PHP applications, your development environment must contain at least three components:

- A base operating system (OS) and server environment (usually Linux)

- A Web server (usually Apache on Linux or IIS on Windows) to intercept HTTP requests and either serve them directly or pass them on to the PHP interpreter for execution

- A PHP interpreter to parse and execute PHP code, and return the results to the Web server

There's also often a fourth *optional but very useful* component:

- A database engine (such as MySQL) that holds application data, accepts connections from the PHP layer, and modifies or retrieves data from the database

An important corollary of this approach is that the PHP code is executed on the server, and not on the client browser. This allows Web developers to write program code that is completely independent of, and thus impervious to, browser quirks—an important advantage over client-side scripting languages, such as JavaScript, which often require complex logic to account for browser-specific differences. Further, because the code is all executed on the server and only the output is sent to the client, it is impossible for users to see the source code of your PHP program—an important security advantage over languages like JavaScript.

Ask the Expert

Q: How much do the components of a PHP development environment cost?

A: The four components described in the preceding section are all open-source projects and, as such, can be downloaded off the Internet at no charge. As a general principle, there are also no fees or charges associated with using these components for either personal or commercial purposes, or for developing and distributing applications that use them. If you do intend to write commercial applications, however, it's a good idea to review the licensing terms that are associated with each of these components; typically, you will find these on the component's Web site as well as in the downloadable archive file.

When all four components—Linux, Apache, MySQL, and PHP—are present, the development environment is referred to as the "LAMP platform."

Creating Your First PHP Script

Now that you know a little bit about PHP, let's dive right in and begin writing some code. By necessity, the scripts you'll be writing in the following sections will be fairly simple—but don't worry, things will get more complicated as you learn more about the language!

If you haven't already done so, this is a good place to boot up your computer, download the newest versions of Apache and PHP, and install them to your development environment. Appendix A of this book has detailed instructions for accomplishing this procedure, and for testing your development system to ensure that all is working as it should post-installation, so flip ahead and come back here once you're ready.

All done? Let's get started!

Writing and Running the Script

PHP scripts are merely plain-text files containing PHP instructions, sometimes combined with other odds and ends—JavaScript, HTML, and so on. So, the simplest way to write a PHP script is to pop open your favorite text editor and create a file containing some PHP code, as follows:

```php
<?php
// this line of code displays a famous quotation
echo 'A horse! A horse! My kingdom for a horse!';
?>
```

Save this file to a location under your Web server's document root, and name it *horse.php*. Then, start up your Web browser, and browse to the URL corresponding to the file location. You should see something like Figure 1-2.

Figure 1-2 The output of the *horse.php* script

Understanding the Script

What happened here? Well, when you requested the script *horse.php,* the Apache Web server received your request, recognized that the file was a PHP script (by means of the .php file extension), and handed it off to the PHP parser and interpreter for further processing. This PHP interpreter then read the instructions between the <?php ... ?> tags, executed them, and passed the results back to the Web server, which in turn sent them back to your browser. The instructions in this instance consisted of a call to PHP's echo statement, which is responsible for displaying output to the user; the output to be displayed is enclosed in quotation marks.

There is some useful information to be gleaned from even this simple PHP script. It should be clear, for example, that all PHP code must be enclosed within <?php ... ?> tags and every PHP statement must end in a semicolon. Blank lines within the PHP tags are ignored by the parser.

Ask the Expert

Q: I wrote the following PHP script (omitting the semicolon terminator), and it worked without generating an error.

```
<?php
echo 'The Queen is dead. Long live the Queen'
?>
```

This contradicts what you said earlier about every PHP statement necessarily ending with a semicolon. Please explain.

A: Omitting the semi-colon at the end of a PHP statement is one of the most common mistakes novice PHP programmers make, and it invariably results in an error message. However, there is one situation—the one you discovered—where you can get away clean even with this omission. A semicolon is not needed to terminate the last line of a PHP block, because the closing ?> includes a semicolon. That's why the script you wrote works without an error.

Note, however, that while you can get away with this omission, omitting the semicolon in this manner is not good programming practice. After all, you never know when you'll need to add something else to the end of your script!

Free-form comments can be incorporated within a PHP script via the same conventions used in JavaScript. Single-line comments must be preceded by the // characters, while multiline comments must be enclosed within a /* ... */ comment block. These comments are excluded from the output of the PHP script. Here are some examples:

```
<?php
// a single-line comment
?>
<?php
/* a multi-line
   comment
   block */
?>
```

Handling Script Errors

The PHP parser has a sharp eye. If your code includes an error, it will—depending on the severity of the error—either display a warning message or stop script execution at the point of error with a notification of what went wrong. Chapter 10 of this book deals with errors and error handling in detail, but it's instructive at this point to see what happens when the PHP parser encounters an error, so that you have a better understanding of how to deal with this situation when it happens to you.

To deliberately generate an error, go back to the *horse.php* script you created earlier and drop in an extra semicolon after the echo keyword, so that the script now looks like this:

```
<?php
// this line of code displays a famous quotation
echo ; 'A horse! A horse! My kingdom for a horse!';
?>
```

Save this file, and browse to it as before. This time, you should see something like Figure 1-3.

As Figure 1-3 illustrates, the PHP parser is quick to catch errors in your code. The error message generated by the parser is quite helpful: it tells you what the error was, as well as the line on which it occurred. This makes it fairly easy—in most cases—to locate and correct the error.

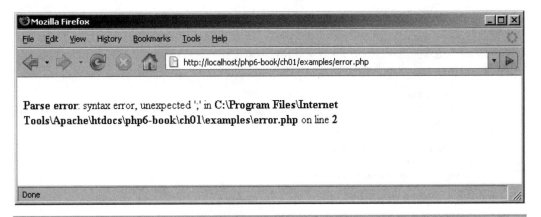

Figure 1-3   The output generated by PHP when it finds a script error

Mixing PHP with HTML

When the PHP parser reads a script, it executes only the code found between PHP tags; everything outside these tags is ignored by the parser and returned "as is." This makes it extremely easy to embed PHP code within an HTML document to create Web pages that have all the formatting bells and whistles of standard HTML but can additionally perform complex calculations or read and manipulate data from external sources (such as databases or Web services).

To see how this works in practice, consider the following code listing:

```
<!DOCTYPE html PUBLIC "-//W3C//DTD XHTML 1.0 Transitional//EN"
    "DTD/xhtml1-transitional.dtd">
<html xmlns="http://www.w3.org/1999/xhtml" xml:lang="en" lang="en">
  <head>
    <title>HTML Color Table</title>
    <style type="text/css">
    body {
        font-family: Verdana sans-serif;
    }
    td {
        border: solid 5px white;
    }
    </style>
  </head>
  <body>
    <h2>Colors with HTML and PHP</h2>
```

(continued)

```
      <table>
        <tr>
          <td>Blue</td>
          <td style="width:40px; background-color:#0000ff"></td>
        </tr>
        <tr>
          <td><?php echo 'Red'; ?></td>
          <td style="width:40px; background-color:<?php echo '#ff0000'; ?>"></td>
        </tr>
<?php
    // this row generated through PHP
    echo "<tr>\n";
    echo "  <td>Green</td>\n";
    echo "  <td style=\"width:40px; background-color:#00ff00\"></td>\n";
    echo "</tr>\n";
?>
      </table>
    </body>
</html>
```

Save this script as *colors.php,* and view it in your Web browser. You should see an HTML page containing a table with three rows and two columns, with one column containing a color and the other its corresponding name (Figure 1-4).

Use your browser's *View Source* command to inspect the HTML code of the page, and you'll see that the PHP parser has interpolated the output of the various echo statements into the HTML source code to create a complete HTML page. This is a very common

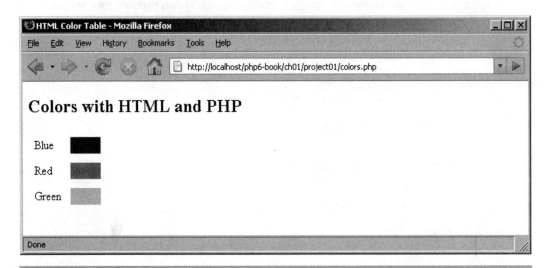

Figure 1-4   A Web page containing colors and color codes, generated by mixing PHP with HTML

technique used for building Web applications with PHP, and you'll see it in almost every example that follows.

Escaping Special Characters

There's one interesting thing about *colors.php* that bears explaining: the numerous backslashes used in the script. Look at the PHP-generated third row of the HTML table, and then at the corresponding HTML source code of the output page, and you'll notice that none of these backslashes make an appearance. Where did they go?

There's a simple explanation for this. As you've already seen, output to be displayed by PHP is wrapped in quotation marks. But what happens when the output to be displayed includes quotation marks of its own, as occurs with the HTML code generated in *colors.php*? If you simply enclose one set of quotation marks within another, PHP will get confused about which quotation marks are to be printed literally, and which ones are simply used to enclose the string value, and will generate a parser error Therefore, to handle these situations, PHP allows you to *escape* certain characters by preceding them with a backslash (\). There so-called *escape sequences* include

Sequence	What It Represents
\n	a line feed character
\t	a tab
\r	a carriage return
\"	a double quotation mark
\'	a single quotation mark

When the parser encounters one of these *escape sequences,* it knows to replace it with the corresponding value before sending it to the output device. Consider, for example, this line of code:

```php
<?php
echo "You said \"Hello\"";
?>
```

PHP knows that the quotation marks preceded with a backslash are to be printed "as is," and it will not confuse them with the quotation marks that signal the beginning and end of a string. This is why you see a backslash before every PHP-generated quotation mark and line feed in *colors.php*.

Ask the Expert

Q: Why does the *colors.php* script use single quotes in some places, and double quotes in others?

A: Escape sequences, such as those for line feeds (\n), carriage returns (\r), and double quotation marks (\"), can only be understood by the PHP parser when they are themselves enclosed in double quotes. If these escape sequences are enclosed in single quotes, they will be printed "as is."

Consider the following code snippets and their output, which illustrate the difference:

```
<?php
// output:
// Welcome
// to
// PHP
echo "Welcome\nto\nPHP";
?>
```

```
<?php
// output: Welcome\nto\nPHP
echo 'Welcome\nto\nPHP';
?>
```

Now, the *colors.php* script is responsible for dynamically generating the HTML code for the last row of the HTML table. This row code must be formatted for easy readability, with `<tr>` and `<td>` elements appearing on different lines. Performing this task requires use of the line feed (\n) escape sequence, which, as explained earlier, is only recognized when enclosed within double quotes. This is why double quotes are used at certain places within the *colors.php* script.

Sample Applications

Obviously, there's a lot more to PHP than just the `echo` statement, and you'll get a crash course in the language's many different capabilities in subsequent chapters. For the moment, though, this is a good place to take a well-earned break, grab some coffee, and reflect on all you've just learned. And just to whet your interest for what's coming up, here's a small sample of the many applications that developers just like you have used PHP for.

phpMyAdmin

The phpMyAdmin (www.phpmyadmin.net/) application is a PHP-based administration tool for the MySQL RDBMS. One of the most popular projects on the SourceForge network, it allows table and record creation and modification, index management, ad hoc SQL query execution, data import and export, and database performance monitoring.

phpBB

The phpBB (www.phpbb.com/) application is a robust, open-source PHP implementation of an online bulletin board system that is both easy to use and simple to administer. It provides a simple, user-friendly discussion board for portal members and includes support for features like message posting and replying, message threading, subject/body search, themes, private messages, and many others.

Gallery

Gallery (http://gallery.menalto.com/) is a highly configurable digital photo archive written in PHP. It supports multiple image galleries and multiple keywords per photo, and it includes features such as automatic thumbnail creation, image captioning and editing, keyword search, and gallery-level authentication.

Ask the Expert

Q: I understand how the backslash is used to mark escape sequences. But what happens if I need to print an actual backslash in my output?

A: The solution to this is fairly simple: use a double backslash!

```php
<?php
echo "This is a backslash: \\";
?>
```

PoMMo

PoMMo (www.pommo.org/) is a mass-mailing application written entirely in PHP. It is particularly useful for managing and sending e-mail messages to one or more subscriber mailing lists, and it also supports the use of customized input forms for the collection of subscriber data. It allows administrators to import and export subscriber data from a MySQL database, and subscribers to manage their subscriptions through an online control panel.

Smarty

Smarty (www.smarty.net/) is a PHP-based framework for separating the business logic of a PHP application from its user interface. It achieves this separation through the use of templates containing output placeholders, which are replaced at run time with actual content. Smarty supports template caching and nesting, pre- and post-rendering filters, and built-in functions to simplify common tasks. It has rapidly become one of the most popular template engines for PHP-based application development.

Squirrelmail

Squirrelmail (www.squirrelmail.org/) is a Web-based mail client written in PHP, with support for both the SMTP and IMAP protocols. It includes the ability to send and receive attachments, manage address book collections, and manipulate server-based mailboxes. The application is highly configurable and can be extended through the use of plug-ins and themes.

eZ Publish

The eZ Publish (www.ez.no/) application is a PHP-based content management system that is suitable for the development of both small, personal Web pages and large, corporate Web sites. It includes support for creating and editing content, tracking changes, building customized publishing workflows, and setting up a "Web shop" with integrated e-commerce functions.

Mantis

Mantis (www.mantisbt.org/) is a Web-based bug-tracking system designed specifically to track and resolve issues for software and other projects. It supports multiple user access levels, multiple projects, and multiple priority levels, and it includes a full-featured search engine and various built-in reports for up-to-date snapshots of a project's status.

Wordpress

Wordpress (www.wordpress.org/) is a well-known Weblog (aka *blog*) publishing tool. It allows users to maintain and publish online diaries of their activities and supports themes, tags, automatic spell-checking, video and photo upload, and built-in spam protection. It's extremely fast, easy to set up, and simple to use—three reasons that have made it popular with millions of bloggers around the world.

Summary

This chapter provided a gentle introduction to the world of PHP, discussing the history and evolution of the language and highlighting some of its unique features and advantages vis-à-vis competing alternatives. It explained the various components of the typical PHP development environment and illustrated how they interact with each other. Finally, it got you started writing PHP code, showing you the basic syntactical rules of the language and explaining how to embed PHP code inside HTML documents using the special `<?php ... ?>` PHP tags through an easy project. These basic skills will serve you well through the next chapter, which gives you a crash course in two of the PHP's fundamental building blocks: variables and operators.

If you'd like to learn more about the topics discussed in this chapter, you'll find the following links useful:

- The official PHP Web site, at **www.php.net**

- PHP usage statistics, at **www.php.net/usage.php**

- A brief history of PHP, at **www.php.net/manual/en/history.php**

- The community behind PHP, at **www.php.net/credits.php**

Chapter 1 Self Test

1. Which are the four components of the LAMP framework?

2. Why is PHP superior to client-side languages such as JavaScript?

3. What does the `echo` statement do?

4. What happens when the PHP parser encounters whitespace or blank lines in a PHP script?

5. What character must necessarily be used to terminate every PHP statement? Name one situation where omitting this termination character does not produce an error.

6. What is an escape sequence? Name three commonly used escape sequences.

7. What will be the output of the following PHP scripts:

A

```php
<?php
        echo                    "Today looks\nbright and sunny"
    ;
?>
```

B

```php
<?php
echo "Ours not to question why;";
echo "Ours but to do and die";
?>
```

8. Find the error in each of the following PHP scripts:

A

```php
<?php
/* print a line of output /
echo 'Hello'
?>
```

B

```php
<?php
echo '<p align="right">Copyright Me, 2008</p>';
?>
```

C

```php
<?php
echo 'Line 1;
?>
```

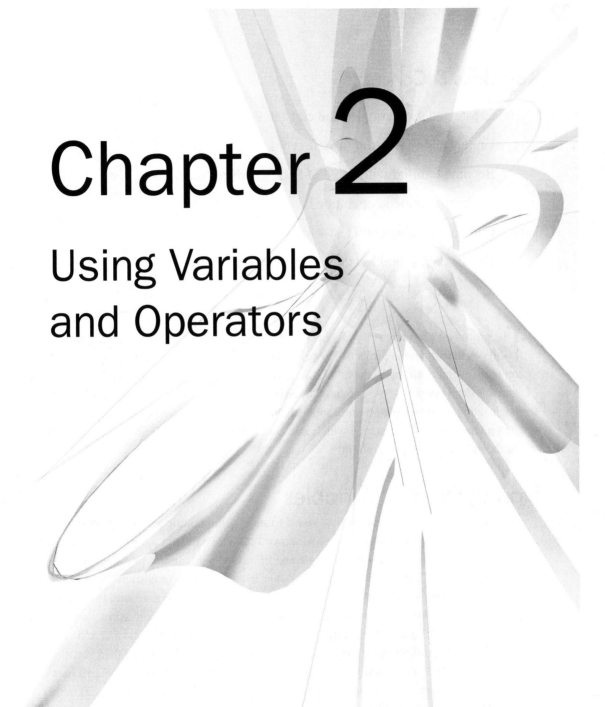

Chapter 2

Using Variables and Operators

Key Skills & Concepts

- Create and use variables and constants

- Understand PHP's simple data types

- Become familiar with some of PHP's built-in functions

- Perform arithmetic operations

- Compare and logically test variables

- Handle data submitted through a Web form

The preceding chapter gave you a gentle introduction to PHP, letting you get your hands dirty with two simple projects. However, as you'll shortly see, PHP is good for much more than simply filling in the blanks in an HTML page. In this chapter, you'll learn about variables and operators, the two basic building blocks of any PHP program, and you'll begin using them to develop more sophisticated programs. You'll also create your very first interactive PHP script, one which asks for, and responds to, a user's input. So without further ado, let's jump straight in!

Storing Data in Variables

A *variable* is simply a container that's used to store both numeric and non-numeric information. And just as with any container, you can move it from place to place, add stuff to it, or empty it out on the floor in a pile and fill it with something completely different.

To stretch the analogy a little further, just as it's a good idea to label every container, so too should you give every variable in your program a name. As a general rule, these names should make sense and should be easy to understand. In the real world, this makes it easier to find things; in the programming world, it makes your code cleaner and easier to understand by others. As someone who's been there, I can tell you that there's nothing more frustrating than spending three hours searching a bunch of boxes for Mom's best china, only to realize it's in the one marked "Miscellaneous" together with an old rubber bone and some crumbly biscuits!

PHP has some simple rules for naming variables. Every variable name must be preceded with a dollar ($) symbol and must begin with a letter or underscore character, optionally followed by more letters, numbers, or underscore characters. Common punctuation characters, such as commas, quotation marks, or periods, are not permitted in variable names; neither are spaces. So, for example, $root, $_num, and $query2 are all valid variable names, while $58%, $1day, and email are all invalid variable names.

Assigning Values to Variables

Assigning a value to a variable in PHP is quite easy: use the equality (=) symbol, which also happens to be PHP's assignment operator. This assigns the value on the right side of the equation to the variable on the left.

To use a variable in a script, simply call it by name in an expression and PHP will replace it with its value when the script is executed. Here's an example:

```
<!DOCTYPE html PUBLIC "-//W3C//DTD XHTML 1.0 Transitional//EN"
    "DTD/xhtml1-transitional.dtd">
<html xmlns="http://www.w3.org/1999/xhtml" xml:lang="en" lang="en">
  <head><title /></head>
  <body>
   <?php
   // assign value to variable
   $name = 'Simon';
   ?>
  <h2>Welcome to <?php echo $name; ?>'s Blog!</h2>
  </body>
</html>
```

In this example, the variable $name is assigned the value 'Simon'. The echo statement is then used to print the value of this variable to the Web page.

You can also assign a variable the value of another variable, or the result of a calculation. The following example demonstrates both these situations:

```
<?php
// assign value to variable
$now = 2008;

// assign variable to another variable
$currentYear = $now;

// perform calculation
$lastYear = $currentYear - 1;

// output: '2007 has ended. Welcome to 2008!'
echo "$lastYear has ended. Welcome to $currentYear!";
?>
```

Ask the Expert

Q: **Is it possible for a variable's name itself to be a variable?**

A: In rare situations, you might find it useful to set a variable's name dynamically, at run time. PHP allows you to do this, by enclosing the dynamic part of the variable name in curly braces. The following example illustrates:

```php
<?php
// set a variable
$attribute = 'price';

// create a new variable
// its name comes dynamically
// from the value of $attribute
${$attribute} = 678;

// output: 678
echo $price;
?>
```

Destroying Variables

To destroy a variable, pass the variable to PHP's aptly named unset() function, as in the following example:

```php
<?php
// assign value to variable
$car = 'Porsche';

// print variable value
// output: 'Before unset(), my car is a Porsche'
echo "Before unset(), my car is a $car";

// destroy variable
unset($car);

// print variable value
// this will generate an 'undefined variable' error
// output: 'After unset(), my car is a '
echo "After unset(), my car is a $car";
?>
```

NOTE

Trying to access or use a variable that's been unset(), as in the preceding script, will result in a PHP "undefined variable" error message. This message may or may not be visible in the output page, depending on how your PHP error reporting level is configured. Refer to Chapter 10 for more information on how PHP errors work.

Alternatively, empty a variable of its contents by assigning PHP's special NULL value to it. You can read more about PHP's NULL data type in the next section, but here's a quick revision of the preceding example to illustrate how it works:

```php
<?php
// assign value to variable
$car = 'Porsche';

// print variable value
// output: 'Before unset(), my car is a Porsche'
echo "Before unset(), my car is a $car";

// assign empty value to variable
$car = null;

// print variable value
// output: 'After unset(), my car is a '
echo "After unset(), my car is a $car";
?>
```

CAUTION

Variable names in PHP are case-sensitive. As a result, $help refers to a different variable than does $HELP or $Help. Forgetting this simple rule is a common cause of frustration among developers new to PHP programming.

Inspecting Variable Contents

PHP offers the var_dump() function, which accepts a variable and X-rays it for you. Here's an example:

```php
<?php
// define variables
$name = 'Fiona';
$age = 28;

// display variable contents
var_dump($name);
var_dump($age);
?>
```

TIP

There's also a `print_r()` function that performs the same function as `var_dump()`, although it returns less information.

Understanding PHP's Data Types

The values assigned to a PHP variable may be of different *data types,* ranging from simple string and numeric types to more complex arrays and objects. You've already seen two of these, strings and numbers, in action in previous examples. Here's a full-fledged example, which introduces three more data types:

```php
<?php
// Boolean
$validUser = true;

// integer
$size = 15;

// floating point
$temp = 98.6;

// string
$cat = 'Siamese';

// null
$here = null;
?>
```

- *Booleans* are the simplest of all PHP data types. Like a switch that has only two states, on and off, it consists of a single value that may be set to either 1 (`true`) or 0 (`false`). In this listing, `$validUser` is a Boolean variable set to `true`.

- PHP also supports two numeric data types: *integers* and *floating-point values.* Floating-point values (also known as *floats* or *doubles*) are decimal or fractional numbers, while integers are round numbers. Both may be less than, greater than, or equal to zero. In this listing, `$size` holds an integer value, while `$temp` holds a floating-point value.

- For non-numeric data, PHP offers the *string* data type, which can hold letters, numbers, and special characters. String values must be enclosed in either single quotes or double quotes. In the previous listing, `$cat` is a string variable containing the value `'Siamese'`.

- You may also encounter the NULL data type, which is a "special" data type first introduced in PHP 4. NULLs are used to represent "empty" variables in PHP; a variable of type NULL is a variable without any data. In the preceding listing, `$here` is NULL.

Ask the Expert

Q: Does PHP support numbers written in hexadecimal, octal, or scientific notation?

A: Yes, yes, and yes. Here are some examples:

```php
<?php
// 8, specified as octal value
$a = 010;

// 1500, specified as hexadecimal value
$b = 0x5dc;

// 690, in scientific notation
$c = 6.9E+2;
?>
```

CAUTION

Many novice PHP developers mistakenly believe that assigning the empty string ' ' to a variable automatically renders it empty. This is untrue, as PHP does not consider a NULL value equivalent to an empty string. To definitely remove a variable's contents, always set it to NULL.

Setting and Checking Variable Data Types

Unlike other programming languages, where a variable's data type must be explicitly defined by the programmer, PHP automatically determines a variable's data type from the content it holds. And if the variable's content changes over the duration of a script, the language will automatically set the variable to the appropriate new data type.

Here's an example which illustrates this *type juggling*:

```php
<?php
// define string variable
$whoami = 'Sarah';

// output: 'string'
echo gettype($whoami);

// assign new integer value to variable
$whoami = 99.8;
```

```
// output: 'double'
echo gettype($whoami);

// destroy variable
unset($whoami);

// output: 'NULL'
echo gettype($whoami);
?>
```

This example introduces PHP's gettype() operator, which is a handy little tool for finding out the type of a particular variable. As the script output demonstrates, the variable $whoami begins life as a string, assigned the value 'Sarah'. It's then assigned the number 99.8, which automatically converts it to a floating-point variable. Following this, the variable is de-initialized with the unset() method, which removes its value and turns it into a NULL. PHP has been the invisible hand behind each of these conversions, internally resetting the data type of $whoami from string to floating-point to null.

This doesn't mean that you're entirely at PHP's mercy, however; it's possible to explicitly set the type of a PHP variable by *casting* a variable to a specific type before using it. Casting is a technique commonly used by Java programmers; to use it, simply specify the desired data type in parentheses on the right side of the assignment equation. Consider the following example, which illustrates turning a floating-point value into an integer value:

```
<?php
// define floating-point variable
$speed = 501.789;

// cast to integer
$newSpeed = (integer) $speed;

// output: 501
echo $newSpeed;
?>
```

In addition to the gettype() function, PHP includes a number of more specialized functions, to test if a variable is of a specific type. Table 2-1 has a list.

TIP

Remember that var_dump() function you met in a previous section? If you look closely at its output, you'll see that in addition to telling you what a variable contains, it also shows you the variable's data type.

Function	Purpose
is_bool()	Tests if a variable holds a Boolean value
is_numeric()	Tests if a variable holds a numeric value
is_int()	Tests if a variable holds an integer
is_float()	Tests if a variable holds a floating-point value
is_string()	Tests if a variable holds a string value
is_null()	Tests if a variable holds a NULL value
is_array()	Tests if a variable is an array
is_object()	Tests if a variable is an object

Table 2-1   PHP Functions to Test Variable Data Types

Using Constants

So far, this chapter has focused mainly on variables, which are good for storing and changing values over the lifetime of a PHP script. But what if you need to store a fixed value, one that remains static over the course of a script? Well, that's when you reach for a *constant.*

As the name suggests, constants are PHP containers for values that remain constant and never change. They're mostly used for data that is known well in advance and that is used, unchanged, in multiple places within your application. Good candidates for constants are debug and log levels, version numbers, configuration flags, and formulae.

Constants are defined using PHP's define() function, which accepts two arguments: the name of the constant, and its value. Constant names must follow the same rules as variable names, with one exception: the $ prefix is not required for constant names.

Here's an example of defining and using a constant in a script:

```php
<?php
// define constants
define ('PROGRAM', 'The Matrix');
define ('VERSION', 11.7);

// use constants
// output: 'Welcome to The Matrix (version 11.7)'
echo 'Welcome to ' . PROGRAM . ' (version ' . VERSION . ')';
?>
```

NOTE
By convention, constant names are usually entirely uppercased; this is to enable their easy identification and differentiation from "regular" variables in a script.

Manipulating Variables with Operators

By themselves, variables are simply containers for information. In order to do anything useful with them, you need *operators*. Operators are symbols that tell the PHP processor to perform certain actions. For example, the addition (+) symbol is an operator that tells PHP to add two variables or values, while the greater-than (>) symbol is an operator that tells PHP to compare two values.

PHP supports more than 50 such operators, ranging from operators for arithmetical operations to operators for logical comparison and bitwise calculations. This section discusses the most commonly used operators.

Ask the Expert

Q: When should I use a variable, and when should I use a constant?

A: Variables are temporary storage; use them for values which are likely to change over the course of the script. Constants are a little more permanent; use them for values that are likely to remain fixed and are referenced multiple times in your script. Unlike variables, constants cannot be unset, nor can their names be generated dynamically.

Performing Arithmetic Operations

PHP supports all standard arithmetic operations, as illustrated by the list of operators in Table 2-2.

Operator	Description
+	Add
−	Subtract
*	Multiply
/	Divide and return quotient
%	Divide and return modulus

Table 2-2 Common Arithmetic Operators

And here's an example illustrating these operators in action:

```php
<?php
// define variables
$x = 10;
$y = 5;
$z = 3;

// add
$sum = $x + $y;
echo "$x + $y = $sum\n";

// subtract
$diff = $x - $y;
echo "$x - $y = $diff\n";

// multiply
$product = $x * $y;
echo "$x * $y = $product\n";

// divide and get quotient
$quotient = $x / $y;
echo "$x / $y = $quotient\n";

// divide and get modulus
$modulus = $x % $y;
echo "$x % $y = $modulus\n";
?>
```

Ask the Expert

Q: **Is there any limit on how large a PHP integer value can be?**

A: Yes there is, but it's pretty high: 2147483647. This limit is defined by PHP in its
`PHP_INT_MAX` constant, so you can check it yourself at any time.

Concatenating Strings

To combine strings, use PHP's concatenation operator, which happens to be a period (.).
The following example illustrates:

```php
<?php
// define variables
$country = 'England';
$city = 'London';
```

```
// combine into single string
// output: 'Welcome to London, the coolest city in all of England'
echo 'Welcome to ' . $city . ', the coolest city in all of ' . $country;
?>
```

Comparing Variables

PHP lets you compare one variable or value with another via its wide range of comparison
operators, listed in Table 2-3.

And here's an example illustrating these operators in action:

```
<?php
// define variables
$p = 10;
$q = 11;
$r = 11.3;
$s = 11;

// test if $q is greater than $p
// returns true
echo ($q > $p);

// test if $q is less than $p
// returns false
echo ($q < $p);

// test if $q is greater than or equal to $s
// returns true
echo ($q >= $s);

// test if $r is less than or equal to $s
// returns false
echo ($r <= $s);
```

Operator	Description
==	Equal to
!=	Not equal to
>	Greater than
>=	Greater than or equal to
<	Less than
<=	Less than or equal to
===	Equal to and of the same type

Table 2-3   Common Comparison Operators

```
// test if $q is equal to $s
// returns true
echo ($q == $s);

// test if $q is equal to $r
// returns false
echo ($q == $r);
?>
```

It's worth making special mention here of the === operator, which is excluded from the preceding example. This operator allows for stricter comparison between variables: it only returns true if the two variables or values being compared hold the same information and are of the same data type. Thus, in the next example, a comparison between $bool and $num would return true when compared with the == operator, but false when compared with the === operator:

```
<?php
// define variables of two types
// but with the same value
$bool = (boolean) 1;
$int = (integer) 1;

// returns true
echo ($bool == $int);

// returns false
echo ($bool === $int);
?>
```

Performing Logical Tests

When building complex conditional expressions—a topic that will be discussed in detail in Chapter 3—you will often come across situations where it's necessary to combine one or more logical tests. PHP's three most commonly used logical operators, listed in Table 2-4, are intended specifically for this situation.

Operator	Description
&&	AND
||	OR
!	NOT

Table 2-4 Common Logical Operators

Logical operators really come into their own when combined with conditional tests, so the following example is illustrative only; you'll find something much meatier to chew on in Chapter 3.

```php
<?php
// define variables
$price = 100;
$size = 18;

// logical AND test
// returns true if both comparisons are true
// returns true here
echo ($price > 50 && $size < 25);

// logical OR test
// returns true if any of the comparisons are true
// returns false here
echo ($price > 150 || $size > 75);

// logical NOT test
// reverses the logical test
// returns false here
echo !($size > 10);
?>
```

Other Useful Operators

There are a few other operators that tend to come in handy during PHP development. First, the addition-assignment operator, represented by the symbol +=, lets you simultaneously add and assign a new value to a variable. The following example illustrates:

```php
<?php
// define variable
$count = 7;

// add 2 and re-assign new value to variable
$count += 2;

// output: 9
echo $count;
?>
```

Here, the expression $count +=7 is equivalent to the expression $count = $count + 2—an addition operation followed by an assignment of the result back to the same variable. In a similar vein, there exist operators for other mathematical and string assignments. Table 2-5 has a list.

Operator	Description
+=	Add and assign
-=	Subtract and assign
*=	Multiply and assign
/=	Divide and assign quotient
%=	Divide and assign modulus
.=	Concatenate and assign (strings only)

Table 2-5   Common Assignment Operators

Here are examples of these in action:

```php
<?php
// define variables
$count = 7;
$age = 60;
$greeting = 'We';

// subtract 2 and re-assign new value to variable
// equivalent to $count = $count - 2
// output: 5
$count -= 2;
echo $count;

// divide by 5 and re-assign new value to variable
// equivalent to $age = $age / 5
// output: 12
$age /= 5;
echo $age;

// add new string and re-assign new value to variable
// equivalent to $greeting = $greeting . 'lcome!'
// output: 'Welcome!'
$greeting .= 'lcome!';
echo $greeting;
?>
```

As you proceed through this book, you'll also comes across the auto-increment and auto-decrement operators, represented by the ++ and -- symbols respectively.

The operators automatically add 1 to, or subtract 1 from, the variable they are applied to. Here's an example:

```php
<?php
// define variable
$count = 19;

// increment
$count++;

// output: 20
echo $count;

// now decrement
$count--;

// output: 19
echo $count;
?>
```

These operators are commonly found in loop counters, another topic that will be discussed in detail in Chapter 3.

Understanding Operator Precedence

Back in math class, you probably learned about BODMAS, a mnemonic that specifies the order in which a calculator or a computer performs a sequence of mathematical operations: Brackets, Order, Division, Multiplication, Addition, and Subtraction. Well, PHP follows a similar set of rules when determining which operators have precedence over others—and learning these rules can save you countless frustrating hours debugging a calculation that looks right, yet somehow always returns the wrong result!

The following list (a short version of a much longer list in the PHP manual) illustrates PHP's most important precedence rules. Operators at the same level have equal precedence.

- `++ --`
- `!`
- `* / %`
- `+ - .`
- `< <= > >=`

- `== != === !==`
- `&&`
- `||`
- `= += -= *= /= .= %= &= |= ^=`

Ask the Expert

Q: PHP's precedence rules are tough to remember. Is there an easier way to tell PHP the order in which I'd like a calculation performed?

A: Yes. Parentheses always have the highest precedence, so wrapping an expression in these will force PHP to evaluate it first. When using multiple sets of parentheses, remember that evaluation begins from the innermost set of parentheses and proceeds outward (rather like peeling an onion from the inside). As an example, consider the expression `(((4 * 8) - 2) / 10)`, which evaluates to 3 with parentheses and `31.8` without.

Try This 2-1 Building a Dollars-to-Euros Converter

Let's now take a quick break from all this theory and try applying some of it to a practical, real-world project: a currency converter for dollars into euros. This project will apply some of what you've learned in previous sections about variables, constants, and arithmetic operators; it'll also come in handy the next time you jet off to Europe on vacation!

Here's the code (*convert.php*):

```
<!DOCTYPE html PUBLIC "-//W3C//DTD XHTML 1.0 Transitional//EN"
  "DTD/xhtml1-transitional.dtd">
<html xmlns="http://www.w3.org/1999/xhtml" xml:lang="en" lang="en">
  <head>
    <title>Project 2-1: USD/EUR Currency Conversion</title>
  </head>
  <body>
    <h2>Project 2-1: USD/EUR Currency Conversion</h2>
    <?php
    // define exchange rate
```

(continued)

```
    // 1.00 USD = 0.70 EUR
    define ('EXCHANGE_RATE', 0.70);

    // define number of dollars
    $dollars = 150;

    // perform conversion and print result
    $euros = $dollars * EXCHANGE_RATE;
    echo "$dollars USD is equivalent to: $euros EUR";
    ?>
  </body>
</html>
```

If you've been following along, this script should be fairly easy to understand. It begins by defining a constant named EXCHANGE_RATE which—surprise, surprise—stores the dollar-to-euro exchange rate (assumed here at 1.00 U.S. dollar to 0.70 euro). Next, it defines a variable named $dollars to hold the number of dollars to be converted, and then it performs an arithmetic operation using the * operator, the $dollars variable, and the EXCHANGE_RATE constant to return the equivalent number of euros. This result is then stored in a new variable named $euros, and printed to the Web page.

Figure 2-1 illustrates what the output looks like.

To convert a different quantity of dollars, simply change the $dollars variable. Go on, give it a whirl and see for yourself!

Figure 2-1 The output of the dollars-to-euros converter

Handling Form Input

So far, all the examples you've seen have had their variables neatly defined at the top of the script listing. However, as your PHP scripts become more complex, this happy situation will change, and you'll need to learn how to interact with user-supplied input. The most common source of this information is a Web form, and PHP comes with a simple mechanism to retrieve information submitted through such forms.

To illustrate, consider the following simple Web form (*choose.html*), which asks you to select a brand of automobile and enter your desired color:

```
<!DOCTYPE html PUBLIC "-//W3C//DTD XHTML 1.0 Transitional//EN"
    "DTD/xhtml1-transitional.dtd">
<html xmlns="http://www.w3.org/1999/xhtml" xml:lang="en" lang="en">
  <head><title /></head>
  <body>
    <h2>Select Your Car</h2>
    <form method="post" action="car.php">
      Type: <br />
      <select name="selType">
        <option value="Porsche 911">Porsche 911</option>
        <option value="Volkswagen Beetle">Volkswagen Beetle</option>
        <option value="Ford Taurus">Ford Taurus</option>
      </select><p />
      Color: <br />
      <input type="text" name="txtColor" /> <p />
      <input type="submit" />
    </form>
  </body>
</html>
```

As forms go, this is a fairly simple one: it has a selection list and an input box. Figure 2-2 illustrates what it looks like.

Notice the `'action'` attribute of this Web form: it references a PHP script named *car.php*. This is the script that receives the data entered into the form once the form is submitted. Notice also the form's `'method'` attribute, which specifies that the submission of data will occur through the POST method.

With these two facts firmly in mind, let's take a look at *car.php* next:

```
<!DOCTYPE html PUBLIC "-//W3C//DTD XHTML 1.0 Transitional//EN"
    "DTD/xhtml1-transitional.dtd">
<html xmlns="http://www.w3.org/1999/xhtml" xml:lang="en" lang="en">
  <head><title /></head>
  <body>
    <h2>Success!</h2>
```

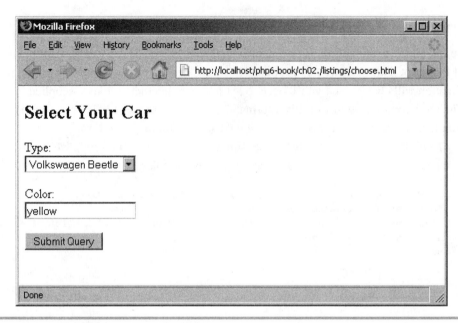

Figure 2-2 A simple form

```php
<?php
// get form input
$type = $_POST['selType'];
$color = $_POST['txtColor'];

// use form input
echo "Your $color $type is ready. Safe driving!";
?>
  </body>
</html>
```

What's going on here? Well, whenever a form is submitted to a PHP script through the POST method, the form's input variables and their values automatically become available to the PHP script through a special container variable named $_POST. Accessing the value entered into a particular form field then becomes as simple as referencing $_POST with the corresponding field's name, as in the preceding script.

Consider, for example, the task of accessing the color entered by the user in the Web form. From the form code, it can be seen that the text input field designated for this data in the form is named 'txtColor'. Therefore, within the PHP script, the value entered into this text input field can be accessed using the syntax $_POST['txtColor'].

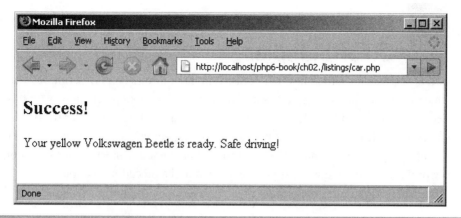

Figure 2-3   The result of submitting the form

This value can then be used in the normal fashion: it may be printed to the Web page, assigned to another variable, or manipulated using one of the many operators discussed in preceding sections.

Figure 2-3 illustrates the result of submitting the form.

In case your Web form submits data using the GET method instead of the POST method, PHP has you covered there as well: form input submitted using the GET method finds a home in the $_GET container variable and may be accessed by referencing $_GET instead of $_POST.

Ask the Expert

Q: I understood the previous sections about variables and how they work, but $_GET and $_POST don't seem to follow those rules. What's going on here?

A: The $_GET and $_POST variables are different from the simple string and numeric variable types you've seen so far in this chapter. They're a more complex type of variable known as an *array*, which can hold more than one value at a time and which also follows different rules for storing and accessing the values within it. Arrays will be discussed extensively in Chapter 4, at which point everything you've just read about $_GET and $_POST will fall into place.

Try This 2-2 Building an Interactive HTML Color Sampler

Now that you've understood how to access form input through a PHP script, let's put together an application that demonstrates this feature in a more practical way. In this project, you'll build an HTML color sampler, a tool that will let you enter RGB color values and will display a swatch of the corresponding color in your Web browser. The RGB color values will be entered into a form and processed with PHP, thus providing a real-world usage example of what you've learned in the preceding section.

First up, the Web form (*color.html*):

```
<!DOCTYPE html PUBLIC "-//W3C//DTD XHTML 1.0 Transitional//EN"
   "DTD/xhtml1-transitional.dtd">
<html xmlns="http://www.w3.org/1999/xhtml" xml:lang="en" lang="en">
  <head>
    <title>Project 2-2: An Interactive HTML Color Sampler</title>
  </head>
  <body>
    <h2>Project 2-2: An Interactive HTML Color Sampler</h2>
    <form method="get" action="display.php">
      R: <input type="text" name="r" size="3" /> <p />
      G: <input type="text" name="g" size="3" /> <p />
      B: <input type="text" name="b" size="3" /> <p />
      <input type="submit" value="Show me" />
    </form>
  </body>
</html>
```

Pretty standard fare here—a Web form with three input fields, one each for the red, green, and blue color components. Notice that this form submits its data to a PHP script named *display.php,* and it uses the GET method (for variety).

Figure 2-4 illustrates what the form looks like.

Next up, the PHP script that accepts the input and uses it to display a color swatch (*display.php*):

```
<!DOCTYPE html PUBLIC "-//W3C//DTD XHTML 1.0 Transitional//EN"
   "DTD/xhtml1-transitional.dtd">
<html xmlns="http://www.w3.org/1999/xhtml" xml:lang="en" lang="en">
  <head>
    <title>Project 2-2: An Interactive HTML Color Sampler</title>
  </head>
  <body>
    <h2>Project 2-2: An Interactive HTML Color Sampler</h2>
    <?php
```

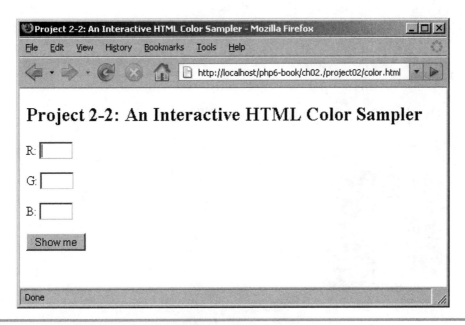

Figure 2-4   A Web form with fields for RGB color values

```
// get input values
$r = $_GET['r'];
$g = $_GET['g'];
$b = $_GET['b'];

// generate RGB string from input
$rgb = $r . ',' . $g . ',' . $b;
?>
   R: <?php echo $r; ?>
   G: <?php echo $g; ?>
   B: <?php echo $b; ?>
<p />
<div style="width:150px; height: 150px;
background-color: rgb(<?php echo $rgb; ?>)" />
</body>
</html>
```

The data entered into the form becomes accessible through the $_GET array (notice that it's $_GET because the GET method was used to submit the form). This data is then swept into three variables by this script: $r, $g, and $b. These are then concatenated into a single string using PHP's concatenation operator (remember him?). This RGB string is then used to set the background color for a <div> element a little further down in the HTML document.

(continued)

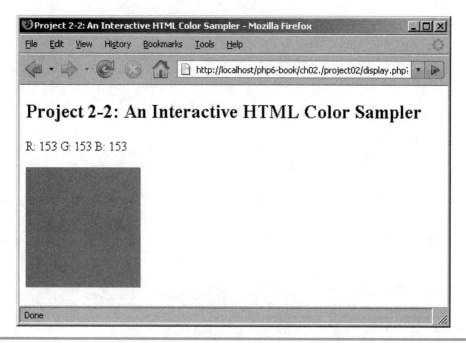

Figure 2-5 The color sample resulting from form submission

The result? When the browser renders the page, you'll see a 150×150 block solid-filled with the color corresponding to the selected RGB values. And if you go back to the Web form and enter a new set of RGB codes, the color will change appropriately . . . hence the "interactive" in "interactive color sampler"!

Figure 2-5 illustrates what happens when you enter the codes 153,153,153 (a light shade of gray, because this page is in black and white).

Table 2-6 has some more RGB color combinations for you to try.

Color	R	G	B
Pink	250	75	200
Orange	255	105	0
Yellow	255	255	0
Green	75	200	60
Brown	100	75	25

Table 2-6 Sample RGB Color Combinations

Summary

This chapter probably took you a little longer to get through than the preceding one, but at the end of it, your knowledge of PHP's basic constructs should have noticeably increased. The chapter began by introducing you to PHP variables and constants, explaining how to name them, assign values to them, use them in a script, and destroy them when done. It gave you a quick introduction to PHP's simple data types and then took you on a whirlwind tour of PHP's arithmetic, string, comparison, and logical operators, using commented examples to explain how each of these operators could be used to manipulate and modify variable contents.

With these basics out of the way, the chapter proceeded to an explanation of how to process form input with PHP, a common task that you'll perform over and over again through the course of this book and, indeed, throughout your career as a PHP developer. Finally, two projects—one demonstrating the use of operators to perform calculations on variables and the other illustrating how easy it is to create an interactive PHP application using form input—showed how this learning can be put to practical use.

The next chapter will build on everything you've learned so far, explaining how you can add intelligence to your PHP scripts through the use of conditional tests, and showing you how PHP's loop constructs can help in performing repetitive actions. Until then, though, spend some time looking at these PHP manual links, which offer more detailed information on the topics discussed in this chapter:

- PHP data types, at **www.php.net/manual/en/language.types.php**
- Type juggling and typecasting in PHP, at **www.php.net/manual/en/language.types.type-juggling.php**
- PHP type comparison tables, at **www.php.net/manual/en/types.comparisons.php**
- Variable basics, at **www.php.net/manual/en/language.variables.php**
- PHP operators and operator precedence, at **www.php.net/manual/en/language.operators.php**
- Accessing form data with PHP, at **www.php.net/manual/en/language.variables.external.php**

Chapter 2 Self Test

1. The PHP function to detect the type of a variable is: _____

2. Identify which of the following variable names are invalid: $24, $IAMHERE, $_error, $^b, ${$var}, $yA_K

3. Write a PHP statement to create a constant value holding the name of your favorite ice-cream flavor.

4. Write a PHP script to initialize a variable and then increment its value by 3.

5. Mark the following statements as true or false:

   A The unset() function de-initializes a variable and removes it from the program's variable space.

   B The PHP expressions $c = '' and $c = null are equivalent.

   C The result of the calculation (56 - 1 * 36 % 7) is 6.

   D The == operator tests two variables for both value and type equality.

   E The OR logical operator has higher precedence than the AND logical operator.

   F The is_numeric() function returns true if passed a floating-point value.

   G Casting a floating-point number to an integer always results in the number being rounded down.

   H Form elements of type 'hidden' are excluded from $_POST and $_GET.

6. What are the values of $x and ABC at the end of the following PHP script?

```php
<?php
$x = 89;
define ('ABC', $x+1);
$x += ABC;
?>
```

7. What is the likely output of the following PHP script?

```php
<?php
$boolean = (integer) true;
$number = 1;
echo (integer) ($boolean === $number);
?>
```

8. What is the likely output of the following PHP script?

```php
<?php
define ('NUM', '7');
$a = NUM;
echo gettype ($a);
?>
```

9. Rewrite the code from Try This 2-1 such that both the exchange rate and the amount to be converted are supplied by the user through a Web form.

10. Write a PHP script that accepts a temperature value in Celsius (C) through a Web form and converts it to the Fahrenheit (F) scale. The conversion formula to use is: $F = (9/5) * C + 32$.

11. Write a PHP script to display the values entered into a Web form that contains:

- One text input field
- One text area
- One hidden field
- One password field
- One selection list
- Two radio buttons
- Two checkboxes

Chapter 3

Controlling
Program Flow

Key Skills & Concepts

- Learn to use conditional statements like `if-else` and `switch-case`

- Automate repetitive tasks with the `while`, `do-while`, and `for` loops

- Gain experience with PHP's built-in string and numeric functions

The PHP programs you saw in the preceding chapter were fairly straightforward: they accepted one or more input values, performed calculations or comparisons with them, and returned a result. In reality, though, PHP programs are never so simple: most programs will need to make complex decisions and execute different operations at run time in accordance with programmer-specified conditions.

In this chapter, you'll learn how to create PHP programs that are more "intelligent" and can perform different actions based on the results of a logical or comparative test. You'll also learn how to automate repetitive actions using loops, and find out more about PHP's built-in functions for working with strings and numbers. To ensure that you're able to apply this learning in the real world, this chapter also lets you test your newly acquired knowledge against four practical projects.

Writing Simple Conditional Statements

In addition to storing and retrieving values in variables, PHP also lets programmers evaluate different conditions during the course of a program and take decisions based on whether these conditions evaluate to true or false. These conditions, and the actions associated with them, are expressed by means of a programming construct called a *conditional statement*. PHP supports different types of conditional statements, each one intended for a particular use.

The if Statement

The simplest of PHP's conditional statements is the `if` statement. This works much like the English-language statement, "if X happens, do Y." Here's a simple example, which contains a conditional statement that checks if the value of the `$number` variable is less than 0 and prints a notification message if so.

```php
<?php
// if number is less than zero
// print message
$number = -88;
if ($number < 0) {
    echo 'That number is negative';
}
?>
```

The key to the if statement is thus the condition to be evaluated, which is always enclosed in parentheses. If the condition evaluates to true, the code within the curly braces is executed; if it evaluates to false, the code within the curly braces is skipped. This true/false test is performed using PHP's comparison operators, which you learned about in the preceding chapter; Table 3-1 quickly recaps them.

The if-else Statement

The if statement is quite basic: it only lets you define what happens when the condition specified evaluates to true. But PHP also offers the if-else statement, an improved version of the if construct that allows you to define an alternative set of actions that the program should take when the condition specified evaluates to false. Using this statement often results in more compact and readable code, because it lets you combine two actions into a single, unified code block. In English, this statement would read, "if X happens, do Y; otherwise, do Z."

Operator	Description
==	Equal to
!=	Not equal to
>	Greater than
>=	Greater than or equal to
<	Less than
<=	Less than or equal to
===	Equal to and of the same type

Table 3-1 Common Comparison Operators

To illustrate, consider this revision of the previous listing:

```php
<?php
// change message depending on whether
// number is less than zero or not
$number = -88;
if ($number < 0) {
    echo 'That number is negative';
} else {
    echo 'That number is either positive or zero';
}
?>
```

Here, an `if-else` statement is used to account for two possible outcomes: a number less than zero, and all other numbers. To see it in action, try running this script once as is, and then again after changing the value of the $number variable to a positive value.

Ask the Expert

Q: Is there a more compact way to write an `if-else` statement?

A: Yes, there is. It involves a little thingamajig called the *ternary operator*. This operator, represented by the question mark (?) symbol, lets you represent an `if-else` conditional statement in a single, compact line of code. To see it in action, consider the following two equivalent scripts:

The Standard if-else Block	The Equivalent Block Using the Ternary Operator

<pre><?php
if ($x < 10) {
 echo 'X is less than 10';
} else {
 echo 'X is more than 10';
}
?></pre>
	<pre><?php
	echo ($x < 10) ? 'X is less than 10' :
	 'X is more than 10';
	?></pre>

Here, the ternary operator selects the code on the left of the colon if the condition evaluates to true, and the code on the right if the condition evaluates to false.

Try This 3-1   Testing Odd and Even Numbers

Now that you know the basics of conditional statements, let's look at an example of how they can be used. The following program will ask the user to enter a number into a Web form, test it to see whether it is odd or even, and return a corresponding message.

Here's the code (*oddeven.php*):

```
<!DOCTYPE html PUBLIC "-//W3C//DTD XHTML 1.0 Transitional//EN"
    "DTD/xhtml1-transitional.dtd">
<html xmlns="http://www.w3.org/1999/xhtml" xml:lang="en" lang="en">
  <head>
    <title>Project 3-1: Odd/Even Number Tester</title>
  </head>
  <body>
    <h2>Project 3-1: Odd/Even Number Tester</h2>
<?php
    // if form not yet submitted
    // display form
    if (!isset($_POST['submit'])) {
?>
    <form method="post" action="oddeven.php">
      Enter value: <br />
      <input type="text" name="num" size="3" />
      <p>
      <input type="submit" name="submit" value="Submit" />
    </form>
<?php
    // if form submitted
    // process form input
    } else {
    // retrieve number from POST submission
    $num = $_POST['num'];

    // test value for even-ness
    // display appropriate message
    if (($num % 2) == 0) {
      echo 'You entered ' . $num . ', which is an even number.';
    } else {
      echo 'You entered ' . $num . ', which is an odd number.';
    }
  }
?>
  </body>
</html>
```

(continued)

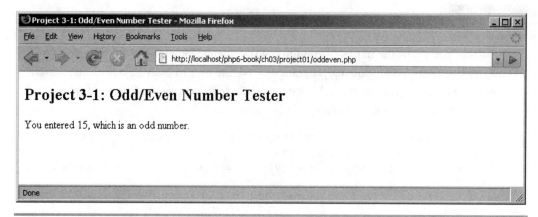

Figure 3-1 Testing odd and even numbers with PHP

This program consists of two sections: the first half generates a Web form for the user to enter a value, while the second half checks whether the value is odd or even and prints an appropriate message. In most cases, these two sections would be in separate files; they've been combined into a single PHP script by the magic of a conditional statement.

How does it work? Well, when the Web form is submitted, the $_POST variable will contain an entry for the <input type='submit'...> element. A conditional test then checks for the presence or absence of this variable: if absent, the program "knows" that the Web form has not been submitted yet and so prints the form's HTML code; if present, the program "knows" that the Web form has been submitted and it then proceeds to test the input value.

Testing the input value for evenness is handled by a second if-else conditional statement. Here, the conditional expression consists of dividing the input value by 2 and testing if the remainder is zero. If this test returns true, one message is printed; else, another message is printed.

Figure 3-1 illustrates what the output of the script looks like.

Writing More Complex Conditional Statements

The if-else statement lets you define actions for two eventualities: a true condition and a false condition. In reality, however, your program may have more than just these two simple outcomes to contend with. For these situations, PHP offers two constructs that allow the programmer to account for multiple possibilities: the `if-elseif-else` statement and the `switch-case` statement.

The if-elseif-else Statement

The `if-elseif-else` statement lets you chain together multiple `if-else` statements, thus allowing the programmer to define actions for more than just two possible outcomes. Consider the following example, which illustrates its use:

```php
<?php
// handle multiple possibilities
// define a different message for each day
$today = 'Tuesday';
if ($today == 'Monday') {
    echo 'Monday\'s child is fair of face.';
} elseif ($today == 'Tuesday') {
    echo 'Tuesday\'s child is full of grace.';
} elseif ($today == 'Wednesday') {
    echo 'Wednesday\'s child is full of woe.';
} elseif ($today == 'Thursday') {
    echo 'Thursday\'s child has far to go.';
} elseif ($today == 'Friday') {
    echo 'Friday\'s child is loving and giving.';
} elseif ($today == 'Saturday') {
    echo 'Saturday\'s child works hard for a living.';
} else {
    echo 'No information available for that day';
}
?>
```

Here, the program will output a different message for each day of the week (as set in the $today variable). Notice also the final `else` branch: this is a "catch-all" branch, which will be triggered if none of the previous conditional statements evaluate to true, and it's a handy way to account for situations that you can't foresee.

There's one important thing to remember about the `if-elseif-else` construct: as soon as one of the conditional statements evaluates to true, PHP will execute the corresponding code, skip the remaining conditional tests, and jump straight to the lines following the entire `if-elseif-else` block. So, even if more than one of the conditional tests evaluates to true, PHP will only execute the code corresponding to the first true test.

The switch-case Statement

An alternative to the `if-elseif-else` statement is the `switch-case` statement, which does almost the same thing: it tests a variable against a series of values until it finds a match, and then executes the code corresponding to that match. Consider the following code listing, which is equivalent to the preceding one:

```php
<?php
// handle multiple possibilities
// define a different message for each day
$today = 'Tuesday';
switch ($today) {
    case 'Monday':
        echo 'Monday\'s child is fair of face.';
        break;
    case 'Tuesday':
        echo 'Tuesday\'s child is full of grace.';
        break;
    case 'Wednesday':
        echo 'Wednesday\'s child is full of woe.';
        break;
    case 'Thursday':
        echo 'Thursday\'s child has far to go.';
        break;
    case 'Friday':
        echo 'Friday\'s child is loving and giving.';
        break;
    case 'Saturday':
        echo 'Saturday\'s child works hard for a living.';
        break;
    default:
        echo 'No information available for that day';
        break;
}
?>
```

The switch-case construct differs from the if-elseif-else construct in one important way. Once PHP finds a case statement that evaluates to true, it executes not only the code corresponding to that case statement, but also the code for all subsequent case statements. If this is not what you want, add a break statement to the end of each case block (as is done in the previous listing) to tell PHP to break out of the switch-case statement block once it executes the code corresponding to the first true case.

Notice also the 'default' case: as the name suggests, this specifies the default set of actions PHP should take if none of the other cases evaluate to true. This default case, like the else branch of the if-elseif-else block, is very useful as a "catch-all" handler for unforeseen situations.

Try This 3-2   ## Assigning Boy Scouts to Tents

Let's now use the `if-elseif-else` statement to create a small application for Scoutmasters everywhere: a Web tool that can automatically assign Scouts to the correct tent during camping expeditions, on the basis of their age. This application presents Scouts with a Web form into which they can enter their age; it then assigns them to one of four tents—Red, Green, Blue, and Black—with other Scouts of approximately the same age.

Here's the code (*tent.php*):

```
<!DOCTYPE html PUBLIC "-//W3C//DTD XHTML 1.0 Transitional//EN"
    "DTD/xhtml1-transitional.dtd">
<html xmlns="http://www.w3.org/1999/xhtml" xml:lang="en" lang="en">
  <head>
    <title>Project 3-2: Tent Assignment</title>
  </head>
  <body>
    <h2>Project 3-2: Tent Assignment</h2>
<?php
    // if form not yet submitted
    // display form
    if (!isset($_POST['submit'])) {
?>
    <form method="post" action="tent.php">
      Enter your age: <br />
      <input type="text" name="age" size="3" />
      <p>
      <input type="submit" name="submit" value="Submit" />
    </form>
<?php
    // if form submitted
    // process form input
    } else {
    // retrieve age from POST submission
    $age = $_POST['age'];

    // assign to one of four tents
    // based on which age "bin" it falls into
    if ($age <= 9) {
        echo "You're in the Red tent.";
    } elseif ($age > 9 && $age <= 11) {
        echo "You're in the Blue tent.";
    } elseif ($age > 11 && $age <= 14) {
        echo "You're in the Green tent.";
```

(continued)

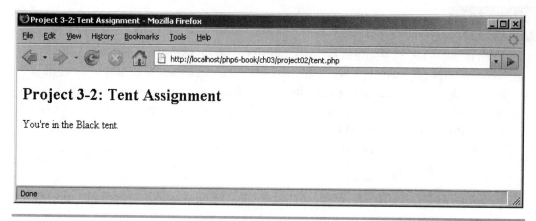

Figure 3-2 The result page, which assigns the user to a tent

```
        } elseif ($age > 14 && $age <= 17) {
            echo "You're in the Black tent.";
        } else {
            echo "You'd better get in touch with the Scoutmaster.";
        }
    }
?>
  </body>
</html>
```

Like the previous project in this chapter, this one too combines the Web form and its result page into a single script, separated by an `if-else` conditional statement. Once the Scout enters his age into the Web form and submits it, an `if-elseif-else` block takes care of defining four age ranges (one for each tent), testing the input age against these ranges, and figuring out which tent is most appropriate for the Scout. The age ranges are: 0–9 (Red tent); 10–11 (Blue tent); 12–14 (Green tent); and 14–17 (Black tent). Scouts over the age of 17 see a message asking them to contact the Scoutmaster to arrange their accommodation.

Figure 3-2 shows the result page of a form submission.

Combining Conditional Statements

PHP allows one conditional statement to be nested within another, to allow for more complex decision-making. To illustrate this, consider the following listing:

```
<?php
// for employees with annual comp <= $15000
```

```
// those with a rating >= 3 get a $5000 bonus
// everyone else gets a $3000 bonus
if ($rating >= 3) {
    if ($salary < 15000) {
        $bonus = 5000;
    }
} else {
    if ($salary < 15000) {
        $bonus = 3000;
    }
}
?>
```

You can also combine conditional statements by using logical operators, such as the && or || operator. You learned about logical operators in the preceding chapter; Table 3-2 quickly recaps the list.

Here's an example of how these logical operators can be used with a conditional statement:

```
<?php
$year = 2008;
// leap years are divisible by 400
// or by 4 but not 100
if (($year % 400 == 0) || (($year % 100 != 0) && ($year % 4 == 0))) {
    echo "$year is a leap year.";
} else {
    echo "$year is not a leap year.";
}
?>
```

Repeating Actions with Loops

Like any good programming language, PHP also supports *loops*—essentially, the ability to repeat a series of actions until a prespecified condition is fulfilled. Loops are an important tool that help in automating repetitive tasks within a program. PHP supports four different

Operator	Description
&&	AND
||	OR
!	NOT

Table 3-2 Common Logical Operators

types of loops, three of which are discussed in the following section (the fourth type is explained in the next chapter).

The while Loop

The easiest type of loop to understand is the while loop, which repeats continuously while a prespecified condition is true. Here's an example, which uses a loop to repeatedly print an 'x' to the output page.

```php
<?php
// repeat continuously until counter becomes 10
// output: 'xxxxxxxxx'
$counter = 1;
while ($counter < 10) {
   echo 'x';
   $counter++;
}
?>
```

Notice the condition enclosed in parentheses; so long as this condition evaluates to true, the code within the curly braces is executed. As soon as the condition becomes false, the loop stops repeating, and the lines following the loop are executed in the usual fashion.

The do-while Loop

With a while loop, the condition to be evaluated is tested at the beginning of each loop iteration. There's also a variant of this loop, the do-while loop, which evaluates the condition at the end of each loop iteration. Here's a revision of the preceding example that illustrates it in action:

```php
<?php
// repeat continuously until counter becomes 10
// output: 'xxxxxxxxx'
$counter = 1;
do {
   echo 'x';
   $counter++;
} while ($counter < 10);
?>
```

The difference in structure should also be apparent: with a do-while loop, the condition to be evaluated now appears at the bottom of the loop block, rather than the beginning.

NOTE

The difference in behavior between a while loop and a do-while loop has one important implication: with a while loop, if the conditional expression evaluates to false on the first pass itself, the loop will never be executed. With a do-while loop, on the other hand, the loop will always be executed once, even if the conditional expression is false, because the condition is evaluated at the end of the loop iteration rather than the beginning.

The for Loop

The while and do-while loops are fairly simple: they repeat for so long as the specified condition remains true. But PHP also supports a more sophisticated type of loop, the for loop, which is useful when you need to execute a set of statements a specific number of times.

The best way to understand a for loop is by looking at some code. Here's a simple example, which lists the numbers between 1 and 10:

```php
<?php
// repeat continuously until counter becomes 10
// output:
for ($x=1; $x<10; $x++) {
  echo "$x ";
}
?>
```

In this listing, the loop begins by initializing the counter variable $x to 1; it then executes the statements that make up the loop. Once it reaches the end of the first loop iteration, it updates the loop counter by adding 1 to it, checks the conditional expression to ensure that the counter hasn't yet reached 10, and executes the loop once more. This process continues until the counter reaches 10 and the conditional expression becomes false.

As this listing illustrates, there are thus three expressions involved in the typical for loop, separated by semicolons and enclosed in parentheses:

- The first of these is an assignment expression, which initializes the loop counter to a specific value—in this case, assigning the value 1 to the variable $x.

- The second is a conditional expression, which must evaluate to either true or false; the loop will continue to execute so long as this condition remains true. Once the condition becomes false, the loop will stop executing.

- The third is again an assignment expression, which is executed at the end of each loop iteration, and which updates the loop counter with a new value—in this case, adding 1 to the value of $x.

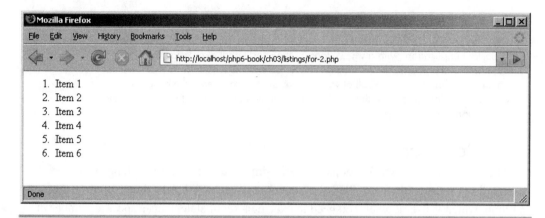

Figure 3-3 A dynamically generated list

Here's another example, this one demonstrating how to use a `for` loop to generate an ordered HTML list:

```php
<?php
// generate ordered list of 6 items
echo "<ol>";
for ($x=1; $x<7; $x++) {
  echo "<li>Item $x</li>";
}
echo "</ol>";
?>
```

Figure 3-3 illustrates what the output looks like.

Combining Loops

Just as with conditional statements, it's also possible to nest one loop inside another. To illustrate, consider the next example, which nests one `for` loop inside another to dynamically generate an HTML table.

```php
<!DOCTYPE html PUBLIC "-//W3C//DTD XHTML 1.0 Transitional//EN"
   "DTD/xhtml1-transitional.dtd">
<html xmlns="http://www.w3.org/1999/xhtml" xml:lang="en" lang="en">
  <head>
    <title></title>
  </head>
  <body>
<?php
// generate an HTML table
// 3 rows, 4 columns
echo "<table border=\"1\">";
```

```
for ($row=1; $row<4; $row++) {
  echo "<tr>";
  for ($col=1; $col<5; $col++) {
    echo "<td>Row $row, Column $col</td>";
  }
  echo "</tr>";
}
echo "</table>";
?>
  </body>
</html>
```

This script utilizes two `for` loops. The outer loop is responsible for generating the table rows, and it runs three times. On each iteration of this outer loop, an inner loop is also triggered; this loop is responsible for generating the cells within each row, and it runs four times. The end result is a table with three rows, each containing four cells. Figure 3-4 displays this result.

Interrupting and Skipping Loops

While on the topic of loops, it's interesting to discuss two PHP statements that allow you to either interrupt a loop or skip a particular iteration of a loop. PHP's `break` statement is aptly named: it allows you to break out of a loop at any point. To illustrate, consider the following loop, which would normally iterate five times but stops after the second iteration due to the `break` statement:

```
<?php
$count = 0;
// loop 5 times
```

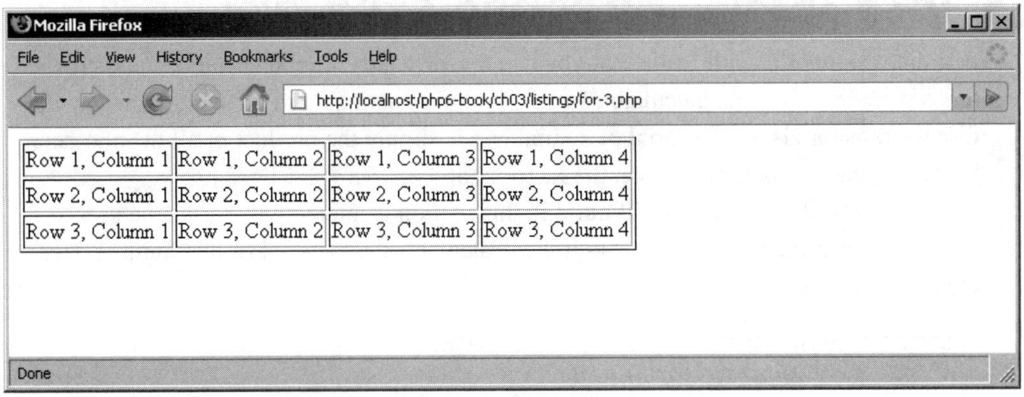

Figure 3-4 A dynamically generated table

```
while ($count <= 4) {
    $count++;
    // when the counter hits 3
    // break out of the loop
    if ($count == 3) {
        break;
    }
    echo "This is iteration #$count <br/>";
}
?>
```

Unlike break, continue doesn't halt processing of the loop; it simply "jumps one" iteration. To see how this works, consider the following loop, which iterates five times but skips the third iteration due to the intervention of the continue statement:

```
<?php
$count = 0;
// loop 5 times
while ($count <= 4) {
    $count++;
    // when the counter hits 3
    // skip to the next iteration
    if ($count == 3) {
        continue;
    }
    echo "This is iteration #$count <br/>";
}
?>
```

Try This 3-3 Building a Factorial Calculator

A simple real-world application that you can try for yourself to better understand how loops work, is a factorial calculator. In case you were snoozing in math class the day they discussed factorials, the factorial of a number n is simply the product of all the numbers between n and 1. So, for example, the factorial of 4 is 4 *3 * 2 * 1 = 24.

The factorial calculator you'll build in this section is interactive: it asks the user to enter a number into a Web form, and it then calculates the factorial of that number. Here's the code (*factorial.php*):

```
<!DOCTYPE html PUBLIC "-//W3C//DTD XHTML 1.0 Transitional//EN"
    "DTD/xhtml1-transitional.dtd">
<html xmlns="http://www.w3.org/1999/xhtml" xml:lang="en" lang="en">
  <head>
    <title>Project 3-3: Factorial Calculator</title>
```

```
    </head>
    <body>
      <h2>Project 3-3: Factorial Calculator</h2>
<?php
    // if form not yet submitted
    // display form
    if (!isset($_POST['submit'])) {
?>
      <form method="post" action="factorial.php">
        Enter a number: <br />
        <input type="text" name="num" size="3" />
        <p>
        <input type="submit" name="submit" value="Submit" />
      </form>
<?php
      // if form submitted
      // process form input
      } else {
      // retrieve number from form input
      $num = $_POST['num'];

      // check that number is positive
      if ($num <= 0) {
        echo 'ERROR: Please enter a number greater than 0';
        exit();
      }

      // calculate factorial
      // by multiplying the number by all the
      // numbers between itself and 1
      $factorial = 1;
      for ($x=$num; $x>=1; $x--) {
        $factorial *= $x;
      }
      echo "Factorial of $num is: $factorial";
    }
?>
    </body>
</html>
```

Most of the work here is performed by the `for` loop. This loop's counter is initialized to the number entered by the user, and the loop then runs backward, decrementing the loop counter by 1 on each iteration. Each time the loop runs, the previously calculated product is multiplied by the current value of the loop counter. The end result is the factorial of the input number.

Figure 3-5 shows the result after submitting the form.

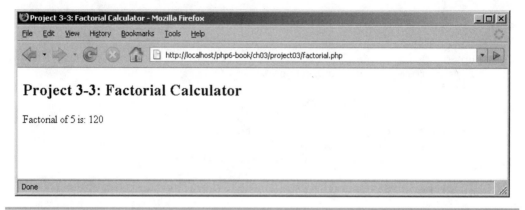

Figure 3-5 The output page, which displays the factorial of the number

Working with String and Numeric Functions

In the preceding chapter, you learned a little bit about PHP's data types, including its operators for string and number manipulation. But PHP lets you do a lot more than simply concatenate strings and add values; the language comes with a full-featured library of built-in functions that let you do everything from reversing and splitting strings to calculating logarithmic values. This section will introduce you to some of these functions.

Using String Functions

PHP has over 75 built-in string manipulation functions, supporting operations ranging from string repetition and reversal to comparison and search-and-replace. Table 3-3 lists some of these functions.

Checking for Empty Strings

The empty() function returns true if a string variable is "empty." Empty string variables are those with the values ' ', 0, '0', or NULL. The empty() function also returns true when used with a non-existent variable. Here are some examples:

```php
<?php
// test if string is empty
// output: true
$str = '';
echo (boolean) empty($str);

// output: true
$str = null;
echo (boolean) empty($str);
```

```
// output: true
$str = '0';
echo (boolean) empty($str);

// output: true
unset($str);
echo (boolean) empty($str);
?>
```

Function	What It Does
empty()	Tests if a string is empty
strlen()	Calculates the number of characters in a string
strrev()	Reverses a string
str_repeat()	Repeats a string
substr()	Retrieves a section of a string
strcmp()	Compares two strings
str_word_count()	Calculates the number of words in a string
str_replace()	Replaces parts of a string
trim()	Removes leading and trailing whitespace from a string
strtolower()	Lowercases a string
strtoupper()	Uppercases a string
ucfirst()	Uppercases the first character of a string
ucwords()	Uppercases the first character of every word of a string
addslashes()	Escapes special characters in a string with backslashes
stripslashes()	Removes backslashes from a string
htmlentities()	Encodes HTML within a string
htmlspecialchars()	Encodes special HTML characters within a string
nl2br()	Replaces line breaks in a string with elements
html_entity_decode()	Decodes HTML entities within a string
htmlspecialchars_decode()	Decodes special HTML characters within a string
strip_tags()	Removes PHP and HTML code from a string

Table 3-3 Common PHP String Functions

Reversing and Repeating Strings

The `strlen()` function returns the number of characters in a string. Here's an example of it in action:

```php
<?php
// calculate length of string
// output: 17
$str = 'Welcome to Xanadu';
echo strlen($str);
?>
```

Reversing a string is as simple as calling the `strrev()` function, as in the next listing:

```php
<?php
// reverse string
// output: 'pets llams enO'
$str = 'One small step';
echo strrev($str);
?>
```

In case you need to repeat a string, PHP offers the `str_repeat()` function, which accepts two arguments—the string to be repeated, and the number of times to repeat it. Here's an example:

```php
<?php
// repeat string
// output: 'yoyoyo'
$str = 'yo';
echo str_repeat($str, 3);
?>
```

Working with Substrings

PHP also allows you to slice a string into smaller parts with the `substr()` function, which accepts three arguments: the original string, the position (*offset*) at which to start slicing, and the number of characters to return from the starting position. The following listing illustrates this in action:

```php
<?php
// extract substring
// output: 'come'
$str = 'Welcome to nowhere';
echo substr($str, 3, 4);
?>
```

NOTE

When using the `substr()` function, the first character of the string is treated as offset 0, the second character as offset 1, and so on.

To extract a substring from the end of a string (rather than the beginning), pass `substr()` a negative offset, as in this revision of the preceding example:

```php
<?php
// extract substring
// output: 'come here'
$str = 'Welcome to nowhere';
echo substr($str, 3, 5) . substr($str, -4, 4);
?>
```

Ask the Expert

Q: Can I retrieve a single character of a string? How?

A: There are two ways to retrieve a single character of a string. The longer way involves using the `substr()` function, as in the next listing:

```php
<?php
// output: 'r'
$str = 'abracadabra';
echo substr($str,2,1);
?>
```

The `substr()` function accepts three arguments: the original string, the offset at which substring extraction should begin, and the number of characters to extract starting from the specified offset. Note that offset counting begins at 0, not 1.

However, PHP also supports a shortcut syntax to accomplish the same thing. This consists of specifying the offset of the character to be retrieved within curly braces, after the variable name. The following listing illustrates:

```php
<?php
// output: 'r'
$str = 'abracadabra';
echo $str{2};
?>
```

Comparing, Counting, and Replacing Strings

If you need to compare two strings, the strcmp() function performs a case-sensitive comparison of two strings, returning a negative value if the first is "less" than the second, a positive value if it's the other way around, and zero if both strings are "equal." Here are some examples of how this works:

```
<?php
// compare strings
$a = "hello";
$b = "hello";
$c = "hEllo";

// output: 0
echo strcmp($a, $b);

// output: 1
echo strcmp($a, $c);
?>
```

PHP's str_word_count() function provides an easy way to count the number of words in a string. The following listing illustrates its use:

```
<?php
// count words
// output: 5
$str = "The name's Bond, James Bond";
echo str_word_count($str);
?>
```

If you need to perform substitution within a string, PHP also has the str_replace() function, designed specifically to perform find-and-replace operations. This function accepts three arguments: the search term, the replacement term, and the string in which to perform the replacement. Here's an example:

```
<?php
// replace '@' with 'at'
// output: 'john at domain.net'
$str = 'john@domain.net';
echo str_replace('@', ' at ', $str);
?>
```

Formatting Strings

PHP's trim() function can be used to remove leading or trailing whitespace from a string; this is quite useful when processing data entered into a Web form. Here's an example:

```php
<?php
// remove leading and trailing whitespace
// output 'a b   c'
$str = '   a b   c   ';
echo trim($str);
?>
```

Changing the case of a string is as simple as calling the `strtolower()` or `strtoupper()` function, as illustrated in the next listing:

```php
<?php
// change string case
$str = 'Yabba Dabba Doo';

// output: 'yabba dabba doo'
echo strtolower($str);

// output: 'YABBA DABBA DOO'
echo strtoupper($str);
?>
```

You can also uppercase the first character of a string with the `ucfirst()` function, or format a string in "word case" with the `ucwords()` function. The following listing demonstrates both these functions:

```php
<?php
// change string case
$str = 'the yellow brigands';

// output: 'The Yellow Brigands'
echo ucwords($str);

// output: 'The yellow brigands'
echo ucfirst($str);
?>
```

Working with HTML Strings

PHP also has some functions exclusively for working with HTML strings. First up, the `addslashes()` function, which automatically escapes special characters in a string with backslashes. Here's an example:

```php
<?php
// escape special characters
// output: 'You\'re awake, aren\'t you?'
$str = "You're awake, aren't you?";
echo addslashes($str);
?>
```

You can reverse the work done by addslashes() with the aptly named stripslashes() function, which removes all the backslashes from a string. Consider the following example, which illustrates:

```
<?php
// remove slashes
// output: 'John D'Souza says "Catch you later".'
$str = "John D\'Souza says \"Catch you later\".";
echo stripslashes($str);
?>
```

The htmlentities() and htmlspecialchars() functions automatically convert special HTML symbols (like < and >) into their corresponding HTML representations (< and &<hairline #>gt;). Similarly, the nl2br() function automatically replaces newline characters in a string with the corresponding HTML line break tag <br />. Here's an example:

```
<?php
// replace with HTML entities
// output: '&lt;div width=&quot;200&quot;&gt;
//          This is a div&lt;/div&gt;'
$html = '<div width="200">This is a div</div>';
echo htmlentities($html);

// replace line breaks with <br/>s
// output: 'This is a bro<br />
//          ken line'
$lines = 'This is a bro
         ken line';
echo nl2br($lines);
?>
```

You can reverse the effect of the htmlentities() and htmlspecialchars() functions with the html_entity_decode() and htmlspecialchars_decode() functions.

Finally, the strip_tags() function searches for all HTML and PHP code within a string and removes it to generate a "clean" string. Here's an example:

```
<?php
// strip HTML tags from string
// output: 'Please log in again'
$html = '<div width="200">Please <strong>log in again</strong></div>';
echo strip_tags($html);
?>
```

Using Numeric Functions

Don't think that PHP's power is limited to strings only: the language has over 50 built-in functions for working with numbers, ranging from simple formatting functions to functions for arithmetic, logarithmic, and trigonometric manipulations. Table 3-4 lists some of these functions.

Doing Calculus

A common task when working with numbers involves rounding them up and down. PHP offers the ceil() and floor() functions for this task, and they're illustrated in the next listing:

```php
<?php
// round number up
// output: 19
$num = 19.7;
echo floor($num);
```

Function	What It Does
ceil()	Rounds a number up
floor()	Rounds a number down
abs()	Finds the absolute value of a number
pow()	Raises one number to the power of another
log()	Finds the logarithm of a number
exp()	Finds the exponent of a number
rand()	Generates a random number
bindec()	Converts a number from binary to decimal
decbin()	Converts a number from decimal to binary
decoct()	Converts a number from decimal to octal
dechex()	Converts a number from decimal to hexadecimal
hexdec()	Converts a number from hexadecimal to decimal
octdec()	Converts a number from octal to decimal
number_format()	Formats a number with grouped thousands and decimals
printf()	Formats a number using a custom specification

Table 3-4   Common PHP Numeric Functions

```
// round number down
// output: 20
echo ceil($num);
?>
```

There's also the abs() function, which returns the absolute value of a number. Here's an example:

```
<?php
// return absolute value of number
// output: 19.7
$num = -19.7;
echo abs($num);
?>
```

The pow() function returns the value of a number raised to the power of another:

```
<?php
// calculate 4 ^ 3
// output: 64
echo pow(4,3);
?>
```

The log() function calculates the natural or base-10 logarithm of a number, while the exp() function calculates the exponent of a number. Here's an example of both in action:

```
<?php
// calculate natural log of 100
// output: 2.30258509299
echo log(10);

// calculate log of 100, base 10
// output: 2
echo log(100,10);

// calculate exponent of 2.30258509299
// output: 9.99999999996
echo exp(2.30258509299);
?>
```

Generating Random Numbers

Generating random numbers with PHP is pretty simple too: the language's built-in rand() function automatically generates a random integer greater than 0. You can constrain it to a specific number range by providing optional limits as arguments. The following example illustrates:

```
<?php
// generate a random number
```

```
echo rand();

// generate a random number between 10 and 99
echo rand(10,99);
?>
```

Converting Between Number Bases

PHP comes with built-in functions for converting between binary, decimal, octal, and hexadecimal bases. Here's an example which demonstrates the bindec(), decbin(), decoct(), dechex(), hexdec(), and octdec() functions in action:

```
<?php
// convert to binary
// output: 1000
echo decbin(8);

// convert to hexadecimal
// output: 8
echo dechex(8);

// convert to octal
// output: 10
echo decoct(8);

// convert from octal
// output: 8
echo octdec(10);

// convert from hexadecimal
// output: 101
echo hexdec(65);

// convert from binary
// output: 8
echo bindec(1000);
?>
```

Formatting Numbers

When it comes to formatting numbers, PHP offers the number_format() function, which accepts four arguments: the number to be formatted, the number of decimal places to display, the character to use instead of a decimal point, and the character to use to separate grouped thousands (usually a comma). Consider the following example, which illustrates:

```
<?php
// format number (with defaults)
```

```
// output: 1,106,483
$num = 1106482.5843;
echo number_format($num);

// format number (with custom separators)
// output: 1?106?482*584
echo number_format($num,3,'*','?');
?>
```

For more control over number formatting, PHP offers the `printf()` and `sprintf()` functions. These functions, though very useful, can be intimidating to new users, and so the best way to understand them is with an example. Consider the next listing, which shows them in action:

```php
<?php
// format as decimal number
// output: 00065
printf("%05d", 65);

// format as floating-point number
// output: 00239.000
printf("%09.3f", 239);

// format as octal number
// output:   10
printf("%4o", 8);

// format number
// incorporate into string
// output: 'I see 8 apples and 26.00 oranges'
printf("I see %4d apples and %4.2f oranges", 8, 26);
?>
```

Both functions accept two arguments, a series of *format specifiers* and the raw string or number to be formatted. The input is then formatted according to the format specifiers and the output either displayed with `printf()` or assigned to a variable with `sprintf()`.

Some common format specifiers are listed in Table 3-5.

You can also combine these format specifiers with a *precision specifier*, which indicates the number of digits to display for floating-point values—for example, `%1.2f` implies that the number should be formatted as a floating-point value with two digits displayed after the decimal point. For smaller numbers, it's also possible to add a *padding specifier*, which tells the function to pad the numbers to a specified length using a custom character. You can see both these types of specifiers in action in the preceding listing.

Specifier	What It Means
%s	String
%d	Decimal number
%x	Hexadecimal number
%o	Octal number
%f	Floating-point number

Table 3-5 Format Specifiers for the `printf()` and `sprintf()` Functions

Try This 3-4 Processing a Member Registration Form

Now that you've seen some of PHP's built-in functions, let's apply some of what you've learned to a practical application: a membership application form for a sports club. This form will ask the applicant to enter various bits of personal information; it will then validate this information and, if acceptable, will formulate and send an e-mail with the applicant's information to the club administrator.

Here's the HTML form (*register.html*):

```
<!DOCTYPE html PUBLIC "-//W3C//DTD XHTML 1.0 Transitional//EN"
   "DTD/xhtml1-transitional.dtd">
<html xmlns="http://www.w3.org/1999/xhtml" xml:lang="en" lang="en">
  <head>
    <title>Project 3-4: Member Registration</title>
  </head>
  <body>
    <h2>Project 3-4: Member Registration</h2>
    <form method="post" action="register.php">
      Name: <br />
      <input type="text" name="name" size="50" />
      <p>
      Address: <br />
      <textarea name="address" rows="5" cols=40></textarea>
      <p>
      Age: <br />
      <input type="text" name="age" size="3" />
      <p>
      Profession: <br />
      <input type="text" name="profession" size="50" />
```

(continued)

```
      <p>
      Residential status: <br />
      <input type="radio" name="resident" value="yes" checked="true" /> Resident
      <input type="radio" name="resident" value="no" /> Non-Resident
      <p>
      <input type="submit" name="submit" value="Submit" />
    </form>
  </body>
</html>
```

This form has five input fields, one each for the applicant's name, address, age, profession, and residential status. Figure 3-6 has a picture of what the form looks like.

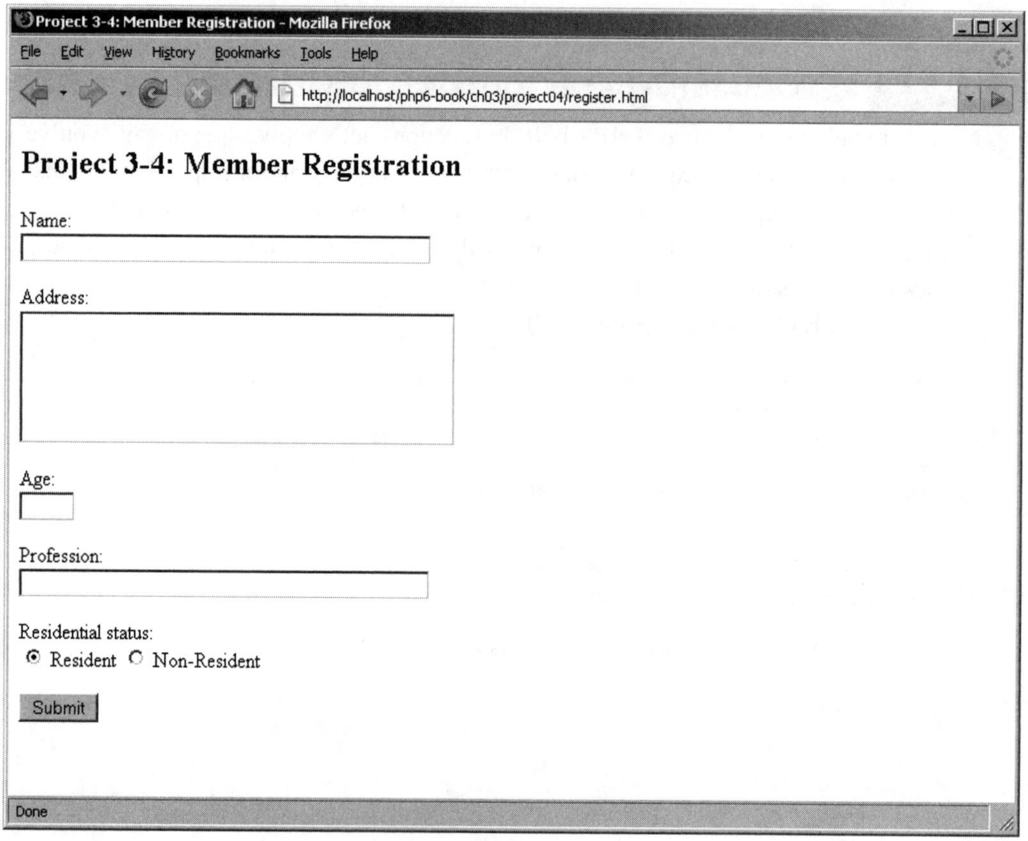

Figure 3-6 A Web-based application form

NOTE

In order to successfully send mail with PHP using the `mail()` function, your *php.ini* configuration file must include some information about the mail server or mail agent to be used. Windows users will need to set the `'SMTP'` and `'smtp_port'` options, while *NIX users may need to set the `'sendmail_path'` option. More information on these options can be obtained from the PHP manual page at www.php.net/mail.

Once the form is submitted, the data entered into it by the applicant is passed to the form processing script (*register.php*) via the POST method. The next listing shows the contents of this script:

```php
<!DOCTYPE html PUBLIC "-//W3C//DTD XHTML 1.0 Transitional//EN"
   "DTD/xhtml1-transitional.dtd">
<html xmlns="http://www.w3.org/1999/xhtml" xml:lang="en" lang="en">
  <head>
    <title>Project 3-4: Member Registration</title>
  </head>
  <body>
    <h2>Project 3-4: Member Registration</h2>
<?php
    // retrieve details from POST submission
    $name = $_POST['name'];
    $address = $_POST['address'];
    $age = $_POST['age'];
    $profession = $_POST['profession'];
    $resident = $_POST['resident'];

    // validate submitted data
    // check name
    if (empty($name)) {
      die('ERROR: Please provide your name.');
    }

    // check address
    if (empty($address)) {
      die('ERROR: Please provide your address.');
    }

    // check age
    if (empty($age)) {
      die('ERROR: Please provide your age');
    } else if ($age < 18 || $age > 60) {
      die('ERROR: Membership is only open to those between 18 and 60 years.');
    }

    // check profession
    if (empty($profession)) {
      die('ERROR: Please provide your profession.');
    }
```

(continued)

```php
// check residential status
if (strcmp($resident, 'no') == 0) {
  die('ERROR: Membership is only open to residents.');
}

// if we get this far
// all the input has passed validation
// formulate and send e-mail message
$to = 'registration@some.domain.com';
$from = 'webmaster@some.domain.com';
$subject = 'Application for membership';
$body = "Name: $name\r\nAddress: $address\r\n
  Age: $age\r\nProfession: $profession\r\n
  Residential status: $resident\r\n";
if(mail($to, $subject, $body, "From: $from")) {
    echo 'Thank you for your application.';
} else {
    die('ERROR: Mail delivery error');
}
?>
  </body>
</html>
```

NOTE

Remember to alter the value of the $to variable in the *register.php* script, to reflect your e-mail address.

This script begins by retrieving the values submitted by the user from $_POST and assigning these values to regular PHP variables. Next, the empty() function is used to test whether they are empty; those which are, generate an error message and cause the script to terminate immediately. Two extra conditional tests are also present in this section: the first for the applicant's age, to filter out applicants younger than 18 or older than 60; and the second for the applicant's residential status, to filter out non-residents.

Assuming all the checks are successful, the script proceeds to create an e-mail message, setting variables for the sender, recipient, message subject, and message body. These variables are then passed to PHP's mail() function, which actually does the hard work of sending the e-mail message. If message transmission is successful, a success notification appears; if not, an error message is generated.

The mail() function is new to you and so deserves a more detailed examination. The mail() function is a built-in PHP function to send an e-mail message, and it accepts four parameters: the recipient e-mail address, the message subject, the message body, and a list of additional message headers (of which the 'From' header is mandatory). It uses these parameters to construct an e-mail message, connect to the specified mail server, and hand the message over to delivery. If handover is successful, `mail()` returns true; otherwise, it returns false.

CAUTION

It's important to understand what the return value of the `mail()` function means. If the `mail()` function returns true, it merely means is that the message was successfully handed over to the mail server for delivery. It *does not* mean that the message was subsequently successfully transmitted to, or received by, the intended recipient (because PHP has no way of tracking the message once it's been handed over to the mail server). Failing to understand this distinction is a common error made by programmers new to PHP.

Also new in this script is the `die()` function: this function provides a convenient way to immediately terminate script processing, usually if an error occurs. You can also pass an optional message to `die()`; this message will be output by PHP at the point of script termination and thus serves as a useful explanation to the user about what went wrong.

Ask the Expert

Q: Can I add a custom header to e-mail messages sent through PHP?

A: Yes. The fourth argument to the `mail()` function is a string containing your custom header, in `header:value` format. If you have more than one custom header to add, separate the headers with `\r\n`. The following example illustrates:

```php
<?php
// define message
$to = 'bacchus@vsnl.com';
$subject = 'Hello';
$body = "This is a test";
// define custom headers
$headers = "From:webmaster@my.domain.com\r\n
 Organization:MyOrg Inc.\r\nX-Mailer:PHP";
if(mail($to, $subject, $body, $headers)) {
  echo 'Your message was sent.';
} else {
  die('ERROR: Mail delivery error');
}
?>
```

Summary

The goal of this chapter was to move you along the learning curve, from building simple, linear programs to creating more sophisticated PHP applications. It began by explaining how you can add intelligence to your PHP scripts through the use of conditional tests, and offered usage examples for PHP's `if`, `if-else`, `if-elseif-else`, and `switch-case` statements. It then proceeded to a discussion of PHP's loop constructs, showing you how easy it is to automate repetitive actions with PHP and introducing you to three common loop types: the `while`, `do-while`, and `for` loops.

The latter half of the chapter took you on a whirlwind tour of PHP's built-in string and numeric functions, using commented examples to explain how to perform tasks ranging from simple string comparison and extraction to more complex number conversion and formatting. And as if all that wasn't enough, this chapter helped you work your way through four projects, each designed to demonstrate practical usage of the concepts taught. Conditional statements, loops, and built-in functions all got a workout in these projects, which ranged the gamut from a simple odd/even number tester to a full-fledged Web application form that included input validation and e-mail message transmission functions.

At the close of this chapter, you now know enough about PHP's basic grammar and syntax to begin writing your own, reasonably complex PHP scripts. The next chapter will help expand your bag of PHP tricks, by introducing you to a new type of PHP variable and also giving you some insight into PHP's date and time manipulation functions. Until then, though, spend some time looking at the links that follow, which offer more detailed information on the topics discussed in this chapter:

- Conditional statements and loops, at
  www.php.net/manual/en/language.control-structures.php

- A discussion of PHP string functions, at **www.php.net/manual/en/ref.strings.php**
  and **www.melonfire.com/community/columns/trog/article.php?id=88**

- PHP math functions, at **www.php.net/manual/en/ref.math.php**

- Sending e-mail with PHP, at **www.php.net/manual/en/ref.mail.php**

- PHP's ternary operator, at **www.php.net/manual/en/language.operators.php**

Chapter 3 Self Test

1. What is the difference between an `if-else` statement and an `if-elseif-else` statement?

2. Write a conditional statement that checks the value of `$city` and displays a message if it is equal to `'Minneapolis'`.

3. Explain the difference between a `while` loop and a `do-while` loop. Illustrate your answer with an example.

4. Using a `while` loop, write a program that prints a multiplication table for the number 8.

5. Rewrite the program from Question 4 using a `for` loop.

6. Name the functions you would use to

   A Decode HTML entities

   B Uppercase a string

   C Round a number down

   D Remove whitespace from a string

   E Generate a random number

   F Reverse a string

   G Count words in a string

   H Count characters in a string

   I Terminate script processing with a custom message

   J Compare two strings

   K Calculate the exponent of a number

   L Convert a decimal number to a hexadecimal value

7. What will be the output of the following line of PHP code:

```php
<?php printf("%09.6f", 7402.4042); ?>
```

8. Given the string `'Mark had a nice day'`, create the new string `'Mark had icecream'`.

Chapter 4

Working with Arrays

Key Skills & Concepts

- Understand the different array types supported by PHP

- Process array contents with the `foreach` loop

- Use arrays with Web forms

- Sort, merge, add, modify, and split arrays using PHP's built-in functions

- Work with dates and times

By now, PHP's simple data types should be old hat to you—you've spent the last few chapters using them, in different permutations and combinations, to create applications of varying complexity and usefulness. But there's a lot more to PHP's data types than strings, numbers, and Booleans; PHP also supports *arrays,* which let you group and manipulate more than one value at a time.

In this chapter, you'll learn all about arrays: how to create them, how to add and edit them, and how to manipulate the values they hold. You'll also learn about a new loop type designed specifically for use with arrays, get a crash course in some of PHP's built-in array functions, and apply your learning to some practical projects.

Storing Data in Arrays

So far, all the variables you've used have held only a single value. Array variables are "special," because they can hold more than one value at a time. This makes them particularly useful for storing related values—for example, a set of fruit names, as in this example:

```php
<?php
// define array
$fruits = array('apple', 'banana', 'pineapple', 'grape');
?>
```

Once you've got an array like this one, a natural question arises: how do you retrieve a particular value? It's quite simple: use index numbers to access the various values stored inside it, with zero representing the first value. Thus, to access the value `'apple'` from the preceding array, you'd use the notation `$fruits[0]`, while the value `'grape'` can be retrieved using the notation `$fruits[3]`.

PHP also supports a slightly different type of array, in which index numbers are replaced with user-defined strings, or "keys." Here's a revised version of the preceding example, which uses keys instead of index numbers:

```php
<?php
// define array
$fruits = array(
   'a' => 'apple',
   'b' => 'banana',
   'p' => 'pineapple',
   'g' => 'grape'
);
?>
```

This type of array is known as an *associative array*. The keys of the array must be unique; each key references a single value, and the key-value relationship is expressed through the `=>` symbol. To access the value `'apple'` from the array, you'd use the notation `$fruits['a']`, while the value `'banana'` can be retrieved using the notation `$fruits['b']`.

Assigning Array Values

PHP's rules for naming array variables are the same as those for regular variables: variable names must be preceded with a dollar ($) symbol and must begin with a letter or underscore character, optionally followed by more letters, numbers, or underscore characters. Punctuation characters and spaces are not allowed within array variable names.

Once you've decided a name for your array, there are two ways of assigning values to it. The first is the method you saw in the preceding section, where the values are all assigned at once, separated with commas. This method creates a standard, number-indexed array. Here's an example:

```php
<?php
// define array
$cars = array(
   'Ferrari',
   'Porsche',
   'Jaguar',
   'Lamborghini',
   'Mercedes'
);
?>
```

The second way to create such an array is to set values individually using index notation. Here's an example, which is equivalent to the preceding one:

```php
<?php
// define array
$cars[0] = 'Ferrari';
$cars[1] = 'Porsche';
$cars[2] = 'Jaguar';
$cars[3] = 'Lamborghini';
$cars[4] = 'Mercedes';
?>
```

Ask the Expert

Q: In all these examples, you've explicitly specified the array index for each assignment statement. What if I don't know what the correct index is? Can I make PHP automatically assign the next available array index to my value?

A: To automatically assign the next available index to an array value, omit the index number in your array assignment statement, as you see here:

```php
<?php
// define array
$cars[] = 'Ferrari';
$cars[] = 'Lamborghini';
?>
```

You can also use both these techniques with associative arrays. To assign all the values of such an array in a single statement, set a key for each value and link the two using the => connector, remembering to separate each key-value pair with commas. Here's an example:

```php
<?php
// define array
$data = array(
  'username' => 'john',
  'password' => 'secret',
  'host' => '192.168.0.1'
);
?>
```

You can also assign values to keys one by one, as in this next example:

```php
<?php
// define array
$data['username'] = 'john';
$data['password'] = 'secret';
$data['host'] = '192.168.0.1';
?>
```

To access a value from an array in a script, simply use the array name and index/key in an expression and PHP will replace it with its value when the script is executed, as with any normal variable. Here's a simple example that illustrates how this works:

```php
<?php
// define array
$data = array(
  'username' => 'john',
  'password' => 'secret',
  'host' => '192.168.0.1'
);

// use array value
echo 'The password is: ' . $data['password'];
?>
```

NOTE
Do you remember the special container variables named $_GET and $_POST that you first encountered in Chapter 2? Well, they're arrays too! When a form is submitted, each element of the form is automatically converted by PHP into a member of either the $_POST or $_GET array (depending on the method of submission).

Modifying Array Values

Modifying an array value is as simple as modifying any other variable value: simply assign a new value to the element using either its index or its key. Consider the following example, which modifies the second element of the $meats array to hold the value 'turkey' instead of 'ham':

```php
<?php
// define array
$meats = array(
  'fish',
  'chicken',
  'ham',
  'lamb'
);
```

```
// change 'ham' to 'turkey'
$meats[2] = 'turkey';
?>
```

To remove an element from an array, use the unset() function on the corresponding key or index:

```
<?php
// define array
$meats = array(
  'fish',
  'chicken',
  'ham',
  'lamb'
);

// remove 'fish'
unset($meats[0]);
?>
```

Ask the Expert

Q: If I remove an element from the middle of an array, what happens to the values on either side?

A: If you remove an element from an array with unset(), PHP will set that array element to NULL but will not automatically re-index the array. If the array is a numerically indexed array, you can re-index it to remove these "holes" in the indexing sequence, by passing the array through PHP's array_multisort() function.

You can also remove an element from an array using the array_pop() or array_push() function; these functions are discussed a little further along in this chapter.

Retrieving Array Size

An important task when using arrays, especially in combination with loops, is finding out how many values the array contains. This is easily accomplished with PHP's count() function, which accepts the array variable as a parameter and returns an integer value indicating how many elements it contains. Here's an example:

```
<?php
// define array
$data = array('Monday', 'Tuesday', 'Wednesday');
```

```
// get array size
echo 'The array has ' . count($data) . ' elements';
?>
```

TIP
Instead of the count() function, you can also use the sizeof() function, which does the same thing.

Ask the Expert

Q: Is there an upper limit on how many elements a PHP array can hold?

A: No. The number of elements in an array is limited only by available memory, as defined in the 'memory_limit' configuration variable in PHP's configuration file.

Nesting Arrays

PHP also allows you to combine arrays, by placing one inside another to an unlimited depth. This can come in handy when dealing with structured, hierarchically arranged information. To illustrate, consider the following example:

```
<?php
// define nested array
$phonebook = array(
  array(
    'name' => 'Raymond Rabbit',
    'tel' => '1234567',
    'email' => 'ray@bunnyplanet.in',
    ),
  array(
    'name' => 'David Duck',
    'tel' => '8562904',
    'email' => 'dduck@duckpond.corp',
    ),
  array(
    'name' => 'Harold Horse',
    'tel' => '5942033',
    'email' => 'kingharold@farmersmarket.horsestuff.com',
  )
);
?>
```

In this example, $phonebook is an array nested two levels deep. The first level is numerically indexed, with each element representing an entry from a phone book. Each of these elements is itself an associative array, holding specific information on the attributes of the corresponding phone book entry, such as the contact's name, phone number, and e-mail address.

To access a value a few levels deep in a nested array, use the correct hierarchical sequence of indices/keys to get to the value. Here's an example, which returns the phone number of the contact 'David Duck':

```php
<?php
// define nested array
$phonebook = array(
  array(
    'name' => 'Raymond Rabbit',
    'tel' => '1234567',
    'email' => 'ray@bunnyplanet.in',
    ),
  array(
    'name' => 'David Duck',
    'tel' => '8562904',
    'email' => 'dduck@duckpond.corp',
    ),
  array(
    'name' => 'Harold Horse',
    'tel' => '5942033',
    'email' => 'kingharold@farmersmarket.horsestuff.com',
    )
);

// access nested value
echo "David Duck's number is: " . $phonebook[1]['tel'];
?>
```

TIP

Want to look inside an array and see what it contains? The var_dump() and print_r() functions discussed in Chapter 2 work just as well on arrays as on other variables. Try them out for yourself and see!

Processing Arrays with Loops and Iterators

Often, your PHP program will need to work its way through an array, performing an operation or calculation on each value it finds. The best way to do this is with a loop, which you learned about in the preceding chapter. Consider the following example, which sets up an array and then iterates over it using a for loop:

```php
<?php
// define array
$cities = array('London', 'Paris', 'Madrid', 'Los Angeles', 'Bombay', 'Jakarta');

// iterate over array
// print each value
for ($i=0; $i<count($cities); $i++) {
  echo $cities[$i] . "\r\n";
}
?>
```

In this listing, a for loop iterates over the $cities array, printing each value found. The loop runs as many times as there are elements in the array; this information is quickly ascertained by a call to the count() function.

The foreach Loop

You might remember that the preceding chapter's discussion of loops was left unfinished, with one loop type still left to be explained. That loop, the foreach loop, was first introduced in PHP 4.0 and is the simplest way of iterating over arrays—not surprising, as that's what it was specifically designed for!

With a foreach loop, each time the loop runs, the current array element is assigned to a temporary variable, which can then be processed in any way you please—printed, copied to another variable, used in a calculation, and so on. Unlike a for loop, a foreach loop doesn't use a counter; it automatically "knows" where it is in the array, and it moves forward continuously until it reaches the end of the array, at which point it automatically halts.

The best way to understand this marvel of automation is with an example. The next listing shows it in action, rewriting the preceding listing to use a foreach loop instead of a for loop:

```php
<?php
// define array
$cities = array('London', 'Paris', 'Madrid', 'Los Angeles', 'Bombay', 'Jakarta');

// iterate over array
// print each value
foreach ($cities as $c) {
  echo "$c \r\n";
}
?>
```

The foreach loop also works with associative arrays, except that for such arrays, it uses two temporary variables (one each for the key and value). The next listing illustrates the difference:

```php
<?php
// define array
$cities = array(
  "United Kingdom" => "London",
  "United States" => "Washington",
  "France" => "Paris",
  "India" => "Delhi"
);

// iterate over array
// print each value
foreach ($cities as $key => $value) {
  echo "$value is in $key. \r\n";
}
?>
```

The Array Iterator

Alternatively, you may prefer to use an ArrayIterator (new in PHP 5.0), which provides a ready-made, extensible tool to loop over array elements. Here's a simple example:

```php
<?php
// define array
$cities = array(
  "United Kingdom" => "London",
  "United States" => "Washington",
  "France" => "Paris",
  "India" => "Delhi"
);

// create an ArrayIterator object
$iterator = new ArrayIterator($cities);

// rewind to beginning of array
$iterator->rewind();

// iterate over array
// print each value
while($iterator->valid()) {
    print $iterator->current() . " is in " . $iterator->key() . ". \r\n";
    $iterator->next();
}
?>
```

In this listing, an ArrayIterator object is initialized with an array variable, and the object's rewind() method is used to reset the internal array pointer to the first element of the array. A while loop, which runs so long as a valid() element exists, can then be used to iterate over the array. Individual array keys are retrieved with the key() method, and their corresponding values are retrieved with the current() method. The next() method moves the internal array pointer forward to the next array element.

NOTE
Don't worry if the syntax used by the ArrayIterator object isn't completely clear to you. Objects are dealt with in some depth in Chapter 5, and the preceding listing will make more sense once you've worked your way through that chapter.

Try This 4-1 Averaging the Grades of a Class

Now that you've understood the basics of working with arrays, let's try a small application that demonstrates their practical utility. In this section, you'll write a small script that accepts an array of values, representing the numerical grades of individual students in a class, and then calculates various summary statistics, including the average and the number of students in the top and bottom 20 percent of the class.

Here's the code (*grades.php*):

```
<!DOCTYPE html PUBLIC "-//W3C//DTD XHTML 1.0 Transitional//EN"
    "DTD/xhtml1-transitional.dtd">
<html xmlns="http://www.w3.org/1999/xhtml" xml:lang="en" lang="en">
  <head>
    <title>Project 4-1: Grade Averaging</title>
  </head>
  <body>
    <h2>Project 4-1: Grade Averaging</h2>
<?php
// define array of grades
// ranging between 1 and 100
$grades = array(
    25, 64, 23, 87, 56, 38, 78, 57, 98, 95,
    81, 67, 75, 76, 74, 82, 36, 39,
    54, 43, 49, 65, 69, 69, 78, 17, 91
);

// get number of grades
$count = count($grades);

// iterate over grades
// calculate total and top/bottom 20%
$total = $top = $bottom = 0;
foreach ($grades as $g) {
  $total += $g;
```

(continued)

```
  if ($g <= 20) {
    $bottom++;
  }

  if ($g >= 80) {
    $top++;
  }
}

// calculate average
$avg = round($total / $count);

// print statistics
echo "Class average: $avg <br />";
echo "Number of students in bottom 20%: $bottom <br />";
echo "Number of students in top 20%: $top <br />";
?>
  </body>
</html>
```

This script begins by defining an array, which holds the grades received by each student in the class. A foreach loop then iterates over the array, generating a cumulative total; this total is then divided by the number of students, retrieved via the count() function, to calculate the class average.

Since the grades range between 1 and 100, it's also not difficult to calculate the number of students in the top and bottom 20 percent of the class. Within the foreach loop, each value is checked to see if it is less than 20 or greater than 80, and the corresponding counter is incremented accordingly. The summary data thus collected is then printed to the Web page, as shown in Figure 4-1.

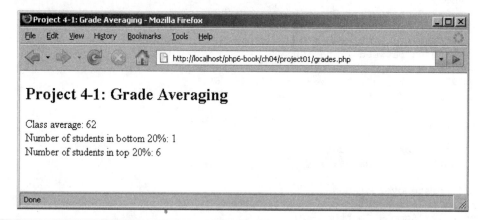

Figure 4-1 The summary statistics generated by the grade averaging program

Using Arrays with Forms

Arrays are particularly potent when used in combination with form elements that support more than one value, such as multiple-selection list boxes or grouped checkboxes. To capture a user's input in an array, simply add square braces to the form element's 'name' to automatically convert it into a PHP array when the form is submitted.

The easiest way to illustrate this is with an example. Consider the following form, which holds a multiple-selection list of popular music artists:

```
<form method="post" action="array-form.php">
    Select your favourite artists: <br />
    <select name="artists[]" multiple="true">
      <option value="Britney Spears">Britney Spears</option>
      <option value="Aerosmith">Aerosmith</option>
      <option value="Black-Eyed Peas">Black-Eyed Peas</option>
      <option value="Diana Ross">Diana Ross</option>
      <option value="Foo Fighters">Foo Fighters</option>
    </select>
    <p>
    <input type="submit" name="submit" value="Submit" />
  </form>
```

Notice the 'name' attribute of the <select> element, which is named artists[]. This tells PHP that, when the form is submitted, all the selected values from the list should be converted into elements of an array. The name of the array will be $_POST['artists'], and it will look something like this:

```
Array
(
    [0] => Britney Spears
    [1] => Black-Eyed Peas
    [2] => Diana Ross
)
```

Try This 4-2   Selecting Pizza Toppings

A practical application will make it easier to understand how PHP interacts with array variables and forms. This next application presents the user with a form containing various pizza toppings and asks the user to select, via checkbox, his or her favorite toppings. Here's the form (*pizza.html*):

```
<!DOCTYPE html PUBLIC "-//W3C//DTD XHTML 1.0 Transitional//EN"
    "DTD/xhtml1-transitional.dtd">
```

(continued)

```
<html xmlns="http://www.w3.org/1999/xhtml" xml:lang="en" lang="en">
  <head>
    <title>Project 4-2: Pizza Topping Selector</title>
  </head>
  <body>
    <h2>Project 4-2: Pizza Topping Selector</h2>
    <form method="post" action="pizza.php">
      Select your favourite pizza toppings: <br />
      <input type="checkbox" name="toppings[]" value="tomato">Tomato</input>
      <input type="checkbox" name="toppings[]" value="onion">Onion</input>
      <input type="checkbox" name="toppings[]" value="jalapenos">Jalapeno
peppers</input>
      <input type="checkbox" name="toppings[]" value="olives">Olives</input>
      <input type="checkbox" name="toppings[]" value="mint">Mint</input>
      <input type="checkbox" name="toppings[]" value="pineapple">Pineapple</input>
      <input type="checkbox" name="toppings[]" value="bacon">Bacon</input>
      <input type="checkbox" name="toppings[]" value="chicken">Chicken</input>
      <input type="checkbox" name="toppings[]" value="ham">Ham</input>
      <input type="checkbox" name="toppings[]" value="anchovies">Anchovies</input>
      <input type="checkbox" name="toppings[]" value="x-cheese">Extra cheese</input>
      <p>
      <input type="submit" name="submit" value="Submit" />
    </form>
  </body>
</html>
```

Figure 4-2 illustrates what the form looks like.

And here's the code for the form submission script (*pizza.php*):

```
<!DOCTYPE html PUBLIC "-//W3C//DTD XHTML 1.0 Transitional//EN"
    "DTD/xhtml1-transitional.dtd">
<html xmlns="http://www.w3.org/1999/xhtml" xml:lang="en" lang="en">
  <head>
    <title>Project 4-2: Pizza Topping Selector</title>
  </head>
  <body>
    <h2>Project 4-2: Pizza Topping Selector</h2>
      You selected the following toppings: <br />
      <ul>
      <?php
      foreach ($_POST['toppings'] as $t) {
        echo "<li>$t</li> \r\n";
      }
      ?>
      </ul>
  </body>
</html>
```

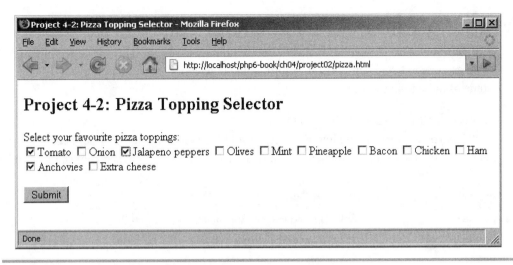

Figure 4-2   A Web form to select pizza toppings

When the Web form is submitted, PHP automatically places all the checked values into the $_POST['toppings'] array. This array can then be processed like any other array—in this case, with a foreach loop that prints the selected toppings in an ordered list. Figure 4-3 illustrates this output.

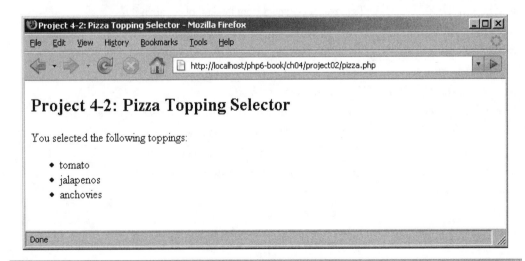

Figure 4-3   The result of submitting the form

Working with Array Functions

PHP has numerous built-in array manipulation functions, supporting operations ranging from array search and comparison to sorting and conversion operations. Table 4-1 lists some of these functions.

Converting Between Strings and Arrays

PHP lets you convert a string into an array, by splitting the string on a user-defined separator and assigning the resulting segments to an array. The PHP function to accomplish this task is

Function	What It Does
explode()	Splits a string into array elements
implode()	Joins array elements into a string
range()	Generates a number range as an array
min()	Finds the smallest value in an array
max()	Finds the largest value in an array
shuffle()	Randomly rearranges the sequence of elements in an array
array_slice()	Extracts a segment of an array
array_shift()	Removes an element from the beginning of an array
array_unshift()	Adds an element to the beginning of an array
array_pop()	Removes an element from the end of an array
array_push()	Adds an element to the end of an array
array_unique()	Removes duplicate elements from an array
array_reverse()	Reverses the sequence of elements in an array
array_merge()	Combines two or more arrays
array_intersect()	Calculates the common elements between two or more arrays
array_diff()	Calculates the difference between two arrays
in_array()	Checks if a particular value exists in an array
array_key_exists()	Checks if a particular key exists in an array
sort()	Sorts an array
asort()	Sorts an associative array by value
ksort()	Sorts an associative array by key
rsort()	Reverse-sorts an array
krsort()	Reverse-sorts an associative array by value
arsort()	Reverse-sorts an associative array by key

Table 4-1   Common PHP Array Functions

the aptly named `explode()` function, which accepts two arguments—the separator and the source string—and returns an array. Here's an example:

```php
<?php
// define string
$str = 'tinker,tailor,soldier,spy';

// convert string to array
// output: ('tinker', 'tailor', 'soldier, 'spy')
$arr = explode(',', $str);
print_r($arr);
?>
```

It's also possible to reverse the process, joining the elements of an array into a single string using user-supplied "glue." The PHP function for this is named `implode()`, and it's illustrated in the next listing:

```php
<?php
// define array
$arr = array('one', 'two', 'three', 'four');

// convert array to string
// output: 'one and two and three and four'
$str = implode(' and ', $arr);
print_r($str);
?>
```

Working with Number Ranges

If you're trying to fill an array with a range of numbers, the `range()` function offers a convenient alternative to manually entering each value. This function accepts two end points and returns an array containing all the numbers between those end points. Here's an example, which generates an array containing all the values between 1 and 1000:

```php
<?php
// define array
$arr = range(1,1000);
print_r($arr);
?>
```

Alternatively, if you already have an array of numbers and are trying to calculate the minimum or maximum of the series, PHP's `min()` and `max()` functions will come in handy—they accept an array of numbers and return the smallest and largest values in the array respectively. The next listing has an example:

```php
<?php
// define array
$arr = array(7, 36, 5, 48, 28, 90, 91, 3, 67, 42);

// get min and max
// output: 'Minimum is 3 and maximum is 91'
echo 'Minimum is ' . min($arr) . ' and maximum is ' . max($arr);
?>
```

Extracting Array Segments

PHP allows you to slice an array into smaller parts with the `array_slice()` function, which accepts three arguments: the original array, the index position (*offset*) at which to start slicing, and the number of elements to return from the starting offset. The following listing illustrates this in action:

```php
<?php
// define array
$rainbow = array('violet', 'indigo', 'blue', 'green', 'yellow',
    'orange', 'red');

// extract 3 central values
// output: ('blue', 'green', 'yellow')
$arr = array_slice($rainbow, 2, 3);
print_r($arr);
?>
```

To extract a segment from the end of an array (rather than the beginning), pass `array_slice()` a negative offset, as in this revision of the preceding example:

```php
<?php
// define array
$rainbow = array('violet', 'indigo', 'blue', 'green', 'yellow',
    'orange', 'red');

// extract 3 central values
// starting from the end
// output: ('blue', 'green', 'yellow')
$arr = array_slice($rainbow, -5, 3);
print_r($arr);
?>
```

Adding and Removing Array Elements

PHP comes with four functions that allow you to add or remove elements from the beginning or end of an array: the `array_unshift()` function adds an element to the beginning of an array; the `array_shift()` function removes the first element of an array; the `array_push()` function adds an element to the end of an array; and the `array_pop()` function removes the last element of an array. The following listing illustrates them all in action:

```php
<?php
// define array
$movies = array('The Lion King', 'Cars', 'A Bug\'s Life');

// remove element from beginning of array
array_shift($movies);

// remove element from end of array
array_pop($movies);

// add element to end of array
array_push($movies, 'Ratatouille');

// add element to beginning of array
array_unshift($movies, 'The Incredibles');

// print array
// output: ('The Incredibles', 'Cars', 'Ratatouille')
print_r($movies);
?>
```

NOTE

The `array_unshift()`, `array_shift()`, `array_push()`, and `array_pop()` functions should be used only with numerically indexed arrays and not with associative arrays. Each of these functions automatically re-indexes the array to account for the value(s) added or removed during its operation.

Removing Duplicate Array Elements

PHP lets you strip an array of duplicate values with its `array_unique()` function, which accepts an array and returns a new array containing only unique values. The next listing illustrates it in action:

```php
<?php
// define array
$duplicates = array('a', 'b', 'a', 'c', 'e', 'd', 'e');
```

```
// remove duplicates
// output: ('a', 'b', 'c', 'e', 'd')
$uniques = array_unique($duplicates);
print_r($uniques);
?>
```

Randomizing and Reversing Arrays

PHP's shuffle() function re-arranges the elements of an array in random order, while its array_reverse() function reverses the order of an array's elements. The following listing illustrates:

```
<?php
// define array
$rainbow = array('violet', 'indigo', 'blue', 'green', 'yellow',
    'orange', 'red');

// randomize array
shuffle($rainbow);
print_r($rainbow);

// reverse array
// output: ('red', 'orange', 'yellow', 'green', 'blue',
//   'indigo', 'violet')
$arr = array_reverse($rainbow);
print_r($arr);
?>
```

Searching Arrays

The in_array() function looks through an array for a specified value and returns true if found. Here's an example, which searches the array $cities for the string 'Barcelona':

```
<?php
// define array
$cities = array('London', 'Paris', 'Barcelona', 'Lisbon', 'Zurich');

// search array for value
echo in_array('Barcelona', $cities);
?>
```

If, instead of values, you'd like to search the keys of an associative array, PHP has you covered there too: the array_key_exists() function looks for a match to the specified search term among an array's keys. The following listing illustrates:

```php
<?php
// define array
$cities = array(
  "United Kingdom" => "London",
  "United States" => "Washington",
  "France" => "Paris",
  "India" => "Delhi"
);

// search array for key
echo array_key_exists('India', $cities);
?>
```

Sorting Arrays

PHP comes with a number of built-in functions designed for sorting array elements in different ways. The first of these is the sort() function, which lets you sort numerically indexed arrays alphabetically or numerically, from lowest to highest value. Here's an example:

```php
<?php
// define array
$data = array(15,81,14,74,2);

// sort and print array
// output: (2,14,15,74,81)
sort($data);
print_r($data);
?>
```

If you're sorting an associative array, though, it's better to use the asort() function, which maintains the correlation between keys and values while sorting. The following listing illustrates this:

```php
<?php
// define array
$profile = array(
  "fname" => "Susan",
  "lname" => "Doe",
  "sex" => "female",
  "sector" => "Asset Management"
);

// sort by value
// output: ('sector' => 'Asset Management',
//   'lname' => 'Doe',
```

```
//   'fname' => 'Susan',
//   'sex' => 'female')
asort($profile);
print_r($profile);
?>
```

Also related to associative arrays is the ksort() function, which uses keys instead of values when performing the sorting. Here's an example:

```
<?php
// define array
$profile = array(
   "fname" => "Susan",
   "lname" => "Doe",
   "sex" => "female",
   "sector" => "Asset Management"
);

// sort by key
// output: ('fname' => 'Susan',
//   'lname' => 'Doe',
//   'sector' => 'Asset Management',
//   'sex' => 'female')
ksort($profile);
print_r($profile);
?>
```

TIP

To reverse the sorted sequence generated by sort(), asort(), and ksort(), use the rsort(), arsort(), and krsort() functions respectively.

Merging Arrays

PHP lets you merge one array into another with its array_merge() function, which accepts one or more array variables. The following listing and output illustrates its use:

```
<?php
// define arrays
$dark = array('black', 'brown', 'blue');
$light = array('white', 'silver', 'yellow');

// merge arrays
// output: ('black', 'brown', 'blue',
//          'white', 'silver', 'yellow')
$colors = array_merge($dark, $light);
print_r($colors);
?>
```

Comparing Arrays

PHP provides two functions to compare arrays: the `array_intersect()` function returns the values common to two arrays, while the `array_diff()` function returns the values from the first array that don't exist in the second. Here's an example, which illustrates both these functions in action:

```php
<?php
// define arrays
$orange = array('red', 'yellow');
$green = array('yellow', 'blue');

// find common elements
// output: ('yellow')
$common = array_intersect($orange, $green);
print_r($common);

// find elements in first array but not in second
// output: ('red')
$unique = array_diff($orange, $green);
print_r($unique);
?>
```

TIP

You can also compare arrays with PHP's equality (==) operator, in much the same way as you would compare other variables.

Try This 4-3   Checking Prime Numbers

Now that you've seen the many ways PHP lets you work with arrays, let's try a small practical example that illustrates some of these built-in functions in action. This application asks the user to enter a series of numbers into a form, and returns a message indicating which of them are prime numbers.

Here's the code (*primes.php*):

```
<!DOCTYPE html PUBLIC "-//W3C//DTD XHTML 1.0 Transitional//EN"
    "DTD/xhtml1-transitional.dtd">
<html xmlns="http://www.w3.org/1999/xhtml" xml:lang="en" lang="en">
  <head>
    <title>Project 4-3: Prime Number Tester</title>
  </head>
  <body>
    <h2>Project 4-3: Prime Number Tester</h2>
```

(continued)

```php
<?php
    // if form not yet submitted
    // display form
    if (!isset($_POST['submit'])) {
?>
    <form method="post" action="primes.php">
      Enter a list of numbers, separated by commas: <br />
      <input type="text" name="num" />
      <p>
      <input type="submit" name="submit" value="Submit" />
    </form>
<?php
    // if form submitted
    // process form input
    } else {
      // retrieve number from POST submission
      // convert to array by splitting on comma
      $numStr = $_POST['num'];
      $numArr = explode(',', $_POST['num']);
      $primes = array();
      $primeFlag = 0;

      // iterate over array
      // get absolute values of each number
      foreach ($numArr as $n) {
        $n = trim(abs($n));

        // test each number for prime-ness:
        // check the number by dividing it
        // by all the numbers between 2 and itself
        // if not perfectly divisible by any,
        // number is prime
        for ($i=2; $i<$n; $i++) {
          $primeFlag = 0;
          if (($n%$i) == 0) {
            break;
          }
          $primeFlag = 1;
        }

        // if prime
        // add to output array
        if ($primeFlag == 1) {
          array_push($primes, $n);
        }
      }
```

```
          // check if any primes were found
          // if yes, sort and remove duplicates from array
          // print message
          if (count($primes) > 0) {
            $primes = array_unique($primes);
            sort($primes);
            echo 'The following numbers are prime: ' . implode($primes, ' ');
          } else {
            echo 'No prime numbers found';
          }
        }
?>
    </body>
</html>
```

Using a technique that should now be familiar to you, this application also combines the Web form and its result page into a single script, separated by an `if-else` conditional statement. The Web form allows the user to enter a series of numbers, separated by commas. Figure 4-4 illustrates what the form looks like.

Once a user enters some numbers into the Web form and submits it, the second half of the script is triggered. It should be clear that this part of the script uses many of the array functions discussed in the preceding section. First, the `explode()` function takes care of extracting the individual numbers from the user's submission into an array, using

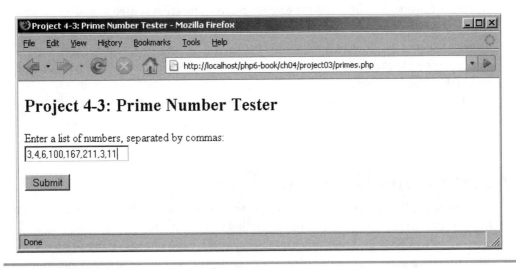

Figure 4-4 A Web form to enter numbers

(continued)

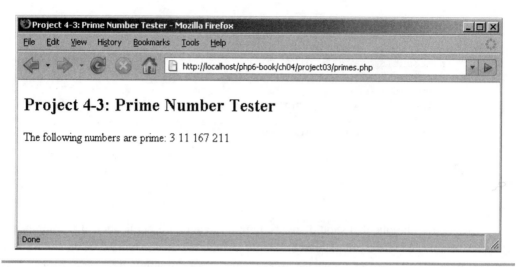

Figure 4-5 The result of the form submission, displaying the prime numbers found

the comma as separator. Next, a `foreach` loop iterates over the array, first calculating the absolute value of each number and then dividing that number by all other numbers between itself and 2 to determine whether or not it is prime.

Assuming the number is not perfectly divisible by at least one other number, the number is considered prime, and the `array_push()` function is used to add it to a new array named `$primes`. Once all the numbers submitted by the user are processed in this manner, the `count()` function is used to check if any primes were found; if yes, the `$primes` array is checked for duplicate values, sorted from lowest to highest value, and sent to the page as output.

Figure 4-5 shows the output after submitting the sequence.

Working with Dates and Times

In addition to allowing you to store multiple values in an array, PHP also comes with a full-featured set of functions for working with dates and times. Although the language does not have a dedicated data type for date and time values, it nevertheless allows programmers a great deal of flexibility when creating, formatting, and manipulating such values.

Ask the Expert

Q: What's a UNIX timestamp?

A: Very simply, a UNIX timestamp for a particular time point represents the number of seconds that have elapsed between midnight on January 1, 1970, and that time point. So, for example, the time point January 5 2008 10:15:00 AM in UNIX timestamp format would be 1199508300.

PHP can automatically turn a date value into a UNIX timestamp with its mktime() function, which accepts day, month, year, hour, minute, and second arguments and returns a UNIX timestamp corresponding to that instant in time.

Generating Dates and Times

Like many other programming languages, PHP represents date/time values in UNIX timestamp format. Generating a timestamp is usually accomplished with the mktime() function, which accepts a series of date and time parameters and converts them into a timestamp. To illustrate, consider the following example, which returns a UNIX timestamp corresponding to January 5 2008 10:15:00 AM:

```
<?php
// return timestamp for Jan 5 2008 10:15
// output: 1199508300
echo mktime(10,15,00,1,5,2008);
?>
```

Calling mktime() without any arguments returns the UNIX timestamp corresponding to the present time:

```
<?php
// return timestamp for now
echo mktime();
?>
```

Another way to get the current date and time is with PHP's getdate() function, which returns an associative array containing information about the current date and time. Here's an example of what this array looks like:

```
Array
(
    [seconds] => 33
    [minutes] => 27
```

```
[hours] => 19
[mday] => 12
[wday] => 1
[mon] => 11
[year] => 2007
[yday] => 315
[weekday] => Monday
[month] => November
[0] => 1194875853
)
```

And here's an example of this function in action:

```php
<?php
// get current date and time as array
$now = getdate();

// output: 'It is now 19:26:23 on 12-11-2007'
echo 'It is now ' . $now['hours'] . ':' . $now['minutes'] . ':'
. $now['seconds'] . ' on ' . $now['mday'] . '-' . $now['mon'] . '-'
. $now ['year'];
?>
```

TIP

Notice that the array returned by getdate() includes a UNIX timestamp representation of the date, at index position 0.

Formatting Dates and Times

In most cases, generating a timestamp is only half the battle: you also need to find a way to display it in human-readable form. That's where PHP's date() function comes in: it allows you to massage that long, ugly timestamp into something that's much more informative. This function accepts two arguments: a formatting string and a timestamp. The formatting string is a sequence of characters, each of which has a special meaning; Table 4-2 has a list of the most commonly used ones.

Using the special characters from Table 4-2, it's possible to format a UNIX timestamp with date() to customize the display of a date/time value. Here are some examples:

```php
<?php
// output: "It is now 12:28 pm 20 Mar 2008"
echo 'It is now ' . date("h:i a d M Y", mktime(12,28,13,3,20,2008));
```

Character	What It Means
d	Day of the month (numeric)
D	Day of the week (string)
l	Day of the week (string)
F	Month (string)
M	Month (string)
m	Month (numeric)
Y	Year
h	Hour (in 12-hour format)
H	Hour (in 24-hour format)
a	AM or PM
i	Minute
s	Second

Table 4-2 Formatting Codes for the `date()` Function

```
// output: "It is now 8:15 14 Feb 2008"
echo 'It is now ' . date("H:i d F Y", mktime(8,15,0,2,14,2008));

// output: "Today's date is Oct-05-2007"
echo 'Today\'s date is ' . date("M-d-Y", mktime(0,0,0,10,5,2007));
?>
```

Useful Date and Time Functions

PHP also supports many other date/time manipulation functions, which allow you to check if a date is valid or convert between time zones. Table 4-3 lists some of these functions.

Function	What It Does
checkdate()	Checks a date for validity
strtotime()	Creates timestamps from English-language descriptions
gmdate()	Expresses a timestamp in GMT

Table 4-3 Common PHP Date Functions

Checking Date Validity

A useful built-in function is the checkdate() function, which accepts a month, day, and year combination and returns a true/false value indicating whether the corresponding date is valid. Consider the following example, which illustrates it by testing the date 30 February 2008:

```php
<?php
// output: 'Date is invalid'
if (checkdate(2,30,2008)) {
  echo 'Date is valid';
} else {
  echo 'Date is invalid';
}
?>
```

Converting Strings to Timestamps

Another very useful function is PHP's strtotime() function, which accepts a string value containing an embedded date or time and converts this into a UNIX timestamp. Here's an example:

```php
<?php
// define string containing date value
// convert it to UNIX timestamp
// re-format it using date()
// output: '07 Jul 08'
$str = 'July 7 2008';
echo date('d M y', strtotime($str));
?>
```

Interestingly, strtotime() also recognizes common time descriptions such as "now", "3 hours ago", "tomorrow", or "next Friday". The following listing illustrates this very useful feature:

```php
<?php
// output: '12 Nov 07'
echo date('d M y', strtotime('now'));

// output: '13 Nov 07'
echo date('d M y', strtotime('tomorrow'));

// output: '16 Nov 07'
echo date('d M y', strtotime('next Friday'));
```

```
// output: '10 Nov 07'
echo date('d M y', strtotime('48 hours ago'));
?>
```

Mapping Day and Month Numbers to Names

The date() function discussed in the preceding section isn't useful only for formatting timestamps into readable date strings; it can also be used to find the weekday name corresponding to a particular date. To do this, simply use the 'D' format character with your timestamp . . . as in the following example, which displays the day that Oct 5 2008 falls on:

```
<?php
// output: 'Sun'
echo date('D', mktime(0,0,0,10,5,2008));
?>
```

You can also do this for month names, by using the date() function's 'F' parameter:

```
<?php
// display list of month names
// output: 'January, February, ... December'
foreach (range(1,12) as $m) {
  $months[] = date('F', mktime(0,0,0,$m,1,0));
}
echo implode($months, ', ');
?>
```

Calculating GMT Time

PHP's gmdate() function works exactly like its date() function, except that it returns GMT representations of formatted date strings, instead of local time representations. To see this in action, consider the following examples, which return GMT equivalents for two local times:

```
<?php
// returns GMT time relative to 'now'
echo gmdate('H:i:s d-M-Y', mktime());

// returns GMT time relative to '00:01 1-Dec-2007'
// output: '18:31:00 30-Nov-2007'
echo gmdate('H:i:s d-M-Y', mktime(0,1,0,12,1,2007));
?>
```

Try This 4-4 Building an Age Calculator

Now that you know a little bit about how PHP deals with dates and times, let's put all this learning to good use with a practical project: a Web application that lets you enter your date of birth and calculates how old you are today, in years and months.

Here's the code (*agecalc.php*):

```
<!DOCTYPE html PUBLIC "-//W3C//DTD XHTML 1.0 Transitional//EN"
    "DTD/xhtml1-transitional.dtd">
<html xmlns="http://www.w3.org/1999/xhtml" xml:lang="en" lang="en">
  <head>
    <title>Project 4-4: Age Calculator</title>
  </head>
  <body>
    <h2>Project 4-4: Age Calculator</h2>
<?php
    // if form not yet submitted
    // display form
    if (!isset($_POST['submit'])) {
?>
    <form method="post" action="agecalc.php">
      Enter your date of birth, in mm/dd/yyyy format: <br />
      <input type="text" name="dob" />
      <p>
      <input type="submit" name="submit" value="Submit" />
    </form>
<?php
    // if form submitted
    // process form input
    } else {
      // split date value into components
      $dateArr = explode('/', $_POST['dob']);

      // calculate timestamp corresponding to date value
      $dateTs = strtotime($_POST['dob']);

      // calculate timestamp corresponding to 'today'
      $now = strtotime('today');

      // check that the value entered is in the correct format
      if (sizeof($dateArr) != 3) {
        die('ERROR: Please enter a valid date of birth');
      }

      // check that the value entered is a valid date
      if (!checkdate($dateArr[0], $dateArr[1], $dateArr[2])) {
        die('ERROR: Please enter a valid date of birth');
      }
```

```
    // check that the date entered is earlier than 'today'
    if ($dateTs >= $now) {
      die('ERROR: Please enter a date of birth earlier than today');
    }

    // calculate difference between date of birth and today in days
    // convert to years
    // convert remaining days to months
    // print output
    $ageDays = floor(($now - $dateTs) / 86400);
    $ageYears = floor($ageDays / 365);
    $ageMonths = floor(($ageDays - ($ageYears * 365)) / 30);
    echo "You are approximately $ageYears years and $ageMonths months old.";
  }
?>
  </body>
</html>
```

Once a user submits his or her date of birth into the Web form (Figure 4-6) in MM/DD/YYYY format, the second half of the script is triggered. The first bit of this section of the program is concerned mostly with error checks. First, the date entered into the form is split into its constituent values of month, day, and year, and the checkdate() function is used to verify whether or not it is valid. Following this, the strtotime() function is used to convert the entered date into a UNIX timestamp; this is then compared with "today" to verify that the date entered is in the past.

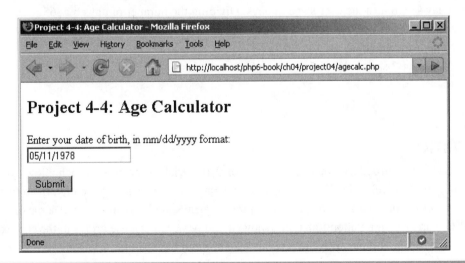

Figure 4-6   A Web form for the user to enter his or her date of birth

(continued)

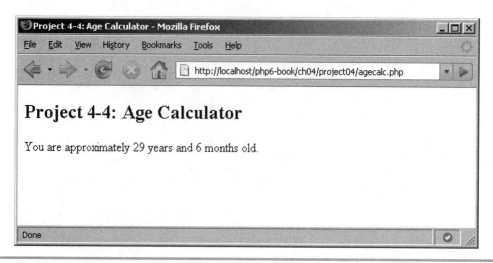

Figure 4-7 The result of the form submission, showing the calculated age

Assuming the date entered into the form passes these error checks, the script proceeds to the calculation stage. First, "today's" timestamp is subtracted from the birth timestamp; as both timestamps are expressed in seconds, the result of this calculation returns the user's age, in seconds. This value is then divided by 86400—the number of seconds in a day—to return the user's age in days. Dividing the number of days by 365 returns the user's age in years. Finally, the fractional part of the age (months) is calculated by dividing the remaining days by 30.

Figure 4-7 shows the output after a form submission.

Summary

This chapter introduced you to a new type of PHP variable, the array, which allows you to group multiple related values together and operate on them as a single entity. In addition to showing you how to create, edit, and process arrays, it also demonstrated some of PHP's array manipulation functions, showed you how you can use arrays in the context of Web forms, and put arrays to practical use through three simple applications. Finally, it explained how to work with temporal data in PHP, illustrating the most commonly used date and time functions and using them to build a simple age calculator.

Arrays are an important addition to your PHP toolkit, and as your scripts become more sophisticated, you'll begin to appreciate how powerful and flexible they really are. To find out more about them, consider visiting the following links:

- Arrays, at **www.php.net/manual/en/language.types.array.php**

- Array operators, at **www.php.net/manual/en/language.operators.array.php**

- Array manipulation functions, at **www.php.net/manual/en/ref.array.php**

- The special $_POST and $_GET arrays, at **www.php.net/manual/en/reserved.variables.php#reserved.variables.get**

- Date and time functions, at **www.php.net/manual/en/ref.datetime.php**

Chapter 4 Self Test

1. What are the two types of PHP arrays, and how do they differ?

2. Name the functions you would use to

   A Remove duplicate elements from an array

   B Add an element to the beginning of an array

   C Sort an array in reverse

   D Count the number of elements in an array

   E Search for a value in an array

   F Display the contents of an array

   G Shuffle the contents of an array

   H Combine two arrays into one

   I Find the common elements between two arrays

   J Convert a string to an array

   K Extract a segment of an array

3. What will be the output of the following line of PHP code:

```php
<?php
sort(array_slice(array_reverse(array_unique(array('b','i','g','f',
'o','o','t'))), 2, 3));
?>
```

4. Using only an array and a `foreach` loop, write a program that prints the days of the week.

5. Write a program that reads an array of numbers and returns a list of all those numbers less than 15.

6. Write a program that reads an array and returns a message indicating whether the array contains only unique values.

Chapter 5

Using Functions and Classes

Key Skills & Concepts

- Learn the benefits of encapsulating code into functions and classes

- Define and use your own functions, arguments, and return values

- Understand local and global variables

- Learn about recursion and variable-length argument lists

- Define and use your own classes, methods, and properties

- Understand OOP concepts of visibility, extensibility, and reflection

As your PHP programs get more complex, you might find yourself repeatedly writing code to perform the same task—for example, testing a number for prime-ness or checking a form field to see if it's empty or not. In these situations, it usually makes sense to turn this code into a reusable component, which can be managed independently and "called upon" as needed from different PHP programs. Not only does this reduce the amount of duplicate code you have to write, but it also makes your scripts leaner, more efficient, and easier to maintain.

PHP offers two constructs to help you reduce code duplication in your programs: *user-defined functions* are reusable code segments that are created by the programmer to perform specific tasks, while *classes* provide a more formal, object-oriented approach to reusability and encapsulation. This chapter will introduce you to both these constructs, using practical examples to illustrate their real-world utility.

Creating User-Defined Functions

In previous chapters, you've been introduced to many of PHP built-in functions for string, number, and array manipulation. However, PHP doesn't only restrict you to its built-in functions; it also lets you define your own. These *user-defined functions* are a neat way for you to create independent, reusable code "packages" that perform specific tasks and can be maintained independently of the main program.

Packaging your code into functions has four important advantages:

- It reduces duplication within a program, by allowing you to extract commonly used routines into a single component. This has the added benefit of making programs smaller, more efficient, and easier to read.

- A function is created once but used many times, often from more than one program. If the function code changes, the changes are implemented in one spot (the function definition) while the function invocations remain untouched. This fact can significantly simplify code maintenance and upgrades, especially when contrasted with the alternative: manually changing every occurrence of the earlier code wherever it occurs (and possibly introducing new errors in the process).

- Debugging and testing a program becomes easier when the program is subdivided into functions, as it becomes easier to trace the source of an error and correct it with minimal impact on the rest of the program.

- Functions encourage abstract thinking, because packaging program code into a function is nothing more or less than understanding how a *specific* task may be encapsulated into a *generic* component. In this sense, functions encourage the creation of more robust and extensible software designs.

Creating and Invoking Functions

There are three components to every function:

- *Arguments,* which serve as inputs to the function
- *Return values,* which are the outputs returned by the function
- The *function body,* which contains the processing code to turn inputs into outputs

To begin with, let's start with a simple example, one that doesn't use either arguments or return values. Consider the following PHP script, which contains a user-defined function to print the current day of the week:

```php
<?php
// function definition
// print today's weekday name
function whatIsToday() {
  echo "Today is " . date('l', mktime());
}

// function invocation
whatIsToday();
?>
```

Function definitions begin with the `function` keyword, followed by the function name and a list of arguments (optional) in parentheses. Curly braces then enclose the main body of the function, which can contain any legal PHP code, including variable definitions, conditional tests, loops, and output statements. Function names must begin with a letter or underscore character, optionally followed by more letters, numbers, or underscore characters; punctuation characters and spaces are not allowed within function names. In the preceding listing, the function is named `whatIsToday()` and its body contains a single statement, which uses `echo` and `date()` to obtain and print the current weekday name.

Of course, defining a function is only half the battle: the other half is using it. In PHP, invoking a function is as simple as calling it by name (and passing it optional arguments, if needed). The main body of the script in the preceding listing does just this: it invokes the function by name and then stands back to see the results.

Ask the Expert

Q: Can I invoke a function before it's been defined?

A: Yes. PHP 4.0 (and better) allow developers to invoke a function even if the corresponding function definition appears later on in the program. This feature is particularly useful for developers who prefer to place their function definitions at the bottom of a PHP script, rather than the top, for easier readability.

Using Arguments and Return Values

A function that always returns the same output is a lot like a radio station that plays the same song all day—not very useful or interesting at all! What you'd really like is the ability to change the music the station plays in response to feedback that you, the listener, provide—in effect, to create an audience request show. In PHP terms, this amounts to creating functions that can accept input values at run time and use these input values to affect the output returned by the function.

That's where *arguments* come in. Arguments are "placeholder" variables within a function definition; they're replaced at run time by values provided to the function from the main program. The processing code within the function then manipulates these values to return the desired result. Since the input to the function will differ each time it is invoked, the output will necessarily differ too.

To illustrate, consider the following listing, which defines a function accepting two arguments and uses these arguments to perform a geometric calculation:

```php
<?php
// function definition
// calculate perimeter of rectangle
// p = 2 * (l+w)
function getPerimeter($length, $width) {
  $perimeter = 2 * ($length + $width);
  echo "The perimeter of a rectangle of length $length
  units and width $width units is: $perimeter units";
}

// function invocation
// with arguments
getPerimeter(4,2);
?>
```

The function in this listing performed a calculation and then printed the result directly to the output page. But what if you want the function to perform its work and, instead of printing the result, do something else with it? Well, in PHP, you can have a function explicitly return a value, like the result of a calculation, to the statement that called it. This is accomplished by using a return statement inside the function, as in the next example:

```php
<?php
// function definition
// calculate perimeter of rectangle
// p = 2 * (l+w)
function getPerimeter($length, $width) {
  $perimeter = 2 * ($length + $width);
  return $perimeter;
}

// function invocation
// with arguments
echo 'The perimeter of a rectangle of length 4 units
and width 2 units is: ' . getPerimeter(4,2) . ' units';
?>
```

You can return multiple values from a function, by placing them all in an array and returning the array. The next example illustrates, by accepting a sentence and returning the individual words, reversed, to the caller as an array:

```php
<?php
// function definition
// break a string into words
```

```php
// reverse and return as an array
function reverseMe($sentence) {
    $words = explode(' ', $sentence);
    foreach ($words as $k => $v) {
      $words[$k] = strrev($v);
    }
    return $words;
}

// function invocation
// output: 'evaH a doog yad'
echo implode(' ', reverseMe('Have a good day'));

// function invocation
// output: 'lliW uoy yrram em'
echo implode(' ', reverseMe('Will you marry me'));
?>
```

NOTE

When PHP encounters a `return` statement inside a function, it halts processing of the function and "returns" control to the main body of the program.

Setting Default Argument Values

As you saw earlier, the arguments that a function expects to receive from the main program are specified in the function's argument list. For convenience, you can assign default values to any or all of these arguments; these default values are used in the event the function invocation is missing some arguments. Here's an example, which generates an e-mail address from supplied username and domain arguments; if the domain argument is missing, a default domain is automatically assigned:

```php
<?php
// function definition
// generate e-mail address from supplied values
function buildAddress($username, $domain = 'mydomain.info') {
    return $username . '@' . $domain;
}

// function invocation
// without optional argument
// output: 'My e-mail address is john@mydomain.info'
echo 'My e-mail address is ' . buildAddress('john');

// function invocation
// with optional argument
```

```
// output: 'My e-mail address is jane@cooldomain.net'
echo 'My e-mail address is ' . buildAddress('jane', 'cooldomain.net');
?>
```

Notice that in the first instance, the function has been called with only a single argument, even though the function definition requires two. However, since a default value is present for the second argument, the missing argument is automatically replaced by said default value, and no errors are generated.

TIP

If only some of your function's arguments have default values assigned to them, place these arguments at the end of the function's argument list. This lets PHP correctly differentiate between missing arguments that don't have default values, and missing arguments that do.

Using Dynamic Argument Lists

A PHP function definition normally has a fixed argument list, where the number of arguments is known in advance. However, PHP also lets you define functions with so-called *variable-length argument lists,* where the number of arguments can change with each invocation of the function. A good example of this is a function that accepts an arbitrary number of arguments, adds them up, and returns the average . . . as illustrated in the following listing:

```
<?php
// function definition
// calculate average of supplied values
function calcAverage() {
  $args = func_get_args();
  $count = func_num_args();
  $sum = array_sum($args);
  $avg = $sum / $count;
  return $avg;
}

// function invocation
// with 3 arguments
// output: 6
echo calcAverage(3,6,9);

// function invocation
// with 8 arguments
// output: 150
echo calcAverage(100,200,100,300,50,150,250,50);
?>
```

Notice that the `calcAverage()` function definition in the previous listing does not include a predefined argument list; rather, the arguments passed to it are retrieved at run time using the `func_num_args()` and `func_get_args()` functions. The `func_num_args()` function returns the number of arguments passed to a function, while the `func_get_args()` function returns the actual argument values, as an array. As illustrated in the preceding listing, both functions come in very handy when dealing with functions that accept an arbitrary number of arguments.

Understanding Variable Scope

A key concept related to user-defined functions in PHP is *variable scope*: the extent of a variable's visibility within the space of a PHP program. By default, variables used within a function are local—their impact is restricted to the function space alone, and they cannot be viewed or manipulated from outside the function in which they exist. To illustrate this, consider the following example:

```php
<?php
// function definition
// change the value of $score
function changeScore() {
  $score = 25;
}

// define a variable in the main program
// print its value
$score = 11;
echo 'Score is: ' . $score;    // output: 11

// run the changeScore() function
changeScore();

// print $score again
echo 'Score is: ' . $score;    // output: 11
?>
```

Here, the variable `$score` is defined in the main program, and the `changeScore()` function contains code to change the value of this variable. However, after running this function, the value of `$score` remains at its original setting, because the changes made to `$score` within the `changeScore()` function remain "local" to the function and do not reflect in the main program.

This "bounding" of variables to within a function space is deliberate: it maintains a degree of separation between the main program and its functions, and it reduces the chances of variables from the main program affecting variables within a function. However, there are certainly occasions when it may be necessary to "import" a variable from the main program into a function, or vice versa. For these situations, PHP offers the `global` keyword: when applied to a variable inside a function, this keyword turns the variable into a global variable, making it visible both inside and outside the function.

The next example illustrates the difference between global and local scope more clearly:

```php
<?php
// function definition
// change the value of $score
function changeScore() {
  global $score;
  $score = 25;
}

// define a variable in the main program
// print its value
$score = 11;
echo 'Score is: ' . $score;    // output: 11

// run the changeScore() function
changeScore();

// print $score again
echo 'Score is: ' . $score;    // output: 25
?>
```

In this revision of the previous listing, the `global` keyword used with the `$score` variable within the `changeScore()` function changes the scope of the variable, increasing its scope to encompass the entire program. As a result, changes made to the variable within the function will reflect in the main program (and vice versa). The output of the script illustrates this fact clearly.

Using Recursive Functions

Another, slightly more complex idea involving functions is *recursion*. A *recursive function* is a function that calls itself repeatedly until a condition is satisfied. Such a function is typically used to solve complex, iterative calculations, or to process deeply nested structures.

To illustrate how a recursive function works, consider the next example, which writes a recursive function to drill down into a nested array and print all of its contents:

```php
<?php
// recursive function definition
// function to print all the values
// in a nested array
function printValues($arr) {
  global $count;
  global $out;

  // check that input is an array
  if (!is_array($arr)) {
    die('ERROR: Input is not an array');
  }

  // iterate through array
  // increment counter by 1 for each value found
  // if value is itself an array:
  // recursively call function to count
  // number of elements in the child array
  // else:
  // add the value found to the output array
  foreach ($arr as $a) {
    if (is_array($a)) {
      printValues($a);
    } else {
      $out[] = $a;
      $count++;
    }
  }

  // return total count and values found to caller
  // as array
  return array('total' => $count, 'values' => $out);
}

// define nested array
$data = array(
  'o' => array(
    'orange',
    'owl',
    'one'),
  't' => array(
```

```
      'tea',
      'ten',
      'tag',
      'twentythree' => array(
        array('twenty', 'three'),
        array('vingt', 'trois', array(
          'red'  =>  'baron',
          'blue' => 'blood'
        ))
      )
    )
  )
);

// count and print values in nested array
$ret = printValues($data);
echo $ret['total'] . ' value(s) found: ';
echo implode(', ', $ret['values']);
?>
```

The output of this example would be

```
12 value(s) found: orange, owl, one, tea, ten,
tag, twenty, three, vingt, trois, baron, blood
```

The core of this example is the printValues() function, which accepts an array as argument. It then loops through this array using a foreach loop, adding each value it finds to an output array named $out. For each such value found, it also increments a counter named $count by 1. In the event that any of the values encountered in this manner is itself an array, printValues() calls itself recursively to process that child array (and any other child arrays found at deeper nesting levels). This process continues until no further values are left to be processed.

Because both $out and $count are global variables, they maintain their values throughout this process. Once the function has completed its work, these two variables are packaged into a single associative array, which is returned to the caller and printed to the output page.

TIP
While recursive functions are often the quickest way to solve a complex calculation, they're not the only way: in most cases, you can accomplish the same thing, albeit less elegantly, by using one or more loops.

Try This 5-1　Calculating GCF and LCM

Now that you've imbibed a fair amount of knowledge about PHP's user-defined functions, let's put that knowledge to the test with a small practical application. This next example invites the user to enter two numbers into a Web form, and calculates the greatest common factor (GCF) and least common multiple (LCM) of the entered numbers.

NOTE

In case you skipped Math class, the GCF of two numbers is the largest factor common to both, while the LCM of two numbers is the smallest multiple common to both. Thus, for example, the GCF of 6 and 10 is 2, while the LCM is 30. Read more about GCF and LCM, including a detailed description of the Euclidean algorithm used in this example, at http://en.wikipedia.org/wiki/Greatest_common_factor and http://en.wikipedia.org/wiki/Least_common_multiple.

Here's the code (*gcf_lcm.php*):

```php
<?php
// function definition
// get GCF of two numbers
function getGCF($a, $b) {
  if ($b == 0) {
    return $a;
  }
  else {
    return getGCF($b, $a % $b);
  }
}

// function definition
// get LCM of two numbers using GCF
function getLCM($a, $b) {
  return ($a * $b) / getGCF($a, $b);
}
?>
<!DOCTYPE html PUBLIC "-//W3C//DTD XHTML 1.0 Transitional//EN"
   "DTD/xhtml1-transitional.dtd">
<html xmlns="http://www.w3.org/1999/xhtml" xml:lang="en" lang="en">
  <head>
    <title>Project 5-1: GCF and LCM</title>
  </head>
  <body>
    <h2>Project 5-1: GCF and LCM</h2>
<?php
    // if form not yet submitted
    // display form
    if (!isset($_POST['submit'])) {
?>
    <form method="post" action="gcf_lcm.php">
      Enter two integers: <br />
```

```
        <input type="text" name="num_1" size="3" />
        <p>
        <input type="text" name="num_2" size="3" />
        <p>
        <input type="submit" name="submit" value="Submit" />
    </form>
<?php
    // if form submitted
    // process form input
    } else {
        $num1 = (int)$_POST['num_1'];
        $num2 = (int)$_POST['num_2'];

        // calculate and print GCF and LCM
        echo "You entered: $num1, $num2";
        echo "<br />";
        echo "The GCF of ($num1, $num2) is: " . getGCF($num1, $num2);
        echo "<br />";
        echo "The LCM of ($num1, $num2) is: " . getLCM($num1, $num2);
    }
?>
  </body>
</html>
```

This script generates a form for the user to enter two numbers (Figure 5-1).

Once the form is submitted, the numbers entered by the user are passed as arguments to the getGCF() and getLCM() functions, which, respectively, calculate and return the GCF and LCM of the number pair to the caller. Figure 5-2 displays the results of one such form submission.

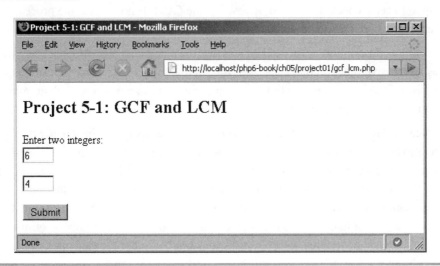

Figure 5-1   A Web form to enter two numbers

(continued)

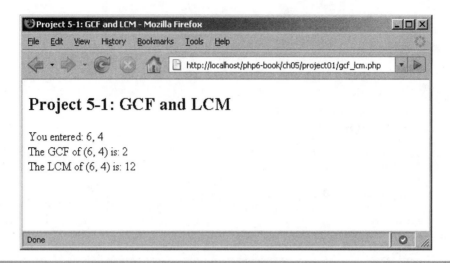

Figure 5-2   The results of the form submission, displaying the calculated GCF and LCM

Since this chapter is all about functions, it's worthwhile spending a few minutes to dissect the getGCF() and getLCM() functions.

1. The getGCF() function accepts two arguments and calculates the GCF value using the Euclidean algorithm. Wikipedia's description of this algorithm, at http://en.wikipedia .org/wiki/Euclidean_algorithm, states: "Given two natural numbers *a* and *b*, not both equal to zero: check if *b* is zero; if yes, *a* is the GCD. If not, repeat the process using, respectively, *b*, and the remainder after dividing *a* by *b*."

   From this description, it should be clear that the Euclidean algorithm can be expressed as a recursive function that calls itself repeatedly, feeding the remainder of the previous division into the next one until the remainder becomes zero. If you look at getGCF(), you'll see that's precisely what it does.

2. Once the GCF has been calculated, the LCM can be easily obtained using the relationship LCM (A,B) = (A*B)/GCF(A,B). This relationship, and its derivation, may also be obtained from Wikipedia, at http://en.wikipedia.org/wiki/Least_common_ multiple—and if you look inside the getLCM() function, you'll see this same calculation in action. You'll notice also that getLCM() internally calls getGCF()—a fine example of inter-function cooperation and an illustration of how functions can be used to break down large complex tasks into smaller, more focused operations.

Creating Classes

In addition to allowing you to create your own functions, PHP also allows you to group related functions together using a *class*. Classes are the fundamental construct behind object-oriented programming (OOP), a programming paradigm that involves modeling program behavior into "objects" and then using these objects as the basis for your applications.

Up until recently, PHP's support for OOP was limited; however, PHP 5.0 introduced a new object model that allowed programmers significantly greater flexibility and ease of use when working with classes and objects. Although OOP is generally considered "too complex" for beginners to attempt, the widespread prevalence and use of objects under PHP 5.1 and PHP 5.2 means that no aspiring PHP programmer can afford to be totally unaware of it.

With this in mind, the following sections will offer a simple introduction to how classes and objects work under PHP. Interested readers are encouraged to learn more by referring to the advanced material suggested at the end of the chapter.

Introducing Classes and Objects

Think of a *class* as a miniature ecosystem: it's a self-contained, independent collection of variables and functions, which work together to perform one or more specific (and usually related) tasks. Variables within a class are called *properties*; functions are called *methods*.

Classes serve as templates for *objects,* which are specific instances of a class. Every object has properties and methods corresponding to those of its parent class. Every object instance is completely independent, with its own properties and methods, and can thus be manipulated independently of other objects of the same class.

To put this in more concrete terms, consider an example: an Automobile class that contain properties for color and make, and methods for acceleration, braking, and turning. It's possible to derive two independent objects from this Automobile class, one representing a Ford and the other a Honda. Each of these objects would have methods for acceleration, braking, and turning, as well as specific values for color and make. Each object instance could also be manipulated independently: for example, you could change the Honda's color without affecting the Ford, or call the Ford's acceleration method without any impact on the Honda.

Figure 5-3 illustrates the relationship between a class and its object instances visually.

Defining and Using Classes

In PHP, classes are defined much like functions: a class definition begins with the `class` keyword, which is followed by the class name and a pair of curly braces. The complete

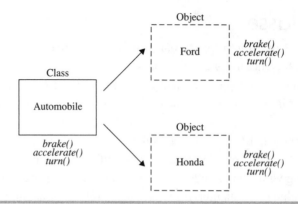

Figure 5-3   The relationship between classes and objects

class definition must be enclosed within these braces; in most cases, this definition consists of property (variable) definitions followed by method (function) definitions.

To see what a class definition looks like, review the following listing: it contains a definition for an Automobile class, with two properties named $color and $make and methods named accelerate(), brake(), and turn():

```php
<?php
// class definition
class Automobile {

  // properties
  public $color;
  public $make;

  // methods
  public function accelerate() {
    echo 'Accelerating...';
  }

  public function brake() {
    echo 'Slowing down...';
  }

  public function turn() {
    echo 'Turning...';
  }
}
?>
```

Once a class has been defined, objects can be created from the class with the new keyword. Class methods and properties can directly be accessed through this object instance. Here's an example, which creates an instance of the Automobile class and assigns it to $car, and then sets the object's properties and invokes object methods (note the -> symbol used to connect objects to their properties or methods):

```php
<?php
// instantiate object
$car = new Automobile;

// set object properties
$car->color = 'red';
$car->make = 'Ford Taurus';

// invoke object methods
$car->accelerate();
$car->turn();
?>
```

To access or change a class method or property from within the class itself, it's necessary to prefix the corresponding method or property name with $this, which refers to "this" class. To see how this works, consider this revision of the preceding example, which sets a class property named $speed and then modifies this property from within the accelerate() and brake() functions:

```php
<?php
// class definition
class Automobile {

  // properties
  public $color;
  public $make;
  public $speed = 55;

  // methods
  public function accelerate() {
    $this->speed += 10;
    echo 'Accelerating to ' . $this->speed . '...';
  }

  public function brake() {
    $this->speed -= 10;
    echo 'Slowing down to ' . $this->speed . '...';
  }
```

```
  public function turn() {
    $this->brake();
    echo 'Turning...';
    $this->accelerate();
  }
}
?>
```

And now, when you invoke these functions, you'll see the effect of changes in $speed:

```
<?php
// instantiate object
$car = new Automobile;

// invoke methods
// output: 'Accelerating to 65...'
//         'Slowing down to 55...'
//         'Turning...'
//         'Accelerating to 65...'
$car->accelerate();
$car->turn();
?>
```

Ask the Expert

Q: Can I look inside an object or class to see its structure?

A: Since PHP 5.0, PHP has included a full-fledged *reflection* API, which lets you peer into any class or object and obtain detailed information on its properties, methods, interfaces, and constants. To use it, instantiate an object of either ReflectionClass or ReflectionObject and pass it the class or object to be X-rayed. Here's an example:

```
<?php
// reflection for class
Reflection::export(new ReflectionClass('Cat'));

// reflection for object
Reflection::export(new ReflectionObject($myCat));
?>
```

Read more about reflection in PHP at www.php.net/manual/en/language.oop5 .reflection.php

Try This 5-2 Encrypting and Decrypting Text

Now that you know the basics of classes and objects, let's run through a brief practical
example. This next listing defines a class named Jumbler, which allows users to encrypt
(and decrypt) text using a simple encryption algorithm and a user-supplied numeric key.
Take a look at the class definition (*jumbler.php*):

```php
<?php
// class definition
class Jumbler {

  // properties
  public $key;

  // methods
  // set encryption key
  public function setKey($key) {
    $this->key = $key;
  }

  // get encryption key
  public function getKey() {
    return $this->key;
  }

  // encrypt
  public function encrypt($plain) {
    for ($x=0; $x<strlen($plain); $x++) {
      $cipher[] = ord($plain[$x]) + $this->getKey() + ($x * $this->getKey());
    }
    return implode('/', $cipher);
  }

  // decrypt
  public function decrypt($cipher) {
    $data = explode('/', $cipher);
    $plain = '';
    for ($x=0; $x<count($data); $x++) {
      $plain .= chr($data[$x] - $this->getKey() - ($x * $this->getKey()));
    }
    return $plain;
  }
}
?>
```

(continued)

This class has a single property and four methods:

- The $key property holds the numeric key entered by the user. This key is used to perform the encryption.
- The setKey() method accepts an argument and sets the $key property to that value.
- The getKey() method returns the value of the $key property.
- The encrypt() function accepts a plain-text string and "jumbles" it using the key.
- The decrypt() function accepts an encrypted string and restores the original plain-text string from it using the key.

A quick word about the internals of the encrypt() and decrypt() methods, before proceeding to a usage example. When encrypt() is invoked with a plain-text string, it steps through the string and calculates a numeric value for each character. The numeric value is the sum of

- The character's ASCII code, as returned by the ord() function
- The numeric key set by the user through the setKey() method
- The product of the numeric key and the character's position in the string

Each number returned after this calculation is added to an array, and once the entire string is processed, the elements of the array are joined into a single string, separated by slashes, with implode().

Table 5-1 has a brief illustration of how the word 'Ant' is converted into the encrypted string '410/800/1151' using this method.

The decryption routine reverses this process: it first splits the encrypted ciphertext string into individual numbers using the slashes as delimiters, and adds them to an array. It then obtains the character corresponding to each number, by subtracting

- The numeric key set by the user through the setKey() method; and
- The product of the numeric key and the character's position in the string

Character $c	Position $p	ord($c)	Key $key	$key * $p	Total
'A'	0	65	345	0	410
'n'	1	110	345	345	800
't'	2	116	345	690	1151

Table 5-1 An Example Encryption Run

from the number, and then using the chr() function to retrieve the ASCII character corresponding to the remainder. The characters returned through this process are concatenated into a single string and returned to the caller.

CAUTION

The encryption routine used by the Jumbler class is illustrative only, and highly insecure—don't even think about using it to secure real-world data.

Now that you've understood how the class works, let's look at how it could be used. This next listing generates a form for the user to enter plaintext or ciphertext, as well as a numeric key, and then uses a Jumbler object to encrypt or decrypt it. Here's the code (*jumbler.php*):

```
<!DOCTYPE html PUBLIC "-//W3C//DTD XHTML 1.0 Transitional//EN"
  "DTD/xhtml1-transitional.dtd">
<html xmlns="http://www.w3.org/1999/xhtml" xml:lang="en" lang="en">
  <head>
    <title>Project 5-2: Encrypting Text</title>
  </head>
  <body>
    <h2>Project 5-2: Encrypting Text</h2>
<?php
    // if form not yet submitted
    // display form
    if (!isset($_POST['submit'])) {
?>
    <form method="post" action="jumbler.php">
      Enter:
      <input type="radio" name="type" value="P" checked>Plaintext</input>
      <input type="radio" name="type" value="C">Ciphertext </input>
      <br />
      <textarea name="text" rows="6" cols="40" wrap="soft"></textarea>
      <p>
      Enter numeric key: <br />
      <input type="text" name="key" size="6" />
      <p>
      <input type="submit" name="submit" value="Submit" />
    </form>
<?php
    // if form submitted
    // process form input
    } else {
      $type = $_POST['type'];
      $text = $_POST['text'];
      $key = (int)$_POST['key'];

      // perform encryption or decryption
      // print output
      $j = new Jumbler;
```

(continued)

```
      $j->setKey($key);
      if ($type == 'C') {
        echo $j->decrypt($text);
      } else {
        echo $j->encrypt($text);
      }
    }
?>
  </body>
</html>
```

The script is quite simple: it generates a Web form containing text fields for the user to enter text and a numeric key, and radio buttons to indicate whether the text being entered is plaintext or ciphertext. On submission, a new instance of the Jumbler class is created, and the key entered by the user is registered with the instance via the `setKey()` method. Depending on the type of text entered, the instance's `encrypt()` or `decrypt()` method is called, and the output is printed back to the page.

Figure 5-4 shows what the Web form looks like, and Figure 5-5 has an example of the encrypted text generated after form submission.

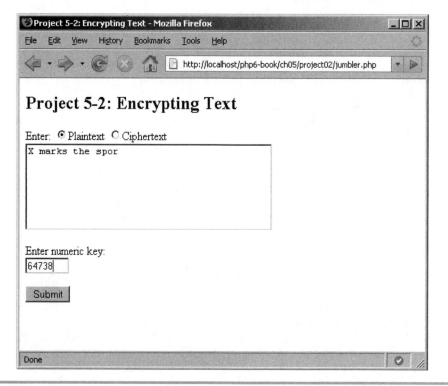

Figure 5-4 A Web form to enter plaintext

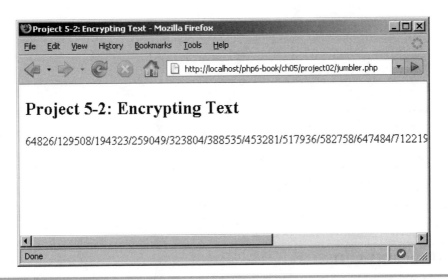

Figure 5-5   The result after encryption

Using Advanced OOP Concepts

PHP's object model also supports many more advanced features, giving developers a great deal of power and flexibility in building OOP-driven applications. This section illustrates three such features: constructors and destructors, extensibility, and visibility.

Using Constructors and Destructors

PHP makes it possible to automatically execute code when a new instance of a class is created, using a special class method called a *constructor*. You can also run code when a class instance ends using a so-called *destructor*. Constructors and destructors can be implemented by defining functions named __construct() and __destruct() within the class, and placing object (de)initialization code within them.

Here's a simple example illustrating how this works:

```php
<?php
// define class
class Machine {

    // constructor
    function __construct() {
        echo "Starting up...\n";
    }
}
```

```
    // destructor
    function __destruct() {
        echo "Shutting down...\n";
    }
}

// create an object
// output: "Starting up..."
$m = new Machine();

// then destroy it
// output: "Shutting down..."
unset($m);
?>
```

Extending Classes

For most developers, extensibility is the most powerful reason for using the OOP paradigm. Put very simply, *extensibility* implies that a new class can be derived from an existing one, inheriting all the properties and methods of the parent class and adding its own new properties and methods as needed. Thus, for example, a Human class could extend a Mammal class, which is itself an extension of a Vertebrate class, with each new extension adding its own features as well as inheriting the features of its parent.

In PHP, extending a class is as simple as attaching the `extends` keyword and the name of the class being extended to a class definition, as in the following example:

```
<?php
class Mammal {
  // class definition
}

class Human extends Mammal {
  // class definition
}
?>
```

With such an extension, all the properties and methods of the parent class become available to the child class and can be used within the class' program logic. To illustrate, consider the following listing:

```
<?php
// parent class definition
class Mammal {
```

```php
  public $age;

  function __construct() {
    echo 'Creating a new ' . get_class($this) . '...';
  }

  function setAge($age) {
    $this->age = $age;
  }

  function getAge() {
    return $this->age;
  }

  function grow() {
    $this->age += 4;
  }
}

// child class definition
class Human extends Mammal {

  public $name;

  function __construct() {
    parent::__construct();
  }

  function setName($name) {
    $this->name = $name;
  }

  function getName() {
    return $this->name;
  }

  function grow() {
    $this->age += 1;
    echo 'Growing...';
  }
}
?>
```

This listing contains two class definitions:

1. Mammal, the parent class, which contains the $age property and the methods
   setAge(), getAge(), and grow();

2. Human, which extends Mammal and inherits all of Mammal's properties and methods. Human contains the additional $name property and the additional methods setName() and getName(); its grow() method overrides the method of the same name in the parent class. Notice also that Human's __construct() method internally calls Mammal's __construct() method; the special keyword parent provides an easy shortcut to refer to the current class' parent.

Here's an example of how you'd use the extended class:

```php
<?php
$baby = new Human;
$baby->setAge(1);
$baby->setName('Tonka');
echo $baby->getName() . ' is now ' . $baby->getAge() . ' year(s) old...';
$baby->grow();
$baby->grow();
echo $baby->getName() . ' is now ' . $baby->getAge() . ' year(s) old.';
?>
```

Figure 5-6 shows the output of this listing.

From the output, it should be clear that even though the class definition for Human doesn't explicitly contain getAge() and setAge() methods, nor the $age property,

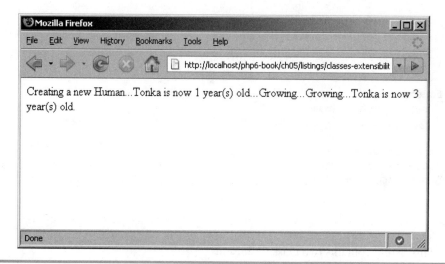

Figure 5-6 Using inherited methods of a class

instances of the Human class can still use these methods, as they are inherited from the parent Mammal class.

Once you begin working with inheritance and extensibility, it's easy to quickly become overwhelmed with long and complex class trees. For this reason, PHP provides an instanceof operator, to test if an object is an instance of a particular class. This operator returns true if the object instance has the named class anywhere in its parent tree. Here's an example of it in action:

```php
<?php
// class tree
class Vertebrate {
}
class Mammal extends Vertebrate {
}
class Human extends Mammal {
}

$baby = new Human;
// output: true
echo ($baby instanceof Vertebrate) ? 'true' : 'false';
?>
```

TIP
There's also the get_class() function, which returns the name of the class from which an object was instantiated, and the get_parent_class() function, which returns the name of its parent.

Adjusting Visibility Settings
In the first part of this chapter, you learned the difference between "local" and "global" scope, and you saw how variables used inside a function are invisible to the main program. When working with classes, PHP allows you to exert even greater control over the *visibility* of object properties and methods. Three levels of visibility exist, ranging from most visible to least visible; these correspond to the public, protected, and private keywords.

You'll have noticed that all the property and method definitions in earlier examples are prefixed with the keyword public; this sets the corresponding class methods and properties to be "public" and allows a caller to manipulate them directly from the main body of the program. This "public" visibility is the default level of visibility for any class member (method or property) under PHP.

If you don't like the thought of this intrusion, you can explicitly mark a particular property or method as `private` or `protected`, depending on how much control you want to cede over the object's internals. "Private" methods and properties are only visible within the class that defines them, while "protected" methods and properties are visible to both their defining class and any child (inherited) classes. Attempts to access these properties or methods outside their visible area typically produces a fatal error that stops script execution.

To see how this works in practice, consider the following example:

```php
<?php
// class tree
class Mammal {
  public $name;
  protected $age;
  private $species;
}
class Human extends Mammal {
}

$mammal = new Mammal;
$mammal->name = 'William';    // ok
$mammal->age = 3;             // fatal error
$mammal->species = 'Whale';   // fatal error

$human = new Human;
$human->name = 'Barry';       // ok
$human->age = 1;              // fatal error
$human->species = 'Boy';      // undefined
?>
```

Try This 5-3   Generating Form Selection Lists

Let's now turn to another example to illustrate some of the more advanced concepts taught in the preceding section. Here, you'll create objects to mimic the `<select>` and `<option>` elements used in a Web form, writing methods that allow you to define such a selection list programmatically from your application. There are three primary objects you'll encounter in the next example: a base Element object and two derived objects named Select and Option.

Let's start with the base Element object, which represents a generic form element:

```php
<?php
// class definition
class Element {
  private $name;
  private $value;
  private $label;
```

```php
  // constructor
  public function __construct() {
  }

  // method: set element 'name'
  public function setName($name) {
    $this->name = $name;
  }

  // method: get element 'name'
  public function getName() {
    return $this->name;
  }

  // method: set element value
  public function setValue($value) {
    $this->value = $value;
  }

  // method: get element value
  public function getValue() {
    return $this->value;
  }

  // method: set English-language element label
  public function setLabel($label) {
    $this->label = $label;
  }

  // method: get element label
  public function getLabel() {
    return $this->label;
  }
}
?>
```

We assume here that every form element has three properties: a name, a value, and a text label. The preceding class definition defines just these properties and also provides "getter" and "setter" methods to change and retrieve these properties.

This Element object serves as the base for other, more focused form elements—such as the Option object, which represents an `<option>` element. Here's the definition:

```php
<?php
// child class definition
class Option extends Element {

  // constructor
  public function __construct($value='', $label='') {
    parent::__construct();
```

(continued)

```php
    $this->setValue($value);
    $this->setLabel($label);
  }

  // method: output HTML for <option> elements
  public function render() {
    echo "<option value=\"" . $this->getValue() . "\">" . $this->getLabel() .
"</option>\n";
  }
}
?>
```

The constructor for an Option accepts two arguments: a value and a label. These two arguments are then used to set the Option's $value and $label properties, via its setValue() and setLabel() methods. Note that these methods are not explicitly defined in the class but actually belong to the Element class; however, due to extensibility, the methods of the parent class are automatically available to its children.

The Option class also adds a new method, render(), which outputs the HTML code necessary to create an <option> element. Notice that this method internally calls getValue() and getLabel(), also methods of its parent, to correctly generate the necessary HTML code.

All that's left now is to define the Select class:

```php
<?php
// child class definition
class Select extends Element {

  protected $options;

  // constructor
  public function __construct() {
    parent::__construct();
    $this->options = array();
  }

  // method: add an option to the list
  public function setOption($option) {
    $this->options[] = $option;
  }

  // method: return all options for the list as array
  private function getOptions() {
    return (array)$this->options;
  }

  // method: output HTML code for <select> element
  public function render() {
```

```
      echo $this->getLabel() . ": <br />\n";
      echo "<select name=\"" . $this->getName() . "\">\n";
      foreach ($this->getOptions() as $opt) {
        echo $opt->render();
      }
      echo "</select>";
    }
  }
?>
```

This class defines a single protected property, $options, as an array. The class also offers the setOption() method, which accepts an Option object and adds it to the $options array; and the render() method, which iterates over the $options array and outputs the HTML code needed for the <select> element. Both the preceding methods are public; however, there's also a getOptions() method, which is a private method only used internally to return the $options array to the caller.

How would you use these objects? Here's an example:

```
<?php
      // generate selection list
      $fruits = new Select();
      $fruits->setLabel('Fruits');
      $fruits->setName('fruit_sel');
      $fruits->setOption(new Option('Oranges', 'Oranges'));
      $fruits->setOption(new Option('Strawberries', 'Strawberries'));
      $fruits->setOption(new Option('Pineapples', 'Pineapples'));
      $fruits->setOption(new Option('Bananas', 'Bananas'));
      $fruits->render();
?>
```

The first step is to initialize an instance of the Select class and assign the element a label and name via the setLabel() and setName() methods—remember that these methods have been inherited from the parent Element class. Next, the Select object's setOption() method is used to assign options to the selection list—each setOption() call is passed an Option object holding the option's label and value. Once all the options have been assigned, the Select object's render() method takes care of actually writing the HTML to the page:

Here's what the HTML output generated by render() looks like:

```
Fruits: <br />
<select name="fruit_sel">
<option value="Oranges">Oranges</option>
<option value="Strawberries">Strawberries</option>
<option value="Pineapples">Pineapples</option>
<option value="Bananas">Bananas</option>
</select>
```

(continued)

Why stop with just one selection list? The nice thing about OOP, after all, is reusability—and so, it's easy to generate multiple selection lists, just by reusing the three classes described previously. Here's an example illustrating this (*select.php*):

```
<!DOCTYPE html PUBLIC "-//W3C//DTD XHTML 1.0 Transitional//EN"
    "DTD/xhtml1-transitional.dtd">
<html xmlns="http://www.w3.org/1999/xhtml" xml:lang="en" lang="en">
  <head>
    <title>Project 5-3: Generating Form Selection Lists</title>
  </head>
  <body>
    <h2>Project 5-3: Generating Form Selection Lists</h2>
<?php
    // if form not yet submitted
    // display form
    if (!isset($_POST['submit'])) {
?>
    <form method="post" action="select.php">
      <?php
      // generate selection list #1
      $fruits = new Select();
      $fruits->setLabel('Fruits');
      $fruits->setName('fruit_sel');
      $fruits->setOption(new Option('Oranges', 'Oranges'));
      $fruits->setOption(new Option('Strawberries', 'Strawberries'));
      $fruits->setOption(new Option('Pineapples', 'Pineapples'));
      $fruits->setOption(new Option('Bananas', 'Bananas'));
      $fruits->render();
      ?>

      <p />

      <?php
      // generate selection list #2
      $metals = new Select();
      $metals->setLabel('Metals');
      $metals->setName('metal_sel');
      $metals->setOption(new Option('Iron', 'Iron'));
      $metals->setOption(new Option('Silver', 'Silver'));
      $metals->setOption(new Option('Gold', 'Gold'));
      $metals->setOption(new Option('Platinum', 'Platinum'));
      $metals->render();
      ?>

      <p />

      <?php
      // generate selection list #3
      $animals = new Select();
      $animals->setLabel('Animals');
```

```
        $animals->setName('animal_sel');
        $animals->setOption(new Option('Lion', 'Lion'));
        $animals->setOption(new Option('Hyena', 'Hyena'));
        $animals->setOption(new Option('Fox', 'Fox'));
        $animals->render();
        ?>
        <p />
        <input type="submit" name="submit" value="Submit" />
      </form>
<?php
    // if form submitted
    // process form input
    } else {
      var_dump($_POST);
    }
?>
  </body>
</html>
```

Figure 5-7 illustrates the output of this listing.

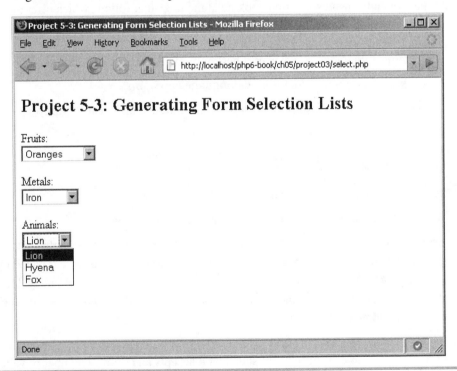

Figure 5-7   A form containing three dynamically generated selection lists

Summary

This chapter introduced you to two fairly advanced constructs: user-defined functions, which allow you to package your PHP code into reusable blocks; and classes, which allow you to group related functions into independent, extensible units. It also gave you a crash course in important software design concepts, such as recursion, encapsulation, inheritance, visibility, and reflection. All of these concepts and techniques were reinforced through the development of three practical examples; you probably found these somewhat more challenging than those in previous chapters, but working through them will almost certainly have moved your PHP skills up a notch.

At the close of this chapter (and this section), you know enough about the basic grammar and syntax of object-oriented programming to recognize and understand its use in third-party code, and also to begin writing modular, OOP-driven scripts of your own. These skills will stand you in good stead as you move into the next section of this book, which focuses on integrating your PHP application with data from other external sources. Until then, though, spend some time looking at the links that follow, which offer more detailed information on the topics discussed in this chapter.

- User-defined functions, at **www.php.net/manual/en/language.functions.php**

- Classes, at **www.php.net/manual/en/language.oop5.php**

- Class visibility, at **www.php.net/manual/en/language.oop5.visibility.php**

 Chapter 5 Self Test

1. State one advantage of using functions.

2. What is the difference between an argument and a return value?

3. Using the relationship `DISTANCE = SPEED * TIME`, write a function that calculates distance given the speed and time. Use this function to find the distance traveled by an aircraft departing from London, England, at 9:30 P.M. and arriving in Bombay, India, at 11 A.M. the next day. Assume the aircraft flies at 910 km/hr and the time difference between London and Bombay is 4.5 hours.

4. Using the property `LCM (P,Q,R,S) = LCM(LCM(LCM(P,Q),R),S)`, extend the LCM/GCF example in this chapter such that it accepts an arbitrary number of values and returns the LCM of the series.

5. What is a constructor?

6. What happens if you attempt to access a private method of a parent class from its child class?

7. What would be the output of the following code?

```php
<?php
class Daddy {
  public function talk() {
    echo get_class($this);
  }
}
class Baby extends Daddy {
  public function play() {
    parent::talk();
  }
}

$a = new Baby;
$a->play();
?>
```

8. Using the Select class defined earlier in this chapter, create a new DateSelect class containing three selection lists, one each for day, month, and year. Demonstrate usage of this class in a Web form.

9. What would be the output of the following PHP code:

```php
<?php
echo date("l d F Y H:i a", mktime(12,15,22,11,17,2008));
?>
```

Part II

Working with Data from Other Sources

Chapter 6

Working with Files and Directories

Key Skills & Concepts

- Learn to read and write disk files

- Process directories recursively

- Copy, move, rename, and delete files and directories

- Work with file paths and attributes

John Donne famously said, "No man is an island," and this maxim holds true for PHP scripts as well. So far, all the examples you've seen have been self-contained, with their source data arriving either from user input or from variables hard-wired into the program body. In reality, though, your PHP script will need to work with data retrieved from disk files, SQL resultsets, XML documents, and many other data sources.

PHP comes with numerous built-in functions to access these data sources and this chapter will get you started on the road to discovering them, by focusing specifically on PHP's file system functions. With 70+ functions available, there's an abundance of options; this chapter will give you a crash course in the most important ones, with both examples and practical projects of reading, writing, and manipulating disk files and directories.

Reading Files

PHP's file manipulation API is extremely flexible: it lets you read files into a string or into an array, from the local file system or a remote URL, by lines, bytes, or characters. The following sections explain all these variants in greater detail.

Reading Local Files

The easiest way to read the contents of a disk file in PHP is with the `file_get_contents()` function. This function accepts the name and path to a disk file, and reads the entire file into a string variable in one fell swoop. Here's an example:

```php
<?php
// read file into string
$str = file_get_contents('example.txt') or die('ERROR: Cannot find file');
echo $str;
?>
```

An alternative method of reading data from a file is PHP's `file()` function, which accepts the name and path to a file and reads the entire file into an array, with each element of the array representing one line of the file. To process the file, all you need do is iterate over the array using a `foreach` loop. Here's an example, which reads a file into an array and then displays it using such a loop:

```php
<?php
// read file into array
$arr = file('example.txt') or die('ERROR: Cannot find file');
foreach ($arr as $line) {
  echo $line;
}
?>
```

Reading Remote Files

Both `file_get_contents()` and `file()` also support reading data from URLs, using either the HTTP or FTP protocol. Here's an example, which reads an HTML file off the Web into an array:

```php
<?php
// read file into array
$arr = file('http://www.google.com') or die('ERROR: Cannot find file');
foreach ($arr as $line) {
  echo $line;
}
?>
```

In case of slow network links, it's sometimes more efficient to read a remote file in "chunks," to maximize the efficiency of available network bandwidth. To do this, use the `fgets()` function to read a specific number of bytes from a file, as in the next example:

```php
<?php
// read file into array (chunks)
$str = '';$fp = fopen('http://www.google.com', 'r') or die('ERROR:
Cannot open file');
while (!feof($fp)) {
  $str .= fgets($fp,512);
}
fclose($fp);
echo $str;
?>
```

This listing introduces four new functions, so let's take a closer look at it. First, the fopen() function: it accepts the name of the source file and an argument indicating whether the file is to be opened in read ('r'), write ('w'), or append ('a') mode, and then creates a pointer to the file. Next, a while loop calls the fgets() function continuously in a loop to read a specific number of bytes from the file and append these bytes to a string variable; this loop continues until the feof() function returns true, indicating that the end of the file has been reached. Once the loop has completed, the fclose() function destroys the file pointer.

NOTE

In order to read remote URLs, the PHP configuration variable 'allow_url_fopen' must be set to true in the PHP configuration file *php.ini*. If this variable is set to false, all attempts to read remote files will fail.

Reading Specific Segments of a File

A final twist involves reading only a specific block of lines from a line—something that can be accomplished with a combination of PHP's fseek() and fgets() functions. Consider the next example, which sets up a user-defined function named readBlock() and accepts three arguments: the filename, the starting line number, and the number of lines to return from the starting point:

```php
<?php
// function definition
// read a block of lines from a file
function readBlock($file, $start=1, $lines=null) {
  // open file
  $fp = fopen($file, 'r') or die('ERROR: Cannot find file');

  // initialize counters
  $linesScanned = 1;
  $linesRead = 0;
  $out = '';

  // loop until end of file
  while (!feof($fp)) {
    // get each line
    $line = fgets($fp);
    // if start position is reached
    // append line to output variable
    if ($linesScanned >= $start) {
      $out .= $line;
      $linesRead++;
      // if max number of lines is defined and reached
```

```
      // break out of loop
      if (!is_null($linesRead) && $linesRead == ($lines)) {
        break;
      }
    }
    $linesScanned++;
  }
  return $out;
}

echo readBlock('example.txt', 3, 4);
?>
```

Within readBlock(), a loop iterates through the file line by line, until the starting line number is reached (a line counter named $linesScanned keeps track of the current line number, incrementing by 1 on each iteration of the loop). Once the starting line is reached, it (and all subsequent lines) are read into a string variable until the specified maximum number of lines are processed or until the end of the file is reached.

Writing Files

The flip side of reading data from files is writing data to them. And PHP comes with a couple of different ways to do this as well. The first is the file_put_contents() function, a close cousin of the file_get_contents() function you read about in the preceding section: this function accepts a filename and path, together with the data to be written to the file, and then writes the latter to the former. Here's an example:

```
<?php
// write string to file
$data = "A fish \n out of \n  water\n";
file_put_contents('output.txt', $data)
 or die('ERROR: Cannot write file');
echo 'Data written to file';
?>
```

If the file specified in the call to file_put_contents() already exists on disk, file_put_contents() will overwrite it by default. If, instead, you'd prefer to preserve the file's contents and simply append new data to it, add the special FILE_APPEND flag to your file_put_contents() function call as a third argument. Here's an example:

```
<?php
// write string to file
$data = "A fish \n out of \n  water\n";
file_put_contents('output.txt', $data, FILE_APPEND)
```

```
    or die('ERROR: Cannot write file');
echo 'Data written to file';
?>
```

An alternative way to write data to a file is to create a file pointer with fopen(), and then write data to the pointer using PHP's fwrite() function. Here's an example of this technique:

```
<?php
// open and lock file
// write string to file
// unlock and close file
$data = "A fish \n out of \n  water\n";
$fp = fopen('output.txt', 'w') or die('ERROR: Cannot open file');
flock($fp, LOCK_EX) or die ('ERROR: Cannot lock file');
fwrite($fp, $data) or die ('ERROR: Cannot write file');
flock($fp, LOCK_UN) or die ('ERROR: Cannot unlock file');
fclose($fp);
echo 'Data written to file';
?>
```

Notice the flock() function from the preceding listing: this function "locks" a file before reading or writing it, so that it cannot be accessed by another process. Doing this reduces the possibility of data corruption that might occur if two processes attempt to write different data to the same file at the same instant. The second parameter to flock() specifies the type of lock: LOCK_EX creates an exclusive lock for writing, LOCK_SH creates a non-exclusive lock for reading, and LOCK_UN destroys the lock.

Ask the Expert

Q: Can I read and write binary files with PHP?

A: Yes. The file_get_contents(), file_put_contents(), and file() functions all read and write data in binary format by default; this lets you use PHP with binary files without worrying that your data will get corrupted.

NOTE
The directory into which you're trying to save the file must already exist, or else PHP will generate a fatal error. You can test if a directory exists with the file_exists() function, discussed later in this chapter.

Try This 6-1 Reading and Writing Configuration Files

Now that you know how to read and write files, let's try creating an application that uses the functions described in the preceding section. Assume for a second that you're developing a Weblog application, and you'd like your users to be able to configure certain aspects of this application's behavior—for example, how many posts appear on the index page or the e-mail address that comments are sent to. In this case, you'd probably need to build a Web-based form that allows users to input these configuration values and saves them to a file that your application can read as needed.

This next listing generates just such a Web form, allowing users to enter values for different configuration values and then saving this information to a disk file. When users revisit the form, the data previously saved to the file is read and used to prefill the form's fields.

Here's the code (*configure.php*):

```php
<!DOCTYPE html PUBLIC "-//W3C//DTD XHTML 1.0 Transitional//EN"
    "DTD/xhtml1-transitional.dtd">
<html xmlns="http://www.w3.org/1999/xhtml" xml:lang="en" lang="en">
  <head>
    <title>Project 6-1: Reading And Writing Configuration Files</title>
  </head>
  <body>
    <h2>Project 6-1: Reading And Writing Configuration Files</h2>
<?php
    // define configuration filename and path
    $configFile = 'config.ini';

    // if form not yet submitted
    // display form
    if (!isset($_POST['submit'])) {

      // set up array with default parameters
      $data = array();
      $data['AdminEmailAddress'] = null;
      $data['DefAuthor'] = null;
      $data['NumPosts'] = null;
      $data['NumComments'] = null;
      $data['NotifyURL'] = null;

      // read current configuration values
      // use them to pre-fill the form
      if (file_exists($configFile)) {
        $lines = file($configFile);
        foreach ($lines as $line) {
          $arr = explode('=', $line);
          $i = count($arr) - 1;
```

(continued)

```php
            $data[$arr[0]] = $arr[$i];
        }
    }
?>
    <form method="post" action="configure.php">
      Administrator email address: <br />
      <input type="text" size="50" name="data[AdminEmailAddress]" value="<?php
echo $data['AdminEmailAddress']; ?>"/>
      <p>
      Default author name: <br />
      <input type="text" name="data[DefAuthor]"  value="<?php echo
$data['DefAuthor']; ?>"/>
      <p>
      Number of posts on index page: <br />
      <input type="text" size="4" name="data[NumPosts]" value="<?php echo
$data['NumPosts']; ?>"/>
      <p>
      Number of anonymous comments: <br />
      <input type="text" size="4" name="data[NumComments]" value="<?php echo
$data['NumComments']; ?>"/>
      <p>
      URL for automatic notification of new posts: <br />
      <input type="text" size="50" name="data[NotifyURL]" value="<?php echo
$data['NotifyURL']; ?>"/>
      <p>
      <input type="submit" name="submit" value="Submit" />
    </form>
<?php
    // if form submitted
    // process form input
    } else {
    // read submitted data
    $config = $_POST['data'];

    // validate submitted data as necessary
    if ((trim($config['NumPosts']) != '' && (int)$config['NumPosts'] <= 0) ||
(trim($config['NumComments']) != '' && (int)$config['NumComments'] <= 0)) {
        die('ERROR: Please enter a valid number');
    }

    // open and lock configuration file for writing
    $fp = fopen($configFile, 'w+') or die('ERROR: Cannot open configuration
file for writing');
    flock($fp, LOCK_EX) or die('ERROR: Cannot lock configuration file for
writing');

    // write each configuration value to the file
    foreach ($config as $key => $value) {
      if (trim($value) != '') {
        fwrite($fp, "$key=$value\n") or die('ERROR: Cannot write [$key] to
configuration file');
      }
    }
```

```
        // close and save file
        flock($fp, LOCK_UN) or die ('ERROR: Cannot unlock file');
        fclose($fp);
        echo 'Configuration data successfully written to file.';
    }
?>
  </body>
</html>
```

This example illustrates a common, and practical, use of PHP's file functions: to read and write configuration files in the context of a Web application. Figure 6-1 illustrates the Web form generated by this script.

Once the form is submitted, the data entered into it arrives in the form of an associative array, whose keys correspond to the configuration variables in use. This data is then validated and a file pointer is opened to the configuration file, *config.ini*. A `foreach` loop then iterates over the array, writing the keys and values to the file pointer in `key=value` format, with each key-value pair on a separate line. The file pointer is then closed, saving the data to disk.

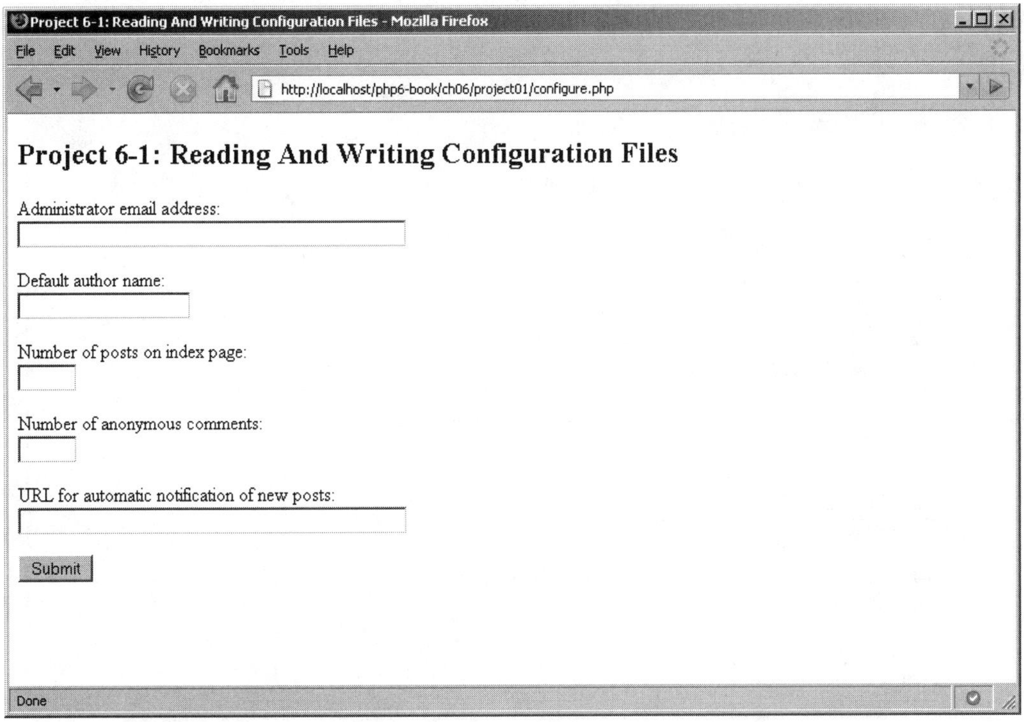

Figure 6-1   A Web form to enter configuration data

(continued)

Here's an example of what *config.ini* would look like after submitting the form in Figure 6-1:

```
AdminEmailAddress=admin@abc.com
DefAuthor=Charles W
NumPosts=8
NumComments=4
```

If a user revisits the Web form, the script first checks if a configuration file named *config.ini* exists in the current directory. If it does, the lines of the file are read into an array with PHP's `file()` function; a `foreach` loop then processes this array, splitting each line on the equality (=) symbol and turning the resulting key-value pairs into an associative array. This array is then used to prefill the form fields, by assigning a value to each input field's `'value'` attribute.

Figure 6-2 illustrates one such Web form, prefilled with data read from the configuration file.

Users are, of course, free to resubmit the form with new data; as explained previously, this submission will then be used to rewrite the configuration file with new values.

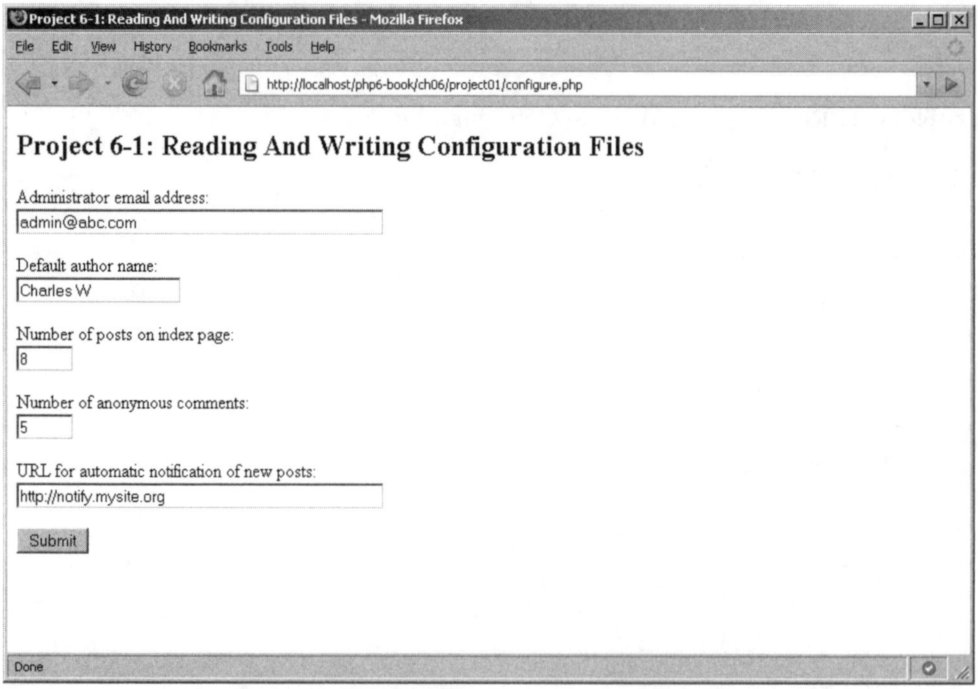

Figure 6-2 A Web form prefilled with data from a configuration file

Processing Directories

PHP also allows developers to work with directories on the file system, iterating through directory contents or moving forward and backward through directory trees. Iterating through a directory is a simple matter of calling PHP's DirectoryIterator object, as in the following example, which uses the DirectoryIterator to read a directory and list each file within it:

```php
<?php
// initialize iterator with name of
// directory to process
$dit = new DirectoryIterator('.');

// loop over directory
// print names of files found
while($dit->valid()) {
  if (!$dit->isDot()) {
    echo $dit->getFilename() . "\n";
  }
  $dit->next();
}

unset($dit);
?>
```

Here, a DirectoryIterator object is initialized with a directory name, and the object's `rewind()` method is used to reset the internal pointer to the first entry in the directory. A `while` loop, which runs so long as a `valid()` entry exists, can then be used to iterate over the directory. Individual filenames are retrieved with the `getFilename()` method, while the `isDot()` method can be used to filter out the entries for the current (`.`) and parent (`..`) directories. The `next()` method moves the internal pointer forward to the next entry.

You can also accomplish the same task with a `while` loop and some of PHP's directory manipulation functions . . . as in the following listing:

```php
<?php
// create directory pointer
$dp = opendir('.') or die ('ERROR: Cannot open directory');

// read directory contents
// print filenames found
while ($file = readdir($dp)) {
  if ($file != '.' && $file != '..') {
    echo "$file \n";
  }
}

// destroy directory pointer
closedir($dp);
?>
```

Here, the `opendir()` function returns a pointer to the directory named in the function call. This pointer is then used by the `readdir()` function to iterate over the directory, returning a single entry each time it is invoked. It's then easy to filter out the `.` and `..` directories, and print the names of the remaining entries. Once done, the `closedir()` function closes the file pointer.

TIP

Also consider PHP's `scandir()` function, which accepts a directory name and returns an array containing a list of the files within that directory together with their sizes. It's then easy to process this array with a `foreach` loop.

In some cases, you might need to process not just the first-level directory, but also its subdirectories and sub-subdirectories. A recursive function, which you learned about in Chapter 5, is usually the best tool for this purpose: consider the next listing, which illustrates one such function in action:

```php
<?php
// function definition
// print names of files in a directory
// and its child directories
function printDir($dir, $depthStr='+') {
  if (file_exists($dir)) {
    // create directory pointer
    $dp = opendir($dir) or die ('ERROR: Cannot open directory');

    // read directory contents
    // print names of files found
    // call itself recursively if directories found
    while ($file = readdir($dp)) {
      if ($file != '.' && $file != '..') {
        echo "$depthStr $dir/$file \n";
        if (is_dir("$dir/$file")) {
          printDir("$dir/$file", $depthStr.'+');
        }
      }
    }

    // close directory pointer
    closedir($dp);
  }
}

// print contents of directory
// and all children
if (file_exists('.')) {
  echo '<pre>';
  printDir('.');
  echo '<pre>';
}
?>
```

The `printDir()` function in this listing might appear complex, but it's actually quite simple. It accepts two arguments: the name of the top-level directory to use, and a "depth string," which indicates, via indentation, the position of a particular file or directory in the hierarchy. Using this input, the function opens a pointer to the named directory and begins processing it with `readdir()`, printing the name of each directory or file found. In the event that a directory is found, the depth string is incremented by an additional character and the `printDir()` function is itself recursively called to process that subdirectory. This process continues until no further files or directories remain to be processed.

Figure 6-3 has an example of the output of this listing.

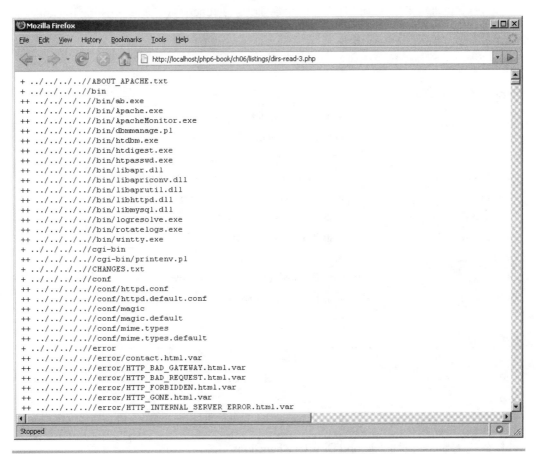

Figure 6-3   An indented directory listing

Performing Other File and Directory Operations

In addition to the tools you've seen in previous sections, PHP comes with a whole range of file and directory manipulation functions, which allow you to check file attributes; copy, move, and delete files; and work with file paths and extensions. Table 6-1 lists some of the important functions in this category.

Checking if a File or Directory Exists

If you try reading or appending to a file that doesn't exist, PHP will typically generate a fatal error. Ditto for attempts to access or read/write from/to a directory that doesn't exist. To avoid these error messages, always check that the file or directory you're attempting to access already exists, with PHP's file_exists() function. The next listing illustrates it in action:

Function	What It Does
file_exists()	Tests if a file or directory exists
filesize()	Returns the size of a file in bytes
realpath()	Returns the absolute path of a file
pathinfo()	Returns an array of information about a file and its path
stat()	Provides information on file attributes and permissions
is_readable()	Tests if a file is readable
is_writable()	Tests if a file is writable
is_executable()	Tests if a file is executable
is_dir()	Tests if a directory entry is a directory
is_file()	Tests if a directory entry is a file
copy()	Copies a file
rename()	Renames a file
unlink()	Deletes a file
mkdir()	Creates a new directory
rmdir()	Removes a directory
include() / require()	Reads an external file into the current PHP script

Table 6-1 Common PHP File and Directory Functions

```php
<?php
// check file
if (file_exists('somefile.txt')) {
  $str = file_get_contents('somefile.txt');
} else {
  echo 'Named file does not exist. ';
}

// check directory
if (file_exists('somedir')) {
  $files = scandir('somedir');
} else {
  echo 'Named directory does not exist.';
}
?>
```

Calculating File Size

To calculate the size of a file in bytes, call the `filesize()` function with the filename as argument:

```php
<?php
// get file size
// output: 'File is 1327 bytes.'
if (file_exists('example.txt')) {
  echo 'File is ' . filesize('example.txt') . ' bytes.';
} else {
  echo 'Named file does not exist. ';
}
?>
```

Finding the Absolute File Path

To retrieve the absolute file system path to a file, use the `realpath()` function, as in the next listing:

```php
<?php
// get file path
// output: 'File path: /usr/local/apache/htdocs/
//               /php-book/ch06/listings/example.txt'
if (file_exists('example.txt')) {
  echo 'File path: ' . realpath('example.txt');
} else {
  echo 'Named file does not exist. ';
}
?>
```

Ask the Expert

Q: Are PHP's file functions case-sensitive with respect to filenames?

A: It depends on the underlying file system. Windows is case-insensitive with respect to filenames, so PHP's file functions are case-insensitive too. However, filenames on *NIX systems are case-sensitive, and so PHP's file functions are case-sensitive too on these systems. Thus, given the file *eXAMple.txt,* the statement `<?php file_exists('example.txt'); ?>` might return false on a *NIX system but true on a Windows system.

You can also use the `pathinfo()` function, which returns an array containing the file's path, name, and extension. Here's an example:

```php
<?php
// get file path info as array
if (file_exists('example.txt')) {
  print_r(pathinfo('example.txt'));
} else {
  echo 'Named file does not exist. ';
}
?>
```

Retrieving File Attributes

You can obtain detailed information on a particular file, including its ownership, permissions, and modification and access times, with PHP's `stat()` function, which returns this information as an associative array. Here's an example:

```php
<?php
// get file information
if (file_exists('example.txt')) {
  print_r(stat('example.txt'));
} else {
  echo 'Named file does not exist. ';
}
?>
```

You can check if a file is readable, writable or executable with the `is_readable()`, `is_writable()`, and `is_executable()` functions. The following example illustrates their usage:

```php
<?php
// get file information
```

```php
// output: 'File is: readable  writable'
if (file_exists('example.txt')) {
  echo 'File is: ';
  // check for readable bit
  if (is_readable('example.txt')) {
    echo ' readable ';
  }
  // check for writable bit
  if (is_writable('example.txt')) {
    echo ' writable ';
  }
  // check for executable bit
  if (is_executable('example.txt')) {
    echo ' executable ';
  }
} else {
  echo 'Named file does not exist. ';
}
?>
```

The `is_dir()` function returns true if the argument passed to it is a directory, while the `is_file()` function returns true if the argument passed to it is a file. Here's an example:

```php
<?php
// test if file or directory
if (file_exists('example.txt')) {
  if (is_file('example.txt')) {
    echo 'It\'s a file.';
  }
  if (is_dir('example.txt')) {
    echo 'It\'s a directory.';
  }
} else {
  echo 'ERROR: File does not exist.';
}
?>
```

Creating Directories

To create a new, empty directory, call the `mkdir()` function with the path and name of the directory to be created:

```php
<?php
if (!file_exists('mydir')) {
  if (mkdir('mydir')) {
    echo 'Directory successfully created.';
```

```
    } else {
      echo 'ERROR: Directory could not be created.';
    }
} else {
  echo 'ERROR: Directory already exists.';
}
?>
```

Copying Files

You can copy a file from one location to another by calling PHP's copy() function with the file's source and destination paths as arguments. Here's an example:

```
<?php
// copy file
if (file_exists('example.txt')) {
  if (copy('example.txt', 'example.new.txt')) {
    echo 'File successfully copied.';
  } else {
    echo 'ERROR: File could not be copied.';
  }
} else {
  echo 'ERROR: File does not exist.';
}
?>
```

It's important to note that if the destination file already exists, the copy() function will overwrite it.

Renaming Files or Directories

To rename or move a file (or directory), call PHP's rename() function with the old and new path names as arguments. Here's an example that renames a file and a directory, moving the file to a different location in the process:

```
<?php
// rename/move file
if (file_exists('example.txt')) {
  if (rename('example.txt', '../example.new.txt')) {
    echo 'File successfully renamed.';
  } else {
    echo 'ERROR: File could not be renamed.';
  }
} else {
  echo 'ERROR: File does not exist.';
}
```

```
// rename directory
if (file_exists('mydir')) {
  if (rename('mydir', 'myotherdir')) {
    echo 'Directory successfully renamed.';
  } else {
    echo 'ERROR: Directory could not be renamed.';
  }
} else {
  echo 'ERROR: Directory does not exist.';
}
?>
```

As with copy(), if the destination file already exists, the rename() function will overwrite it.

CAUTION
PHP will only allow you to copy, delete, rename, create, and otherwise manipulate a file or directory if the user "owning" the PHP script has the privileges necessary to perform the task.

Removing Files or Directories
To remove a file, pass the filename and path to PHP's unlink() function, as in the following example:

```
<?php
// delete file
if (file_exists('dummy.txt')) {
  if (unlink('dummy.txt')) {
    echo 'File successfully removed.';
  } else {
    echo 'ERROR: File could not be removed.';
  }
} else {
  echo 'ERROR: File does not exist.';
}
?>
```

To remove an empty directory, PHP offers the rmdir() function, which does the reverse of the mkdir() function. If the directory isn't empty, though, it's necessary to first remove all its contents (including all subdirectories) and only then call the rmdir() function to remove the directory. You can do this manually, but a recursive function is usually more efficient—here's an example, which demonstrates how to remove a directory and all its children:

```php
<?php
// function definition
// remove all files in a directory
function removeDir($dir) {
  if (file_exists($dir)) {
    // create directory pointer
    $dp = opendir($dir) or die ('ERROR: Cannot open directory');

    // read directory contents
    // delete files found
    // call itself recursively if directories found
    while ($file = readdir($dp)) {
      if ($file != '.' && $file != '..') {
        if (is_file("$dir/$file")) {
          unlink("$dir/$file");
        } else if (is_dir("$dir/$file")) {
          removeDir("$dir/$file");
        }
      }
    }

    // close directory pointer
    // remove now-empty directory
    closedir($dp);
    if (rmdir($dir)) {
      return true;
    } else {
      return false;
    }
  }
}

// delete directory and all children
if (file_exists('mydir')) {
  if (removeDir('mydir')) {
    echo 'Directory successfully removed.';
  } else {
    echo 'ERROR: Directory could not be removed.';
  }
} else {
  echo 'ERROR: Directory does not exist.';
}
?>
```

Here, the removeDir() function is a recursive function that accepts one input argument: the name of the top-level directory to remove. The function begins by creating a pointer to the directory with `opendir()` and then iterating over the directory's contents with a `while` loop—you've seen this technique in a previous section of this chapter. For each directory entry found, the `is_file()` and `is_dir()` methods are used to determine if the entry is a file or a sub-directory; if the former, the `unlink()` function is used to delete the file and if the latter, the `removeDir()` function is called recursively to again process the subdirectory's contents. This process continues until no files or subdirectories are left; at this point, the top-level directory is empty and can be removed with a quick `rmdir()`.

Reading and Evaluating External Files

To read and evaluate external files from within your PHP script, use PHP's `include()` or `require()` function. A very common application of these functions is to include a standard header, footer, or copyright notice across all the pages of a Web site. Here's an example:

```
<!DOCTYPE html PUBLIC "-//W3C//DTD XHTML 1.0 Transitional//EN"
   "DTD/xhtml1-transitional.dtd">
<html xmlns="http://www.w3.org/1999/xhtml" xml:lang="en" lang="en">
   <head>
     <title></title>
   </head>
   <body>
     <?php require('header.php'); ?>
     <p/>
     This is the page body.
     <p/>
     <?php include('footer.php'); ?>
   </body>
</html>
```

Here, the script reads two external files, *header.php* and *footer.php,* and places the contents of these files at the location of the `include()` or `require()` call. It's important to note that any PHP code to be evaluated within the files included in this manner must be enclosed within `<?php ... ?>` tags.

Ask the Expert

Q: What is the difference between `include()` and `require()`?

A: Fairly simple: a missing `include()` will generate a warning but allow script execution to continue, whereas a missing `require()` will generate a fatal error that halts script execution.

Try This 6-2   Creating a Photo Gallery

Let's now try another practical example, this one using what you've learned about manipulating directories and using different file functions. This next listing scans a specified directory for digital photographs and dynamically generates a Web page to display these images—a digital photo gallery, if you will. Here's the code (*gallery.php*):

```
<!DOCTYPE html PUBLIC "-//W3C//DTD XHTML 1.0 Transitional//EN"
   "DTD/xhtml1-transitional.dtd">
<html xmlns="http://www.w3.org/1999/xhtml" xml:lang="en" lang="en">
  <head>
    <title>Project 6-2: Creating An Image Gallery</title>
  </head>
  <style type="text/css">
  ul {
        list-style-type: none;
  }

  li {
      float: left;
      padding: 10px;
      margin: 10px;
      font: bold 10px Verdana, sans-serif;
  }

  img {
      display: block;
      border: 1px solid #333300;
      margin-bottom: 5px;
      }
  </style>
  <body>
    <h2>Project 6-2: Creating An Image Gallery</h2>
    <ul>
<?php
    // define location of photo images
    // this must be a location accessible by the script owner
    $photosDir = './photos';

    // define which file extensions are images
    $photosExt = array('gif', 'jpg', 'jpeg', 'tif', 'tiff', 'bmp', 'png');

    // initialize array to hold filenames of images found
    $photosList = array();
```

```php
    // read directory contents
    // build photo list
    if (file_exists($photosDir)) {
      $dp = opendir($photosDir) or die ('ERROR: Cannot open directory');
      while ($file = readdir($dp)) {
        if ($file != '.' && $file != '..') {
          $fileData = pathinfo($file);
          if (in_array($fileData['extension'], $photosExt)) {
            $photosList[] = "$photosDir/$file";
          }
        }
      }
      closedir($dp);
    } else {
      die ('ERROR: Directory does not exist.');
    }

    // iterate over photo list
    // display each image and filename
    if (count($photosList) > 0) {
      for ($x=0; $x<count($photosList); $x++) {
?>
        <li>
          <img height="150" width="200"
            src="<?php echo $photosList[$x]; ?>" />
          <?php echo basename($photosList[$x]); ?><br/>
          <?php echo round(filesize($photosList[$x])/1024) . ' KB'; ?>
        </li>
<?php
      }
    } else {
      die('ERROR: No images found in directory');
    }
?>
    </ul>
  </body>
</html>
```

This listing begins by defining the path to the directory containing your digital images; you'll need to modify this to reflect your local system in order for the listing to work. It also sets up an array named $photosExt containing common file extensions for digital photographs; this information is useful when searching for image files in the named directory.

Having set up these two variables, the listing uses PHP's opendir() and readdir() functions to iterate over the specified directory and process each entry in it. If an entry's file extension is found to match an element from $photosExt, the file and path are added

(continued)

to a separate $photosList array. This process continues until all the entries in the named directory are processed.

Assuming at least one image has been found, the next (and final) step is to generate the HTML code to display the images on a Web page. This is accomplished by iterating over $photosList with a foreach loop and generating an <img /> tag for each file found in it, together with the image's filename and file size in kilobytes. The image references thus created are formatted as elements of a horizontal HTML list, such that they appear neatly arranged on the final output page.

Figure 6-4 illustrates the output of this listing. As the listing illustrates, it's quite easy to use PHP's directory and file functions to iterate through a directory and process the files found within it.

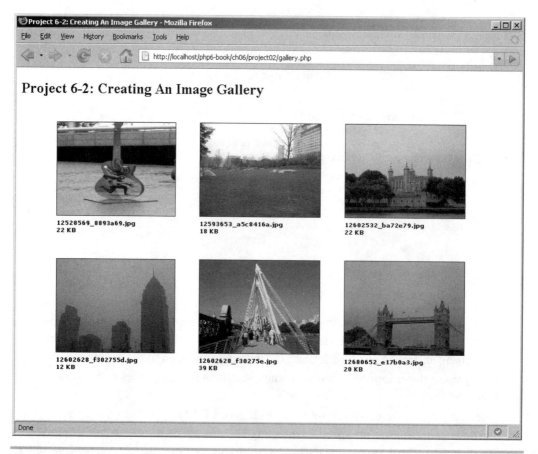

Figure 6-4 A dynamically generated Web photo gallery

Summary

Reading and writing files are basic tasks that any PHP developer should know how to accomplish; this chapter covered both these tasks, and many more. It began with a demonstration of how to read local and remote files, as well as how to create new files or append data to existing ones. It then moved on to directory manipulation under PHP and explained many of PHP's file and directory functions, illustrating each with a brief example. Two projects—reading and writing a configuration file, and creating a Web-based photo gallery—assisted in applying this learning in a practical context.

To read more about the topics discussed in this chapter, consider visiting the following links:

- Working with files and directories, at **www.melonfire.com/community/columns/ trog/article.php?id=208** and **www.melonfire.com/community/columns/trog/ article.php?id=211**

- File system functions, at **www.php.net/manual/en/ref.filesystem.php**

- Directory functions, at **www.php.net/manual/en/ref.dir.php**

 # Chapter 6 Self Test

1. Name the functions you would use to

   A Obtain the absolute path to a file

   B Delete a file

   C Retrieve the size of a file

   D Read the contents of a file into an array

   E Check if a file is writable

   F Check if a directory exists

   G Read the contents of a directory into an array

   H Write a string to a file

   I Create a new directory

   J Delete a directory

   K Create a pointer to a directory

   L Check if a directory entry is a file

2. Why would you use the `flock()` function?

3. Write a PHP script to count the number of lines in a file.

4. Write a PHP script to read a file, reverse its contents, and write the result back to a new file.

5. Write a PHP script to look through the current directory and rename all the files with extension *.txt* to extension *.xtx.*

6. Using the `removeDir()` recursive function in this chapter as model, write a recursive function to copy the contents of one directory to another.

7. Write a PHP script to read the current directory and return a file list sorted by last modification time. (Hint: The PHP function to return the last modification time of a file is `filemtime()`).

Chapter 7

Working with Databases and SQL

Key Skills & Concepts

- Learn database concepts and Structured Query Language

- Add, edit, delete, and view records using MySQL and SQLite databases

- Retrieve database records with PHP

- Validate and save user input to a database with PHP

- Write portable database-driven programs

One of the reasons for PHP's popularity as a Web scripting language is its support for a wide range of relational database systems. This support makes it easy for Web developers to create data-driven Web sites and to prototype new Web applications quickly and efficiently, with minimal fuss and muss.

PHP supports more than fifteen different database engines, including Microsoft SQL Server, IBM DB2, PostgreSQL, MySQL, and Oracle. Until PHP 5, this support was offered through native database extensions, each with its own functions and features; however, this made it hard for developers to change from one database engine to another. PHP 5 rectified this situation by introducing a common API for database access: the PHP Data Objects (PDO) extension, which provides a unified interface to working with databases and helps developers manipulate different databases in a consistent manner.

In PHP 5.3, the PDO extension has been further improved, with support for new database engines and further optimizations for security and performance. For backward compatibility, the native database extensions also continue to be supported. Because you'll often find yourself having to choose between a native extension (which may be faster or offer more features) or PDO (which offers portability and consistency across database engines), this chapter covers both options: it introduces you to PDO and also discusses two of PHP's most popular native extensions, the MySQL Improved extension and the SQLite extension.

Introducing Databases and SQL

In the Internet age, information is no longer represented in filing cabinets; instead, it's stored as digital ones and zeros in electronic databases, which are data storage "containers" that impose a certain structure on information. Not only do these electronic databases take up less physical space than their wood-and-metal counterparts, but they also come packed with tools to help users quickly filter and retrieve information using different criteria. In particular, most electronic databases today are *relational databases,* which allow users to define relationships between different database tables for more effective search and analysis.

There are a large number of database management systems currently available, some commercial and some free. You've probably already heard of some of them: Oracle, Microsoft Access, MySQL, and PostgreSQL. These database systems are powerful, feature-rich software applications, capable of organizing and searching millions of records at very high speeds; as such, they're widely used by businesses and government offices, often for mission-critical purposes.

Before getting into the nitty-gritty of manipulating database records with PHP, it's essential to first have a clear understanding of basic database concepts. If you're new to databases, the following sections provide a grounding in the basics and also let you get your hands dirty with a practical exercise in Structured Query Language (SQL). This information will be helpful to understand the more advanced material in subsequent sections.

Understanding Databases, Records, and Primary Keys

Every database is composed of one or more *tables.* These tables, which structure data into rows and columns, impose organization on the data. Figure 7-1 illustrates a typical table.

This table contains sales figures for various locations, with each row, or *record,* holding information for a different location and year. Each record is itself subdivided into columns, or *fields,* with each field holding a different fragment of information. This tabular structure makes it easy to search the table for records matching particular *criteria*: for example, all locations with sales greater than $10,000, or sales for all locations in the year 2008.

The records in a table are not arranged in any particular order—they can be sorted alphabetically, by year, by sales total, by location, or by any other criteria you choose to specify. To make it easy to identify a specific record, therefore, it becomes necessary

ID	Year	Location	Sales ($)
1	2007	Dallas	9495
2	2007	Chicago	8574
3	2007	Washington	12929
4	2007	New York	13636
5	2007	Los Angeles	8748
6	2007	Boston	3478
7	2008	Dallas	15249
8	2008	Chicago	19433
9	2008	Washington	3738
10	2008	New York	12373
11	2008	Los Angeles	16162
12	2008	Boston	4745

Figure 7-1   An example table

to add a unique identifying attribute to each record, such as a serial number or sequence code. In the preceding example, each record is identified by a unique "record ID" field; this field is referred to as the *primary key* for that table.

TIP

An easy way to understand these concepts is with an analogy. Think of a database as a library, and each table as a bookshelf within this library. A record is thus the electronic representation of a book on a shelf, with the title of the book serving as the record's primary key. In the absence of this title, it would be impossible to easily distinguish one book from another. (The only way to do so would be to open each book and investigate its contents—a time-consuming process, which the primary key helps you avoid!)

Once you've got information into a table, you typically want to use it to answer specific questions—for example, how many locations had sales greater than $5000 in 2008? These questions are known as *queries,* and the results returned by the database in response to these queries are known as *result sets.* Queries are performed using the Structured Query Language.

Understanding Relationships and Foreign Keys

You already know that a single database can hold multiple tables. In a relational database system, these tables can be linked to each other by one or more common fields, called *foreign keys.* These foreign keys make it possible to create one-to-one or one-to-many relationships between different tables, and combine data from multiple tables to create more comprehensive result sets.

To illustrate, consider Figure 7-2, which shows three linked tables.

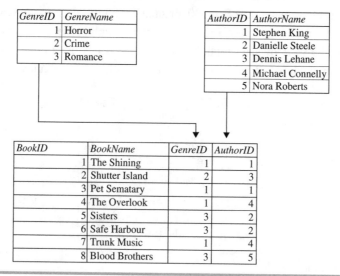

GenreID	GenreName
1	Horror
2	Crime
3	Romance

AuthorID	AuthorName
1	Stephen King
2	Danielle Steele
3	Dennis Lehane
4	Michael Connelly
5	Nora Roberts

BookID	BookName	GenreID	AuthorID
1	The Shining	1	1
2	Shutter Island	2	3
3	Pet Sematary	1	1
4	The Overlook	1	4
5	Sisters	3	2
6	Safe Harbour	3	2
7	Trunk Music	1	4
8	Blood Brothers	3	5

Figure 7-2 Table relationships

Figure 7-2 shows three tables, containing information on authors (Table A), genres (Table G), and books (Table B) respectively. Tables G and B are fairly straightforward: they contain a list of genre and author names respectively, with each record identified by a unique primary key. Table B is a little more complex: each book in the table is linked to a specific genre by means of the genre's primary key (from Table G) and to a specific author via the author's primary key (from Table A).

By following these keys to their respective source tables, it's easy to identify the author and genre for a specific book. For example, it can be seen that the title "The Shining" is written by "Stephen King" and belongs to the genre "Horror." Similarly, starting from the other end, it can be seen that the author "Michael Connelly" has written two books, "The Overlook" and "Trunk Music."

Relationships such as the ones seen in Figure 7-2 form the foundations of a relational database system. Linking tables using foreign keys is also more efficient than the alternative: while creating a single everything-but-the-kitchen-sink table to hold all your information might appear convenient at first glance, updating such a table is always a manual (and error-prone) process of finding every occurrence of a particular value and replacing it with a new value. Breaking information up into independent tables and linking these tables with foreign keys ensures that a particular piece of information appears once, and only once, in your database; this eliminates redundancies, simplifies changes (by localizing them to a single location), and makes the database more compact and manageable.

The process of streamlining a database by defining and implementing one-to-one and one-to-many relationships between its component tables is known as *database normalization,* and it's a key task faced by any database engineer when creating a new database. In the normalization process, the database engineer also identifies cross-relationships and incorrect dependencies between tables, and optimizes data organization so that SQL queries perform at their maximum efficiency. A number of *normal forms* are available to help you test the extent to which your database is normalized; these normal forms provide useful guidelines to help ensure that your database design is both structurally consistent and efficient.

Understanding SQL Statements

Structured Query Language, or SQL, is the standard language used to communicate with a database, add or change records and user privileges, and perform queries. The language, which became an ANSI standard in 1989, is currently used by almost all of today's commercial RDBMSs.

SQL statements fall into one of three categories:

- **Data Definition Language (DDL)** DDL consists of statements that define the structure and relationships of a database and its tables. Typically, these statements are used to create, delete, and modify databases and tables; specify field names and types; and set indexes.

- **Data Manipulation Language (DML)** DML statements are related to altering and extracting data from a database. These statements are used to add records to, and delete records from, a database; perform queries; retrieve table records matching one or more user-specified criteria; and join tables together using their common fields.

- **Data Control Language (DCL)** DCL statements are used to define access levels and security privileges for a database. You would use these statements to grant or deny user privileges; assign roles; change passwords; view permissions; and create rulesets to protect access to data.

SQL commands resemble spoken English, which makes the language easy to learn. The syntax is quite intuitive as well: every SQL statement begins with an "action word," like DELETE, INSERT, ALTER, or DESCRIBE, and ends with a semicolon. Whitespace, tabs, and carriage returns are ignored. Here are a few examples of valid SQL statements:

```
CREATE DATABASE library;
SELECT movie FROM movies WHERE rating > 4;
DELETE FROM cars WHERE year_of_manufacture < 1980;
```

Table 7-1 lists the syntax for some common SQL statements, with explanations.

SQL Statement	What It Does
CREATE DATABASE database-name	Creates a new database
CREATE TABLE table-name (field1, field2, ...)	Creates a new table
INSERT INTO table-name (field1, field2, ...) VALUES (value1, value2, ...)	Inserts a new record into a table with specified values
UPDATE table-name SET field1=value1, field2=value2, ... [WHERE condition]	Updates records in a table with new values
DELETE FROM table-name [WHERE condition]	Deletes records from a table
SELECT field1, field2, ... FROM table-name [WHERE condition]	Retrieves matching records from a table
RENAME table-name TO new-table-name	Renames a table
DROP TABLE table-name	Deletes a table
DROP DATABASE database-name	Deletes a database

Table 7-1 Common SQL Statements

Ask the Expert

Q: How widely supported is SQL?

A: SQL is both an ANSI and ISO standard, and is widely supported by all standards-compliant SQL database systems. That said, many database vendors have also extended "standard" SQL with proprietary extensions, in order to offer customers an improved feature set or better performance. These extensions differ from vendor to vendor, and SQL statements that use these extensions may not work in the same fashion on all database systems. Therefore, it's always wise to check your database system's documentation and understand which, if any, proprietary extensions it offers and how these extensions affect the SQL statements that you write.

Try This 7-1 Creating and Populating a Database

Now that you've understood the basics, let's try a hands-on exercise that should get you familiar with using databases and SQL. In this section, you'll use the interactive MySQL command-line client to create a database and tables, add and edit records, and generate result sets matching various criteria.

NOTE
Throughout the following exercise, boldface type indicates commands that you should enter at the MySQL command-line prompt. Commands can be entered in either uppercase or lowercase. Before beginning with the exercise, ensure that you have installed, configured, and tested the MySQL database system according to the instructions in Appendix A of this book.

Begin by starting up the MySQL command-line client and connecting to the MySQL database with your username and password:

```
shell> mysql -u user -p
Password: ******
```

If all went well, you'll see a welcome message and an interactive SQL prompt, like this:

```
mysql>
```

You can now proceed to enter SQL statements at this prompt. These statements will be transmitted to, and executed on, the MySQL server, and the results will be displayed on the lines following the prompt. Remember to end each statement with a semicolon.

(continued)

Creating the Database

Since all tables are stored in a database, the first step is to create one, using the CREATE DATABASE statement:

```
mysql> CREATE DATABASE music;
Query OK, 1 row affected (0.05 sec)
```

Next, select this newly minted database as the default for all future commands with the USE statement:

```
mysql> USE music;
Database changed
```

Adding Tables

Once you've got your database initialized, it's time to add some tables to it. The SQL command to accomplish this is the CREATE TABLE statement, which requires a table name and a detailed description of the table's fields. Here's an example:

```
mysql> CREATE TABLE artists (
    -> artist_id INT(4) NOT NULL PRIMARY KEY AUTO_INCREMENT,
    -> artist_name VARCHAR (50) NOT NULL,
    -> artist_country CHAR (2) NOT NULL
    -> );
Query OK, 0 rows affected (0.07 sec)
```

This statement creates a table named *artists* with three fields, *artist_id, artist_name,* and *artist_country*. Notice that each field name is followed by a *type declaration*; this declaration identifies the type of data that the field will hold, whether string, numeric, temporal, or Boolean. MySQL supports a number of different data types, and the most important ones are summarized in Table 7-2.

There are a few additional constraints (*modifiers*) that are set for the table in the preceding statement:

- The NOT NULL modifier ensures that the field cannot accept a NULL value after each field definition.

- The PRIMARY KEY modifier marks the corresponding field as the table's primary key.

- The AUTO_INCREMENT modifier, which is only available for numeric fields, tells MySQL to automatically generate a value for this field every time a new record is inserted into the table, by incrementing the previous value by 1.

Field Type	Description
INT	A numeric type that can accept values in the range of –2147483648 to 2147483647
DECIMAL	A numeric type with support for floating-point or decimal numbers
DATE	A date field in the YYYY-MM-DD format
TIME	A time field in the HH:MM:SS format
DATETIME	A combined date/time type in the YYYY-MM-DD HH:MM:SS format
YEAR	A field specifically for year displays in the range 1901 to 2155, in either YYYY or YY formats
TIMESTAMP	A timestamp type, in YYYYMMDDHHMMSS format
CHAR	A string type with a maximum size of 255 characters and a fixed length
VARCHAR	A string type with a maximum size of 255 characters and a variable length
TEXT	A string type with a maximum size of 65535 characters
BLOB	A binary type for variable data
ENUM	A string type that can accept one value from a list of previously defined possible values
SET	A string type that can accept zero or more values from a set of previously defined possible values

Table 7-2 MySQL Data Types

Now, go ahead and create two more tables using these SQL statements:

```
mysql> CREATE TABLE ratings (
    -> rating_id INT(2) NOT NULL PRIMARY KEY,
    -> rating_name VARCHAR (50) NOT NULL
    -> );
Query OK, 0 rows affected (0.13 sec)

mysql> CREATE TABLE songs (
    -> song_id INT(4) NOT NULL PRIMARY KEY AUTO_INCREMENT,
    -> song_title VARCHAR(100) NOT NULL,
    -> fk_song_artist INT(4) NOT NULL,
    -> fk_song_rating INT(2) NOT NULL
    -> );
Query OK, 0 rows affected (0.05 sec)
```

Adding Records

Adding a record to a table is a simple matter of calling the INSERT statement with appropriate values. Here's an example, which adds a record to the *artists* table by specifying values for the *artist_id* and *artist_name* fields:

```
mysql> INSERT INTO artists (artist_id, artist_name, artist_country)
    -> VALUES ('1', 'Aerosmith', 'US');
Query OK, 1 row affected (0.00 sec)
```

(continued)

You'll remember, from the preceding section, that the *artist_id* field was marked with the AUTO_INCREMENT flag. This is a MySQL extension to standard SQL, which tells MySQL to automatically assign a value to this field if it's left unspecified. To see this in action, try adding another record using the following statement:

```
mysql> INSERT INTO artists (artist_name, artist_country)
    -> VALUES ('Abba', 'SE');
Query OK, 1 row affected (0.00 sec)
```

In a similar vein, add some records to the *ratings* table:

```
mysql> INSERT INTO ratings (rating_id, rating_name) VALUES (4, 'Good');
Query OK, 1 row affected (0.00 sec)
mysql> INSERT INTO ratings (rating_id, rating_name) VALUES (5, 'Excellent');
Query OK, 1 row affected (0.00 sec)
```

And some to the *songs* table:

```
mysql> INSERT INTO songs (song_title, fk_song_artist, fk_song_rating)
    -> VALUES ('Janie\'s Got A Gun', 1, 4);
Query OK, 1 row affected (0.04 sec)
mysql> INSERT INTO songs (song_title, fk_song_artist, fk_song_rating)
    -> VALUES ('Crazy', 1, 5);
Query OK, 1 row affected (0.00 sec)
```

Notice that the records in the *songs* table are linked to records in the *artists* and *ratings* tables via foreign keys. You'll see these foreign key relationships in action in the next section.

NOTE
The code archive for this book has a full list of SQL INSERT statements to populate the three tables used in this exercise. Run these statements and complete building the tables before proceeding to the next section.

Executing Queries
Once the data is in the database, it's time to do something with it. SQL allows you to search for records matching specific criteria using the SELECT statement. Here's an example, which returns all the records from the artists table:

```
mysql> SELECT artist_id, artist_name FROM artists;
+-----------+-------------+
| artist_id | artist_name |
+-----------+-------------+
|         1 | Aerosmith   |
|         2 | Abba        |
|         3 | Timbaland   |
|         4 | Take That   |
|         5 | Girls Aloud |
|         6 | Cubanismo   |
+-----------+-------------+
6 rows in set (0.00 sec)
```

In most cases, you will want to add filters to your query, to reduce the size of your result set and ensure that it contains only records matching certain criteria. This is accomplished by adding a WHERE clause to your SELECT statement together with one or more conditional expressions. Here's an example, which lists only artists from the United States:

```
mysql> SELECT artist_id, artist_name FROM artists
    -> WHERE artist_country = 'US';
+-----------+-------------+
| artist_id | artist_name |
+-----------+-------------+
|         1 | Aerosmith   |
|         3 | Timbaland   |
+-----------+-------------+
2 rows in set (0.00 sec)
```

All the standard comparison operators you're already familiar with from PHP are supported by SQL. The preceding example demonstrated the equality (=) operator; this next one demonstrates the greater-than-or-equal-to (>=) operator, by listing all those songs with ratings of 4 or higher:

```
mysql> SELECT song_title, fk_song_rating FROM songs
    -> WHERE fk_song_rating >= 4;
+--------------------+----------------+
| song_title         | fk_song_rating |
+--------------------+----------------+
| Janie's Got A Gun  |              4 |
| Crazy              |              5 |
| En Las Delicious   |              5 |
| Pray               |              4 |
| Apologize          |              4 |
| SOS                |              4 |
| Dancing Queen      |              4 |
+--------------------+----------------+
7 rows in set (0.00 sec)
```

(continued)

You can combine conditional expressions using the AND, OR, and NOT logical operators (just like with regular PHP conditional statements). Here's an example, which lists artists from the United States or United Kingdom:

```
mysql> SELECT artist_name, artist_country FROM artists
    -> WHERE artist_country = 'US'
    -> OR artist_country = 'UK';
+--------------+----------------+
| artist_name  | artist_country |
+--------------+----------------+
| Aerosmith    | US             |
| Timbaland    | US             |
| Take That    | UK             |
| Girls Aloud  | UK             |
+--------------+----------------+
4 rows in set (0.02 sec)
```

Ordering and Limiting Result Sets

If you'd like to see the data from a table ordered by a specific field, SQL offers the ORDER BY clause. This clause lets you define the field name to sort against and the sort direction (ascending or descending).

For example, to see an alphabetically sorted song list, use the following SQL statement:

```
mysql> SELECT song_title FROM songs
    -> ORDER BY song_title;
+---------------------------+
| song_title                |
+---------------------------+
| Another Crack In My Heart |
| Apologize                 |
| Babe                      |
| Crazy                     |
| Dancing Queen             |
| En Las Delicious          |
| Gimme Gimme Gimme         |
| Janie's Got A Gun         |
| Pray                      |
| SOS                       |
| Sure                      |
| Voulez Vous               |
+---------------------------+
12 rows in set (0.04 sec)
```

To reverse-sort the list, add the additional DESC modifier, as in the next example:

```
mysql> SELECT song_title FROM songs
    -> ORDER BY song_title DESC;
+--------------------------+
| song_title               |
+--------------------------+
| Voulez Vous              |
| Sure                     |
| SOS                      |
| Pray                     |
| Janie's Got A Gun        |
| Gimme Gimme Gimme        |
| En Las Delicious         |
| Dancing Queen            |
| Crazy                    |
| Babe                     |
| Apologize                |
| Another Crack In My Heart |
+--------------------------+
12 rows in set (0.00 sec)
```

SQL also lets you limit how many records appear in the result set with the LIMIT keyword, which accepts two parameters: the record offset to start at (beginning with 0) and the number of records to display. For example, to display rows 4–9 (inclusive) of a result set, use the following statement:

```
mysql> SELECT song_title FROM songs
    -> ORDER BY song_title
    -> LIMIT 3,6;
+-------------------+
| song_title        |
+-------------------+
| Crazy             |
| Dancing Queen     |
| En Las Delicious  |
| Gimme Gimme Gimme |
| Janie's Got A Gun |
| Pray              |
+-------------------+
5 rows in set (0.00 sec)
```

Using Wildcards

The SQL SELECT statement also supports a LIKE clause, which can be used to search within text fields using wildcards. There are two types of wildcards allowed in a LIKE

(continued)

clause: the % character, which is used to signify zero or more occurrences of a character, and the _ character, which is used to signify exactly one occurrence of a character.

The following example illustrates a LIKE clause in action, searching for song titles with the character 'g' in them:

```
mysql> SELECT song_id, song_title FROM songs
    -> WHERE song_title LIKE '%g%';
+---------+--------------------+
| song_id | song_title         |
+---------+--------------------+
|       1 | Janie's Got A Gun  |
|       7 | Apologize          |
|       8 | Gimme Gimme Gimme   |
|      10 | Dancing Queen      |
+---------+--------------------+
4 rows in set (0.00 sec)
```

Joining Tables

So far, all the queries you've seen have been concentrated on a single table. But SQL also allows you to query two or more tables at a time, and display a combined result set. This is technically referred to as a *join,* since it involves "joining" different tables at common fields (the foreign keys) to create new views of the data.

TIP

When joining tables, prefix each field name with the name of the table it belongs to, in order to avoid confusion in case fields in different tables share the same name.

Here's an example of joining the *songs* and *artists* tables together using the common *artist_id* field (the WHERE clause is used to map the common fields to each other):

```
mysql> SELECT song_id, song_title, artist_name FROM songs, artists
    -> WHERE songs.fk_song_artist = artists.artist_id;
+---------+--------------------+--------------+
| song_id | song_title         | artist_name  |
+---------+--------------------+--------------+
|       1 | Janie's Got A Gun  | Aerosmith    |
|       2 | Crazy              | Aerosmith    |
|       8 | Gimme Gimme Gimme   | Abba         |
|       9 | SOS                | Abba         |
|      10 | Dancing Queen      | Abba         |
|      11 | Voulez Vous        | Abba         |
|       7 | Apologize          | Timbaland    |
|       4 | Sure               | Take That    |
```

```
|        5 | Pray                       | Take That    |
|        6 | Another Crack In My Heart  | Take That    |
|       12 | Babe                       | Take That    |
|        3 | En Las Delicious           | Cubanismo    |
+----------+----------------------------+--------------+
12 rows in set (0.00 sec)
```

And here's an example of joining all three tables together and then filtering the result set even further to include only those songs with a rating of 4 or higher and with non-U.S. artists:

```
mysql> SELECT song_title, artist_name, rating_name
    -> FROM songs, artists, ratings
    -> WHERE songs.fk_song_artist = artists.artist_id
    -> AND songs.fk_song_rating = ratings.rating_id
    -> AND ratings.rating_id >= 4
    -> AND artists.artist_country != 'US';
+------------------+-------------+-------------+
| song_title       | artist_name | rating_name |
+------------------+-------------+-------------+
| En Las Delicious | Cubanismo   | Excellent   |
| Pray             | Take That   | Good        |
| SOS              | Abba        | Good        |
| Dancing Queen    | Abba        | Good        |
+------------------+-------------+-------------+
4 rows in set (0.02 sec)
```

Modifying and Removing Records

Just as you INSERT records into a table, so too can you delete records with the DELETE statement. Typically, you would select a specific subset of rows to be deleted by adding the WHERE clause to the DELETE statement, as in the next example, which deletes all those songs with a rating less than or equal to 3:

```
mysql> DELETE FROM songs
    -> WHERE fk_song_rating <= 3;
Query OK, 5 rows affected (0.02 sec)
```

There's also an UPDATE statement, which can be used to change the contents of a record; this too accepts a WHERE clause, so that you can apply changes to only those records matching specific criteria. Consider the following example, which changes the rating 'Excellent' to 'Fantastic':

```
mysql> UPDATE ratings SET rating_name = 'Fantastic'
    -> WHERE rating_name = 'Excellent';
Query OK, 1 row affected (0.00 sec)
Rows matched: 1  Changed: 1  Warnings: 0
```

(continued)

You can alter multiple fields by separating them with commas. Here's an example that updates a particular song record in the *songs* table, changing both its title and its rating:

```
mysql> UPDATE songs SET song_title = 'Waterloo',
    -> fk_song_rating = 5
    -> WHERE song_id = 9;
Query OK, 1 row affected (0.00 sec)
Rows matched: 1  Changed: 1  Warnings: 0
```

Ask the Expert

Q: I'm using ____ database and it doesn't support the ____ field type. What do I do now?

A: Different databases have different syntax for field data types. For example, MySQL calls integer fields INT, while SQLite calls the same fields INTEGER. However, almost all databases will support—at a minimum—data types for integer values, floating-point values, string values, binary values, and NULL values. All you need to do is look up your database documentation and figure out the syntax to correctly use these data types in your SQL statements.

Q: Why do I need to list all the required fields in my SELECT statement? Can't I use the * wildcard to get back all available fields?

A: While SQL does support the asterisk (*) wildcard to represent "all fields in a table," it is preferable to always explicitly name the fields that you would like to see in the result set. This allows the application to survive structural changes in its table(s), and is also usually more memory-efficient because the result set will not contain unwanted or irrelevant data.

Using PHP's MySQLi Extension

As explained previously, PHP allows developers to interact with databases in two ways: by using a customized database-specific extension, or by using the database-neutral PHP Data Objects (PDO) extension. While the PDO extension is more portable, many developers still find it preferable to use the native database extension, especially when the native extension offers better performance or more features than the PDO version.

Of the various database engines supported by PHP, the most popular one by far is MySQL. It's not difficult to understand why: both PHP and MySQL are open-source projects, and by using them together, developers can benefit from huge savings on the licensing costs of commercial alternatives. Historically, too, PHP has offered out-of-the-box support for MySQL since PHP 3, and it only makes sense to leverage off the tremendous amount of thought PHP and MySQL developers have put into making sure that the two packages work together seamlessly and smoothly.

In addition to supporting MySQL through the PHP Data Objects extension (discussed in the next section), PHP also includes a custom MySQL extension named MySQL Improved (MySQLi). This extension provides both speed and feature benefits over the PDO version and is a good choice for MySQL-specific development projects. The following sections discuss this extension in greater detail.

Retrieving Data

In the preceding section, you create a database table and used a SELECT query to retrieve a result set from it. Now, do the same thing using PHP, as in the following script:

```php
<?php
// attempt database connection
$mysqli = new mysqli("localhost", "user", "pass", "music");
if ($mysqli === false) {
  die("ERROR: Could not connect. " . mysqli_connect_error());
}

// attempt query execution
// iterate over result set
// print each record and its fields
// output: "1:Aerosmith \n 2:Abba \n ..."
$sql = "SELECT artist_id, artist_name FROM artists";
if ($result = $mysqli->query($sql)) {
  if ($result->num_rows > 0) {
    while($row = $result->fetch_array()) {
      echo $row[0] . ":" . $row[1] . "\n";
    }
    $result->close();
  } else {
    echo "No records matching your query were found.";
  }
} else {
  echo "ERROR: Could not execute $sql. " . $mysqli->error;
}

// close connection
$mysqli->close();
?>
```

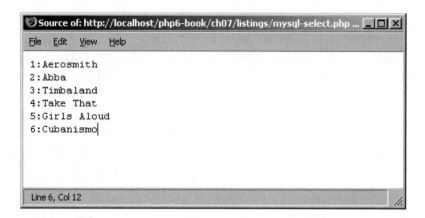

Figure 7-3 Retrieving records from a MySQL database with PHP

Figure 7-3 illustrates what the output of this script should look like.

As you can see, using PHP to get data from a database involves several steps, which are described here:

1. In order to begin communication with the MySQL database server, you first need to open a connection to the server. All communication between PHP and the database server takes place through this connection.

   In order to initialize this connection, initialize an instance of the MySQLi class and pass the object constructor four arguments: the host name of the MySQL server to connect to, a valid username and password to gain access to it, and the name of the database to use.

   Assuming the connection attempt is successful, this object instance represents the database connection for all future operations and exposes methods for querying, fetching, and processing result sets. If the connection attempt is unsuccessful, the object instance will become false; an error message explaining the reason for failure can now be obtained by calling the `mysqli_connect_error()` function.

TIP
If the database server and the Web server are both running on the same physical machine, you can use `localhost` as the server name.

2. The next step is to create and execute the SQL query. This is accomplished by calling the MySQLi object's `query()` method and passing it the query to be executed. If the query was unsuccessful, the method returns Boolean false, and an error message explaining the cause of failure is stored in the MySQLi object's `'error'` property.

3. If, on the other hand, the query is successful and returns one or more records, the return value of the `query()` method is another object, this one an instance of the MySQLi_ Result class. This object represents the result set returned by the query, and it exposes various methods for processing the individual records in the result set.

One such method is the `fetch_array()` method. Each time `fetch_array()` is invoked, it returns the next record in the result set as an array. This makes the `fetch_array()` method very suitable for use in a `while` or `for` loop. The loop counter determines how many times the loop should run; this value is obtained from the MySQLi_Result object's `'num_rows'` property, which stores the number of rows returned by the query. Individual fields from the record can be accessed as array elements, using either the field index or the field name.

CAUTION
The `'num_rows'` property is only meaningful when used with queries that return data, such as SELECT queries; it shouldn't be used with INSERT, UPDATE, or DELETE queries.

4. Each result set returned after a query occupies some amount of memory. Thus, once the result set has been processed, it's a good idea to destroy the MySQLi_Result object, and free up the used memory, by calling the object's `close()` method. And once you've completed working with the database, it's also a good idea to destroy the main MySQLi object in a similar manner, by calling its `close()` method.

Returning Records as Arrays and Objects
The preceding listing demonstrated one method of processing a result set: the `fetch_array()` method of the MySQLi_Result object. This method returns each record from the result set as an array containing both numerically indexed and string-indexed keys; this allows developers the convenience of referring to individual fields of each record either by index or by field name.

The preceding listing demonstrated how to retrieve individual fields using the field index number. The following listing, which is equivalent to the preceding one, performs the same task using field names:

```php
<?php
// attempt database connection
$mysqli = new mysqli("localhost", "user", "pass", "music");
```

```php
if ($mysqli === false) {
  die("ERROR: Could not connect. " . mysqli_connect_error());
}

// attempt query execution
// iterate over result set
// print each record and its fields
// output: "1:Aerosmith \n 2:Abba \n ..."
$sql = "SELECT artist_id, artist_name FROM artists";
if ($result = $mysqli->query($sql)) {
  if ($result->num_rows > 0) {
    while($row = $result->fetch_array()) {
      echo $row['artist_id'] . ":" . $row['artist_name'] . "\n";
    }
    $result->close();
  } else {
    echo "No records matching your query were found.";
  }
} else {
  echo "ERROR: Could not execute $sql. " . $mysqli->error;
}

// close connection
$mysqli->close();
?>
```

However, there's also a third way of retrieving records: as objects, using the `fetch_object()` method. Here, each record is represented as an object, and the fields of a record are represented as object properties. Individual fields can then be accessed using standard `$object->property` notation. The following listing illustrates this approach:

```php
<?php
// attempt database connection
$mysqli = new mysqli("localhost", "user", "pass", "music");
if ($mysqli === false) {
  die("ERROR: Could not connect. " . mysqli_connect_error());
}

// attempt query execution
// iterate over result set
// print each record and its fields
// output: "1:Aerosmith \n 2:Abba \n ..."
$sql = "SELECT artist_id, artist_name FROM artists";
if ($result = $mysqli->query($sql)) {
  if ($result->num_rows > 0) {
    while($row = $result->fetch_object()) {
      echo $row->artist_id . ":" . $row->artist_name . "\n";
    }
```

```php
      $result->close();
    } else {
      echo "No records matching your query were found.";
    }
  } else {
    echo "ERROR: Could not execute $sql. " . $mysqli->error;
  }

// close connection
$mysqli->close();
?>
```

Adding or Modifying Data

It's equally simple to perform a query that changes the data in the database, be it an INSERT, UPDATE, or DELETE. The following example illustrates, by adding a new record to the artists table:

```php
<?php
// attempt database connection
$mysqli = new mysqli("localhost", "user", "pass", "music");
if ($mysqli === false) {
  die("ERROR: Could not connect. " . mysqli_connect_error());
}

// attempt query execution
// add a new record
// output: "New artist with id:7 added."
$sql = "INSERT INTO artists (artist_name, artist_country) VALUES
('Kylie Minogue', 'AU')";
if ($mysqli->query($sql) === true) {
  echo 'New artist with id:'  . $mysqli->insert_id . ' added.';
} else {
  echo "ERROR: Could not execute query: $sql. " . $mysqli->error;
}

// close connection
$mysqli->close();
?>
```

As you'll see, this is not very different from the programming needed to perform a SELECT query. In fact, it's a little simpler because there's no result set to process; all that's needed is to test the return value of the query() method and check if the query was successfully executed or not. Notice also the use of a new property, the 'insert_id' property: this property returns the ID generated by the last INSERT query (only useful if the table into which the INSERT occurred contained an auto-incrementing field).

How about updating an existing record? All that's needed is to change the SQL query string:

```php
<?php
// attempt database connection
$mysqli = new mysqli("localhost", "user", "pass", "music");
if ($mysqli === false) {
  die("ERROR: Could not connect. " . mysqli_connect_error());
}

// attempt query execution
// add a new record
// output: "1 row(s) updated."
$sql = "UPDATE artists SET artist_name = 'Eminem', artist_country = 'US' WHERE artist_id = 7";
if ($mysqli->query($sql) === true) {
  echo $mysqli->affected_rows . ' row(s) updated.';
} else {
  echo "ERROR: Could not execute query: $sql. " . $mysqli->error;
}

// close connection
$mysqli->close();
?>
```

When performing an UPDATE or DELETE, the number of rows affected by the statement will be stored in the MySQLi object's 'affected_rows' property. The preceding listing shows this property in use.

Using Prepared Statements

In the event that you need to execute a particular query multiple times with different values—for example, a series of INSERT statements—the MySQL database server supports *prepared statements,* which offer a more efficient means of accomplishing this task than repeatedly calling the $mysqli->query() method.

Essentially, a prepared statement is an SQL query template containing placeholder variables for the values to be inserted or modified. This statement is stored on the database server and invoked as often as needed, with the placeholders replaced with actual values on each execution. Because the statement is stored on the database server, a prepared statement is typically faster for batch operations that involve running the same SQL query over and over with different values.

Ask the Expert

Q: How do prepared statements offer better performance?

A: In the normal course, every time an SQL statement is executed on the database server, the server must parse the SQL code and check its syntax and structure before allowing it to execute. With a prepared statement, the SQL statement is stored in a temporary location on the database server and thus only needs to be parsed and validated once. Further, every time the statement is executed, only the placeholder values need to be transmitted to the server instead of the complete statement.

To see a prepared statement in action, consider the following script, which inserts multiple songs into the database using a prepared statement with PHP's MySQLi extension:

```php
<?php
// define values to be inserted
$songs = array(
  array('Patience', 4, 3),
  array('Beautiful World', 4, 4),
  array('Shine', 4, 4),
  array('Hold On', 4, 3),
);

// attempt database connection
$mysqli = new mysqli("localhost", "user", "pass", "music");
if ($mysqli === false) {
  die("ERROR: Could not connect. " . mysqli_connect_error());
}

// prepare query template
// execute multiple times
$sql = "INSERT INTO songs (song_title, fk_song_artist, fk_song_rating)
VALUES (?, ?, ?)";
if ($stmt = $mysqli->prepare($sql)) {
  foreach ($songs as $s) {
    $stmt->bind_param('sii', $s[0], $s[1], $s[2]);
    if ($stmt->execute()) {
      echo "New song with id: "  . $mysqli->insert_id . " added.\n";
    } else {
      echo "ERROR: Could not execute query: $sql. " . $mysqli->error;
    }
  }
}
```

```
} else {
  echo "ERROR: Could not prepare query: $sql. " . $mysqli->error;
}

// close connection
$mysqli->close();
?>
```

As this listing illustrates, using a prepared statement involves a different procedure from the one you're used to seeing from previous examples.

To use a prepared statement, it is necessary to first define the SQL query string that will be executed multiple times. This query string typically contains one or more placeholders, denoted by question marks (?). These placeholders will be replaced by actual values on each execution of the statement. The query string with its placeholders is then passed to the MySQLi object's prepare() method, which checks the SQL for errors and returns a MySQLi_Stmt object representing the prepared statement.

Executing the prepared statement is now a matter of performing two actions, usually within a loop:

1. *Bind the values to the prepared statement.* The values to be interpolated into the statement must be *bound* to their placeholders with the MySQLi_Stmt object's bind_param() method. The first argument to this method must be an ordered string sequence indicating the data types of the values to be interpolated (*s* for string, *i* for integer, *d* for double-precision number); this argument is then followed by the actual values. In the preceding listing, the string 'sii' indicates that the values to be interpolated into the prepared statement will be, in sequence, a string type (the song title), an integer type (the artist foreign key), and an integer type (the rating foreign key).

2. *Execute the prepared statement.* Once the values have been bound to their placeholders, the prepared statement is executed by calling MySQLi_Stmt object's execute() method. This method replaces the placeholders in the prepared statement with actual values and executes it on the server.

Thus, using a prepared statement offers performance benefits when you need to execute the same statement multiple times, with only the values changing on each execution. Most popular databases, including MySQL, PostgreSQL, Oracle, and InterBase, support prepared statements, and this feature should be used where available to make your SQL batch operations more efficient.

Handling Errors

If your database code doesn't work as expected, don't worry—the MySQLi extension comes with a bunch of functions that can tell you why. You've already seen these in action at various places in previous listings, but here's a complete list:

- The MySQLi object's `'error'` property holds the last error message generated by the database server.

- The MySQLi object's `'errno'` property holds the last error code returned by the database server.

- The `mysqli_connect_error()` function returns the error message generated by the last (failed) connection attempt.

- The `mysqli_connect_errno()` function returns the error code generated by the last (failed) connection attempt.

TIP
To make your application more robust to errors, and to make it easier to find and resolve bugs, it's a good idea to use these error-handling functions liberally within your code.

Try This 7-2   Adding Employees to a Database

Now that you know the basics of using PHP's MySQLi extension, let's apply what you learned in the preceding section to a "real" application. The application here is a Web form, which allows a user to enter employee names and designations into a MySQL-based employee database. Values entered into the form are validated and sanitized using PHP, and transformed into database records using the PHP MySQLi extension.

To begin building this application, first fire up your MySQL command-line client and initialize an empty database:

```
mysql> CREATE DATABASE employees;
Query OK, 1 row affected (0.20 sec)
```

Next, create a table to hold the employee records:

```
mysql> USE employees;
Database changed
mysql> CREATE TABLE employees (
```

(continued)

```
    -> id INT(4) NOT NULL AUTO_INCREMENT PRIMARY KEY,
    -> name VARCHAR(255) NOT NULL,
    -> designation VARCHAR(255) NOT NULL
    -> );
Query OK, 0 rows affected (0.26 sec)
```

All done? The next step is to build a Web form to accept employee data—in this case, each employee's name and designation. On submission, the form processor will check the input and, if valid, generate an INSERT query to write it to the database table created in the preceding step.

Here's the script (*employee.php*):

```
<!DOCTYPE html PUBLIC "-//W3C//DTD XHTML 1.0 Transitional//EN"
    "DTD/xhtml1-transitional.dtd">
<html xmlns="http://www.w3.org/1999/xhtml" xml:lang="en" lang="en">
  <head>
    <title>Project 7-2: Adding Employees to a Database</title>
    <style type="text/css">
    div#message {
      text-align:center;
      margin-left:auto;
      margin-right:auto;
      width:40%;
      border: solid 2px green
    }
    </style>
  </head>
  <body>
    <h2>Project 7-2: Adding Employees to a Database</h2>
    <h3>Add New Employee</h3>
<?php
    // if form submitted
    // process form input
    if (isset($_POST['submit'])) {
      // attempt connection to MySQL database
      $mysqli = new mysqli("localhost", "user", "pass", "employees");
      if ($mysqli === false) {
        die("ERROR: Could not connect to database. " . mysqli_connect_error());
      }

      // open message block
      echo '<div id="message">';

      // retrieve and check input values
      $inputError = false;
      if (empty($_POST['emp_name'])) {
```

```php
      echo 'ERROR: Please enter a valid employee name';
      $inputError = true;
    } else {
      $name = $mysqli->escape_string($_POST['emp_name']);
    }

    if ($inputError != true && empty($_POST['emp_desig'])) {
      echo 'ERROR: Please enter a valid employee designation';
      $inputError = true;
    } else {
      $designation = $mysqli->escape_string($_POST['emp_desig']);
    }

    // add values to database using INSERT query
    if ($inputError != true) {
    $sql = "INSERT INTO employees (name, designation)
            VALUES ('$name', '$designation')";
      if ($mysqli->query($sql) === true) {
        echo 'New employee record added with ID: '  . $mysqli->insert_id;
      } else {
        echo "ERROR: Could not execute query: $sql. " . $mysqli->error;
      }
    }

    // close message block
    echo '</div>';

    // close connection
    $mysqli->close();
  }
?>
  </div>

  <form action="employee.php" method="POST">
    Employee name: <br />
    <input type="text" name="emp_name" size="40" />
    <p/>
    Employee designation: <br />
    <input type="text" name="emp_desig" size="40" />
    <p/>
    <input type="submit" name="submit" value="Submit" />
  </form>

  </body>
</html>
```

When this script is invoked, it generates a Web form with fields for an employee's name and designation. Figure 7-4 demonstrates what the initial form looks like.

(continued)

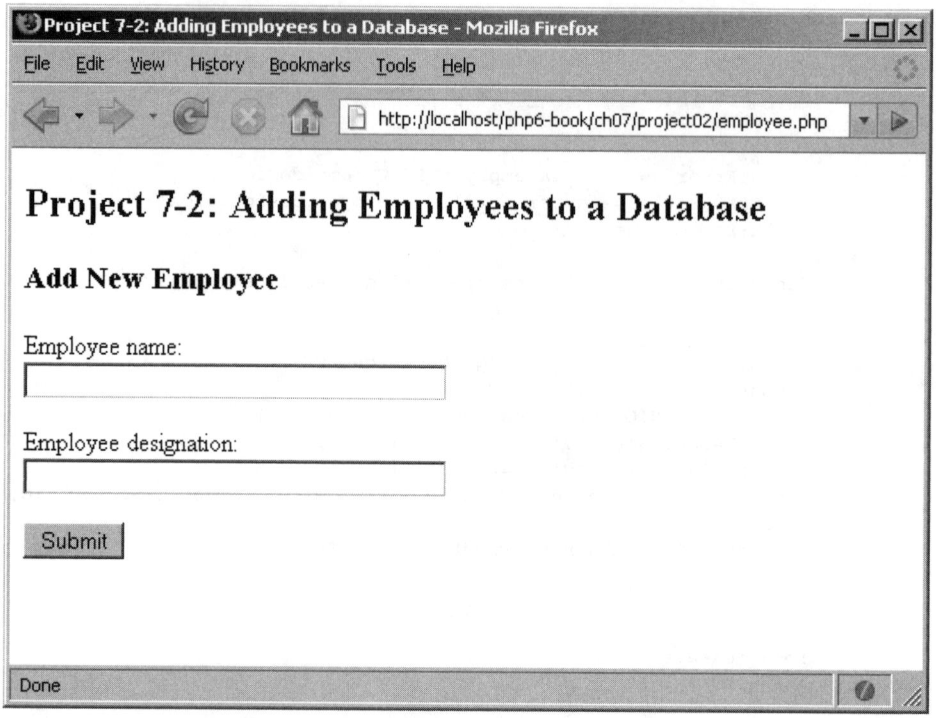

Figure 7-4 A Web form to enter a new employee

When this form is submitted, the script proceeds to initialize a new MySQLi object and open a connection to the MySQL database server. It then checks the form fields to ensure that they contain valid input values. If they do, each input value is "sanitized" using the MySQLi object's escape_string() method, which automatically escapes special characters in the input as a prelude to inserting it into the database, and then interpolated into an INSERT query, which is executed via the object's query() method to save the values to the database. Errors, if any, are displayed using the MySQLi object's error property.

Figure 7-5 demonstrates the output when a record is successfully added and Figure 7-6 demonstrates the output when an input field fails validation.

So that was pretty easy. Now, how about revising this script so that, in addition to allowing you to add new employees to the database, it also displays the existing employee records from the database? This isn't very difficult—add another call to the query()

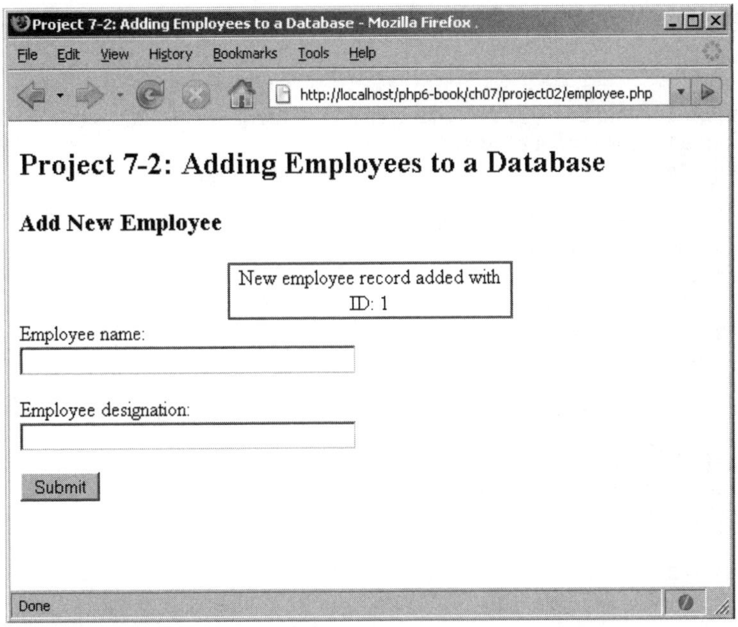

Figure 7-5 The results of successfully adding a new employee to the database

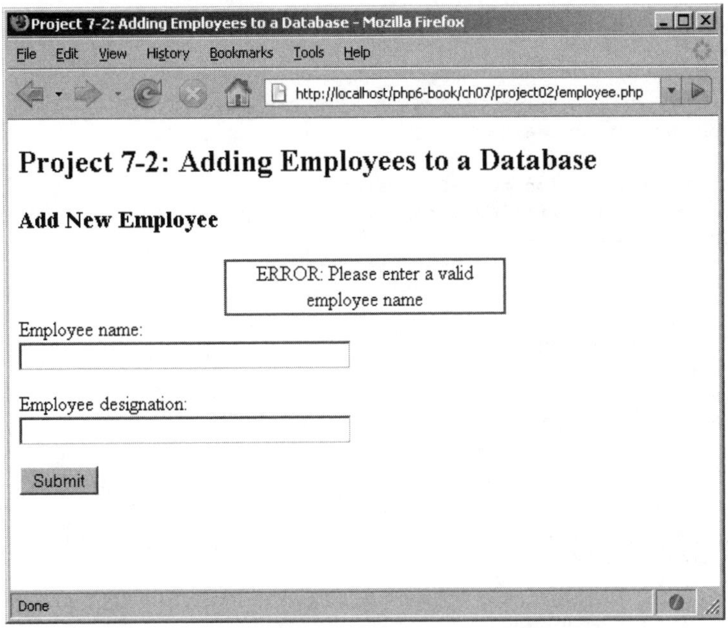

Figure 7-6 The output after invalid data is submitted through the Web form

(continued)

method, this time with a SELECT query, and process the result set using a loop. Here's the revised code:

```
<!DOCTYPE html PUBLIC "-//W3C//DTD XHTML 1.0 Transitional//EN"
   "DTD/xhtml1-transitional.dtd">
<html xmlns="http://www.w3.org/1999/xhtml" xml:lang="en" lang="en">
  <head>
    <title>Project 7-2: Adding Employees to a Database</title>
    <style type="text/css">
    div#message {
      text-align:center;
      margin-left:auto;
      margin-right:auto;
      width:40%;
      border: solid 2px green;
    }
    table {
      border-collapse: collapse;
      width: 320px;
    }
    tr.heading {
      font-weight: bolder;
    }
    td {
      border: 1px solid black;
      padding: 0 0.5em;
    }
    </style>
  </head>
  <body>
    <h2>Project 7-2: Adding Employees to a Database</h2>
    <h3>Add New Employee</h3>
<?php
    // attempt connection to MySQL database
    $mysqli = new mysqli("localhost", "user", "pass", "employees");
    if ($mysqli === false) {
      die("ERROR: Could not connect to database. " . mysqli_connect_error());
    }

    // if form submitted
    // process form input
    if (isset($_POST['submit'])) {
      // open message block
      echo '<div id="message">';

      // retrieve and check input values
      $inputError = false;
      if (empty($_POST['emp_name'])) {
```

```php
      echo 'ERROR: Please enter a valid employee name';
      $inputError = true;
    } else {
      $name = $mysqli->escape_string($_POST['emp_name']);
    }

    if ($inputError != true && empty($_POST['emp_desig'])) {
      echo 'ERROR: Please enter a valid employee designation';
      $inputError = true;
    } else {
      $designation = $mysqli->escape_string($_POST['emp_desig']);
    }

    // add values to database using INSERT query
    if ($inputError != true) {
    $sql = "INSERT INTO employees (name, designation)
            VALUES ('$name', '$designation')";
      if ($mysqli->query($sql) === true) {
        echo 'New employee record added with ID: '  . $mysqli->insert_id;
      } else {
        echo "ERROR: Could not execute query: $sql. " . $mysqli->error;
      }
    }

    // close message block
    echo '</div>';
  }
?>
  </div>

  <form action="employee.php" method="POST">
    Employee name: <br />
    <input type="text" name="emp_name" size="40" />
    <p/>
    Employee designation: <br />
    <input type="text" name="emp_desig" size="40" />
    <p/>
    <input type="submit" name="submit" value="Submit" />
  </form>

  <h3>Employee Listing</h3>
<?php
    // get records
    // format as HTML table
    $sql = "SELECT id, name, designation FROM employees";
    if ($result = $mysqli->query($sql)) {
      if ($result->num_rows > 0) {
        echo "<table>\n";
        echo "  <tr class=\"heading\">\n";
        echo "    <td>ID</td>\n";
        echo "    <td>Name</td>\n";
        echo "    <td>Designation</td>\n";
```

(continued)

```
      echo "   </tr>\n";
      while($row = $result->fetch_object()) {
        echo "  <tr>\n";
        echo "      <td>" . $row->id . "</td>\n";
        echo "      <td>" . $row->name . "</td>\n";
        echo "      <td>" . $row->designation . "</td>\n";
        echo "  </tr>\n";
      }
      echo "</table>";
      $result->close();
    } else {
      echo "No employees in database.";
    }
  } else {
    echo "ERROR: Could not execute query: $sql. " . $mysqli->error;
  }

  // close connection
  $mysqli->close();
?>
  </body>
</html>
```

This version of the script now sports a SELECT query, which retrieves the records from the employees table as objects and processes them using a loop. These records are formatted as an HTML table and printed below the Web form. A useful side effect of this arrangement is that new employee records saved through the form will be immediately reflected in the HTML table once the form is submitted.

Figure 7-7 illustrates the revised output of the script.

Using PHP's SQLite Extension

At this point, you know how to hook a PHP script up to a MySQL database and retrieve, add, edit, and delete records from it. However, MySQL isn't the only game in town— PHP 5.x also includes built-in support for SQLite, a lightweight, efficient alternative to MySQL. This section discusses SQLite and PHP's SQLite extension in greater detail.

Introducing SQLite

SQLite is a fast, efficient database system that offers a viable alternative to MySQL, especially for small- to medium-sized applications. However, unlike MySQL, which contains a large number of interrelated components, SQLite is fully self-contained in a

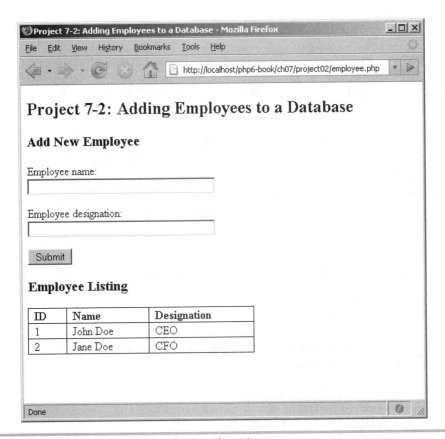

Figure 7-7 A Web page displaying the list of employees

single library file. It's also significantly smaller in size than MySQL—the command-line version of SQLite weighs in at under 200KB—and supports all the standard SQL commands you're used to. MySQL and SQLite also differ in their licensing policies: unlike MySQL, SQLite source code is completely public-domain, which means that developers can use and distribute it however they choose, in both commercial and non-commercial products.

SQLite's small size belies its capabilities, however. It supports databases up to two terabytes in size and can actually produce better performance than MySQL in certain situations. Part of this is for architectural reasons: SQLite reads and writes records directly from and to database files on disk and so incurs less performance overhead than MySQL, which operates a client-server architecture that may be affected by network-level variables.

NOTE

In the following exercise, boldface type indicates commands that you should enter at the SQLite command-line prompt. Commands can be entered in either uppercase or lowercase. Before beginning with the exercise, ensure that you have installed, configured, and tested the SQLite database system according to the instructions in Appendix A of this book.

SQLite supports all the standard SQL statements you've grown to know and love over the preceding two sections: SELECT, INSERT, DELETE, UPDATE, and CREATE TABLE. The following example illustrates, by replicating the MySQL database tables used in the preceding section using SQLite. Begin by starting up the SQLite command-line client and creating a new SQLite database file in the current directory, named *music.db*:

```
shell> sqlite music.db
```

If all went well, you'll see a welcome message and an interactive SQL prompt, like this:

```
sqlite>
```

You can now proceed to enter SQL statements at this prompt. Begin by creating a table to hold artist information:

```
sqlite> CREATE TABLE artists (
   ...> artist_id INTEGER NOT NULL PRIMARY KEY,
   ...> artist_name TEXT NOT NULL,
   ...> artist_country TEXT NOT NULL
   ...> );
```

Unlike MySQL, which offers a wide range of different data types for its fields, SQLite supports just four types; these are summarized in Table 7-3.

Field Type	Description
INTEGER	A numeric type for signed integer values
REAL	A numeric type for floating-point values
TEXT	A string type
BLOB	A binary type

Table 7-3 SQLite Data Types

What is more important, SQLite is a "typeless" database engine. This means that fields in an SQLite database need not be associated with a specific type, and even if they are, they can still hold values of a type different than what is specified. The only exception to this rule are fields of type `INTEGER PRIMARY KEY`: these fields are "auto-number" fields that generate unique numeric identifiers for the records in a table, similar to MySQL's `AUTO_INCREMENT` fields.

With these facts in mind, go ahead and create the remaining two tables using these SQL statements:

```
sqlite> CREATE TABLE ratings (
   ...> rating_id INTEGER NOT NULL PRIMARY KEY,
   ...> rating_name TEXT NOT NULL
   ...> );

sqlite> CREATE TABLE songs (
   ...> song_id INTEGER NOT NULL PRIMARY KEY,
   ...> song_title TEXT NOT NULL,
   ...> fk_song_artist INTEGER NOT NULL,
   ...> fk_song_rating INTEGER NOT NULL
   ...> );
```

Next, populate the tables with some records:

```
sqlite> INSERT INTO artists (artist_id, artist_name, artist_country)
   ...> VALUES ('1', 'Aerosmith', 'US');
sqlite> INSERT INTO artists (artist_name, artist_country)
   ...> VALUES ('Abba', 'SE');

sqlite> INSERT INTO ratings (rating_id, rating_name)
   ...> VALUES (4, 'Good');
sqlite> INSERT INTO ratings (rating_id, rating_name)
   ...> VALUES (5, 'Excellent');

sqlite> INSERT INTO songs (song_title, fk_song_artist, fk_song_rating)
   ...> VALUES ('Janie''s Got A Gun', 1, 4);
sqlite> INSERT INTO songs (song_title, fk_song_artist, fk_song_rating)
   ...> VALUES ('Crazy', 1, 5);
```

NOTE

The code archive for this book has a full list of SQL INSERT statements to populate the three tables used in this exercise. Run these statements and complete building the tables before proceeding.

Once you're done, try a SELECT statement:

```
sqlite> SELECT artist_name, artist_country FROM artists
   ...> WHERE artist_country = 'US'
   ...> OR artist_country = 'UK';
Aerosmith|US
Timbaland|US
Take That|UK
Girls Aloud|UK
```

SQLite fully supports SQL joins—here's an example:

```
sqlite> SELECT song_title, artist_name, rating_name
   ...> FROM songs, artists, ratings
   ...> WHERE songs.fk_song_artist = artists.artist_id
   ...> AND songs.fk_song_rating = ratings.rating_id
   ...> AND ratings.rating_id >= 4
   ...> AND artists.artist_country != 'US';
En Las Delicious|Cubanismo|Fantastic
Pray|Take That|Good
SOS|Abba|Fantastic
Dancing Queen|Abba|Good
```

Retrieving Data

Retrieving records from an SQLite database with PHP is not very different from retrieving them from a MySQL database. The following PHP script illustrates the process using the *music.db* database created in the preceding section:

```php
<?php
// attempt database connection
$sqlite = new SQLiteDatabase('music.db') or die ("Could not open database");

// attempt query execution
// iterate over result set
// print each record and its fields
// output: "1:Aerosmith \n 2:Abba \n ..."
$sql = "SELECT artist_id, artist_name FROM artists";
if ($result = $sqlite->query($sql)) {
  if ($result->numRows() > 0) {
    while($row = $result->fetch()) {
      echo $row[0] . ":" . $row[1] . "\n";
    }
  } else {
    echo "No records matching your query were found.";
  }
} else {
  echo "ERROR: Could not execute $sql. " . sqlite_error_string($sqlite->lastError());
}

// close connection
unset($sqlite);
?>
```

This script performs the following actions:

1. It opens the SQLite database file for data operations, by initializing an instance of the SQLiteDatabase class and passing the object constructor the full path to the database file. If this database file cannot be found, an empty database file will be created with the supplied name (assuming the script has write privileges to the corresponding directory).

2. The next step is to create and execute the SQL query. This is accomplished by calling the SQLiteDatabase object's query() method and passing it the query to be executed. Depending on whether or not the query was successful, the function returns true or false; in the event of a failure, the error code corresponding to reason for failure can be obtained by calling the SQLiteDatabase object's lastError() method. The sqlite_error_string() function converts this error code into a human-readable error message.

TIP
There's a close similarity between these steps and the steps you followed to use the MySQL extension in the preceding section.

3. If, on the other hand, the query is successful and returns one or more records, the return value of the query() method is another object, this one an instance of the SQLiteResult class. This object represents the result set returned by the query, and it exposes various methods for processing the individual records in the result set.

    This script uses the fetch() method, which returns the next record in the result set as an array each time it is invoked. Used in a loop, this method provides a convenient way to iterate over the entire result set, one record at a time. Individual fields from the record can be accessed as array elements, using either the field index or the field name. The number of records in the result set can be retrieved via the SQLiteResult object's numRows() method.

4. Once the entire result set has been processed and no further database operations are to take place, it's a good idea to close the database handle, and free the memory occupied by it, by destroying the SQLiteDatabase object.

Retrieving Records as Arrays and Objects
The SQLiteResult object's fetch() method accepts an additional modifier, which controls how result set records are fetched. This modifier can be any one of the values SQLITE_NUM (to return each record as a numerically indexed array), SQLITE_ASSOC

(to return each record as an associative array), or SQLITE_BOTH (to return each record as both a numerically indexed and an associative array and the default option). Here's an example, which illustrates these modifiers in action while producing output equivalent to the preceding one:

```php
<?php
// attempt database connection
$sqlite = new SQLiteDatabase('music.db') or die ("Could not open database");

// attempt query execution
// print records using different styles
// output: "1:Aerosmith \n 2:Abba \n ..."
$sql = "SELECT artist_id, artist_name FROM artists";
if ($result = $sqlite->query($sql)) {

  // retrieve record as numeric array
  $row = $result->fetch(SQLITE_NUM);
  echo $row[0] . ":" . $row[1] . "\n";

  // retrieve record as associative array
  $row = $result->fetch(SQLITE_ASSOC);
  echo $row['artist_id'] . ":" . $row['artist_name'] . "\n";

  // retrieve record as object
  $row = $result->fetchObject();
  echo $row->artist_id . ":" . $row->artist_name . "\n";

} else {
  echo "ERROR: Could not execute $sql. " . sqlite_error_string($sqlite->lastError());
}

// close connection
unset($sqlite);
?>
```

It's also possible to return each record as an object, by replacing fetch() with the fetchObject() method. Here's an example equivalent to the preceding listing, except retrieving field values as object properties instead of array elements:

```php
<?php
// attempt database connection
$sqlite = new SQLiteDatabase('music.db') or die ("Could not open database");
```

```php
// attempt query execution
// iterate over result set
// print each record and its fields
// output: "1:Aerosmith \n 2:Abba \n ..."
$sql = "SELECT artist_id, artist_name FROM artists";
if ($result = $sqlite->query($sql)) {
  if ($result->numRows() > 0) {
    while($row = $result->fetchObject()) {
      echo $row->artist_id . ":" . $row->artist_name . "\n";
    }
  } else {
    echo "No records matching your query were found.";
  }
} else {
  echo "ERROR: Could not execute $sql. " . sqlite_error_string($sqlite-
>lastError());
}

// close connection
unset($sqlite);
?>
```

An interesting feature of the SQLite extension is the ability to retrieve *all* the records from the result set at once as a nested set of arrays, via the SQLiteResult object's `fetchAll()` method. A `foreach` loop can then iterate over this nested collection, retrieving records one after another. The following example illustrates this procedure in action:

```php
<?php
// attempt database connection
$sqlite = new SQLiteDatabase('music.db') or die ("Could not open database");

// attempt query execution
// iterate over result set
// print each record and its fields
// output: "1:Aerosmith \n 2:Abba \n ..."
$sql = "SELECT artist_id, artist_name FROM artists";
if ($result = $sqlite->query($sql)) {
  $data = $result->fetchAll();
  if (count($data) > 0) {
    foreach ($data as $row) {
      echo $row[0] . ":" . $row[1] . "\n";
    }
  } else {
    echo "No records matching your query were found.";
  }
```

```
} else {
  echo "ERROR: Could not execute $sql. " . sqlite_error_string($sqlite-
>lastError());
}

// close connection
unset($sqlite);
?>
```

CAUTION

The fetchAll() method returns the complete result set as a nested set of arrays, which are stored in system memory until completely processed. To avoid running out of memory, don't use this method if your query is likely to return a large number of records.

Adding or Modifying Data

For queries that don't return a result set, such as INSERT, UPDATE, and DELETE queries, the SQLite extension offers the queryExec() method. The following example illustrates it in action, by adding a new record to the *artists* table:

```
<?php
// attempt database connection
$sqlite = new SQLiteDatabase('music.db') or die ("Could not open database");

// attempt query execution
// add a new record
// output: "New artist with id:8 added."
$sql = "INSERT INTO artists (artist_name, artist_country) VALUES ('James
Blunt', 'UK')";
if ($sqlite->queryExec($sql) == true) {
  echo 'New artist with id:' . $sqlite->lastInsertRowid() . ' added.';
} else {
  echo "ERROR: Could not execute $sql. " . sqlite_error_string($sqlite-
>lastError());
}

// close connection
unset($sqlite);
?>
```

Depending on whether or not the query succeeded, queryExec() returns true or false; it's easy to test this return value and print a success or failure message. If the record was inserted into a table with an INTEGER PRIMARY KEY field, SQLite will have automatically assigned the record a unique identifying number. This number can be retrieved with the SQLiteDatabase object's lastInsertRowid() method, as illustrated in the preceding listing.

CAUTION

For INSERTs, UPDATEs, and DELETEs to work, remember that your PHP script *must* have write privileges for the SQLite database file.

When performing an UPDATE or DELETE query, the number of rows affected by the query can likewise be retrieved via the SQLiteDatabase object's changes() method. The following example demonstrates, by updating the song ratings in the database and returning a count of the records affected:

```php
<?php
// attempt database connection
$sqlite = new SQLiteDatabase('music.db') or die ("Could not open database");

// attempt query execution
// update record
// output: "3 row(s) updated."
$sql = "UPDATE songs SET fk_song_rating = 4 WHERE fk_song_rating = 3";
if ($sqlite->queryExec($sql) == true) {
  echo $sqlite->changes() . ' row(s) updated.';
} else {
  echo "ERROR: Could not execute $sql. " . sqlite_error_string($sqlite-
>lastError());
}

// close connection
unset($sqlite);
?>
```

Handling Errors

Both the query() and queryExec() methods return false if an error occurs during query preparation or execution. It's easy to check the return value of these methods and retrieve the code corresponding to the error by calling the SQLiteDatabase object's lastError() method. Unfortunately, this error code isn't very useful by itself; so, for a textual description of what went wrong, wrap the call to lastError() in the sqlite_error_string() function, as most of the preceding examples do.

Try This 7-3 Creating a Personal To-Do List

Now that you've got a handle on SQLite, how about using it in a practical application: a personal to-do list that you can update and view through your Web browser. This to-do list will allow you to enter tasks and due dates, assign priorities to tasks, edit task descriptions, and mark tasks as complete. It's a little more complicated than applications you've worked on so far, as it includes quite a few moving parts; however, if you've been following along until this point, you shouldn't find it too hard to figure out.

To begin, create a new SQLite database named *todo.db,* and add an empty table to hold task descriptions and dates:

```
shell> sqlite todo.db
sqlite> CREATE TABLE tasks (
   ...> id INTEGER PRIMARY KEY,
   ...> name TEXT NOT NULL,
   ...> due TEXT NOT NULL,
   ...> priority TEXT NOT NULL
   ...> );
```

This table has four fields, one each for the record ID, the task name, the due date for the task, and the task's priority.

Next, create a Web form to add new tasks to this database (*save.php*):

```
<!DOCTYPE html PUBLIC "-//W3C//DTD XHTML 1.0 Transitional//EN"
   "DTD/xhtml1-transitional.dtd">
<html xmlns="http://www.w3.org/1999/xhtml" xml:lang="en" lang="en">
  <head>
    <title>Project 7-3: Creating a Personal To-Do List</title>
    <style type="text/css">
    div#message {
      text-align:center;
      margin-left:auto;
      margin-right:auto;
      width:40%;
      border: solid 2px green
    }
    </style>
  </head>
  <body>
    <h2>Project 7-3: Creating a Personal To-Do List</h2>
    <h3>Add New Task</h3>

    <?php
    // if form not submitted
    // generate new form
```

```php
if (!isset($_POST['submit'])) {
?>

<form method="post" action="save.php">
  Description: <br />
  <input type="text" name="name" />
  <p>
  Date due (dd/mm/yyyy): <br />
  <input type="text" name="dd" size="2" />
  <input type="text" name="mm" size="2" />
  <input type="text" name="yy" size="4" />
  <p>
  Priority: <br />
  <select name="priority">
    <option name="High">High</option>
    <option name="Medium">Medium</option>
    <option name="Low">Low</option>
  </select>
  <p>
  <input type="submit" name="submit" value="Save" />
</form>

<?php
} else {
// if form submitted
// attempt database connection
$sqlite = new SQLiteDatabase('todo.db') or die ("Could not open
database");

// check and sanitize input
$name = !empty($_POST['name']) ? sqlite_escape_string
($_POST['name']) : die('ERROR: Task name is required');
$dd = !empty($_POST['dd']) ? sqlite_escape_string((int)
$_POST['dd']) : die('ERROR: Task due date is required');
$mm = !empty($_POST['mm']) ? sqlite_escape_string((int)
$_POST['mm']) : die('ERROR: Task due date is required');
$yy = !empty($_POST['yy']) ? sqlite_escape_string((int)
$_POST['yy']) : die('ERROR: Task due date is required');
$date = checkdate($mm, $dd, $yy) ? mktime(0, 0, 0, $mm,
$dd, $yy) : die('ERROR: Task due date is invalid');
$priority = !empty($_POST['priority']) ? sqlite_escape_string
($_POST['priority']) : die('ERROR: Task priority is required');

// attempt query execution
// add a new record
$sql = "INSERT INTO tasks (name, due, priority) VALUES ('$name',
'$date', '$priority')";
```

(continued)

```
        if ($sqlite->queryExec($sql) == true) {
          echo '<div id="message">Task record successfully added to
database.</div>';
        } else {
          echo "ERROR: Could not execute $sql. " . sqlite_error_
string($sqlite->lastError());
        }

        // close connection
        unset($sqlite);
      }
      ?>

  </body>
</html>
```

Figure 7-8 illustrates what this Web form looks like.

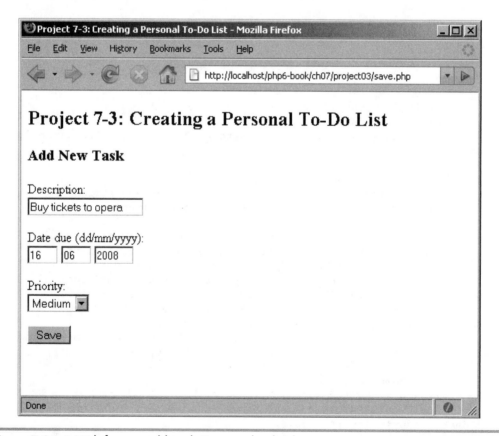

Figure 7-8   A Web form to add to-do items to the database

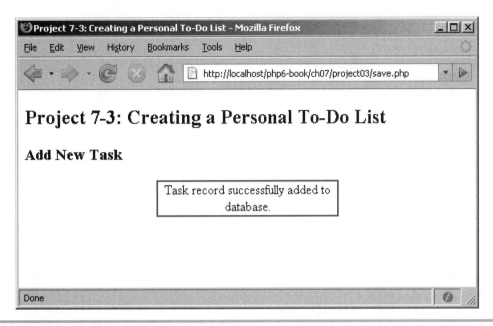

Figure 7-9   The results of adding a new to-do item to the database

When a user submits this form, the data entered is first validated to ensure that all required fields are present. Values entered into the three date field are also checked with PHP's `checkdate()` function, to ensure that together they form a valid date. The input is then further sanitized by passing it through the `sqlite_escape_string()` function, which automatically escapes special characters in the input, and saved to the database using an `INSERT` query.

Figure 7-9 illustrates the output of successfully adding a new task to the database.

So that takes care of adding tasks to the to-do list. Now, how about viewing them? As you will probably have guessed by now, this is simply a matter of using a `SELECT` query to retrieve all the records from the database, and then format the resulting information such that it is suitable for display on a Web page. Here's the relevant code (*list.php*):

```
<!DOCTYPE html PUBLIC "-//W3C//DTD XHTML 1.0 Transitional//EN"
   "DTD/xhtml1-transitional.dtd">
<html xmlns="http://www.w3.org/1999/xhtml" xml:lang="en" lang="en">
  <head>
    <title>Project 7-3: Creating a Personal To-Do List</title>
    <style type="text/css">
    div#message {
      text-align:center;
```

(continued)

```css
     margin-left:auto;
     margin-right:auto;
     width:60%;
     border: solid 2px green
   }
   table {
border-collapse: collapse;
width: 500px;
   }
   tr.heading {
font-weight: bolder;
   }
   td {
border: 1px solid black;
padding: 1em;
   }
   tr.high {
     background: #cc1111;
   }
   tr.medium {
     background: #00aaaa;
   }
   tr.low {
     background: #66dd33;
   }
   a {
     color: black;
     border: outset 2px black;
     text-decoration: none;
     padding: 3px;
   }
   </style>
 </head>
 <body>
   <h2>Project 7-3: Creating a Personal To-Do List</h2>
   <h3>Task List</h3>
```

```php
<?php
// attempt database connection
$sqlite = new SQLiteDatabase('todo.db') or die ("Could not open
database");

// get records
// format as HTML table
$sql = "SELECT id, name, due, priority FROM tasks ORDER BY due";
if ($result = $sqlite->query($sql)) {
  if ($result->numRows() > 0) {
```

```
    echo "<table>\n";
    echo "  <tr class=\"heading\">\n";
    echo "     <td>Description</td>\n";
    echo "     <td>Due date</td>\n";
    echo "     <td></td>\n";
    echo "  </tr>\n";
    while($row = $result->fetchObject()) {
      echo "  <tr class=\"" . strtolower($row->priority) . "\">\n";
      echo "     <td>" . $row->name . "</td>\n";
      echo "     <td>" . date('d M Y',$row->due) . "</td>\n";
      echo "     <td><a href=\"mark.php?id=" . $row->id . "\">Mark as
Done</a></td>\n";
      echo "  </tr>\n";
    }
    echo "</table>";
  } else {
    echo '<div id="message">No tasks listed in database.</div>';
  }
} else {
  echo 'ERROR: Could not execute query: $sql. ' . sqlite_error_
string($sqlite->lastError());
}

// close connection
unset($sqlite);
?>

  <p/>
  <a href="save.php">Add New Task</a>

  </body>
</html>
```

Nothing too taxing here: the script merely executes a SELECT query with exec(), and then iterates over the result set, printing the records found as rows of an HTML table. Notice that depending on the *priority* field of each record, the corresponding HTML table row is color-coded in red, green, or blue.

Figure 7-10 illustrates a sample of the output.

You'll see something else in the figure: each item in the to-do list comes with an option to 'Mark as Done'. This option points to yet another PHP script, *mark.php,* which is responsible for removing the corresponding record from the database. Look closely at the URL to *mark.php,* and you'll see that the record ID is being passed along as well, as the variable $id. Within *mark.php,* this ID will be accessible through the $_GET array, as $_GET['id'].

(continued)

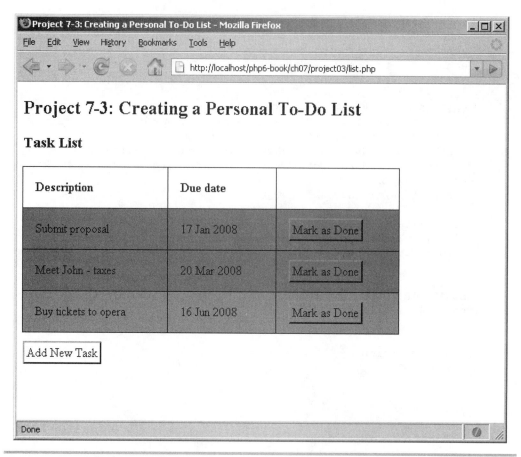

Figure 7-10 A Web page displaying to-do list items, sorted by due date

What does *mark.php* do? Nothing too complex—it simply uses the record ID passed to it in $_GET to formulate and execute a DELETE query, which removes the record from the database. Here's the code (*mark.php*):

```
<!DOCTYPE html PUBLIC "-//W3C//DTD XHTML 1.0 Transitional//EN"
    "DTD/xhtml1-transitional.dtd">
<html xmlns="http://www.w3.org/1999/xhtml" xml:lang="en" lang="en">
  <head>
    <title>Project 7-3: Creating a Personal To-Do List</title>
    <style type="text/css">
    div#message {
```

```
          text-align:center;
          margin-left:auto;
          margin-right:auto;
          width:40%;
          border: solid 2px green
      }
    </style>
  </head>
  <body>
    <h2>Project 7-3: Creating a Personal To-Do List</h2>
    <h3>Remove Completed Task</h3>

    <?php
    if (isset($_GET['id'])) {
      // attempt database connection
      $sqlite = new SQLiteDatabase('todo.db') or die ("Could not open
database");

      // check and sanitize input
      $id = !empty($_GET['id']) ? sqlite_escape_string((int)$_
GET['id']) : die('ERROR: Task ID is required');

      // delete record
      $sql = "DELETE FROM tasks WHERE id = '$id'";
      if ($sqlite->queryExec($sql) == true) {
        echo '<div id="message">Task record successfully removed from
database.</div>';
      } else {
        echo "ERROR: Could not execute $sql. " . sqlite_error_
string($sqlite->lastError());
      }

      // close connection
      unset($sqlite);
    } else {
      die ('ERROR: Task ID is required');
    }
    ?>

  </body>
</html>
```

Figure 7-11 illustrates the output of successfully removing a task from the database.

And now, when you revisit *list.php,* your to-do list will no longer display the item that you marked done. Simple, isn't it!

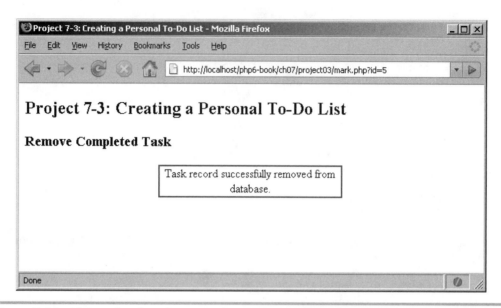

Figure 7-11 The results of marking a to-do item as complete

Using PHP's PDO Extension

In the previous sections, you learned how to integrate your PHP application with both MySQL and SQLite databases. As you will have seen, the MySQLi and SQLite extensions use differently named methods to do their work; as a result, switching from one database system to another essentially involves rewriting all your database code to use the new methods. That's why PHP also offers the database-neutral PHP Data Objects (PDO) extension, which offers greater portability and can significantly reduce the effort involved in switching from one database system to another.

The following sections discuss the PDO extension in greater detail, providing information on how it can be used to connect to different database systems, perform queries, process result sets, and handle connection or query errors. Most of the examples assume a MySQL database system; however, as you'll see, PDO-based programs require minimal modification to work with other database systems, including SQLite.

Retrieving Data

PDO works by providing a standard set of functions for common database operations such as connecting, querying, result set processing and error handling, and internally translating these functions to native API calls understood by the database in use. To illustrate how it works, consider the following example, which executes a SELECT query and displays the records found:

```php
<?php
// attempt a connection
try {
    $pdo = new PDO('mysql:dbname=music;host=localhost', 'user', 'pass');
} catch (PDOException $e) {
    die("ERROR: Could not connect: " . $e->getMessage());
}

// create and execute SELECT query
$sql = "SELECT artist_id, artist_name FROM artists";
if ($result = $pdo->query($sql)) {
  while($row = $result->fetch()) {
    echo $row[0] . ":" . $row[1] . "\n";
  }
} else {
  echo "ERROR: Could not execute $sql. " . print_r($pdo->errorInfo());
}

// close connection
unset($pdo);
?>
```

As this listing illustrates, using PDO to get data from a database involves steps similar to those you've seen in previous sections:

1. The first step is to initialize an instance of the PDO class and pass the object constructor three arguments: a Data Source Name (DSN) string indicating the type of database to connect to as well as other database-specific options, a valid database username, and the corresponding password. The DSN string varies from database to database; you can typically obtain the exact format for this string from the database's documentation.

   Table 7-4 lists some common DSN string formats.

Database	DSN String
MySQL	`'mysql:host=host;port=port;dbname=db'`
SQLite	`'sqlite:path/to/database/file'`
PostgreSQL	`'pgsql:host=host port=port dbname=db user=user password=pass'`
Oracle	`'oci:dbname=//host:port/db'`
Firebird	`'firebird:User=user;Password=pass;Database=db; DataSource=host;Port=port'`

Table 7-4 Common DSN Strings

If the connection attempt is unsuccessful, an exception will be raised; this exception can be caught and handled using PHP's exception-handling mechanism (more details on exceptions can be obtained from Chapter 10 of this book).

2. Assuming a successful connection, the next step is to formulate an SQL query and execute it using PDO's query() method. The return value of this method is a resultset, represented by a PDOStatement object. The contents of the resultset can be processed using the object's fetch() method, which returns the next record in the resultset as an array (both associative and indexed). Individual fields from the record can be accessed as array elements in a loop, using either the field index or the field name.

Ask the Expert

Q: How do I calculate the number of records in my resultset with PDO?

A: Unlike the MySQL and SQLite extensions, PDO does not offer a built-in method or property to directly retrieve the number of records in a returned resultset. This is because not all database systems return this information, and so PDO cannot provide this information in a portable manner. Should you still require this information, however, the recommended approach to this task in the PHP manual is to execute a SELECT COUNT(*) ... statement with your desired query and retrieve the first field of the resultset, which will hold the number of records matching the query. For more information, review the discussion at www.php.net/manual/en/function.PDOStatement-rowCount.php.

The PDOStatement object's fetch() method accepts an additional modifier, which controls how result set records are fetched. Some valid values for this modifier are listed in Table 7-5.

Modifier	What It Does
PDO::FETCH_NUM	Returns each record as a numerically indexed array
PDO::FETCH_ASSOC	Returns each record as an associative array keyed on the field name
PDO::FETCH_BOTH	Returns each record as both a numerically indexed array and an associative array (default value)
PDO::FETCH_OBJ	Returns each record as an object with properties corresponding to the field names
PDO::FETCH_LAZY	Returns each record as a numerically indexed array, associative array, and object

Table 7-5 Modifiers to PDO's fetch() Method

The following listing illustrates these modifiers in action:

```php
<?php
// attempt a connection
try {
    $pdo = new PDO('mysql:dbname=music;host=localhost', 'user', 'pass');
} catch (PDOException $e) {
    die("ERROR: Could not connect: " . $e->getMessage());
}

// create and execute SELECT query
$sql = "SELECT artist_id, artist_name FROM artists";
if ($result = $pdo->query($sql)) {

  // retrieve record as numeric array
  $row = $result->fetch(PDO::FETCH_NUM);
  echo $row[0] . ":" . $row[1] . "\n";

  // retrieve record as associative array
  $row = $result->fetch(PDO::FETCH_ASSOC);
  echo $row['artist_id'] . ":" . $row['artist_name'] . "\n";

  // retrieve record as object
  $row = $result->fetch(PDO::FETCH_OBJ);
  echo $row->artist_id . ":" . $row->artist_name . "\n";

  // retrieve record using combination of styles
  $row = $result->fetch(PDO::FETCH_LAZY);
  echo $row['artist_id'] . ":" . $row->artist_name . "\n";

} else {
  echo "ERROR: Could not execute $sql. " . print_r($pdo->errorInfo());
}

// close connection
unset($pdo);
?>
```

Adding and Modifying Data

PDO also makes it easy to perform INSERT, UPDATE, and DELETE queries with its exec() method. This method, which is designed for one-off SQL queries that change the database, returns the number of records affected by the query. Here's an example of using it to insert and delete a record:

```php
<?php
// attempt a connection
try {
    $pdo = new PDO('mysql:dbname=music;host=localhost', 'user', 'pass');
} catch (PDOException $e) {
    die("ERROR: Could not connect: " . $e->getMessage());
}

// create and execute INSERT query
$sql = "INSERT INTO artists (artist_name, artist_country) VALUES ('Luciano
Pavarotti', 'IT')";
$ret = $pdo->exec($sql);
if ($ret === false) {
  echo "ERROR: Could not execute $sql. " . print_r($pdo->errorInfo());
} else {
  $id = $pdo->lastInsertId();
  echo 'New artist with id: ' . $id . ' added.';
}

// create and execute DELETE query
$sql = "DELETE FROM artists WHERE artist_country = 'IT'";
$ret = $pdo->exec($sql);
if ($ret === false) {
  echo "ERROR: Could not execute $sql. " . print_r($pdo->errorInfo());
} else {
  echo 'Deleted ' . $ret . ' record(s).';
}

// close connection
unset($pdo);
?>
```

This listing uses the exec() method twice, first to insert a new record and then to delete records matching a specified condition. If the query passed to exec() is unsuccessful, exec() returns false; if not, it returns the number of records affected by the query. Notice also the script's use of the PDO object's lastInsertId() method, which returns the ID generated by the last INSERT command if the table contains an auto-incrementing field.

TIP

If no records are affected by the query executed by the exec() method, the method will return zero. Don't confuse this with the Boolean false value returned by exec() if the query fails. To avoid confusion, the PHP manual recommends always testing the return value of exec() with the === operator instead of the == operator.

Using Prepared Statements

PDO also supports prepared statements, via its `prepare()` and `execute()` methods. The following example illustrates, using a prepared statement to add various songs to the database:

```php
<?php
// define values to be inserted
$songs = array(
  array('Voulez-Vous', 2, 5),
  array('Take A Chance On Me', 2, 3),
  array('I Have A Dream', 2, 4),
  array('Thank You For The Music', 2, 4),
);

// attempt a connection
try {
    $pdo = new PDO('mysql:dbname=music;host=localhost', 'user', 'pass');
} catch (PDOException $e) {
    die("ERROR: Could not connect: " . $e->getMessage());
}

// create and execute SELECT query
$sql = "INSERT INTO songs (song_title, fk_song_artist, fk_song_rating) VALUES
(?, ?, ?)";
if ($stmt = $pdo->prepare($sql)) {
  foreach ($songs as $s) {
    $stmt->bindParam(1, $s[0]);
    $stmt->bindParam(2, $s[1]);
    $stmt->bindParam(3, $s[2]);
    if ($stmt->execute()) {
      echo "New song with id: "  . $pdo->lastInsertId() . " added.\n";
    } else {
      echo "ERROR: Could not execute query: $sql. " . print_r
($pdo->errorInfo());
    }
  }

} else {
  echo "ERROR: Could not prepare query: $sql. " . print_r($pdo->errorInfo());
}

// close connection
unset($pdo);
?>
```

If you compare the preceding script with a similar script from the previous section on MySQLi, you'll see a marked resemblance. Like before, this script too defines an SQL query template containing an INSERT statement, containing placeholders instead of actual values, and then turns this template into a prepared statement using the PDO object's prepare() method.

If successful, prepare() returns a PDOStatement object representing the prepared statement. The values to be interpolated into the statement are then bound to the placeholders by repeatedly calling the PDOStatement object's bindParam() method with two arguments, the position of the placeholder and the variable to bind to it. Once the variables are bound, the PDOStatement object's execute() method takes care of actually executing the prepared statement with the correct values.

NOTE

When using prepared statements with PDO, it's important to note that the performance benefits of these statements will only be available if the underlying database natively supports these statements. For databases that don't support prepared statements, PDO will internally convert calls to prepare() and execute() into standard SQL statements and no performance benefits will accrue in these cases.

Handling Errors

When performing database operations with PDO, errors may occur during either the connection phase or the query execution phase. PDO offers robust tools to handle both these types of errors.

Connection Errors

If PDO is unable to connect to the named database using the supplied DSN, username, and password, it automatically generates a PDOException. This exception can be trapped using PHP's standard exception-handling mechanism (discussed in detail in Chapter 10), and an error message explaining the cause of error can be retrieved from the exception object.

Query Execution Errors

If an error occurs during query preparation or execution, PDO provides information on the error via its errorInfo() method. This method returns an array containing three elements: the SQL error code, a database error code, and a human-readable error message (also generated by the underlying database). It's easy to process this array and print the appropriate elements from it within the error-handling section of your script.

Try This 7-4   Building a Login Form

Let's now put PDO through its paces with another practical application, one you're likely to encounter again and again in your PHP development: a login form. This application will generate a Web form for users to enter their usernames and passwords; it will then verify this input against credentials stored in a database and allow or reject the login attempt. In the first instance, this application will use a MySQL database; later on, however, you'll see just how portable PDO code is, when we switch the application over to an SQLite database.

Using a MySQL Database

To begin, fire up your MySQL command-line client and create a table to hold usernames and passwords, as follows:

```
mysql> CREATE DATABASE app;
Query OK, 0 rows affected (0.07 sec)
mysql> USE app;
Query OK, 0 rows affected (0.07 sec)
mysql> CREATE TABLE users (
    -> id int(4) NOT NULL AUTO_INCREMENT,
    -> username VARCHAR(255) NOT NULL,
    -> password VARCHAR(255) NOT NULL,
    -> PRIMARY KEY  (id));
Query OK, 0 rows affected (0.07 sec)
```

At this point, it's also a good idea to "seed" the table by entering some usernames and passwords. For simplicity, we'll keep the passwords the same as the usernames, but encrypt them so that they're shielded from casual viewers (and not-so-casual hackers):

```
mysql> INSERT INTO users (username, password)
    -> VALUES ('john', ' $1$Tk0.gh4.$42EZDbQ4mOfmXMq.0m1tS1');
Query OK, 1 row affected (0.21 sec)

mysql> INSERT INTO users (username, password)
    -> VALUES ('jane', '$1$.15.tR/.$XK1KW1Wzqy0UuMFKQDHH00');
Query OK, 1 row affected (0.21 sec)
```

(continued)

Now, all that's needed is a login form, and some PHP code to read the values entered into the form and test them against the values in the database. Here's the code (*login.php*):

```
<!DOCTYPE html PUBLIC "-//W3C//DTD XHTML 1.0 Transitional//EN"
  "DTD/xhtml1-transitional.dtd">
<html xmlns="http://www.w3.org/1999/xhtml" xml:lang="en" lang="en">
  <head>
    <title>Project 7-4: Building A Login Form</title>
  </head>
  <body>
    <h2>Project 7-4: Building A Login Form</h2>
<?php
    // if form not yet submitted
    // display form
    if (!isset($_POST['submit'])) {
?>
    <form method="post" action="login.php">
      Username: <br />
      <input type="text" name="username" />
      <p>
      Password: <br />
      <input type="password" name="password" />
      <p>
      <input type="submit" name="submit" value="Log In" />
    </form>

<?php
    // if form submitted
    // check supplied login credentials
    // against database
    } else {
      $username = $_POST['username'];
      $password = $_POST['password'];

      // check input
      if (empty($username)) {
        die('ERROR: Please enter your username');
      }
      if (empty($password)) {
        die('ERROR: Please enter your password');
      }

      // attempt database connection
      try {
        $pdo = new PDO('mysql:dbname=test;host=localhost',
'user', 'pass');
      } catch (PDOException $e) {
```

```php
        die("ERROR: Could not connect: " . $e->getMessage());
      }

      // escape special characters in input
      $username = $pdo->quote($username);

      // check if usernames exists
      $sql = "SELECT COUNT(*) FROM users WHERE username = $username";
      if ($result = $pdo->query($sql)) {
        $row = $result->fetch();
        // if yes, fetch the encrypted password
        if ($row[0] == 1) {
          $sql = "SELECT password FROM users WHERE
username = $username";
          // encrypt the password entered into the form
          // test it against the encrypted password stored in
the database
          // if the two match, the password is correct
          if ($result = $pdo->query($sql)) {
            $row = $result->fetch();
            $salt = $row[0];
            if (crypt($password, $salt) == $salt) {
              echo 'Your login credentials were successfully
verified.';
            } else {
              echo 'You entered an incorrect password.';
            }
          } else {
            echo "ERROR: Could not execute $sql. " . print_r
($pdo->errorInfo());
          }
        } else {
          echo 'You entered an incorrect username.';
        }
      } else {
        echo "ERROR: Could not execute $sql. " . print_r
($pdo->errorInfo());
      }

      // close connection
      unset($pdo);
    }
?>
  </body>
</html>
```

Figure 7-12 illustrates what the login form looks like.

(continued)

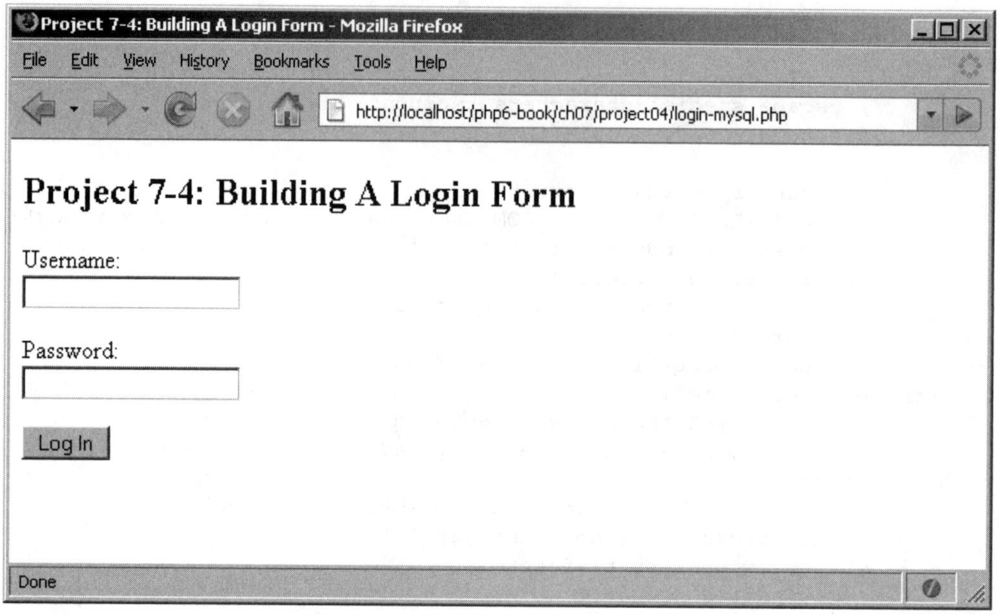

Figure 7-12 A Web-based login form

When this form is submitted, the second half of the script comes into play. This performs a number of steps:

1. It checks the form input to ensure that both the username and the password are present, and halts script execution with an error message if either one is absent. It also escapes special characters in the input using PDO's quote() method.

2. It opens a connection to the database and performs a SELECT query to check if a matching username is present in the database. If this check returns false, it generates the error message "You entered an incorrect username."

3. If the username is present, the script then proceeds to test the password. Because the password is encrypted using a one-way encryption scheme, this test cannot be performed directly; the only way to do this is to re-encrypt the user's password, as entered in the form, and test the result against the version stored in the database. If the two encrypted strings match, it implies that the password entered is correct.

Figure 7-13   The results of entering an incorrect password into the login form

4. Depending on the results of the test, the script then generates either the message 'You entered an incorrect password.' or 'Your login credentials were successfully verified.'

Figure 7-13 illustrates the result of entering an incorrect password and Figure 7-14 illustrates the result of entering a correct password.

Figure 7-14   The results of entering a correct password into the login form

Ask the Expert

Q: How did you generate the encrypted passwords used in this example?

A: The encrypted password strings used in this example were generated with PHP's `crypt()` function, which uses a one-way encryption scheme to encrypt any string passed to it as input. A one-way encryption scheme renders the original password irrecoverable (hence the term "one-way"). The encryption is based on a unique key or salt, which can be optionally provided to the function as a second argument; in its absence, PHP automatically generates a salt.

The original password is no longer recoverable after being passed through `crypt()`, and so performing password validation later against a user-supplied value is a two-step process: first, re-encrypt the user-supplied value with the same salt used in the original encryption process and then, test if the two encrypted strings match. That's precisely what the form processing script in this example does.

Switching to a Different Database

Now, let's assume that external reasons force you to switch over from MySQL to SQLite. The first thing you'll need to do is create a database table to hold all the user account information. So, fire up your SQLite client and replicate the database created in the preceding section (name the database file *app.db*):

```
sqlite> CREATE TABLE users (
   -> id INTEGER PRIMARY KEY,
   -> username TEXT NOT NULL,
   -> password TEXT NOT NULL
   -> );

sqlite> INSERT INTO users (username, password)
   -> VALUES ('john', ' $1$Tk0.gh4.$42EZDbQ4mOfmXMq.Om1tS1');
sqlite> INSERT INTO users (username, password)
   -> VALUES ('jane', '$1$.15.tR/.$XK1KW1Wzqy0UuMFKQDHH00');
```

The next step is to update your application's code so that it communicates with this SQLite database instead of the MySQL database. Because you're using PDO, this update consists of changing one—that's right, *one*—line in your PHP script: the DSN passed to the PDO object constructor. Here's the relevant segment of code:

```php
<?php
    // attempt database connection
    try {
        $pdo = new PDO('sqlite:app.db');
```

```
    } catch (PDOException $e) {
        die("ERROR: Could not connect: " . $e->getMessage());
    }
?>
```

And now, when you try logging in, your application will work exactly as it did before, except that now it will use the SQLite database instead of the MySQL database. Try it for yourself and see!

This portability is precisely why PDO is gaining popularity among PHP developers; it makes the entire process of switching from one database system to another an extremely simple one, reducing both development and testing time and the associated cost.

Summary

PHP's database support is one of the biggest reasons for its popularity, and this chapter covered all the ground necessary for you to get started with this important language feature. It began by introducing you to basic database concepts, and teaching you the basics of Structured Query Language. It then rapidly proceeded to a discussion of PHP's most popular database extensions: the MySQLi extension, the SQLite extension, and the Portable Database Objects (PDO) extension. The discussion included both practical information and code examples of querying and modifying databases with PHP to get you started using these extensions in your daily development.

To read more about the topics discussed in this chapter, consider visiting the following links:

- Database concepts, at
  www.melonfire.com/community/columns/trog/article.php?id=52

- SQL basics, at **www.melonfire.com/community/columns/trog/article.php?id=39** and **www.melonfire.com/community/columns/trog/article.php?id=44**

- More information on SQL joins, at
  www.melonfire.com/community/columns/trog/article.php?id=148

- The MySQL Web site, at **www.mysql.com**

- The SQLite Web site, at **www.sqlite.org**

- PHP's MySQLi extension, at **www.php.net/mysqli**

- PHP's SQLite extension, at **www.php.net/sqlite**

- PHP's PDO extension, at **www.php.net/pdo**

Chapter 7 Self Test

1. Mark the following statements as true or false:

   A SQL table joins can only take place between foreign and primary key fields.

   B MySQL support is new to PHP.

   C The ORDER BY clause is used to sort the fields of an SQL result set.

   D PRIMARY KEY fields can hold null values.

   E It is possible to override the value generated by SQLite for an INTEGER PRIMARY KEY field.

   F Prepared statements can be used only for INSERT operations.

2. Correctly identify the SQL command for each of the following database operations:

   A Delete a database

   B Update a record

   C Delete a record

   D Create a table

   E Select a database for use

3. What is database normalization, and why is it useful?

4. Name one advantage and one disadvantage of using a database abstraction library like PDO instead of a native database extension.

5. Using the PDO extension, write a PHP script to add new songs to the *songs* table developed in this chapter. Allow users to select the song's artist and rating from drop-down form selection lists populated with the contents of the *artists* and *ratings* tables.

6. Using PHP's MySQLi extension, write a PHP script to create a new database table with four fields of your choice. Then, do the same task with an SQLite database table using PHP's SQLite extension.

7. Manually populate the MySQL database tables created in the preceding assignment with 7–10 records of your choice. Then, write a PDO-based script to read the contents of this table and migrate the data found therein to the SQLite database table also created in the preceding assignment. Use a prepared statement.

Chapter 8

Working with XML

Key Skills & Concepts

- Understand basic XML concepts and technologies

- Understand PHP's SimpleXML and DOM extensions

- Access and manipulate XML documents with PHP

- Create new XML documents from scratch using PHP

- Integrate third-party RSS feeds in a PHP application

- Convert between SQL and XML using PHP

The Extensible Markup Language (XML) is a widely accepted standard for data description and exchange. It allows content authors to "mark up" their data with customized machine-readable tags, thereby making data easier to classify and search. XML also helps enforce a formal structure on content, and it provides a portable format that can be used to easily exchange information between different systems.

PHP has included support for XML since PHP 4, but it was only in PHP 5 that the various XML extensions in PHP were standardized to use a common XML parsing toolkit. This chapter introduces you to two of PHP's most useful and powerful XML processing extensions—SimpleXML and DOM—and includes numerous code examples and practical illustrations of using XML in combination with PHP-based applications.

Introducing XML

Before getting into the nitty-gritty of manipulating XML files with PHP, it's instructive to spend some time getting familiar with XML. If you're new to XML, the following section provides a grounding in basic XML, including an overview of XML concepts and technologies. This information will be helpful to understand the more advanced material in subsequent sections.

XML Basics

Let's begin with a very basic question: what is XML, and why is it useful?

XML is a language that helps document authors describe the data in a document, by "marking it up" with custom tags. These tags don't come from a predefined list; instead,

XML encourages authors to create their own tags and structure, suited to their own particular requirements, as a way to increase flexibility and usability. This fact, coupled with the Recommendation status bestowed on it by the W3C in 1998, has served to make XML one of the most popular ways to describe and store structured information on (and off) the Web.

XML data is physically stored in text files. This makes XML documents very portable, because every computer system can read and process text files. Not only does this facilitate data sharing, but it also allows XML to be used in a wide variety of applications. For example, the Rich Site Summaries (RSS) and Atom Weblog feed formats are both based on XML, as is Asynchronous JavaScript and XML (AJAX) and the Simple Object Access Protocol (SOAP).

Ask the Expert

Q: **What programs can I use to create or view an XML file?**

A: On a UNIX/Linux system, both vi and emacs can be used to create XML documents, while Notepad remains a favorite on Windows systems. Both Microsoft Internet Explorer and Mozilla Firefox have built-in XML support and can read and display an XML document in a hierarchical tree view.

Anatomy of an XML Document

Internally, an XML document is made up of various components, each one serving a specific purpose. To understand these components, consider the following XML document, which contains a recipe for spaghetti bolognese:

```
1.   <?xml version='1.0'?>
2.   <recipe>
3.     <ingredients>
4.       <item quantity="250" units="gm">Beef mince</item>
5.       <item quantity="200" units="gm">Onions</item>
6.       <item quantity="75" units="ml">Red wine</item>
7.       <item quantity="12">Tomatoes</item>
8.       <item quantity="2" units="tbsp">Parmesan cheese</item>
9.       <item quantity="200" units="gm">Spaghetti</item>
10.    </ingredients>
11.    <method>
12.      <step number="1">Chop and fry the onions.</step>
13.      <step number="2">Add the mince to the fried onions &amp;
continue frying.</step>
```

```
14.      <step number="3">Puree the tomatoes and blend them into the
mixture with the wine.</step>
15.      <step number="4">Simmer for an hour.</step>
16.      <step number="5">Serve on top of cooked pasta with Parmesan
cheese.</step>
17.    </method>
18. </recipe>
```

This XML document contains a recipe, broken up into different sections; each section is further "marked up" with descriptive tags to precisely identify the type of data contained within it. Let's look at each of these in detail.

1. Every XML document must begin with a declaration that states the version of XML being used; this declaration is referred to as the *document prolog,* and it can be seen in Line 1 of the preceding XML document. In addition to the version number, this document prolog may also contain character encoding information and Document Type Definition (DTD) references (for data validation).

2. The document prolog is followed by a nested series of *elements* (Lines 2–18). Elements are the basic units of XML; they typically consist of a pair of opening and closing tags that enclose some textual content. Element names are user-defined; they should be chosen with care, as they are intended to describe the content sandwiched between them. Element names are case-sensitive and must begin with a letter, optionally followed by more letters and numbers. The outermost element in an XML document— in this example, the element named <recipe> on Line 2—is known as the *document element* or the *root element.*

3. The textual data enclosed within elements is known, in XML parlance, as *character data.* This character data can consist of strings, numbers, and special characters (with some exceptions: angle brackets and ampersands within textual data should be replaced with the entities <, $gt;, and & respectively to avoid confusing the XML parser when it reads the document). Line 13, for example, uses the & entity to represent an ampersand within its character data.

4. Finally, elements can also contain *attributes,* which are name-value pairs that hold additional information about the element. Attribute names are case-sensitive and follow the same rules as element names. The same attribute name cannot be used more than once within the same element, and attribute values should always be enclosed in quotation marks. Lines 4–9 and 12–16 in the example document illustrate the use of attributes to provide additional descriptive information about the element to which they are attached; for example, the 'units' attribute specifies the unit measure for each ingredient.

XML documents can also contain various other components: namespaces, processing instructions, and CDATA blocks. These are a little more complex, and you won't see them in any of the examples used in this chapter; however, if you're interested in learning more about them, take a look at the links at the end of the chapter for more detailed information and examples.

Ask the Expert

Q: Can I create elements that don't contain anything?

A: Sure. The XML specification supports elements that hold no content and therefore do not require a closing tag. To close these elements, simply add a slash to the end of the opening tag, as in the following code snippet:

```
The line breaks <br /> here.
```

Well-Formed and Valid XML

The XML specification makes an important distinction between well-formed and valid documents.

- A *well-formed document* follows all the rules for element and attribute names, contains all essential declarations, contains one (and only one) root element, and follows a correctly nested element hierarchy below the root element. All the XML documents you'll see in this chapter are well-formed documents.

- A *valid document* is one which meets all the conditions of being well-formed and also conforms to additional rules laid out in a Document Type Definition (DTD) or XML Schema. This chapter doesn't discuss DTDs or XML Schemas in detail, so you won't see any examples of this type of document; however, you'll find many examples of such documents online, and in the resource links at the end of the chapter.

XML Parsing Methods

Typically, an XML document is processed by a software application known as an XML parser. This parser reads the XML document using one of two approaches, the Simple API for XML (SAX) approach or the Document Object Model (DOM) approach:

- A SAX parser works by traversing an XML document sequentially, from beginning to end, and calling specific user-defined functions as it encounters different types of XML constructs. Thus, for example, a SAX parser might be programmed to call one function to process an attribute, another one to process a starting element, and yet a third one to process character data. The functions called in this manner are responsible for actually processing the XML construct found, and any information stored within it.

- A DOM parser, on the other hand, works by reading the entire XML document in one fell swoop and converting it to a hierarchical "tree" structure in memory. The parser can then be programmed to traverse the tree, jumping between "sibling" or "child" branches of the tree to access specific pieces of information.

Each of these methods has pros and cons: SAX reads XML data in "chunks" and is efficient for large files, but it requires the programmer to create customized functions to handle the different elements in an XML file. DOM requires less customization but can rapidly consume memory for its actions and so is often unsuitable for large XML data files. The choice of method thus depends heavily on the requirements of the application in question.

XML Technologies

As XML's popularity has increased, so too has the list of technologies that use it. Here are a few that you might have heard about already:

- **XML Schema**   XML Schemas define the structure and format of XML documents, allowing for more flexible validation and support for datatyping, inheritance, grouping, and database linkage.

- **XLink**   XLink is a specification for linking XML data structures together. It allows for more sophisticated link types than regular HTML hyperlinks, including links with multiple targets.

- **XPointer**   XPointer is a specification for navigating the hierarchical tree structure of an XML document, easily finding elements, attributes, and other data structures within the document.

- **XSL**   The Extensible Stylesheet Language (XSL) applies formatting rules to XML documents and "transforms" them from one format to another.

- **XHTML**   XHTML combines the precision of XML markup with the easy-to-understand tags of HTML to create a newer, more standards-compliant version of HTML.

- **XForms**   XForms separates the information gathered in a Web form from the form's appearance, allowing for more stringent validation and easier reuse of forms in different media.

- **XML Query**   XML Query allows developers to query XML document and generate result sets, in much the same way that SQL is used to query and retrieve database records.

- **XML Encryption and XML Signature**   XML Encryption is a means of encrypting and decrypting XML documents, and representing the resulting data. It is closely related to XML Signature, which provides a way to represent and verify digital signatures with XML.

- **SVG**   Scalable Vector Graphics (SVG) uses XML to describe vector or raster graphical images, with support for alpha masks, filters, paths, and transformations.

- **MathML**   MathML uses XML to describe mathematical expressions and formulae, such that they can be easily rendered by Web browsers.

- **SOAP**   The Simple Object Access Protocol (SOAP) uses XML to encode requests and responses between network hosts using HTTP.

Ask the Expert

Q: When should I use an attribute, and when should I use an element?

A: Both attributes and elements contain descriptive data, so it's often a matter of judgment as to whether a particular piece of information is better stored as an element or as an attribute. In most cases, if the information is hierarchically structured, elements are more appropriate containers; on the other hand, attributes are better for information that is ancillary or does not lend itself to a formal structure.

For a more formal discussion of this topic, take a look at the IBM developerWorks article at www.ibm.com/developerworks/xml/library/x-eleatt.html, which discusses the issues involved in greater detail.

Try This 8-1   Creating an XML Document

Now that you know the basics of XML, let's put that knowledge to the test by creating a well-formed XML document and viewing it in a Web browser. This document will describe a library of books using XML. Each entry in the document will contain information on a book's title, author, genre, and page count.

(continued)

To create this XML document, pop open your favorite text editor and enter the following markup (*library.xml*):

```xml
<?xml version="1.0"?>
<library>
  <book id="1" genre="horror" rating="5">
    <title>The Shining</title>
    <author>Stephen King</author>
    <pages>673</pages>
  </book>
  <book id="2" genre="suspense" rating="4">
    <title>Shutter Island</title>
    <author>Dennis Lehane</author>
    <pages>390</pages>
  </book>
  <book id="3" genre="fantasy" rating="5">
    <title>The Lord Of The Rings</title>
    <author>J. R. R. Tolkien</author>
    <pages>3489</pages>
  </book>
  <book id="4" genre="suspense" rating="3">
    <title>Double Cross</title>
    <author>James Patterson</author>
    <pages>308</pages>
  </book>
  <book id="5" genre="horror" rating="4">
    <title>Ghost Story</title>
    <author>Peter Straub</author>
    <pages>389</pages>
  </book>
  <book id="6" genre="fantasy" rating="3">
    <title>Glory Road</title>
    <author>Robert Heinlein</author>
    <pages>489</pages>
  </book>
  <book id="7" genre="horror" rating="3">
    <title>The Exorcist</title>
    <author>William Blatty</author>
    <pages>301</pages>
  </book>
  <book id="8" genre="suspense" rating="2">
    <title>The Camel Club</title>
    <author>David Baldacci</author>
    <pages>403</pages>
  </book>
</library>
```

Save this file to a location under your Web server's document root, and name it *library.xml*. Then, start up your Web browser, and browse to the URL corresponding to the file location. You should see something like Figure 8-1.

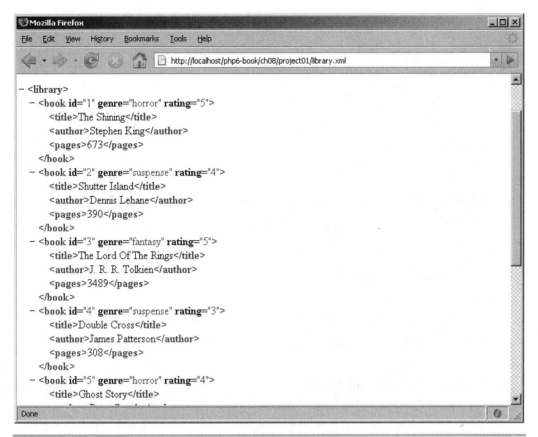

Figure 8-1 An XML document, as seen in Mozilla Firefox

Using PHP's SimpleXML Extension

Although PHP has support for both DOM and SAX parsing methods, by far the easiest way to work with XML data in PHP is via its SimpleXML extension. This extension, which is enabled by default in PHP 5, provides a user-friendly and intuitive interface to reading and processing XML data in a PHP application.

Working with Elements

SimpleXML represents every XML document as an object and turns the elements within it into a hierarchical set of objects and object properties. Accessing a particular element now becomes as simple as using `parent->child` notation to traverse the object tree until that element is reached.

To illustrate how this works in practice, consider the following XML file (*address.xml*):

```
<?xml version='1.0'?>
<address>
  <street>13 High Street</street>
  <county>Oxfordshire</county>
  <city>
    <name>Oxford</name>
    <zip>OX1 1BA</zip>
  </city>
  <country>UK</country>
</address>
```

Here's a PHP script that uses SimpleXML to read this file and retrieve the city name and ZIP code:

```
<?php
// load XML file
$xml = simplexml_load_file('address.xml') or die ("Unable to load XML!");

// access XML data
// output: 'City: Oxford \n Postal code: OX1 1BA\n'
echo "City: " . $xml->city->name . "\n";
echo "Postal code: " . $xml->city->zip . "\n";
?>
```

To read an XML file with SimpleXML, use the `simplexml_load_file()` function and pass it the disk path to the target XML file. This function will then read and parse the XML file and, assuming it is well-formed, return a SimpleXML object representing the document's root element. This object is only the top level of a hierarchical object tree that mirrors the internal structure of the XML data: elements below the root element are represented as properties or child objects and can thus be accessed using the standard `parentObject->childObject` notation.

TIP

If your XML data is in a string variable instead of a file, use the `simplexml_load_string()` function to read it into a SimpleXML object.

Multiple instances of the same element at the same level of the XML document tree are represented as arrays. These can easily be processed using PHP's loop constructs. To illustrate, consider this next example, which reads the *library.xml* file developed in the preceding section and prints the title and author names found within it:

```
<?php
// load XML file
$xml = simplexml_load_file('library.xml') or die ("Unable to load XML!");
```

```
// loop over XML data as array
// print book titles and authors
// output: 'The Shining is written by Stephen King. \n ...'
foreach ($xml->book as $book) {
  echo $book->title . "  is written by " . $book->author . ".\n";
}
?>
```

Here, a `foreach` loop iterates over the <book> objects generated from the XML data, printing each object's `'title'` and `'author'` properties.

You can also count the number of elements at particular level in the XML document with a simple call to `count()`. The next listing illustrates, counting the number of <book>s in the XML document:

```
<?php
// load XML file
$xml = simplexml_load_file('library.xml') or die ("Unable to load XML!");

// loop over XML data as array
// print count of books
// output: '8 book(s) found.'
echo count($xml->book) . ' book(s) found.';
?>
```

Working with Attributes

If an XML element contains attributes, SimpleXML has an easy way to get to these as well: attributes and values are converted into keys and values of a PHP associative array and can be accessed like regular array elements.

To illustrate, consider the following example, which reads the *library.xml* file from the preceding section and prints each book title found, together with its `'genre'` and `'rating'`:

```
<?php
// load XML file
$xml = simplexml_load_file('library.xml') or die ("Unable to load XML!");

// access XML data
// for each book
// retrieve and print 'genre' and 'rating' attributes
// output: 'The Shining \n Genre: horror \n Rating: 5 \n\n ...'
foreach ($xml->book as $book) {
  echo $book->title . "\n";
  echo "Genre: " . $book['genre'] . "\n";
  echo "Rating: " . $book['rating'] . "\n\n";
}
?>
```

In this example, a `foreach` loop iterates over the `<book>` elements in the XML data, turning each into an object. Attributes of the book element are represented as elements of an associative array and can thus be accessed by key: the key `'genre'` returns the value of the `'genre'` attribute, and the key `'rating'` returns the value of the `'rating'` attribute.

Try This 8-2 Converting XML to SQL

Now that you know how to read XML elements and attributes, let's look at a practical example of SimpleXML in action. This next program reads an XML file and converts the data within it into a series of SQL statements, which can be used to transfer the data into a MySQL or other SQL-compliant database.

Here's the sample XML file (*inventory.xml*):

```xml
<?xml version='1.0'?>
<items>
  <item sku="123">
    <name>Cheddar cheese</name>
    <price>3.99</price>
  </item>
  <item sku="124">
    <name>Blue cheese</name>
    <price>5.49</price>
  </item>
  <item sku="125">
    <name>Smoked bacon (pack of 6 rashers)</name>
    <price>1.99</price>
  </item>
  <item sku="126">
    <name>Smoked bacon (pack of 12 rashers)</name>
    <price>2.49</price>
  </item>
  <item sku="127">
    <name>Goose liver pate</name>
    <price>7.99</price>
  </item>
  <item sku="128">
    <name>Duck liver pate</name>
    <price>6.49</price>
  </item>
</items>
```

And here's the PHP code that converts this XML data into SQL statements (*xml2sql.php*):

```php
<?php
// load XML file
$xml = simplexml_load_file('inventory.xml') or die ("Unable to load XML!");

// loop over XML <item> elements
// access child nodes and interpolate with SQL statement
foreach ($xml as $item) {
  echo "INSERT INTO items (sku, name, price) VALUES ('" . addslashes($item['sku']) .
"','" . addslashes($item->name) . "','" . addslashes($item->price) . "');\n";
}
?>
```

This script should be simple to understand if you've been following along: it iterates over all the <item> elements in the XML document, using object->property notation to access each item's <name> and <price>. The 'sku' attribute of each <item> is similarly accessed via the 'sku' key of each item's attribute array. The values retrieved in this fashion are then interpolated into an SQL INSERT statement.

This statement would normally then be supplied to a function such as mysql_ query() or sqlite_query() for insertion into a MySQL or SQLite database; for purposes of this example, it's simply printed to the output device.

Figure 8-2 illustrates the output of this script.

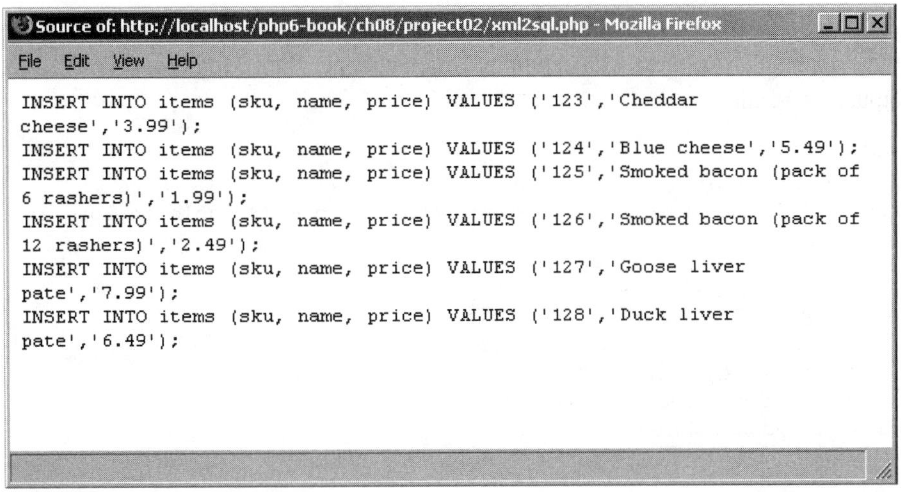

Figure 8-2 Converting XML to SQL with SimpleXML

Altering Element and Attribute Values

With SimpleXML, it's easy to change the content in an XML file: simply assign a new value to the corresponding object property using PHP's assignment operator (=). To illustrate, consider the following PHP script, which changes the title and author of the second book in *library.xml* and then outputs the revised XML document:

```php
<?php
// load XML file
$xml = simplexml_load_file('library.xml') or die ("Unable to load XML!");

// change element values
// set new title and author for second book
$xml->book[1]->title = 'Invisible Prey';
$xml->book[1]->author = 'John Sandford';

// output new XML string
header('Content-Type: text/xml');
echo $xml->asXML();
?>
```

Here, SimpleXML is used to access the second <book> element by index, and the values of the <title> and <author> elements are altered by setting new values for the corresponding object properties. Notice the asXML() method, which is new in this example: it converts the nested hierarchy of SimpleXML objects and object properties back into a regular XML string.

Changing attribute values is just as easy: assign a new value to the corresponding key of the attribute array. Here's an example, which changes the sixth book's 'rating' and outputs the result:

```php
<?php
// load XML file
$xml = simplexml_load_file('library.xml') or die ("Unable to load XML!");

// change attribute values
// set new rating for sixth book
$xml->book[5]{'rating'} = 5;

// output new XML string
header('Content-Type: text/xml');
echo $xml->asXML();
?>
```

Adding New Elements and Attributes

In addition to allowing you to alter element and attribute values, SimpleXML also lets you dynamically add new elements and attributes to an existing XML document. To illustrate, consider the next script, which adds a new <book> to the *library.xml* XML data:

```php
<?php
// load XML file
$xml = simplexml_load_file('library.xml') or die ("Unable to load XML!");

// get the last book 'id'
$numBooks = count($xml->book);
$lastID = $xml->book[($numBooks-1)]{'id'};

// add a new <book> element
$book = $xml->addChild('book');

// get the 'id' attribute
// for the new <book> element
// by incrementing $lastID by 1
$book->addAttribute('id', ($lastID+1));

// add 'rating' and 'genre' attributes
$book->addAttribute('genre', 'travel');
$book->addAttribute('rating', 5);

// add <title>, <author> and <page> elements
$title = $book->addChild('title', 'Frommer\'s Italy 2007');
$author = $book->addChild('author', 'Various');
$page = $book->addChild('pages', 820);

// output new XML string
header('Content-Type: text/xml');
echo $xml->asXML();
?>
```

Every SimpleXML object exposes an addChild() method (for adding new child elements) and an addAttribute() method (for adding new attributes). Both these methods accept a name and a value, generate the corresponding element or attribute, and attach it to the parent object within the XML hierarchy.

These methods are illustrated in the preceding listing, which begins by reading the existing XML document into a SimpleXML object. The root element of this XML document is stored in the PHP object $xml. The listing then needs to calculate the ID to be assigned to the new <book> element: it does this by counting the number of <book> elements already present in the XML document, accessing the last such element, retrieving that element's 'id' attribute, and adding 1 to it.

With that formality out of the way, the listing then dives into element and attribute creation proper:

1. It starts off by attaching a new <book> element to the root element, by invoking the $xml object's addChild() method. This method accepts the name of the element to be created and (optionally) a value for that element. The resultant XML object is stored in the PHP object $book.

2. With the element created, it's now time to set its 'id', 'genre', and 'rating' attributes. This is done via the $book object's addAttribute() method, which also accepts two arguments—the attribute name and value—and sets the corresponding associative array keys.

3. Once the outermost <book> element is fully defined, it's time to add the <title>, <author>, and <pages> elements as children of this <book> element. This is easily done by again invoking the addChild() method, this time of the $book object.

4. Once these child objects are defined, the object hierarchy is converted to an XML document string with the asXML() method.

Figure 8-3 illustrates what the output looks like.

Creating New XML Documents

You can also use SimpleXML to create a brand-spanking-new XML document from scratch, by initializing an empty SimpleXML object from an XML string, and then using the addChild() and addAttribute() methods to build the rest of the XML document tree. Consider the following example, which illustrates the process:

```php
<?php
// load XML from string
$xmlStr = "<?xml version='1.0'?><person></person>";
$xml = simplexml_load_string($xmlStr);

// add attributes
$xml->addAttribute('age', '18');
$xml->addAttribute('sex', 'male');

// add child elements
$xml->addChild('name', 'John Doe');
$xml->addChild('dob', '04-04-1989');

// add second level of child elements
$address = $xml->addChild('address');
```

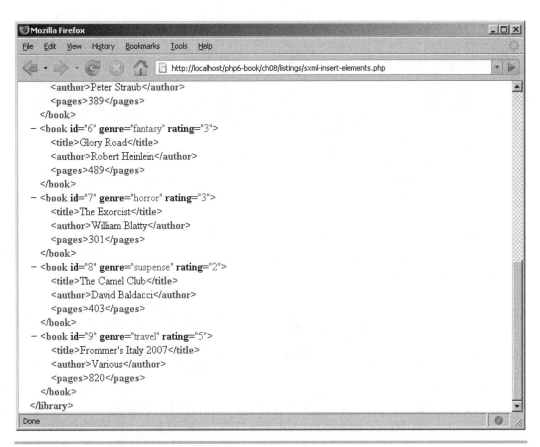

Figure 8-3 Inserting elements into an XML tree with SimpleXML

```
$address->addChild('street', '12 A Road');
$address->addChild('city', 'London');

// add third level of child elements
$country = $address->addChild('country', 'United Kingdom');
$country->addAttribute('code', 'UK');

// output new XML string
header('Content-Type: text/xml');
echo $xml->asXML();
?>
```

This PHP script is similar to what you've already seen in the preceding section, with one important difference: instead of grafting new elements and attributes on to a preexisting XML document tree, this one generates an XML document tree entirely from scratch!

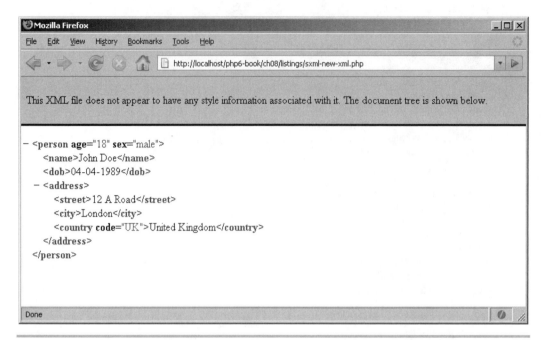

Figure 8-4 Dynamically generating a new XML document with SimpleXML

The script begins by initializing a string variable to hold the XML document prolog and root element. The `simplexml_load_string()` method takes care of converting this string into a SimpleXML object representing the document's root element. Once this object has been initialized, it's a simple matter to add child elements and attributes to it, and to build the rest of the XML document tree programmatically. Figure 8-4 shows the resulting XML document tree.

Try This 8-3 Reading RSS Feeds

RDF Site Summary (RSS) is an XML-based format originally devised by Netscape to distribute information about the content on its My.Netscape.com portal. Today, RSS is extremely popular on the Web as a way to distribute content; many Web sites offer RSS "feeds" that contain links and snippets of their latest news stories or content, and most browsers come with built-in RSS readers, which can be used to read and "subscribe" to these feeds.

An RSS document follows all the rules of XML markup and typically contains a list of resources (URLs), marked up with descriptive metadata. Here's an example:

```
<?xml version="1.0" encoding="utf-8"?>
<rss>
  <channel>
    <title>Feed title here</title>
    <link>Feed URL here</link>
    <description>Feed description here</description>
    <item>
      <title>Story title here</title>
      <description>Story description here</description>
      <link>Story URL here</link>
      <pubDate>Story timestamp here</pubDate>
    </item>
    <item>
      ...
    </item>
  </channel>
</rss>
```

As this sample document illustrates, an RSS document opens and closes with the `<rss>` element. A `<channel>` block contains general information about the Web site providing the feed; this is followed by multiple `<item>` elements, each of which represents a different content unit or news story. Each of these `<item>` elements further contains a title, a URL, and a description of the item.

Given this well-defined and hierarchical structure, parsing an RSS feed with SimpleXML is extremely simple. That's precisely what this next script does: it connects to a URL hosting a live RSS feed, retrieves the XML-encoded feed data, parses it, and converts it to an HTML page suitable for viewing in any Web browser. Here's the code (*rss2html.php*):

```
<!DOCTYPE html PUBLIC "-//W3C//DTD XHTML 1.0 Transitional//EN"
   "DTD/xhtml1-transitional.dtd">
<html xmlns="http://www.w3.org/1999/xhtml" xml:lang="en" lang="en">
  <head>
    <title>Project 8-3: Reading RSS Feeds</title>
    <style type="text/css">
    div.heading {
      font-weight: bolder;
    }
    div.story {
      background-color: white;
      border: 1px solid black;
```

(continued)

```
      width: 320px;
      height: 200px;
      margin: 20px;
    }
  div.headline a {
      font-weight: bolder;
      color: orange;
      margin: 5px;
    }
  div.body {
      margin: 5px;
    }
  div.timestamp {
      font-size: smaller;
      font-style: italic;
      margin: 5px;
    }
  ul {
      list-style-type: none;
    }
  li {
      float: left;
    }
    </style>
  </head>
  <body>
    <h2>Project 8-3: Reading RSS Feeds</h2>
<?php
// read newsvine.com's RSS feed for top technology news stories
$xml = simplexml_load_file("http://www.newsvine.com/_feeds/rss2
 /tag?id=technology") or die("ERROR: Cannot read RSS feed");
?>
    <h3 style="heading"><?php echo $xml->channel->title; ?></h3>
    <ul>
<?php
// iterate over list of stories
// print each story's title, URL and timestamp
// and then the story body
foreach ($xml->channel->item as $item) {
?>
      <li>
        <div class="story">
          <div class="headline">
            <a href="<?php echo $item->link; ?>">
              <?php echo $item->title; ?>
            </a>
          </div>
```

```
            <div class="timestamp"><?php echo $item->pubDate; ?></div>
            <div class="body"><?php echo $item->description; ?></div>
        </div>
      </li>
<?php
}
?>
    </ul>
  </body>
</html>
```

This script begins by using SimpleXML's `simplexml_load_file()` method to connect to a remote URL—in this case, an RSS feed hosted by NewsVine.com—and convert the XML data found therein to a SimpleXML object. It then uses SimpleXML's ability to loop over node collections to quickly retrieve each news story's title, URL, timestamp, and body; marks these bits of information up with HTML; and prints them to the page.

Figure 8-5 illustrates what the output might look like.

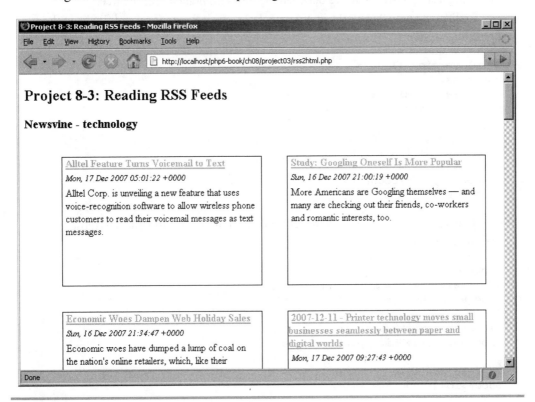

Figure 8-5 Parsing an RSS feed with SimpleXML

Using PHP's DOM Extension

Now, while PHP's SimpleXML extension is easy to use and understand, it's not very good for anything other than the most basic XML manipulation. For more complex XML operations, it's necessary to look further afield, to PHP's DOM extension. This extension, which is also enabled by default in PHP 5, provides a sophisticated toolkit that complies with the DOM Level 3 standard and brings comprehensive XML parsing capabilities to PHP.

Working with Elements

The DOM parser works by reading an XML document and creating objects to represent the different parts of that document. Each of these objects comes with specific methods and properties, which can be used to manipulate and access information about it. Thus, the entire XML document is represented as a "tree" of these objects, with the DOM parser providing a simple API to move between the different branches of the tree.

To illustrate how this works in practice, let's revisit the *address.xml* file from the preceding section:

```
<?xml version='1.0'?>
<address>
  <street>13 High Street</street>
  <county>Oxfordshire</county>
  <city>
    <name>Oxford</name>
    <zip>OX1 1BA</zip>
  </city>
  <country>UK</country>
</address>
```

Here's a PHP script that uses the DOM extension to parse this file and retrieve the various components of the address:

```php
<?php
// initialize new DOMDocument
$doc = new DOMDocument();

// disable whitespace-only text nodes
$doc->preserveWhiteSpace = false;

// read XML file
$doc->load('address.xml');

// get root element
$root = $doc->firstChild;
```

```
// get text node 'UK'
echo "Country: " . $root->childNodes->item(3)->nodeValue . "\n";

// get text node 'Oxford'
echo "City: " . $root->childNodes->item(2)->childNodes->
 item(0)->nodeValue . "\n";

// get text node 'OX1 1BA'
echo "Postal code: " . $root->childNodes->item(2)->childNodes->
 item(1)->nodeValue . "\n";

// output: 'Country: UK \n City: Oxford \n Postal code: OX1 1BA'
?>
```

A quick glance, and it's clear that we're not in SimpleXML territory any longer. With PHP's DOM extension, the first step is always to initialize an instance of the DOMDocument object, which represents an XML document. Once this object has been initialized, it can be used to parse an XML file via its load() method, which accepts the disk path to the target XML file.

The result of the load() method is a tree containing DOMNode objects, with every object exposing various properties and methods for accessing its parent, child, and sibling nodes. For example, every DOMNode object exposes a parentNode property, which can be used to access its parent node, and a childNodes property, which returns a collection of its child nodes. In a similar vein, every DOMNode object also exposes nodeName and nodeValue properties, which can be used to access the node's name and value respectively. It's thus quite easy to navigate from node to node of the tree, retrieving node values at each stage.

To illustrate the process, consider the preceding script carefully. Once the XML document has been load()-ed, it calls the DOMDocument object's firstChild property, which returns a DOMNode object representing the root element <address>. This DOMNode object, in turn, has a childNodes property, which returns a collection of all the child elements of <address>. Individual elements of this collection can be accessed via their index position using the item() method, with indexing starting from zero. These elements are again represented as DOMNode objects; as such, their names and values are therefore accessible via their nodeName and nodeValue properties.

Thus, the element <country>, which is the fourth child element under <address>, is accessible via the path $root->childNodes->item(3), and the text value of this element, 'UK', is accessible via the path $root->childNodes->item(3)->nodeValue. Similarly, the element <name>, which is the first child of the <city> element, is accessible via the path $root->childNodes->item(2)->childNodes->item(0), and the text value 'Oxford' is accessible via the path $root->childNodes->item(2)->childNodes->item(0)->nodeValue.

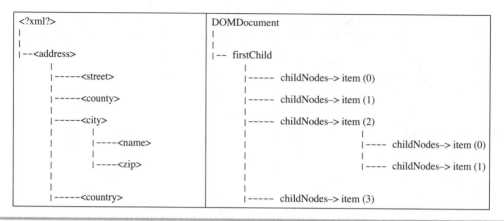

Figure 8-6 DOM relationships

Figure 8-6 should make these relationships clearer, by mapping the XML document tree from *address.xml* to the DOM methods and properties used in this section.

Ask the Expert

Q: When I process an XML document using the DOM, there often appear to be extra text nodes in each node collection. However, when I access these nodes, they appear to be empty. What's going on?

A: As per the DOM specification, all document whitespace, including carriage returns, must be treated as a text node. If your XML document contains extra whitespace, or if your XML elements are neatly formatted and indented on separate lines, this whitespace will be represented in your node collections as apparently empty text nodes. In the PHP DOM API, you can disable this behavior by setting the DOMDocument->preserveWhiteSpace property to 'false', as the examples in this section do.

An alternative approach—and one that can come in handy when you're faced with a deeply nested XML tree—is to use the DOMDocument object's getElementsByTagName() method to directly retrieve all elements with a particular name. The output of this method is a collection of matching DOMNode objects; it's then easy to iterate over the collection with a foreach loop and retrieve the value of each node.

If your document happens to have only one instance of each element—as is the case with *address.xml*—using getElementsByTagName() can serve as an effective shortcut to the traditional tree navigation approach. Consider the following example, which produces the same output as the preceding listing using this approach:

```php
<?php
// initialize new DOMDocument
$doc = new DOMDocument();

// disable whitespace-only text nodes
$doc->preserveWhiteSpace = false;

// read XML file
$doc->load('address.xml');

// get collection of <country> elements
$country = $doc->getElementsByTagName('country');
echo "Country: " . $country->item(0)->nodeValue . "\n";

// get collection of <name> elements
$city = $doc->getElementsByTagName('name');
echo "City: " . $city->item(0)->nodeValue . "\n";

// get collection of <zip> elements
$zip = $doc->getElementsByTagName('zip');
echo "Postal code: " . $zip->item(0)->nodeValue . "\n";

// output: 'Country: UK \n City: Oxford \n Postal code: OX1 1BA'
?>
```

In this example, the getElementsByTagName() method is used to return a DOMNode collection representing all elements with the name <country> in the first instance. From the XML document tree, it's clear that the collection will contain only one DOMNode object. Accessing the value of this node is then simply a matter of calling the collection's item() method with argument 0 (for the first index position) to get the DOMNode object, and then reading its nodeValue property.

In most cases, however, your XML document will not have only one instance of each element. Take, for example, the *library.xml* file you've seen in previous sections, which contains multiple instances of the <book> element. Even in such situations, the getElementsByTagName() method is useful to quickly and efficiently create a subset of matching nodes, which can be processed using a PHP loop. To illustrate, consider this next example, which reads *library.xml* and prints the title and author names found within it:

```php
<?php
// initialize new DOMDocument
$doc = new DOMDocument();

// disable whitespace-only text nodes
$doc->preserveWhiteSpace = false;

// read XML file
$doc->load('library.xml');

// get collection of <book> elements
// for each <book>, get the value of the <title> and <author> elements
// output: 'The Shining is written by Stephen King. \n ...'
$books = $doc->getElementsByTagName('book');
foreach ($books as $book) {
  $title = $book->getElementsByTagName('title')->item(0)->nodeValue;
  $author = $book->getElementsByTagName('author')->item(0)->nodeValue;
  echo  "$title is written by $author.\n";
}
?>
```

In this case, the first call to getElementsByTagName() returns a collection representing all the <book> elements from the XML document. It's then easy to iterate over this collection with a foreach() loop, processing each DOMNode object and retrieving the value of the corresponding <title> and <author> elements with further calls to getElementsByTagName().

TIP
You can return a collection of all the elements in a document by calling DOMDocument-> getElementsByTagName(*).

To find out how many elements were returned by a call to getElementsByTagName(), use the resulting collection's length property. Here's an example:

```php
<?php
// initialize new DOMDocument
$doc = new DOMDocument();

// disable whitespace-only text nodes
$doc->preserveWhiteSpace = false;
```

```
// read XML file
$doc->load('library.xml');

// get collection of <book> elements
// return a count of the total number of <book> elements
// output: '8 book(s) found.'
$books = $doc->getElementsByTagName('book');
echo $books->length . ' book(s) found.';
?>
```

Working with Attributes

The DOM also includes extensive support for attributes: every DOMElement object comes with a getAttribute() method, which accepts an attribute name and returns the corresponding value. Here's an example, which prints each book's rating and genre from *library.xml*:

```
<?php
// initialize new DOMDocument
$doc = new DOMDocument();

// disable whitespace-only text nodes
$doc->preserveWhiteSpace = false;

// read XML file
$doc->load('library.xml');

// get collection of <book> elements
// for each book
// retrieve and print 'genre' and 'rating' attributes
// output: 'The Shining \n Genre: horror \n Rating: 5 \n\n ...'
$books = $doc->getElementsByTagName('book');
foreach ($books as $book) {
  $title = $book->getElementsByTagName('title')->item(0)->nodeValue;
  $rating = $book->getAttribute('rating');
  $genre = $book->getAttribute('genre');
  echo "$title\n";
  echo "Genre: $genre\n";
  echo "Rating: $rating\n\n";
}
?>
```

What if you don't know the attribute name but simply want to process all attributes of an element? Well, every DOMElement has an attributes property, which returns a collection of all the element's attributes. It's easy to iterate over this collection to retrieve each attribute's name and value. The following example demonstrates, by revising the preceding script to use this approach:

```php
<?php
// initialize new DOMDocument
$doc = new DOMDocument();

// disable whitespace-only text nodes
$doc->preserveWhiteSpace = false;

// read XML file
$doc->load('library.xml');

// get collection of <book> elements
// for each book
// retrieve and print all attributes
// output: 'The Shining \n id: 1 \n genre: horror \n rating: 5 \n\n ...'
$books = $doc->getElementsByTagName('book');
foreach ($books as $book) {
  $title = $book->getElementsByTagName('title')->item(0)->nodeValue;
  echo "$title\n";
  foreach ($book->attributes as $attr) {
    echo "$attr->name: $attr->value \n";
  }
  echo "\n";
}
?>
```

Try This 8-4   Recursively Processing an XML Document Tree

If you plan to work with XML and PHP in the future, this next project will almost certainly come in handy some day: it's a simple program that starts at the root of the XML document tree and works its way through to the ends of its branches, processing every element and attribute it finds on the way. Given the tree-like nature of an XML document, the most efficient way to accomplish this task is with a recursive function—and given the wealth of information supplied by the DOM, writing such a function is quite easy.

Assume for a moment that the XML document to be processed looks like this (*inventory.xml*):

```xml
<?xml version='1.0'?>
<objects>
  <object color="red" shape="square">
```

```
    <length units="cm">5</length>
  </object>
  <object color="red" shape="circle">
    <radius units="px">7</radius>
  </object>
  <object color="green" shape="triangle">
    <base units="in">1</base>
    <height units="in">2</height>
  </object>
  <object color="blue" shape="triangle">
    <base units="mm">100</base>
    <height units="mm">50</height>
  </object>
  <object color="yellow" shape="circle">
    <radius units="cm">18</radius>
  </object>
</objects>
```

And here's the PHP code to recursively process this (or any other) XML document using the DOM:

```
<!DOCTYPE html PUBLIC "-//W3C//DTD XHTML 1.0 Transitional//EN"
    "DTD/xhtml1-transitional.dtd">
<html xmlns="http://www.w3.org/1999/xhtml" xml:lang="en" lang="en">
  <head>
    <title>Project 8-4: Recursively Processing An XML Document</title>
  </head>
  <body>
    <h2>Project 8-4: Recursively Processing An XML Document</h2>
    <pre>
<?php
// recursive function to process XML node collection
function xmlProcess($node, $depthMarker) {

  // process this node's children
  foreach ($node->childNodes as $n) {
    switch ($n->nodeType) {

      // for elements, print element name
      case XML_ELEMENT_NODE:
        echo "$depthMarker <b>$n->nodeName</b> \n";
        // if the element has attributes
        // list their names and values
        if ($n->attributes->length > 0) {
          foreach ($n->attributes as $attr) {
            echo "$depthMarker  <i>attr</i>: $attr->name => $attr->value \n";
          }
        }
        break;
```

(continued)

```
    // for text data, print value
    case XML_TEXT_NODE:
      echo "$depthMarker <i>text</i>: \"$n->nodeValue\" \n";
      break;
  }

  // if this node has a further level of sub-nodes
  // increment depth marker
  // run recursively
  if ($n->hasChildNodes()) {
    xmlProcess($n, $depthMarker . DEPTH_CHAR);
  }
  }
}
}
// end function definition

// define the character used for indentation
define ('DEPTH_CHAR', ' ');

// initialize DOMDocument
$doc = new DOMDocument();

// disable whitespace-only text nodes
$doc->preserveWhiteSpace = false;

// read XML file
$doc->load('objects.xml');

// call recursive function with root element
xmlProcess($doc->firstChild, DEPTH_CHAR);
?>
    </pre>
  </body>
</html>
```

In this program, the user-defined xmlProcess() function is a recursive function that works by accepting a DOMNode object as input, retrieving a collection of this node's children by reading the object's childNodes property, and iterating over this collection with a foreach loop. Depending on whether the current node is an element node or a text node, it prints either the node name or the node value. If the node is an element node, it performs an additional step of checking for attributes and printing those as necessary. A "depth string" is used to indicate the hierarchical position of the node in the output; this string is automatically incremented every time the loop runs.

Having completed all these tasks, the last action of the function is to check whether the current node has any children; if it does, it calls itself recursively to process the next level of the node tree. The process continues until no further nodes remain to be processed.

Figure 8-7 illustrates the output of the program when xmlProcess() is called with the document's root element as input argument.

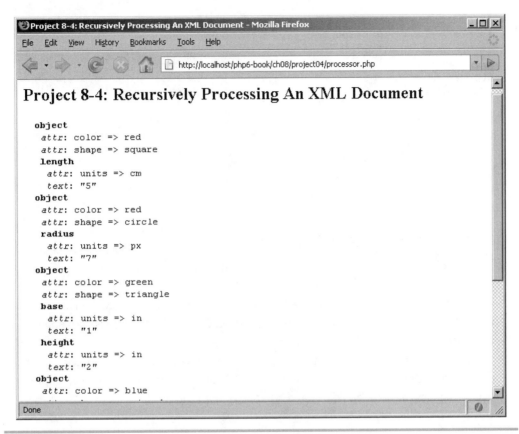

Figure 8-7 Recursively processing an XML document with the DOM

Altering Element and Attribute Values

Under the DOM, changing the value of an XML element is quite simple: navigate to the DOMNode object representing the element and alter its nodeValue property to reflect the new value. To illustrate, consider the following PHP script, which changes the title and author of the second book in *library.xml*, and then outputs the revised XML document:

```php
<?php
// initialize new DOMDocument
$doc = new DOMDocument();

// disable whitespace-only text nodes
$doc->preserveWhiteSpace = false;

// read XML file
$doc->load('library.xml');
```

```php
// get collection of <book> elements
$books = $doc->getElementsByTagName('book');

// change the <title> element of the second <book>
$books->item(1)->getElementsByTagName('title')->item(0)->nodeValue =
'Invisible Prey';

// change the <author> element of the second <book>
$books->item(1)->getElementsByTagName('author')->item(0)->nodeValue =
'John Sandford';

// output new XML string
header('Content-Type: text/xml');
echo $doc->saveXML();
?>
```

Here, the `getElementsByTagName()` method is used to first obtain a collection of
<book> elements and navigate to the second element in this collection (index position: 1).
It's then used again, to obtain references to DOMNode objects representing the <title>
and <author> element. The `nodeValue` properties of these objects are then assigned
new values using PHP's assignment operator, and the revised XML tree is converted back
into a string with the DOMDocument object's `saveXML()` method.

Changing attribute values is just as easy: assign a new value to an attribute using the
corresponding DOMElement object's `setAttribute()` method. Here's an example,
which changes the sixth book's `'rating'` and outputs the result:

```php
<?php
// initialize new DOMDocument
$doc = new DOMDocument();

// disable whitespace-only text nodes
$doc->preserveWhiteSpace = false;

// read XML file
$doc->load('library.xml');

// get collection of <book> elements
$books = $doc->getElementsByTagName('book');

// change the 'genre' element of the fifth <book>
$books->item(4)->setAttribute('genre', 'horror-suspense');

// output new XML string
header('Content-Type: text/xml');
echo $doc->saveXML();
?>
```

Creating New XML Documents

The DOM comes with a full-fledged API for creating new XML documents, or for grafting elements, attributes, and other XML structures on to an existing XML document tree. This API, which is much more sophisticated than that offered by SimpleXML, should be your first choice when dynamically creating or modifying an XML document tree through PHP.

The best way to illustrate this API is with an example. Consider the following script, which sets up a new XML file from scratch:

```php
<?php
// initialize new DOMDocument
$doc = new DOMDocument('1.0');

// create and attach root element <schedule>
$root = $doc->createElement('schedule');
$schedule = $doc->appendChild($root);

// create and attach <course> element under <schedule>
$course = $doc->createElement('course');
$schedule->appendChild($course);

// create and attach <title> element under <course>
// add a value for the <title> element
$title = $doc->createElement('title');
$titleData = $doc->createTextNode('Macro-Economics');
$course->appendChild($title);
$title->appendChild($titleData);

// create and attach <teacher> element under <course>
// add a value for the <teacher> element
$teacher = $doc->createElement('teacher');
$teacherData = $doc->createTextNode('Professor Q. Draw');
$course->appendChild($teacher);
$teacher->appendChild($teacherData);

// create and attach <credits> element under <course>
// add a value for the <credits> element
$credits = $doc->createElement('credits');
$creditData = $doc->createTextNode('4');
$course->appendChild($credits);
$credits->appendChild($creditData);

// attach an attribute 'transferable' to the <credits> element
// set a value for the attribute
$transferable = $doc->createAttribute('transferable');
```

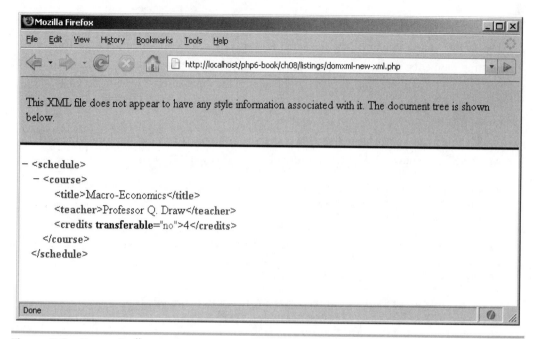

Figure 8-8 Dynamically generating a new XML document with the DOM

```
$credits->appendChild($transferable);
$credits->setAttribute('transferable', 'no');

// format XML output
$doc->formatOutput = true;

// output new XML string
header('Content-Type: text/xml');
echo $doc->saveXML();
?>
```

Figure 8-8 illustrates the XML document generated by this script.

This script introduces some new methods, all related to dynamically creating XML nodes and attaching them to an XML document tree. There are two basic steps involved in this process:

1. Create an object representing the XML structure you wish to add. The base DOMDocument object exposes create...() methods corresponding to each of the primary XML structures: createElement() for element objects, createAttribute() for attribute objects, and createTextNode() for character data.

2. Attach the newly minted object at the appropriate point in the document tree, by calling the parent's `appendChild()` method.

The previous listing illustrates these steps, following a specific sequence to arrive at the result tree shown in Figure 8-8.

1. It begins by first initializing a DOMDocument object named `$doc` and then calling its `createElement()` method to generate a new DOMElement object named `$schedule`. This object represents the document's root element; as such, it is attached to the base of the DOM tree by calling the `$doc->appendChild()` method.

2. One level below the root `<schedule>` element comes a `<course>` element. In DOM terms, this is accomplished by creating a new DOMElement object named `$course` with the DOMDocument object's `createElement()` method, and then attaching this object to the tree under the `<schedule>` element by calling `$schedule->appendChild()`.

3. One level below the `<course>` element comes a `<title>` element. Again, this is accomplished by creating a DOMElement object named `$title` and then attaching this object under `<course>` by calling `$course->appendChild()`. There's a twist here, though: the `<title>` element contains the text value `'Macro-Economics'`. To create this text value, the script creates a new DOMTextNode object via the `createTextNode()` object, populates it with the text string, and then attaches it as a child of the `<title>` element by calling `$title->appendChild()`.

4. The same thing happens a little further along, when creating the `<credits>` element. Once the element and its text value have been defined and attached to the document tree under the `<course>` element, the `createAttribute()` method is used to create a new DOMAttr object to represent the attribute `'transferable'`. This attribute is then attached to the `<credits>` element by calling `$credits->appendChild()`, and a value is assigned to the attribute in the normal fashion, by calling `$credits->setAttribute()`.

Converting Between DOM and SimpleXML

An interesting feature in PHP is the ability to convert XML data between DOM and SimpleXML. This is accomplished by means of two functions: the `simplexml_import_dom()` function, which accepts a DOMElement object and returns a SimpleXML object, and the `dom_import_simplexml()` function, which does the reverse. The following example illustrates this interoperability:

```php
<?php
// initialize new DOMDocument
$doc = new DOMDocument();

// disable whitespace-only text nodes
$doc->preserveWhiteSpace = false;

// read XML file
$doc->load('library.xml');

// get collection of <book> elements
$books = $doc->getElementsByTagName('book');

// convert the sixth <book> to a SimpleXML object
// print title of sixth book
// output: 'Glory Road'
$sxml = simplexml_import_dom($books->item(5));
echo $sxml->title;
?>
```

Try This 8-5 Reading and Writing XML Configuration Files

Now that you know how to read and create XML document trees programmatically, let's use this knowledge in an application that's increasingly popular these days: XML-based configuration files, which use XML to mark up an application's configuration data.

The next listing illustrates this in action, generating a Web form that allows users to configure an oven online by entering configuration value for temperature, mode, and heat source. When the form is submitted, the data entered by the user is converted to XML and saved to a disk file. When users revisit the form, the data previously saved to the file is read and used to prefill the form's fields.

Here's the code (*configure.php*):

```php
<!DOCTYPE html PUBLIC "-//W3C//DTD XHTML 1.0 Transitional//EN"
    "DTD/xhtml1-transitional.dtd">
<html xmlns="http://www.w3.org/1999/xhtml" xml:lang="en" lang="en">
  <head>
    <title>Project 8-5: Reading And Writing XML Configuration Files</title>
  </head>
```

```php
  <body>
    <h2>Project 8-5: Reading And Writing XML Configuration Files</h2>
    <h3 style="background-color: silver">Oven Configuration</h3>
<?php
    // define configuration file name and path
    $configFile = 'config.xml';

    // if form not yet submitted
    // display form
    if (!isset($_POST['submit'])) {

      // set up array with default parameters
      $data = array();
      $data['mode'] = null;
      $data['temperature'] = null;
      $data['duration'] = null;
      $data['direction'] = null;
      $data['autooff'] = null;

      // read current configuration values
      // use them to pre-fill the form
      if (file_exists($configFile)) {
        $doc = new DOMDocument();
        $doc->preserveWhiteSpace = false;
        $doc->load($configFile);
        $oven = $doc->getElementsByTagName('oven');
        foreach ($oven->item(0)->childNodes as $node) {
          $data[$node->nodeName] = $node->nodeValue;
        }
      }
    }
?>
    <form method="post" action="configure.php">
      Mode: <br />
      <select name="data[mode]">
        <option value="grill" <?php echo ($data['mode'] == 'grill') ?
'selected' : null; ?>>Grill</option>
        <option value="bake" <?php echo ($data['mode'] == 'bake') ?
'selected' : null; ?>>Bake</option>
        <option value="toast" <?php echo ($data['mode'] == 'toast') ?
'selected' : null; ?>>Toast</option>
      </select>

      <p>

      Temperature: <br />
      <input type="text" size="2" name="data[temperature]"  value="<?php echo
$data['temperature']; ?>"/>

      <p>
```

(continued)

```
       Duration (minutes): <br />
       <input type="text" size="2" name="data[duration]" value="<?php echo
$data['duration']; ?>"/>

       <p>

       Heat source and direction: <br />
       <input type="radio" name="data[direction]" value="top-down" <?php echo
($data['direction'] == 'top-down') ? 'checked' : null; ?>>Top, downwards</input>
       <input type="radio" name="data[direction]" value="bottom-up" <?php echo
($data['direction'] == 'bottom-up') ? 'checked' : null; ?>>Bottom, upwards
</input>
       <input type="radio" name="data[direction]" value="both" <?php echo
($data['direction'] == 'both') ? 'checked' : null; ?>>Both</input>

       <p>

       Automatically power off when done:
       <input type="checkbox" name="data[autooff]" value="yes" <?php echo
($data['autooff'] == 'yes') ? 'checked' : null; ?>/>

       <p>

       <input type="submit" name="submit" value="Submit" />
    </form>
<?php
    // if form submitted
    // process form input
    } else {
    // read submitted data
    $config = $_POST['data'];

    // validate submitted data as necessary

    if ((trim($config['temperature']) == '') || (trim($config['temperature'])
!= '' && (int)$config['temperature'] <= 0)) {
       die('ERROR: Please enter a valid oven temperature');
    }

    if ((trim($config['duration']) == '') || (trim($config['duration']) != ''
&& (int)$config['duration'] <= 0)) {
       die('ERROR: Please enter a valid duration');
    }

    // generate new XML document
    $doc = new DOMDocument();

    // create and attach root element <configuration>
    $root = $doc->createElement('configuration');
    $configuration = $doc->appendChild($root);
```

```
      // create and attach <oven> element under <schedule>
      $oven = $doc->createElement('oven');
      $configuration->appendChild($oven);

      // write each configuration value to the file
      foreach ($config as $key => $value) {
        if (trim($value) != '') {
          $elem = $doc->createElement($key);
          $text = $doc->createTextNode($value);
          $oven->appendChild($elem);
          $elem->appendChild($text);
        }
      }

      // format XML output
      // save XML file
      $doc->formatOutput = true;
      $doc->save($configFile) or die('ERROR: Cannot write configuration file');
      echo 'Configuration data successfully written to file.';
    }
?>
  </body>
</html>
```

Figure 8-9 illustrates the Web form generated by this script.

Once this form is submitted, the data entered into it arrives in the form of an associative array, whose keys correspond to XML element names. This data is first validated, and the DOM API is then used to generate a new XML document tree containing these elements and their values. Once the tree is completely generated, the DOMDocument object's save() function is used to write the XML to a disk file.

Here's an example of what the XML output file *config.xml* would look like after submitting the form in Figure 8-9:

```
<?xml version="1.0"?>
<configuration>
  <oven>
    <mode>toast</mode>
    <temperature>22</temperature>
    <duration>1</duration>
    <direction>bottom-up</direction>
    <autooff>yes</autooff>
  </oven>
</configuration>
```

If a user revisits the Web form, the script first checks if a configuration file named *config.xml* exists in the current directory. If it does, the XML data in the file is read into a new DOMDocument object with the load() method and converted into an associative

(continued)

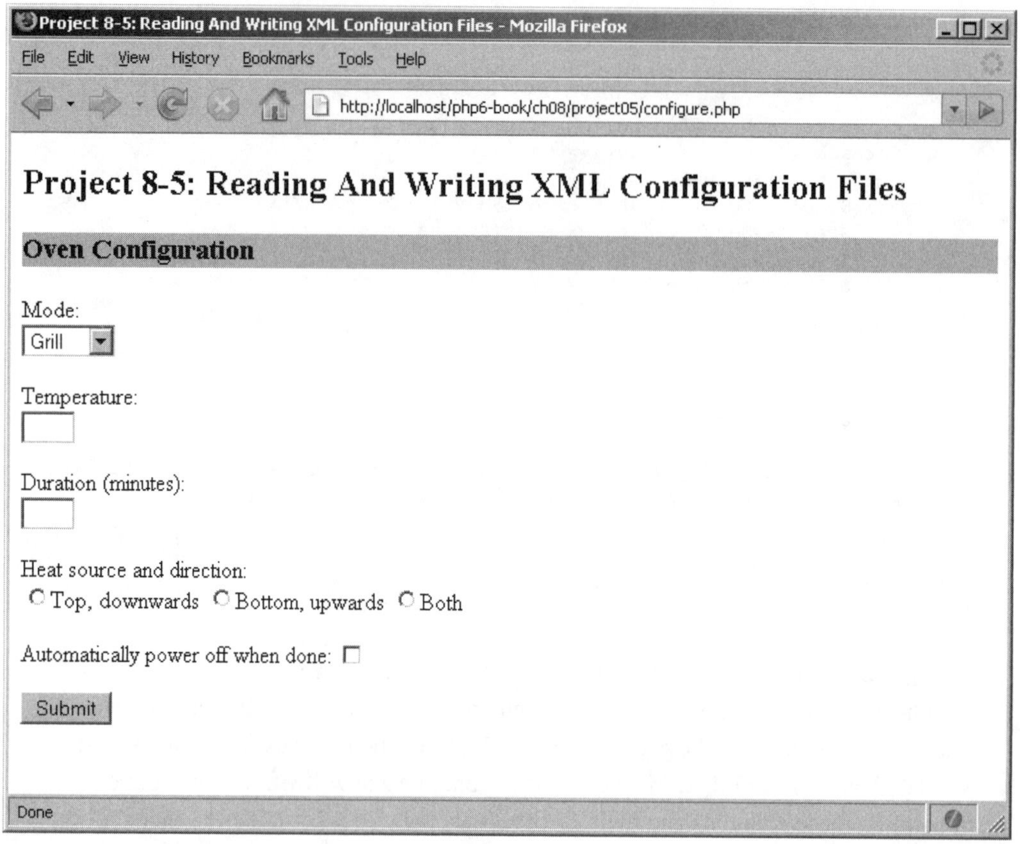

Figure 8-9 A Web form for configuration data

array by iterating over the list of child nodes in a loop. The various radio buttons, check boxes, and selection lists in the form are then checked or preselected, depending on the values in this array.

Figure 8-10 illustrates the form, prefilled with data read from the XML configuration file.

If the user submits the Web form with new values, these new values will again be encoded in XML and used to rewrite the configuration file. Because the configuration is expressed in XML, any application that has XML parsing capabilities can read and use this data. XML, when used in this fashion, thus provides a way to transfer information between applications, even if they're written in different programming languages or run on incompatible operating systems.

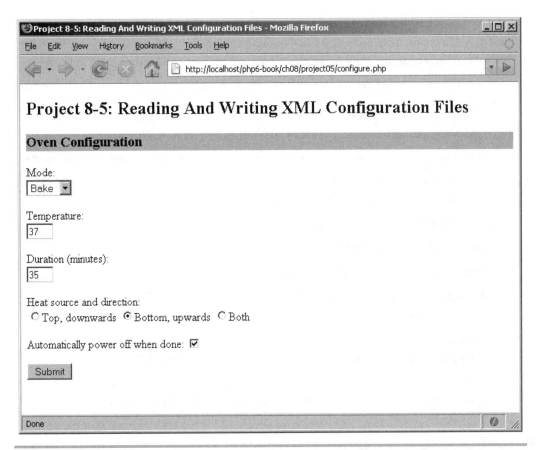

Figure 8-10   The same Web form, prefilled with configuration data

Summary

At the end of this chapter, you should know enough to begin writing PHP programs that can successfully interact with XML-encoded data. This chapter began with an introduction to XML, explaining basic XML structures like elements, attributes, and character data, and providing a crash course in XML technologies and parsing methods. It then proceeded into a discussion of two of PHP's most popular extensions for XML processing, the SimpleXML and DOM extensions, and showed you how each of these extensions could be used to access element and attribute values, create node collections, and programmatically generate or change XML document trees. Various projects, ranging from an XML-to-SQL converter to an RSS feed parser, were used to illustrate practical applications of the interface between XML and PHP.

XML is an extensive topic, and the material in this chapter barely begins to scratch its surface. However, there are many excellent tutorials and articles on XML and PHP on the Web, and links to some of these are presented here, should you be interested in learning more about this interesting and continually changing field:

- XML basics, at **www.melonfire.com/community/columns/trog/article.php?id=78** and **www.melonfire.com/community/columns/trog/article.php?id=79**

- XPath basics, at **www.melonfire.com/community/columns/trog/article.php?id=83**

- XSL basics, at **www.melonfire.com/community/columns/trog/article.php?id=82** and **www.melonfire.com/community/columns/trog/article.php?id=85**

- SimpleXML functions, at **www.php.net/simplexml**

- DOM API functions in PHP, at **www.php.net/dom**

- The DOM specification, at **www.w3.org/DOM/**

- Building XML documents using PHP and PEAR, at **www.melonfire.com/community/columns/trog/article.php?id=180**

- Serializing XML, at **www.melonfire.com/community/columns/trog/article.php?id=244**

- Performing XML-based Remote Procedure Calls (RPC) with PHP, at **www.melonfire.com/community/columns/trog/article.php?id=274**

Chapter 8 Self Test

1. What are the two methods of parsing an XML document, and how do they differ?

2. Name two characteristics of a well-formed XML document.

3. Given the following XML document (*email.xml*), write a program to retrieve and print all the e-mail addresses from the document using SimpleXML:

```
<?xml version='1.0'?>
<data>
  <person>
    <name>Clone One</name>
    <email>one@domain.com</name>
  </person>
  <person>
    <name>Clone SixtyFour</name>
    <email>sixtyfour@domain.com</name>
  </person>
```

```
<person>
  <name>Clone Three</name>
  <email>three@domain.com</name>
</person>
<person>
  <name>Clone NinetyNine</name>
  <email>ninetynine@domain.com</name>
</person>
</data>
```

4. Given the following XML document (*tree.xml*), suggest three different ways to retrieve the text value 'John' using the DOM:

```
<?xml version='1.0'?>
<tree>
  <person type="grandpa" />
  <person type="grandma" />
  <children>
    <person type="pa" />
    <person type="ma" />
    <children>
      <person type="bro">
        <name>John</name>
      </person>
      <person type="sis">
        <name>Jane</name>
      </person>
    </children>
  </children>
</tree>
```

5. Write a program to count the number of elements in an XML file. Use the DOM.

6. Write a program to process the *library.xml* file from earlier in this chapter, increase each book's rating by 1, and print the revised output. Use SimpleXML.

7. Write a program that connects to a MySQL database and retrieves the contents of any one of its tables as an XML file. Use the DOM.

Chapter 9

Working with Cookies, Sessions, and Headers

Key Skills & Concepts

- Understand how cookies work

- Set and use your own cookies to create "sticky" pages

- Share data between pages with sessions and session variables

- Manipulate the user's browser by sending it customized HTTP headers

You probably already know that the Hypertext Transfer Protocol (HTTP) is the standard protocol used to transfer data between your browser and the various Web sites you visit. What you may not know, however, is that HTTP is a "stateless" protocol, which treats each request for a Web page as a unique and independent transaction, with no relationship whatsoever to the transactions that preceded it. To work around this problem, most Web sites use cookies or sessions to "maintain state," in order to offer enhanced services—for example, shopping carts or automatic restoration of personal settings—to site users.

PHP includes full-featured support for cookies and sessions. Using this built-in support, it's easy to create sessions and cookies, store and retrieve user-specific data in them, manipulate them from within your PHP application, and even send custom headers to the user's browser to alter its default behavior. This chapter will show you how, with some practical examples of how useful these features can be when building Web sites and applications.

Working with Cookies

Cookies aren't particularly difficult to get your mind around, but there are some basic concepts you need to be familiar with before you begin writing your own cookie-handling code. The following section will introduce you to these basic concepts.

Cookie Basics

In its simplest form, a *cookie* is a text file saved to a user's system by a Web site. This file contains information that the site can retrieve on the user's next visit, thereby allowing the site to "recognize" the user and provide an enhanced set of features customized to that specific user. Common examples of such features include displaying site content that is personalized according to the user's settings, maintaining a record of the content previously viewed by the user, and integrating personal user information into site display and layout.

Because cookies facilitate data transfer between a user and a remote Web site, they've often been vilified in the media as "insecure" and "bad." In truth, much of this is exaggeration: while cookies (like any other technology) can certainly be misused, most Web sites' usage of cookies is harmless and can be directly linked to enhancing the user experience. In addition, cookies also have some important security features, as follows:

- A cookie can only be read by the Web site or domain that created it.
- A single domain cannot set more than 20 cookies.
- A single cookie cannot exceed 4 kilobytes in size.
- The maximum number of cookies that may be set on a user's system is 300.

CAUTION
Since cookies are stored on the user's hard drive, developers have very little control over them. If a user decides to "turn off" cookie support in his or her browser, your cookies will simply not be saved. Therefore, if data persistence is an important feature of your Web site, have a backup plan (such as server-side cookies or sessions) ready as well.

Cookie Attributes

A typical Web site cookie contains fewer ingredients than the baked variety—five, to be precise. Table 9-1 has a list.

1. Every cookie contains a name-value pair, which represents the variable name and corresponding value to be stored in the cookie.

Attribute	Description	Example
`name=value`	The cookie name and value	`'email=myself@some.domain.com'`
`expires`	The validity of the cookie	`'expires=Friday, 25-Jan-08 23:59:50 IST'`
`domain`	The domain associated with the cookie	`'domain=.thiswebsite.com'`
`path`	The domain path associated with the cookie	`'path=/'`
`secure`	If present, a secure HTTP connection is required to read the cookie	`'secure'`

Table 9-1 Cookie Attributes

2. A cookie's `'expires'` attribute defines how long the cookie is valid for. Setting this attribute's value to a date in the past will usually cause the browser to delete the cookie.

3. A cookie's `'domain'` attribute defines the domain name to be associated with the cookie. Only this domain will be able to access the information in the cookie.

4. A cookie's `'path'` attribute defines which sections of the domain specified in the `'domain'` attribute can access the cookie. Setting this to the server root (/) allows the entire domain access to the information stored in the cookie.

5. A cookie's `'secure'` attribute indicates whether a secure HTTP connection is mandatory before the cookie can be accessed.

Cookie Headers

Cookies are transmitted between the user's browser and a remote Web site by means of HTTP headers. For example, to set a cookie, a Web site must send the user's browser a `'Set-Cookie:'` header containing the necessary attributes. The following example illustrates the headers sent to create two cookies for a domain:

```
Set-Cookie: username=john; path=/; domain=.thiswebsite.com;
expires=Friday, 25-Jan-08 23:59:50 IST
Set-Cookie: location=UK; path=/; domain=.thiswebsite.com;
expires=Friday, 25-Jan-08 23:59:50 IST
```

Similarly, if a particular cookie is valid for a Web site and path, the user's browser automatically includes the cookie information in a `'Cookie:'` header when requesting the site URL. Using the preceding example, when the user next visits the thiswebsite.com domain, the browser will automatically include the following header in its request:

```
Cookie: username=john; location=UK
```

Ask the Expert

Q: Can I read the cookies stored on my system?

A: Cookies are text files stored on your system and, as such, can be read with any text editor. The exact location of the cookie repository on your system depends on which browser and operating system you're using. As an example, under Microsoft Windows, Internet Explorer stores its cookies as separate files under *C:/Documents and Settings/[username]/cookies,* while Mozilla Firefox stores all its cookies in a single file at *C:/Documents and Settings/[username]/Application Data/Mozilla/ Firefox/Profiles/[profilename]/cookies.txt.*

Setting Cookies

PHP's cookie-manipulation API is very simple: it consists of a single function, setcookie(), which can be used to both set and remove cookies. This function accepts six arguments: the cookie's name and value, its expiry date in UNIX timestamp format, its domain and path, and a Boolean flag for the 'secure' attribute. The function returns true if the cookie header was successfully transmitted to the user's system; however, this does not indicate if the cookie was successfully set or not (if the user's browser is set to reject all cookies, a cookie header might be successfully transmitted but the cookie might not actually be set on the user's system).

Here's an example, which sets a cookie containing the user's e-mail address:

```php
<?php
// set a cookie
setcookie('email', 'john@somewebsite.com', mktime()+129600, '/');
?>
```

It's possible to set multiple cookies, simply by calling setcookie() once for each cookie. Here's an example, which sets three cookies with different validity periods and paths:

```php
<?php
// set multiple cookies
setcookie('username', 'whitewhale', mktime()+129600, '/');
setcookie('email', 'john@somewebsite.com', mktime()+86400, '/');
setcookie('role', 'moderator', mktime()+3600, '/admin');
?>
```

CAUTION
Because cookies are set using HTTP headers, calls to setcookie() must precede any output generated by your script. A failure to adhere to this rule will not only prevent the cookie from being set, but will also generate a series of PHP error messages.

Reading Cookies

Cookies set for a domain become available in the special $_COOKIE associative array in PHP scripts running on that domain. These cookies may be accessed using standard array notation. Here's an example:

```php
<?php
// read cookie
if (isset($_COOKIE['email'])) {
  echo 'Welcome back, ' . $_COOKIE['email'] . '!';
} else {
  echo 'Hello, new user!';
}
?>
```

Removing Cookies

To delete a cookie, use `setcookie()` with its name to set the cookie's expiry date to a value in the past, as shown here:

```php
<?php
// remove cookie
$ret = setcookie('role', 'moderator', mktime()-1600, '/admin');
if ($ret) {
  echo 'Cookie headers successfully transmitted.';
}
?>
```

Try This 9-1   Saving and Restoring User Preferences

Let's now build a simple application that uses cookies to save and restore user preferences. The Web form in the next listing asks the user to select his or her preferences on a long flight, and stores these preferences in a cookie on the user's system. When the user returns to the page, the previously set preferences are read from the cookie and automatically restored.

Here's the code (*flight-prefs.php*):

```php
<?php
// if form submitted
// write cookie with settings
if (isset($_POST['submit'])) {
  $ret1 = (isset($_POST['name'])) ? setcookie('name', $_POST['name'],
mktime() + 36400, '/') : null;
  $ret2 = (isset($_POST['seat'])) ? setcookie('seat', $_POST['seat'],
mktime() + 36400, '/') : null;
  $ret3 = (isset($_POST['meal'])) ? setcookie('meal', $_POST['meal'],
mktime() + 36400, '/') : null;
  $ret4 = (isset($_POST['offers'])) ? setcookie('offers', implode(',',
$_POST['offers']), mktime() + 36400, '/') : null;
}

// read cookie and assign cookie values
// to PHP variables
$name = isset($_COOKIE['name']) ? $_COOKIE['name'] : '';
$seat = isset($_COOKIE['seat']) ? $_COOKIE['seat'] : '';
$meal = isset($_COOKIE['meal']) ? $_COOKIE['meal'] : '';
$offers = isset($_COOKIE['offers']) ? explode(',',$_COOKIE['offers'])
: array();
?>
```

```
<!DOCTYPE html PUBLIC "-//W3C//DTD XHTML 1.0 Transitional//EN"
   "DTD/xhtml1-transitional.dtd">
<html xmlns="http://www.w3.org/1999/xhtml" xml:lang="en" lang="en">
  <head>
    <title>Project 9-1: Saving and Restoring User Preferences</title>
  </head>
  <body>
    <h2>Project 9-1: Saving and Restoring User Preferences</h2>
    <h3>Set Your Flight Preferences</h3>
    <?php
    // if form submitted
    // display success message
    if (isset($_POST['submit'])) {
    ?>
    Thank you for your submission.
    <?php
    // if form not submitted
    // display form
    } else {
    ?>
    <form method="post" action="flight-prefs.php">
      Name: <br />
      <input type="text" size="20" name="name" value="<?php echo
$name; ?>" />

      <p>

      Seat selection: <br />
      <input type="radio" name="seat" value="aisle" <?php echo
($seat == 'aisle') ? 'checked' : ''; ?>>Aisle</input>
      <input type="radio" name="seat" value="window" <?php echo
($seat == 'window') ? 'checked' : ''; ?>>Window</input>
      <input type="radio" name="seat" value="center" <?php echo
($seat == 'center') ? 'checked' : ''; ?>>Center</input>

      <p>

      Meal selection: <br />
      <input type="radio" name="meal" value="normal-veg" <?php echo
($meal == 'normal-veg') ? 'checked' : ''; ?>>Vegetarian</input>
      <input type="radio" name="meal" value="normal-nveg" <?php echo
($meal == 'normal-nveg') ? 'checked' : ''; ?>>Non-vegetarian</input>
      <input type="radio" name="meal" value="diabetic" <?php echo
($meal == 'diabetic') ? 'checked' : ''; ?>>Diabetic</input>
      <input type="radio" name="meal" value="child" <?php echo
($meal == 'child') ? 'checked' : ''; ?>>Child</input>
```

(continued)

```
      <p>

      I'm interested in special offers on flights from: <br />
      <input type="checkbox" name="offers[]" value="LHR" <?php echo
in_array('LHR', $offers) ? 'checked' : ''; ?>>London (Heathrow)</
input>
      <input type="checkbox" name="offers[]" value="CDG" <?php echo
in_array('CDG', $offers) ? 'checked' : ''; ?>>Paris</input>
      <input type="checkbox" name="offers[]" value="CIA" <?php echo
in_array('CIA', $offers) ? 'checked' : ''; ?>>Rome (Ciampino)</input>
      <input type="checkbox" name="offers[]" value="IBZ" <?php echo
in_array('IBZ', $offers) ? 'checked' : ''; ?>>Ibiza</input>
      <input type="checkbox" name="offers[]" value="SIN" <?php echo
in_array('SIN', $offers) ? 'checked' : ''; ?>>Singapore</input>
      <input type="checkbox" name="offers[]" value="HKG" <?php echo
in_array('HKG', $offers) ? 'checked' : ''; ?>>Hong Kong</input>
      <input type="checkbox" name="offers[]" value="MLA" <?php echo
in_array('MLA', $offers) ? 'checked' : ''; ?>>Malta</input>
      <input type="checkbox" name="offers[]" value="BOM" <?php echo
in_array('BOM', $offers) ? 'checked' : ''; ?>>Bombay</input>

      <p>

      <input type="submit" name="submit" value="Submit" />
    </form>
    <?php
    }
    ?>
  </body>
</html>
```

This Web form contains various fields for the user to enter his or her name, select a seat and meal type, and sign up for special offers. Figure 9-1 illustrates what this Web form looks like.

When this form is submitted, the choices selected by the user are saved to cookies on the user's system. As a result, every time the user revisits the Web form, this cookie data is automatically read by PHP into the $_COOKIE array. The Web form can then use this cookie data to preselect and prefill the form fields according to the user's last submission, thus appearing to "remember" the user's settings on his or her next visit.

The cookies themselves are stored on the user's system and may be viewed using any text editor. Some browsers also let you view cookies using built-in tools. For example, in Mozilla Firefox, you can view the contents of all cookies set on your system through the Tools I Options I Privacy I Show Cookies menu, as illustrated in Figure 9-2.

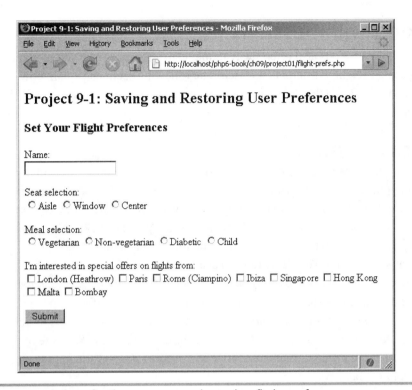

Figure 9-1 A Web form for the user to enter his or her flight preferences

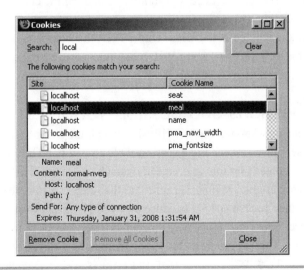

Figure 9-2 Viewing a cookie in Mozilla Firefox

Working with Sessions

Like cookies, sessions also offer a way to maintain state for a Web site or application, albeit using a slightly different approach. The following sections explain how sessions work under PHP, and the PHP functions to create and use sessions within a Web application.

Session Basics

By now, you know what cookies are: text files stored on a user's system that help a Web site or application recognize the user and retrieve specific information about him or her. The problem with cookies is that they're not very secure: because they're stored on the client, it's possible for any reasonably adept user to open the cookie file and read or modify the information stored within it, sometimes to malicious ends.

That's why many Web sites prefer to use *sessions*. Sessions work much like cookies, except that the information used to maintain state is stored on the server, rather than on the client. In a session-based environment, every client is identified through a unique number—a so-called *session identifier*—and this unique number is used to link each client with its information on the server. Every time the client visits the Web site or application, the site reads the client's session identifier and restores state information from a data repository on the server.

Under this system, state information is stored in an SQL database or text file on the server; as a result, users cannot access or modify it, making the entire system that much more secure. The *session identifier* itself may be stored on the client in a cookie, or it may be passed from page to page in the URL. Under PHP, this cookie is named PHPSESSID.

The following sections discuss the PHP functions to create sessions, register and use session variables, and destroy sessions.

Creating Sessions and Session Variables

It's easy to begin a new session under PHP: simply call the session_start() function to create a new session and generate a session ID for the client. Once a session has been created, it becomes possible to create and attach any number of *session variables* to the session; these are like regular variables, in that they can store textual or numeric information, but they're also special because they remain extant over the duration of the session, as the user clicks his or her way through different pages of the site.

Session variables are "registered" by saving them as key-value pairs of the $_SESSION associative array. Like $_POST and $_GET, this array is always available in the global scope and may be accessed directly at any point in your PHP script.

To see how sessions and session variables work, consider the following script, which creates a new client session and registers two session variables:

```php
<?php
// start session
session_start();

// register session variables
$_SESSION['name'] = 'Ronald';
$_SESSION['species'] = 'Rabbit';
?>
```

CAUTION

The `session_start()` function typically sets a cookie containing the session ID on the client system. Therefore, as with the `setcookie()` function, calls to `session_start()` must precede any output generated by the script. This is because of restrictions in the HTTP protocol that require cookie headers to be sent before any script output.

It's now possible to access these session variables from any other page on the same Web domain. To do so, create a new PHP script, recreate the session by calling `session_start()` and then try accessing the values of the `$_SESSION` associative array, as in the next example:

```php
<?php
// start session
session_start();

// read session variables
// output: 'Welcome back, Ronald Rabbit'
echo 'Welcome back, ' . $_SESSION['name'] . ' ' . $_SESSION['species'] ;
?>
```

Ask the Expert

Q: Help! My session variables aren't being saved. What do I do now?

A: If your session variables aren't being correctly registered, there are a couple of possibilities you could look into before giving up and calling the session police:

- By default, PHP saves session data on the server to the */tmp* directory. However, if you're using Microsoft Windows, this directory will not exist, and your sessions will not be correctly saved. To rectify this, open the PHP configuration file, *php.ini,* and edit the `'session.save_path'` variable to reflect your system's temporary directory.

(continued)

- By default, PHP sets a cookie on the user's system with the session identifier. If the user's browser is set to reject all cookies, this session identifier will not be set and session information will not be maintained from page to page. To rectify this, you can instead pass the session identifier from page to page as part of the URL string (although this is less secure) by setting the `'session.use_trans_sid'` variable in the PHP configuration file to true.

- Every PHP session has a *timeout value*—a duration, measured in seconds, of how long the session should remain "alive" in the absence of any user activity. In some cases, this timeout value may be set too low for your application, resulting in sessions being automatically destroyed too soon. You can adjust this timeout value by changing the `'session.gc_maxlifetime'` variable in the PHP configuration file.

Removing Sessions and Session Variables

To unregister a specific session variable, simply unset the corresponding key of the $_SESSION array:

```php
<?php
// start session
session_start();

// erase session variable
unset($_SESSION['name']);
?>
```

Alternatively, to unregister all session variables and erase the session, use the session_destroy() function:

```php
<?php
// start session
session_start();

// erase session
session_destroy();
?>
```

It's important to notice that before you can destroy a session with session_destroy(), you need to first recreate the session environment (so that there is something to destroy) with session_start().

Try This 9-2 Tracking Previous Visits to a Page

Let's now put all this theory in context, by building a simple application that demonstrates how sessions work. This next example uses a session to record every visit made by a user to a Web page. On each visit, the script prints the dates and times of all previous visits and adds a record for the current visit to the session.

Here's the code (*visits.php*):

```php
<?php
// start session
session_start();
?>
<!DOCTYPE html PUBLIC "-//W3C//DTD XHTML 1.0 Transitional//EN"
    "DTD/xhtml1-transitional.dtd">
<html xmlns="http://www.w3.org/1999/xhtml" xml:lang="en" lang="en">
  <head>
    <title>Project 9-2: Tracking Previous Visits To A Page</title>
  </head>
  <body>
    <h2>Project 9-2: Tracking Previous Visits To A Page</h2>
    <?php
    if (!isset($_SESSION['visits'])) {
      echo 'This is your first visit.';
    } else {
      echo 'You previously visited this page on: <br/>';
      foreach ($_SESSION['visits'] as $v) {
        echo date('d M Y h:i:s', $v) . '<br/>';
      }
    }
    ?>
  </body>
</html>
<?php
// add current date/time stamp to session array
$_SESSION['visits'][] = mktime();
?>
```

To see this script in action, visit the Web page a few times, and you should see a growing list containing records of all your previous visits. This list remains available so long as you don't close the browser window—so even if you visit a few other sites and then return to this script, you'll still see the records of all your previous visits. Once you close the browser, however, the session cookie will be destroyed and the list will begin anew.

(continued)

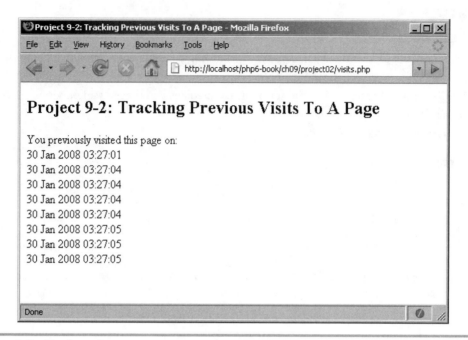

Figure 9-3 Tracking previous visits to a Web page

Figure 9-3 illustrates a sample of what you might see.

This script works by creating a session every time a user visits the page, and storing the timestamp of the user's visits in the session variable `$_SESSION['visits']`. On each subsequent visit, the session is recreated, the array containing the timestamps of previous visits is restored, and a `foreach` loop is used to iterate over this array and print its records in human-readable date and time format.

Using HTTP Headers

In previous sections, you've seen how PHP automatically sends the user's browser headers to set cookies. However, as a PHP developer, these aren't the only headers you can send; PHP lets you send the user's browser any header supported by the HTTP protocol, via its `header()` function.

Perhaps the most commonly used header is the `'Location:'` header, used to transparently redirect the user's browser to a different URL. Here's an example of it in action:

```php
<?php
// redirect to www.php.net
header('Location: http://www.php.net');
?>
```

You can also send other headers—for example, `'Cache-Control:'` or `'Content-Encoding:'` headers—as in the next example:

```php
<?php
// control caching
header('Cache-Control: no-cache');

// set content-type
header('Content-Type: text/xml');

// set content-encoding
echo "<?xml version='1.0'?><doc><element/></doc>";
?>
```

As you now know, sending an HTTP header after the script has already generated output will produce an error. You can avoid this error by first testing if any headers have already been sent, via PHP's headers_sent() function. Consider the following example, which illustrates:

```php
<?php
// check if headers sent
// if no, send headers
// if yes, display error message
if (!headers_sent()) {
  header('Cache-Control: no-cache');
  header('Content-Type: text/plain');
  echo 'Headers sent.';
} else {
  die ('ERROR: Cannot send headers!');
}
?>
```

TIP

For a complete list of headers supported by the HTTP protocol, take a look at the protocol specification at www.w3.org/Protocols/rfc2616/rfc2616.html, or the Wikipedia page at en.wikipedia.org/wiki/List_of_HTTP_headers.

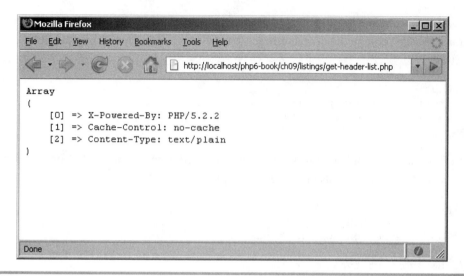

Figure 9-4 A list of HTTP headers that will be sent to the client

To obtain a complete list of HTTP headers that will be sent to the user's browser, use the headers_list() function. Here's an example:

```php
<?php
// control caching
header('Cache-Control: no-cache');

// set content-type
header('Content-Type: text/plain');

// print header list
print_r(headers_list());
?>
```

Figure 9-4 illustrates the output of this script.

Try This 9-3 Building a Better Login Form

In Chapter 7, you built a login form that dynamically interacted with a MySQL database to verify user credentials. Now, let's juice that form up a little with sessions, cookies, and headers. This next example will enhance the login form from Chapter 7 to remember the username entered into it, and to restrict access to certain pages only to logged-in users.

Assuming that you've set up the MySQL database according to the instructions in Chapter 7, here's the revised login form (*login.php*):

```php
<?php
// if form not yet submitted
// display form
if (!isset($_POST['submit'])) {
  $username = (isset($_COOKIE['name'])) ? $_COOKIE['name'] : '';
?>
<!DOCTYPE html PUBLIC "-//W3C//DTD XHTML 1.0 Transitional//EN"
   "DTD/xhtml1-transitional.dtd">
<html xmlns="http://www.w3.org/1999/xhtml" xml:lang="en" lang="en">
  <head>
    <title>Project 9-3: Building A Better Login Form</title>
  </head>
  <body>
    <h2>Project 9-3: Building A Better Login Form</h2>
    <form method="post" action="login.php">
      Username: <br />
      <input type="text" name="username" value="<?php echo $username; ?>"/>
      <p>
      Password: <br />
      <input type="password" name="password" />
      <p>
      <input type="checkbox" name="sticky" checked />
      Remember me
      <p>
      <input type="submit" name="submit" value="Log In" />
    </form>
  </body>
</html>
<?php
// if form submitted
// check supplied login credentials
// against database
} else {
  $username = $_POST['username'];
  $password = $_POST['password'];

  // check input
  if (empty($username)) {
    die('ERROR: Please enter your username');
  }
  if (empty($password)) {
    die('ERROR: Please enter your password');
  }

  // attempt database connection
  try {
    $pdo = new PDO('mysql:dbname=app;host=localhost', 'user', 'pass');
  } catch (PDOException $e) {
```

(continued)

```php
    die("ERROR: Could not connect: " . $e->getMessage());
  }

  // escape special characters in input
  $username = $pdo->quote($username);

  // check if usernames exists
  $sql = "SELECT COUNT(*) FROM users WHERE username = $username";
  if ($result = $pdo->query($sql)) {
    $row = $result->fetch();
    // if yes, fetch the encrypted password
    if ($row[0] == 1) {
      $sql = "SELECT password FROM users WHERE username = $username";
      // encrypt the password entered into the form
      // test it against the encrypted password stored in the database
      // if the two match, the password is correct
      if ($result = $pdo->query($sql)) {
        $row = $result->fetch();
        $salt = $row[0];
        if (crypt($password, $salt) == $salt) {
          // password correct
          // start a new session
          // save the username to the session
          // if required, set a cookie with the username
          // redirect the browser to the main application page
          session_start();
          $_SESSION['username'] = $username;
          if ($_POST['sticky']) {
            setcookie('name', $_POST['username'], mktime()+86400);
          }
          header('Location: main.php');
        } else {
          echo 'You entered an incorrect password.';
        }
      } else {
        echo "ERROR: Could not execute $sql. " . print_r($pdo->errorInfo());
      }
    } else {
      echo 'You entered an incorrect username.';
    }
  } else {
    echo "ERROR: Could not execute $sql. " . print_r($pdo->errorInfo());
  }

  // close connection
  unset($pdo);
}
?>
```

Figure 9-5 illustrates what the login form looks like.

When this form is submitted, the second half of the script verifies the username and password against the values stored in the database, using the procedure previously

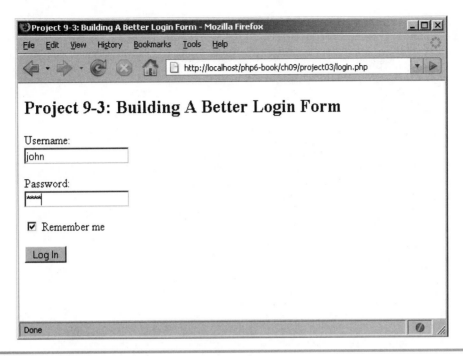

Figure 9-5 A Web form to log in to an application

explained in Chapter 7. There are some important differences, though: in this version, instead of simply generating a success message if the supplied username and password are valid, the script starts a new session and registers the username as a session variable.

Next, the script checks if the "Remember Me" option on the Web form was selected. If it was, the script sets a cookie on the user's system to store the username for subsequent logins. The next time the user visits this page, the cookie set in the previous step will be automatically read, and the form will be prefilled with the username. Once the session and cookie have both been set, the script uses the `header()` function to redirect the user's browser to the application's main page, *main.php*.

This is only half the story, though. In order to restrict access to logged-in users only, it's necessary to check for the presence of a valid session on other pages of the site. To illustrate how this works, look at the application's main page (*main.php*), which implements one such check:

```php
<?php
// recreate session
// check if user has logged in
// if not, display an error message and halt processing
```

(continued)

```
session_start();
if (!isset($_SESSION['username'])) {
  die('ERROR: You attempted to access a restricted page. Please <a
href="login.php">log in</a>.');
}
?>
<!DOCTYPE html PUBLIC "-//W3C//DTD XHTML 1.0 Transitional//EN"
   "DTD/xhtml1-transitional.dtd">
<html xmlns="http://www.w3.org/1999/xhtml" xml:lang="en" lang="en">
  <head>
    <title>Project 9-3: Building A Better Login Form</title>
  </head>
  <body>
    <h2>Project 9-3: Building A Better Login Form</h2>
    This is the main application page.
    <p/>
    You will only see this page after a successful login.
    <p/>
  </body>
</html>
```

Figure 9-6 illustrates what logged-in users would see.

And Figure 9-7 illustrates what users attempting to access this page without logging in would see.

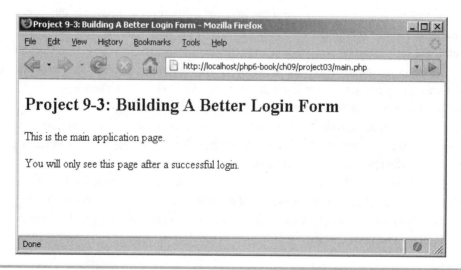

Figure 9-6 The result of successfully logging in

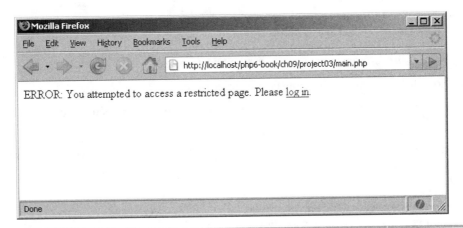

Figure 9-7   The result of accessing a secure page without first logging in

Summary

This chapter demonstrated two of PHP's most useful and sophisticated features: the ability to work around restrictions in the HTTP protocol and the ability to maintain state through sessions and cookies. These features are commonly used by developers to improve and enhance the user experience on PHP-enabled Web sites, and as you saw over the preceding pages, they're quite easy to implement as well.

In addition to a discussion of the theory behind sessions, cookies, and headers, this chapter also included practical examples to put the theory in context. A common Web task—allowing only logged-in users to access parts of a Web site—was used to demonstrate how sessions, cookies, and headers can be used together to build a functional and secure application.

To read more about the topics discussed in this chapter, consider visiting the following links:

- Cookies in PHP, at **www.php.net/setcookie**

- Sessions in PHP, at **www.php.net/session**

- HTTP headers in PHP, at **www.php.net/header**

Chapter 9 Self Test

1. What is the difference between a session and a cookie?

2. How do you remove a previously set cookie?

3. How do you register a session variable? And how do you access its value on a different page?

4. What is wrong with the following PHP script? Without running it, what is the likely output?

```php
<?php
echo 'Redirecting you...';
header('Location: http://www.php.net');
?>
```

5. Write a program that counts how many times a user has visited a particular page:

   A Within the same session

   B Over different sessions

6. Review the last project in this chapter. Then, enhance it by writing a PHP script that logs users out of the application and redirects them back to the login form.

Part III

Security and Troubleshooting

Chapter 10

Handling Errors

Key Skills & Concepts

- Understand PHP's error levels

- Control which errors are displayed in your PHP script

- Bypass PHP's default error handler and divert errors to a custom function

- Understand how to generate and handle exceptions

- Automatically log errors to a file or e-mail address

- Generate a backtrace to debug script errors

A common misconception, especially among less experienced developers, is that a "good" program is one that works without errors. In fact, this is not strictly true: a better definition might be that a good program is one that anticipates all possible error conditions ahead of time and deals with them in a consistent and correct manner.

Writing "intelligent" programs that conform to this definition is as much art as science. Experience and imagination play an important role in assessing potential causes of error and defining corrective action, but no less important is the programming language itself, which defines the tools and functions available to trap and resolve errors.

Fortunately, PHP is no slouch in this department: the language comes with a sophisticated framework to help developers catch errors and take remedial action. This chapter will introduce you to this framework, teaching you about the PHP 5.3 exception model and showing you how to create customized error handling routines tailored to your PHP application's requirements.

Handling Script Errors

As you've worked your way through the projects in this book, you'll undoubtedly have had a few accidents: a misplaced brace here, a missing semicolon there, perhaps a wrongly invoked function somewhere else. And you'll have noticed that PHP is actually quite good about pointing out these errors. In some cases, PHP would have generated an error message but continued executing your script; in other, more serious cases, it would have halted script execution with a message indicating the line number that caused the error.

The type of errors just described are "script-level" errors; they arise when the PHP engine encounters defects in the syntax or structure of a PHP script. Typically, they only become visible once PHP actually starts parsing and executing a script. To illustrate, try creating and running the following script:

```php
<?php
// try dividing by zero
echo 45/0;

// try calling an undefined function
echo someFunc();
?>
```

The output of this script should look something like Figure 10-1.

As Figure 10-1 illustrates, this script generated two types of errors: a "warning" about the attempt to divide by zero, and a "fatal error" about the attempt to invoke an undefined function. In fact, PHP errors can broadly be classified into three main categories, as listed in Table 10-1.

There's a clear hierarchy to PHP's error messages: notices are less serious than warnings, which in turn are less serious that fatal errors. By default, PHP only displays warnings and fatal errors in script output (although, as you will shortly see, you can change this default behavior so that even notices are visible in script output). Errors can

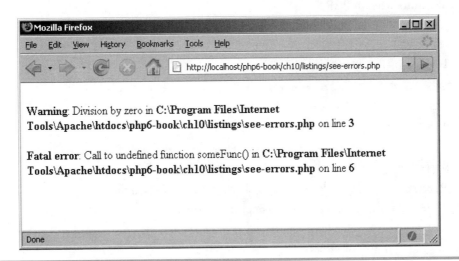

Figure 10-1   An example of a PHP error page

Error Type	Description	Example
Notices	Non-critical errors that don't stop PHP from executing a script	Accessing a variable that hasn't been initialized
Warnings	More serious errors that require attention but still don't stop script execution (although some parts of the script may function incorrectly)	Reading a file that doesn't exist in the stated path
Fatal errors	Syntax errors, or critical errors that force PHP to stop executing a script	Instantiating an object of an undefined class

Table 10-1   PHP Error Categories

arise at various stages during a script's lifetime—at startup, at parse time, at compile time, or at run time—and so PHP also makes internal distinctions between these various stages. Collectively, this adds up to twelve different error levels (plus two "special" levels), represented by named constants. A complete list of these error levels can be obtained from www.php.net/manual/en/ref.errorfunc.php#errorfunc.constants; Table 10-2 lists the ones you'll be using most often.

Most of these error levels are easy to understand. The only ones you might have trouble with are the E_USER error levels, which are set aside for custom application-level errors. Don't worry about these, as they've largely been supplanted by the new exception model introduced in PHP 5.

Error Level	Description
E_PARSE	Fatal parse errors
E_NOTICE	Non-fatal run-time errors (notices)
E_WARNING	Non-fatal run-time errors (warnings)
E_ERROR	Fatal run-time errors that force script termination
E_USER_NOTICE	User-defined non-fatal application errors (notices)
E_USER_WARNING	User-defined non-fatal application errors (warnings)
E_USER_ERROR	User-defined fatal application errors
E_STRICT	Non-fatal run-time errors arising from legacy/deprecated PHP syntax
E_ALL	All errors

Table 10-2   PHP Error Levels

Controlling Error Reporting

You can control which errors are displayed in script output with a built-in PHP function called `error_reporting()`. This function accepts one or more of the named constants from Table 10-2 and tells the script to report only errors that match that type. There's one exception, however: parsing errors (`E_PARSE`) that arise from syntactical defects in a PHP script cannot be hidden using the `error_reporting()` function.

To see this in action, consider the following rewrite of one of the earlier scripts to "hide" non-fatal errors:

```php
<?php
// only display fatal errors
error_reporting(E_ERROR);
echo 45/0;
?>
```

In this case, when the script executes, no warning will be generated even though the script attempts to perform division by zero.

Ask the Expert

Q: What does the `E_STRICT` error level do?

A: At the `E_STRICT` error level, PHP inspects your code at run time and automatically generates recommendations about how it may be improved. Using `E_STRICT` can often provide a heads-up on functions that will break in a future version of PHP, and using it is recommended to improve the long-term maintainability of your code.

You can also use `error_reporting()` to turn off reporting of run-time fatal errors, as in the following example:

```php
<?php
// only display warnings
error_reporting(E_WARNING);
echo someFunc();
?>
```

It's important to realize that `error_reporting()` doesn't automatically make your script error-free; all it does is hide errors of a certain type. As a case in point, although the preceding script will not display a visible error message, it will still generate a fatal error, and script execution will still stop at the point of error.

You can also pass `error_reporting()` a combination of error levels, to customize PHP's error reporting system even further. For example, consider the following script, which only reports notices and fatal errors, but not warnings:

```php
<?php
// only display notices and fatal errors
error_reporting(E_NOTICE | E_ERROR);
echo $var;  // notice
echo 45/0;  // warning
echo someFunc();  // fatal
?>
```

It is also possible to selectively turn off error reporting, on a per-function basis, by prefixing the function call with the @ operator. For example, the following code snippet would normally generate a fatal error because `someFunction()` doesn't exist:

```php
<?php
// call a non-existent function
someFunction();
?>
```

However, this error could be suppressed by placing an @ symbol before the function call, like this:

```php
<?php
// call a non-existent function
@someFunction();
?>
```

Using a Custom Error Handler

By default, when a script error is triggered, PHP's built-in error handler identifies the error type, displays an appropriate error message (based on the `error_reporting()` setting), and optionally halts script execution (if the error is fatal). The message generated by the error handler uses a standard template: it indicates the error type, the reason for the error, and the file name and line number where the error was generated (see Figure 10-1 for an example).

As your PHP applications become more complex, however, this default error handling mechanism may often end up being inadequate. For example, you might wish to customize the template used by the error handler to display more or less information, or you might wish to log the error to a file or database instead of displaying it to the user. For all these situations, PHP offers the `set_error_handler()` function, which allows you to replace PHP's built-in error handler with your own.

The set_error_handler() function accepts a single argument: the name of the user-defined function that should be invoked when an error occurs. This custom function must be capable of accepting a minimum of two mandatory arguments (the error type and the corresponding descriptive message) and up to three additional arguments (the filename, the line number where the error occurred, and a dump of the variable space at the time of error).

NOTE

A custom error handler cannot intercept fatal errors (E_ERROR), parsing errors (E_PARSE), or legacy code notifications (E_STRICT).

To illustrate how this works, consider the following example. Here, a user-defined error handling function replaces PHP's built-in handler, dynamically generating a custom error page:

```
<!DOCTYPE html PUBLIC "-//W3C//DTD XHTML 1.0 Transitional//EN"
    "DTD/xhtml1-transitional.dtd">
<html xmlns="http://www.w3.org/1999/xhtml" xml:lang="en" lang="en">
  <head>
    <title></title>
    <style type="text/css">
    .notice {
      font-weight: bolder;
      color: purple;
    }
    .warning {
      font-weight: bolder;
      font-size: larger;
      color: red;
    }
    </style>
  </head>
  <body>
<?php
// divert errors to custom error handler
set_error_handler('myHandler');

// report all errors
error_reporting(E_ALL);

// generate some errors
echo $var;        // notice
echo 23/0;        // warning
```

```
// custom error handler
function myHandler($type, $msg, $file, $line, $context) {
  $text = "An error occurred on line $line while processing your
request.<p>
          Please visit our <a href=http://www.domain.dom>home page</a>
and try again.";
  switch($type) {
    case E_NOTICE:
      echo "<div class=\"notice\">$text</div><p>";
      break;

    case E_WARNING:
      echo "<div class=\"warning\">$text</div><p>";
      break;
  }
}
?>
  </body>
</html>
```

Here, the set_error_handler() function automatically diverts all errors to the user-defined function myHandler(). When an error occurs, this function is passed the error type, error message, file, and line number where the error occurred, along with the variable context. It then displays a custom error page containing the line number of the error in either purple (notices) or red (warnings), and manually halts script execution. Figure 10-2 illustrates the output.

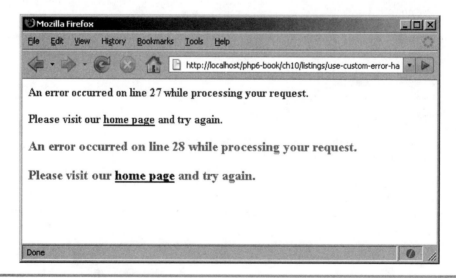

Figure 10-2 An error page generated by a custom error handler

Ask the Expert

Q: How do I restore PHP's default error handling mechanism once I've called `set_error_handler()`?

A: There are two ways to do this. The simplest method is to use PHP's `restore_error_handler()` function. This function restores the last error handler in use before `set_error_handler()` was called; in most cases, this will be PHP's default error handler.

Another option is to have the custom error handler return false; this will force the error to be transferred back to PHP's default handler for processing in the normal manner. This technique is particularly handy if you need to pass errors through a custom function first for preprocessing or logging, and you'll see an example in the section entitled "Logging Errors."

Try This 10-1   Generating a Clean Error Page

PHP's default error handler merely displays information about an error. Often, this error message appears while an output page is being generated, disrupting page layout and creating unnecessary user confusion and stress (see Figure 10-3 for an example of such a page). However, by replacing the default error handler with a custom function, it's possible to easily resolve this problem by generating a "clean" error page while simultaneously logging script errors to a database for later review. This next example will show you how to do this.

To begin, create a new SQLite database, and a table to hold error information, as shown here:

```
shell> sqlite app.db
sqlite> CREATE TABLE errors (
   ...> id INTEGER PRIMARY KEY,
   ...> date TEXT NOT NULL,
   ...> error TEXT NOT NULL,
   ...> script TEXT NOT NULL,
   ...> line TEXT NOT NULL
   ...> );
```

Next, define a custom error handler that intercepts all script errors and writes them to this table using PDO, as in the following script (*app.php*):

```
<?php
// report all errors
error_reporting(E_ALL);
```

(continued)

Figure 10-3 Error output interspersed with page content

```
// use custom handler
set_error_handler('myHandler');

// create an output buffer
ob_start();

// define a custom handler
// which logs errors to the database
// then generates an error page
function myHandler($type, $msg, $file, $line, $context) {
  // log error to database
  $db = 'app.db';
  $pdo = new PDO("sqlite:$db");
  $msg = $pdo->quote($msg);
  $file = $pdo->quote($file);
  $line = $pdo->quote($line);
```

```php
  $date = $pdo->quote(date('d-M-Y h:i:s', mktime()));
  $sql = "INSERT INTO errors (date, error, script, line) VALUES ($date, $msg,
$file, $line)";
  $pdo->exec($sql);

  // reset and close the output buffer
  // generate a new error page
  ob_end_clean();
  $errorPage = '
  <!DOCTYPE html PUBLIC "-//W3C//DTD XHTML 1.0 Transitional//EN"
     "DTD/xhtml1-transitional.dtd">
  <html xmlns="http://www.w3.org/1999/xhtml" xml:lang="en" lang="en">
    <head>
       <title>Error Page</title>
    </head>
    <body>
       <div style="border:solid 1px black; padding:10px; width:50%; height:50%;
margin:auto; top:0; bottom:0; right:0; left:0; position:absolute">
         <h2>Oops!</h2>
         This script encountered an internal error and was unable to execute.
         The error has been logged and will be rectified as soon as possible.
         Until then, please return to the home page and select another activity.
       </div>
    </body>
  </html>';
  echo $errorPage;
  exit();
}
?>
<!DOCTYPE html PUBLIC "-//W3C//DTD XHTML 1.0 Transitional//EN"
   "DTD/xhtml1-transitional.dtd">
<html xmlns="http://www.w3.org/1999/xhtml" xml:lang="en" lang="en">
  <head>
     <title>Project 10-1: Generating a Custom Error Page</title>
  </head>
  <body>
<?php
// output some page text
echo "<h1>Hello and welcome to this page.</h1>";

// generate warning (file not found)
include('missingfile.php');

// output some page text
echo "Goodbye.";

// dump output buffer
ob_end_flush();
?>
  </body>
</html>
```

(continued)

In addition to components you're already familiar with (PDO and custom error handlers), this script also introduces a new animal: PHP's output control functions. As the name suggests, these functions provide a way for developers to exercise a high degree of control over the output generated by a PHP script.

PHP's output control functions work by diverting all the output generated by a script to a special *output buffer* in memory, instead of sending it directly to the client browser. The contents of this buffer remain in memory until they are explicitly made visible to the user; alternatively, they may be erased simply by resetting the buffer.

There are three main functions to learn about in PHP's output control API:

- The ob_start() function initializes an output buffer and prepares it to intercept the output of a script. Needless to say, this function should be called before any output is generated by the script.

- The ob_end_flush() function ends output buffering and sends the current contents of the output buffer to the output device (usually the user's browser).

- The ob_end_clean() function ends output buffering and clears the current contents of the output buffer.

With all this theory in mind, let's return to the preceding script to see how output buffers can help to produce cleaner error pages. A quick glance at the script, and you'll see that it begins by initializing a new output buffer with ob_start(), and a custom error handler with set_error_handler(). Any output generated by the script will now be stored in the output buffer until it is released to the client via a call to ob_end_flush().

Now, consider what happens when an error occurs in the script. First, the custom error handler will intercept this error, open a PDO handle to the SQLite database file created in the previous step, and convert the error (notice or warning) into an SQL INSERT query. This query will then be used to save the error to the database via PDO's exec() method, together with the exact date and time. Then, the call to ob_end_clean() will flush the output buffer, send a custom error page to the browser, and terminate script execution.

As a result of these actions, even if there was a Web page being constructed on the fly when the error occurred, it will never see the light of day, as it will be discarded and replaced by the custom error page. If, on the other hand, the script executes without any errors, the final call to ob_end_flush() will take care of sending the full and final page to the browser.

Figure 10-4 A clean error page

And now, when you run the script, instead of the mangled output previously shown in Figure 10-3, you should see a much cleaner error page. Figure 10-4 illustrates what you'll probably see.

While you're at it, also look in the SQLite table. You should be able to see the error messages thrown by the script, as shown here:

```
1|13-Feb-2008 06:25:30|Undefined variable: myVar|/ch10/project01/
app.php|28
2|13-Feb-2008 06:25:30|include(missingfile.php): failed to open
stream: No such file or directory| /ch10/project01/app.php|31
3|13-Feb-2008 06:25:30|include(): Failed opening 'missingfile.php' for
inclusion (include_path='. ')|/ch10/project01/app.php|31
```

A setup like this makes it easy for an administrator or developer to maintain a permanent record of script errors and return to this record at any time to view or audit errors, while also ensuring that the user experience is consistent and uncomplicated.

Ask the Expert

Q: What happens if the custom error handling function itself contains an error?

A: If the custom error handler itself contains an error, the error will be propagated upward to PHP's default error handling mechanism. So, for example, if the code inside a custom error handler generates a warning, this warning will be reported per PHP's current error reporting level and handled by PHP's default error handler.

Using Exceptions

In addition to errors, PHP 5 also introduced a new exception model, similar to that used by other programming languages like Java and Python. In this exception-based approach, program code is wrapped in a `try` block, and exceptions generated by it are "caught" and resolved by one or more `catch` blocks. Because multiple `catch` blocks are possible, developers can trap different types of exceptions and handle each type differently.

To illustrate how this works, consider the following listing, which attempts to access a non-existent array element using an ArrayIterator:

```php
<?php
// define array
$cities = array(
  "United Kingdom" => "London",
  "United States" => "Washington",
  "France" => "Paris",
  "India" => "Delhi"
);

// try accessing a non-existent array element
// generates an OutOfBoundsException
// output: 'Exception: Seek position 10 is out of range'
try {

  $iterator = new ArrayIterator($cities);
  $iterator->seek(10);

} catch (Exception $e) {
  echo 'ERROR: An exception occurred in your script.';
}
?>
```

When PHP encounters code wrapped within a `try-catch` block, it first attempts to execute the code within the `try` block. If this code is processed without any exceptions being generated, control transfers to the lines following the `try-catch` block. However, if an exception is generated while running the code within the `try` block (as happens in the preceding listing), PHP stops execution of the block at that point and begins checking each catch block to see if there is a handler for the exception. If a handler is found, the code within the appropriate catch block is executed and then the lines following the try block are executed; if not, a fatal error is generated and script execution stops at the point of error.

Every Exception object includes some additional information that can be used for debugging the source of the error. This information can be accessed via the Exception object's built-in methods and includes a descriptive error message, an error code, the filename and line number that caused the error, and a *backtrace* of the function invocations leading to the error. Table 10-3 lists these methods.

And the following revision of the preceding listing illustrates these methods in use:

```php
<?php
// define array
$cities = array(
  "United Kingdom" => "London",
  "United States" => "Washington",
  "France" => "Paris",
  "India" => "Delhi"
);

// try accessing a non-existent array element
// generates an OutOfBoundsException
try {

  $iterator = new ArrayIterator($cities);
  $iterator->seek(10);

} catch (Exception $e) {
  echo "ERROR: Something went wrong!\n";
  echo "Error message: " . $e->getMessage() . "\n";
  echo "Error code: " . $e->getCode() . "\n";
  echo "File name: " . $e->getFile() . "\n";
  echo "Line: " . $e->getLine() . "\n";
  echo "Backtrace: " . $e->getTraceAsString() . "\n";
}
?>
```

Method Name	What It Does
getMessage()	Returns a message describing what went wrong
getCode()	Returns a numeric error code
getFile()	Returns the disk path and name of the script that generated the exception
getLine()	Returns the line number that generated the exception
getTrace()	Returns a backtrace of the calls that led to the error, as an array
getTraceAsString()	Returns a backtrace of the calls that led to the error, as a string

Table 10-3   Methods of the PHP Exception Object

TIP

It's possible to handle different types of exceptions differently, by creating multiple catch blocks and assigning different actions to each one. You'll see an example of this a little further along in the chapter.

Now, if you think about it, you might be tempted to conclude that exceptions are simply old wine in a new bottle. After all, the capabilities already described seem quite easy to replicate using a custom error handler, as described in the preceding section. In reality, though, this exception-based approach is far more sophisticated than it appears, because it offers the following additional benefits:

- In the traditional model, it's necessary to check the return value of every function called to identify if an error occurred and take corrective action. This can produce unnecessarily complicated code and deeply nested code blocks. In the exception-based model, a single catch block can be used to trap any error that occurs in the preceding code block. This eliminates the need for multiple cascading error tests, and it produces simpler and more readable code.

- The traditional model is prescriptive by nature: it requires the developer to think through all possible errors that might occur, and write code to handle each of these possibilities. By contrast, the exception-based approach is more flexible. A generic exception handler works like a safety net, catching and handling even those errors for which no specific handling code has been written. This only helps to make application code more robust and resilient to unforeseen situations.

- Because the exception model used an object-based approach, developers can use OOP concepts of inheritance and extensibility to subclass the base Exception object and create different Exception objects for different types of exceptions. This makes it possible to distinguish between different types of errors, and to handle each type differently.

- The exception-based approach forces developers to make hard decisions about how to handle different types of errors. Unlike in the traditional model, where developers can easily omit (by accident or design) tests to check the return value of functions, exceptions are not so easy to ignore. By requiring developers to create and populate catch blocks, the exception model forces them to think about the causes and consequences of errors and ultimately results in better design and more robust implementation.

The only downside? Exceptions were introduced only in PHP 5, and as a result, they're natively generated only by newer language extensions, such as SimpleXML, PHP Data Objects (PDO), Service Data Objects (SDO), and Standard PHP Library (SPL). For all other PHP functions, it's necessary to check the function's return value for errors and manually convert it into an exception.

Manually creating, or *raising*, exceptions in this manner is a task for PHP's throw statement. This statement needs to be passed a descriptive error message, and an optional error code; it then generates an Exception object using these parameters and makes the message and code available to the exception handler. The process is illustrated in the following listing:

```php
<?php
// set file name
// attempt to copy and then delete file
$file = 'dummy.txt';
try {

  if (!file_exists($file)) {
    throw new Exception("File '$file' was not found.");
  }
  if (file_exists("$file.new")) {
    throw new Exception("Destination file '$file.new' already exists.");
  }
  if (!copy($file, "$file.new")) {
    throw new Exception("File '$file' could not be copied.");
  }
  if (!unlink($file)) {
    throw new Exception("File '$file' could not be removed.");
  }

} catch (Exception $e) {
  echo 'Oops! Something bad happened on line ' . $e->getLine() . ': ' .
$e->getMessage();
  exit();
}
echo 'SUCCESS: File operation successful.';
?>
```

Here, depending on the results of various file operations, a new exception is manually thrown by the script. This exception is then caught by the generic exception handler, and information specific to the error is extracted and displayed to the user.

Using Custom Exceptions

A more sophisticated approach is to subclass the generic Exception object and create specific Exception objects for each possible error. This approach is useful when you need to treat different types of exceptions differently, as it allows you to use a separate catch block (and separate handling code) for each exception type. Here's a revision of the preceding example, which illustrates this approach.

```php
<?php
// subclass Exception
class MissingFileException extends Exception { }
class DuplicateFileException extends Exception { }
class FileIOException extends Exception { }

// set file name
// attempt to copy and then delete file
$file = 'dummy.txt';
try {

  if (!file_exists($file)) {
    throw new MissingFileException($file);
  }
  if (file_exists("$file.new")) {
    throw new DuplicateFileException("$file.new");
  }
  if (!copy($file, "$file.new")) {
    throw new FileIOException("$file.new");
  }
  if (!unlink($file)) {
    throw new FileIOException($file);
  }

} catch (MissingFileException $e) {
  echo 'ERROR: Could not find file \'' . $e->getMessage() . '\'';
  exit();
} catch (DuplicateFileException $e) {
  echo 'ERROR: Destination file \'' . $e->getMessage() . '\' already exists';
  exit();
} catch (FileIOException $e) {
  echo 'ERROR: Could not perform file input/output operation on file \'' .
$e->getMessage() . '\'';
  exit();
} catch (Exception $e) {
  echo 'Oops! Something bad happened on line ' . $e->getLine() . ': ' . $e-
>getMessage();
  exit();
}
echo 'SUCCESS: File operation successful.';
?>
```

This script extends the base Exception class to create three new Exception types, each representing a different possible error. A separate `catch` block for each Exception now makes it possible to customize how each of these three Exceptions is treated. The last `catch` block is a generic "catch-all" handler: exceptions that are not handled by the more specific blocks above it will fall through to, and be dealt with by, this handler.

Ask the Expert

Q: I've seen that uncaught exceptions generate a fatal error that causes the script to end abruptly. Can I change this?

A: Yes and no. PHP offers the `set_exception_handler()` function, which allows you to replace PHP's default exception handler with your own custom code, in much the same way as `set_error_handler()` does. However, there's an important caveat to be aware of here. As you've seen, PHP's default exception handler displays a notification and then terminates script exception. Using a custom exception handler allows limited control over this behavior: while you can change the manner and appearance of the notification display, you can't make the script continue executing beyond the point where the exception was generated.

The moral of the story, then, is that an uncaught exception will *always* result in script termination. That's why it's a good idea to always include a generic `catch` block in your exception-handling code to catch *all* exceptions thrown by your script, regardless of type.

Try This 10-2   Validating Form Input

Now that you have a basic understanding of how exceptions work, as well as how to throw and catch custom exceptions, let's apply this learning to a small project that demonstrates these tools in practice. This next example allows the user to place an order for some fine art, by selecting an artist, medium, and price range. The order is then validated, formatted into an e-mail message, and handed to the mail server for delivery. Errors in this process are handled using custom exception handlers, producing code that's simpler to read and easier to maintain.

Here's the code (*art.php*):

```
<!DOCTYPE html PUBLIC "-//W3C//DTD XHTML 1.0 Transitional//EN"
    "DTD/xhtml1-transitional.dtd">
<html xmlns="http://www.w3.org/1999/xhtml" xml:lang="en" lang="en">
  <head>
    <title>Project 10-2: Validating Form Input</title>
```

(continued)

```
      <style type="text/css">
      div.success {
        width:200px;
        padding:5px;
        border:solid 1px black;
        color:green;
      }
      div.error {
        width:400px;
        padding:5px;
        border:solid 1px black;
        color:red;
      }
      </style>
  </head>
  <body>
      <h2>Project 10-2: Validating Form Input</h2>
      <h3 style="background-color: silver">Purchase Fine Art</h3>
<?php
      // if form not yet submitted
      // display form
      if (!isset($_POST['submit'])) {
?>
      <form method="post" action="art.php">
        Artist: <br />
        <select name="artist">
          <option value="">--select one--</option>
          <option value="Picasso">Picasso</option>
          <option value="Van Gogh">van Gogh</option>
          <option value="Chagall">Chagall</option>
          <option value="Degas">Degas</option>
          <option value="Monet">Monet</option>
          <option value="Matisse">Matisse</option>
        </select>

        <p>

        Medium: <br />
        <select name="medium">
          <option value="">--select one--</option>
          <option value="oil">Oil</option>
          <option value="watercolor">Watercolor</option>
          <option value="ink">Ink</option>
        </select>

        <p>

        Price between: <br />
        <input type="text" size="4" name="min"/> and <input type="text"
size="5" name="max"/>
```

```
      <p>

      Email address: <br />
      <input type="text" size="25" name="email"/>

      <p>
      <input type="submit" name="submit" value="Submit" />
    </form>
<?php
    // if form submitted
    // process form input
    } else {
      error_reporting(E_ERROR);

      // define exception classes
      class InputException extends Exception { }
      class LogicalException extends Exception { }
      class MailException extends Exception { }

      // get form input
      $artist = $_POST['artist'];
      $medium = $_POST['medium'];
      $min = $_POST['min'];
      $max = $_POST['max'];
      $email = $_POST['email'];

      try {

        // validate form input
        if (empty($artist)) {
          throw new InputException('Artist');
        }
        if (empty($medium)) {
          throw new InputException('Medium');
        }
        if (empty($email)) {
          throw new InputException('Email address');
        }
        if (empty($min) || empty($max) || (int)$min <= 0 || (int)$max <= 0) {
          throw new InputException('Price');
        }
        if ($max < $min) {
          throw new LogicalException('Maximum price cannot be less than
minimum price');
        }

        // send email with selection
        $subject = 'Purchase order';
        $to = $email;
        $from = $email;
```

(continued)

```php
    $body = "
      ORDER DETAILS: \r\n\r\n
      Artist: $artist \r\n
      Medium: $medium \r\n
      Price: Between $min and $max \r\n
    ";
    if (!mail($to, $subject, $body, "From:$from")) {
      throw new MailException();
    }

    // print success message
    echo '<div class="success">SUCCESS: Order processed!</div>';

  } catch (InputException $e) {
    echo '<div class="error">ERROR: Please provide a valid value for the
field marked \'' . $e->getMessage() . '\'</div>';
    exit();
  } catch (LogicalException $e) {
    echo '<div class="error">ERROR: '. $e->getMessage() . '</div>';
    exit();
  } catch (MailException $e) {
    echo '<div class="error">ERROR: Unable to deliver email message</
div>';
    file_put_contents('error.log', '[' . date("d-M-Y h:i:s", mktime()) .
'] Mail delivery error to: ' . $e->getMessage() . "\n", FILE_APPEND);
    exit();
  } catch (Exception $e) {
    echo '<div class="error">'. $e->getMessage() . ' on line ' . $e-
>getLine() . '</div>';
    exit();
  }

}
?>
  </body>
</html>
```

The first half of this script simply generates a Web form for the user to make his or her selections, as in Figure 10-5.

Once the form is submitted, the script turns off error reporting for all but fatal errors and defines three new exception types: InputException for errors in form input, LogicalException for errors in input logic, and MailException for errors in mail delivery. These exceptions are simple extensions of the generic Exception object, with no added flavor.

Next, a try block is used to encapsulate the script's processing logic. First, the various input fields are tested for consistency; errors in field data generate either an InputException or a LogicalException. Once the data has been validated, it's formatted into an e-mail message, which is transmitted using PHP's mail() function. If the

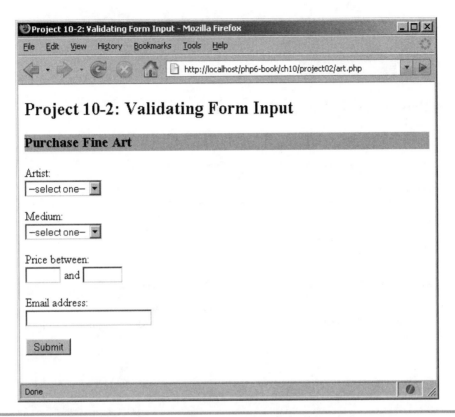

Figure 10-5 A Web form for the user to place an order for fine art

`mail()` function returns false, indicating that message transmission was unsuccessful, a MailException is raised; if not, a success message is printed.

The various exceptions generated by the processing logic aren't just ignored; instead, four `catch` blocks (one each for the three defined exception types and one generic) trap these exceptions, print appropriate user notification of the error, and halt script processing. Each of the exceptions is handled slightly differently, to illustrate just how customized each exception-handling routine can be: for example, MailExceptions are logged to a file with the date, time, and recipient e-mail address, and InputExceptions and LogicalExceptions produce different error messages.

Figure 10-6 illustrates the result when an InputException is generated.

And Figure 10-7 illustrates the result when mail transmission fails and a MailException is generated.

(continued)

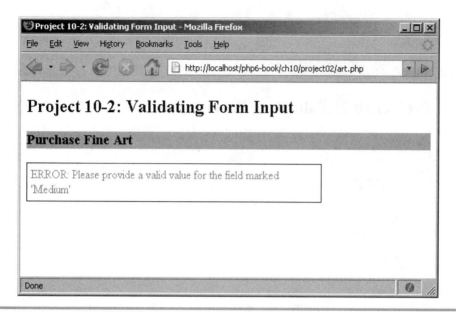

Figure 10-6 The result of catching an InputException when processing the Web form

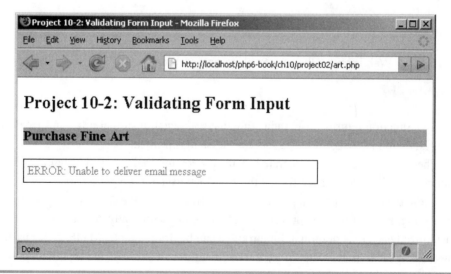

Figure 10-7 The result of catching a MailException when processing the Web form

Logging Errors

In addition to trapping and handling errors at run time, it's also usually a good idea to maintain a semipermanent record of the errors that were generated by an application, for debugging or inspection purposes. That's where PHP's error_log() function comes in: it allows you to send error messages to a disk file or e-mail address as they occur.

The error_log() function needs a minimum of two arguments: the error message to be logged and an integer value indicating the log destination. This integer value may be 0 (the system log file), 1 (an e-mail address), or 3 (a disk file). An e-mail address or disk file path should be specified as a third argument to error_log() as needed.

Here's an example that demonstrates how this works:

```php
<?php
// attempt database connection
$mysqli = new mysqli("localhost", "user", "pass", "music");
if (mysqli_connect_error()) {
  error_log("ERROR: Could not connect. " . mysqli_connect_error() . "\n", 3,
'debug.log');
  die("ERROR: Could not connect. " . mysqli_connect_error());
}

// attempt query execution
// iterate over result set
// print each record and its fields
// output: "1:Aerosmith \n 2:Abba \n ..."
$sql = "SELECT artist_id, artist_name FROM artists";
if ($result = $mysqli->query($sql)) {
  if ($result->num_rows > 0) {
    while($row = $result->fetch_array()) {
      echo $row['artist_id'] . ":" . $row['artist_name'] . "\n";
    }
    $result->close();
  } else {
    echo "No records matching your query were found.";
  }
} else {
  error_log("ERROR: Could not execute $sql. " . $mysqli->error . "\n", 3,
'debug.log');
  echo "ERROR: Could not execute $sql. " . $mysqli->error;
}

// close connection
$mysqli->close();
?>
```

Assuming an incorrect user name or password, this script will log the following message to the file *debug.log*:

```
ERROR: Could not connect. Access denied for user 'user'@'localhost'
(using password: YES)
```

It's quite easy to combine this error logging facility with a custom error handler to ensure that all script errors get logged to a file. Here's an example that demonstrates this:

```php
<?php
// custom handler
function myHandler($type, $msg, $file, $line, $context) {
    error_log("[" . date("d-M-Y h:i:s", mktime()) . "] $msg on line
$line of $file\n", 3, 'debug.log');
    return false;
}

// report all errors
error_reporting(E_ALL);

// set custom handler
set_error_handler("myHandler");

// trigger E_NOTICE (undefined variable)
echo $someVar;

// trigger E_WARNING (missing file)
include("common.php");
?>
```

In this script, all notices and warnings generated by the code will first be automatically logged to the file *debug.log* with a timestamp. Following this, the custom handler returns false; this is deliberately done to return control back to PHP's default error handler and have the error handled in the normal manner.

Debugging Errors

With more complex applications, it becomes necessary to encapsulate commonly used tasks into independent components (functions and classes) and import these as needed into your PHP scripts. While this approach certainly improves the maintainability of your code, it can prove to be a burden when things aren't working as they should. For example, it's quite possible for an error in one component to affect the correct function of other components, and tracing this error back through the call stack is often a long (and frustrating) experience.

To reduce the pain involved in this process, there are various tools you can use. The first is provided by PHP itself, in the form of the debug_print_backtrace() function. This function prints a list of all the function calls leading up to a particular error, to help you identify the source quickly. To illustrate it in action, consider the following script, which contains a deliberate error:

```php
<?php
// custom error handler
// prints a stack trace if an error occurs
function myHandler($type, $msg) {
  debug_print_backtrace();
  exit();
}

class Page {
  public function __construct($num1, $num2) {
    $ex = new Example($num1, $num2);
  }
}

class Example {
  public function __construct($a, $b) {
    $this->a = $a+1;
    $this->b = $b-1;
    $this->run();
  }

  public function run() {
    return $this->a/$this->b;
  }
}

set_error_handler('myHandler');
$page = new Page(10,1);
echo 'Code execution successful';
?>
```

Here, the script will generate a "division by zero" warning, not because of an error in the Page class definition, but because of a warning generated by the run() method further down in the call stack. Figure 10-8 illustrates the error message one would normally see in this case.

Debugging such an error in practice can become fairly messy, especially when the function and class definitions are held in separate files. However, because the error handler in this script automatically prints a backtrace when an error occurs, it's not too difficult to identify the function that's causing the error. Figure 10-9 illustrates the revised output, showing the backtrace.

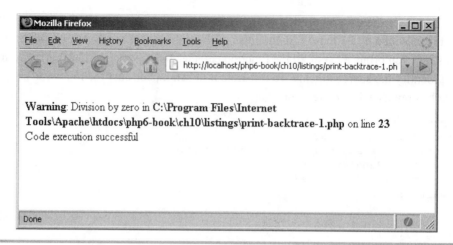

Figure 10-8 A PHP error without additional debugging information

TIP

To enhance PHP's core engine so that it automatically adds backtrace output to every error message, try adding the free Xdebug extension to your PHP build. For more information and installation instructions, visit www.xdebug.com/.

An even more sophisticated approach involves the use of the PHP Debug class, which is freely available from www.php-debug.com/. This class provides a useful framework for tracing script execution, watching and dumping variables, calculating execution times, and performing other common debugging tasks.

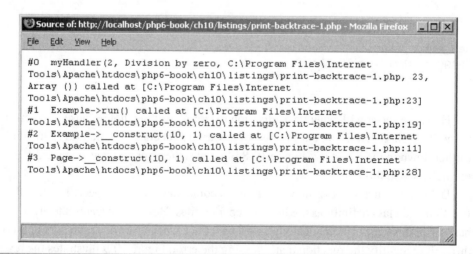

Figure 10-9 A PHP error enhanced with a backtrace

To use this class, download it and place the class files in your application directory. Then, revise the preceding listing to use it, as follows:

```php
<?php
// custom error handler
// prints a stack trace if an error occurs
function myHandler($type, $msg, $file, $line, $context) {
  global $debug;
  $debug->error($msg);
  echo '
  <!DOCTYPE html PUBLIC "-//W3C//DTD XHTML 1.0 Transitional//EN"
     "DTD/xhtml1-transitional.dtd">
  <html xmlns="http://www.w3.org/1999/xhtml" xml:lang="en" lang="en">
    <head>
      <title>Error Page</title>
      <link rel="stylesheet" type="text/css" href="./PHP_Debug-1.0.0/
css/html_table.css" />
    </head>
    <body>
  ';
  $debug->display();
  echo '
    </body>
  </html>
  ';
  exit();
}

// add debug hooks to classes and functions
class Page {
  public function __construct($num1, $num2) {
    global $debug;
    $debug->add('Entering Page::__construct');
    $debug->dump($this);
    $debug->dump(func_get_args(), 'method args');
    $ex = new Example($num1, $num2);
  }
}

class Example {
  public function __construct($a, $b) {
    global $debug;
    $debug->add('Entering Example::__construct');
    $debug->dump($this);
    $debug->dump(func_get_args(), 'method args');
    $this->a = $a+1;
```

```
        $this->b = $b-1;
        $this->run();
    }

    public function run() {
        global $debug;
        $debug->add('Entering Example::run');
        $debug->dump($this);
        $debug->dump(func_get_args(), 'method args');
        return $this->a/$this->b;
    }
}

// configure and read PHP_Debug files
ini_set('include_path', './PHP_Debug-1.0.0/;');
include 'PHP_Debug-1.0.0/PHP/Debug.php';
include 'PHP_Debug-1.0.0/PHP/Debug/Renderer/HTML/TableConfig.php';
$options = array(
        'render_type'            => 'HTML',
        'render_mode'            => 'Table',
        'replace_errorhandler' => false,
);
$debug = new PHP_Debug($options);
set_error_handler('myHandler');

// start running code
$page = new Page(10,1);
echo 'Code execution successful';
?>
```

The PHP_Debug class provides an object with various facilities to help developers debug a script. For instance, the object's add() method can be used to trace script execution by generating messages at user-defined points in the script, such as when entering a function or a loop. Similarly, the dump() method may be used to log the value of a variable at a given instant of time, while the display() method can be used to send all the debugging output to the output device. In the preceding listing, this display() method is used by the custom error handler if an error occurs, to automatically generate a neatly formatted backtrace of all the calls leading up to the error.

Figure 10-10 illustrates the output of the preceding listing.

As Figure 10-10 illustrates, PHP_Debug can provide a much more sophisticated record of the function calls leading up to an error than PHP's vanilla debug_print_backtrace() function.

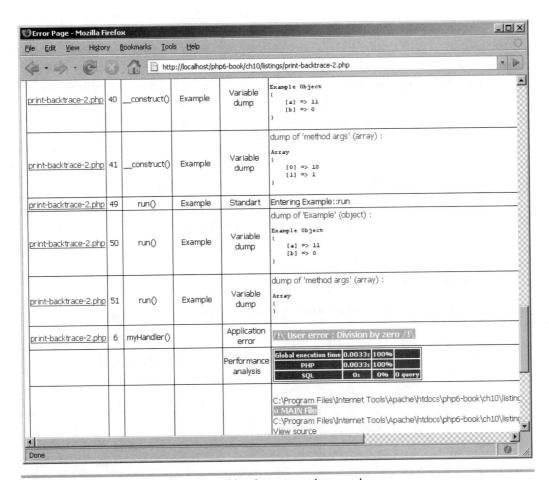

Figure 10-10 A backtrace generated by the PHP_Debug package

Summary

At the end of this chapter, you should have a much clearer idea of how PHP's error-handling framework works, as well as how you can customize it to suit the needs of your particular application. This chapter discussed two models: the earlier error-based model, and the newer exception model introduced with PHP 5. Ease of use and extensibility help the PHP 5 exception model score over the earlier, less primitive techniques; however, because it's not as well supported in the core libraries, most application development demands a judicious mix of the two approaches.

In addition to teaching you all about errors and exceptions, this chapter also introduced you to some of PHP's utility functions for error logging and debugging, and it demonstrated a third-party tool, the PHP_Debug package, to obtain detailed backtrace information when errors occur. Finally, two projects—a database error logger and a form input validator—demonstrated how all this theory can be used in practice.

To learn more about the topics covered in this chapter, consider visiting the following links:

- Exceptions, at **www.php.net/exceptions**

- Error handling functions, at **www.php.net/errorfunc**

- The official PHP_Debug Web site, at **www.php-debug.com**

Chapter 10 Self Test

1. Name two benefits of using the exception-based model.

2. Which types of script errors cannot be caught with a custom error handler?

3. What is an output buffer? How is it useful? Provide a working example that demonstrates its usefulness.

4. Which error handler will be active after the last line of each of the following code blocks is executed:

```php
<?php
set_error_handler('handlerA');
restore_error_handler();
?>

<?php
set_error_handler('handlerA');
set_error_handler('handlerB');
set_error_handler('handlerA');
restore_error_handler();
restore_error_handler();
?>
```

5. Using a custom error handler, illustrate how PHP notices and warnings may be converted to exceptions.

6. Write a program to automatically e-mail every uncaught exception in a script to an administrator.

Chapter 11

Securing PHP

Key Skills & Concepts

- Become familiar with security issues around PHP applications

- Prevent common types of attacks by sanitizing input and output

- Increase the security of your application files, databases, and sessions

- Learn to validate strings, numbers, and dates

- Begin using regular expressions for input validation

- Learn about PHP's security settings

Over the last few chapters, you've learned a great deal about getting and using data from external sources in your PHP applications. You've successfully processed data submitted through online forms, connected your Web pages to a database for dynamic page generation, and retrieved information encoded in XML.

Now, while integrating with all these external data sources can make your PHP applications more relevant and useful, there do remain some risks to be aware of. Insecure PHP applications are vulnerable to attack by malicious users, while improperly validated application input can cause calculations and reports to go wrong. Not only can these vulnerabilities cause significant data corruption and loss, but they can also be embarrassing in the extreme to the proud application developer.

That's where this chapter comes in. Over the next few pages, it will introduce you to various techniques that you can use to validate your application's input, thereby making it more secure and robust. Additionally, it will offer practical examples of input and output sanitization, discuss some of the important security-related variables in the PHP configuration file, and point you to various online resources where you can learn more about PHP application security.

Sanitizing Input and Output

As a Web application developer, there's one unhappy fact that you'll have to learn to live with: there are always going to be people out there who get their chuckles from finding loopholes in your code and exploiting these loopholes for malicious purposes.

Most of the time, these exploits consist of sending your application cleverly disguised input that "tricks" it into doing something it really, really shouldn't. A common example of this type of exploit is the "SQL injection attack," wherein an attacker remotely manipulates your database with an SQL query embedded inside form input. Therefore, one of the most important things a developer must do before using any input supplied by the user, is "sanitize" it by removing any special characters or symbols from it.

In a similar vein, if your application will be using data retrieved from remote sources, it's necessary to always "clean" this data before displaying it to the user. A failure to do this might allow attackers to embed malicious content in your Web pages without your knowledge. A common example of this type of exploit is the "cross-site scripting attack," wherein an attacker is able to gain access to sensitive user data by piggybacking malicious JavaScript code or HTML form code into your Web pages. With this in mind, it's always essential to pass output through a sanitization routine before making it available to the user.

Fortunately, PHP comes with various functions to assist developers in the twin tasks of sanitizing input and output. Here's a brief list:

- The addslashes() function escapes special characters (like quotes and backslashes) in input so that it can be safely entered into a database. Alternatively, use MySQLi's real_escape_string() method to sanitize input before inserting it into a MySQL database, or the sqlite_escape_string() function on input intended for an SQLite database.

- The strip_tags() function enables developers to strip all the HTML and PHP tags out of a string, returning only the ASCII content. This can be useful to remove potentially malicious code from both user input and remote data.

- The htmlentities() function takes care of replacing special characters like ", &, <, and > with their corresponding HTML entity values. By translating these special characters and preventing them from being interpreted as HTML code by the client, this function is very useful to "defang" data and render it incapable of affecting the display or functionality of a Web page.

Here's an example of using the real_escape_string() method and the strip_tags() function to defang user input before saving to a MySQL database:

```php
<?php
// attempt database connection
$mysqli = new mysqli("localhost", "user", "pass", "music");
if ($mysqli === false) {
  die("ERROR: Could not connect. " . mysqli_connect_error());
}
```

```php
// escape input values
if (isset($_POST['artist']) && !empty($_POST['artist'])) {
  $artist = $mysqli->real_escape_string(htmlspecialchars($_
POST['artist']));
}

if (isset($_POST['country']) && !empty($_POST['country'])) {
  $country = $mysqli->real_escape_string(htmlspecialchars($_
POST['country']));
}

// attempt query execution
// add a new record
// output: "New artist with id:7 added."
$sql = "INSERT INTO artists (artist_name, artist_country)
  VALUES ('$artist', '$country')";
if ($mysqli->query($sql) === true) {
  echo 'New artist with id:'  . $mysqli->insert_id . ' added.';
} else {
  echo "ERROR: Could not execute query: $sql. " . $mysqli->error;
}

// close connection
$mysqli->close();
?>
```

And here's an example of sanitizing form input with the `htmlentities()` function:

```php
<?php
// define array of sanitized data
$sanitized = array();

// strip tags from POST input
if (isset($_POST['name']) && !empty($_POST['name'])) {
  $sanitized['name'] = htmlentities($_POST['name']);
}

// processing code //
?>
```

Finally, here's an example of sanitizing potentially dangerous output before displaying it to the user:

```php
<?php
// define array of sanitized data
$sanitized = array();

// get remote data
```

```
$out = 'He<script>document.location.href=
  "http://go.somewhere.bad.com/";</script>llo';

// convert all special characters to entities
// before using it
$sanitized['out'] = htmlentities($out);

echo $out; // unsafe
echo $sanitized['out']; // safe
?>
```

Securing Data

In addition to sanitizing input, it's also important to ensure that your application does not inadvertently allow users to view or manipulate its private files or databases. The following sections discuss some techniques you can use to protect access to configuration files and other data sources.

Securing Configuration Files

Unless you explicitly configure your Web server to deny access to certain file types, any file located under the server's document root can be accessed by a remote user. This makes Web applications, which often store their configuration files with the rest of the application code under the server's document root, particularly vulnerable to unauthorized remote access.

An easy way to plug this security hole is to always store sensitive configuration data outside the Web server document root, and read it into your application as needed via a call to `require()` or `include()`. Because both these functions accept file system (rather than HTTP) paths, they can import files from directories that are not part of the server's document root, thereby making it harder for an attacker to gain access to configuration data.

Here's an example of how this might be done:

```
<?php
// server doc root is: /var/www/html/
// config file stored in: /var/www/apps/conf/

// your script can read this path
include_once '/var/www/apps/conf/myapp.conf'; // will work

// an attacker accessing the same path over HTTP cannot
file_get_contents('http://localhost/../apps/conf/myapp.conf'); // will fail
?>
```

> **NOTE**
>
> In order for this to work, the directory holding the configuration file must have its permission bits set such that its files can be read or written by the user owning the Web server process. This is particularly relevant on *NIX development systems.

Securing Database Access

A common reason for not securing database access is that it is "difficult" and "complicated." This is not strictly true. In most cases, there are some simple steps you can take to make it harder for attackers to gain access to your database, dramatically reducing the risk to your sensitive information. Because the database most commonly used with PHP is MySQL, the following three suggestions are directly relevant to MySQL; however, they can be easily applied to any other RDBMS as well.

● **Give users only the level of access they need**   Most databases, including MySQL, allow precise control over the level of access granted to individual users of the database system. There's a good reason to make use of this privilege system and only grant users as much access as they need: if users are granted blanket permissions to the entire database, a single compromised user account could result in significant data loss or theft. MySQL offers the GRANT and REVOKE commands to control a user's privilege level; different commands are available for other database systems.

The recommended approach here is to define a separate database user for each PHP application, and grant this user access only to the database(s) used by that application. This ensures that even if one application is compromised and its database access credentials stolen by an attacker, the extent of damage that can be wrought as a result will be limited and not affect other databases on the same server.

● **Use secure passwords**   When MySQL is first installed, access to the database server is restricted to the administrator ('root'). By default, this user account is initialized with an empty password, allowing free access to anyone. It's surprising how often this obvious security hole is overlooked by novice developers, who remain unaware of the dangers inherent in continuing with the default setting. With MySQL, the default password can be changed using the *mysqladmin* tool; the procedure differs for other database systems.

To improve security, then, it's a good idea to reset the database server's default administrator password at installation time, and then disseminate it to only the select handful of people who really need to know it. An administrator password that's widely known is highly insecure; the old adage "loose lips sink ships" is at least as true in this context as it was during World War II.

- **Disable remote access** The most common configuration for a LAMP development platform has the database server and Web server hosted on the same physical system. In this case, it's possible to significantly reduce the risk of a remote attack, by allowing only "local" access to the database server and blocking all remote connections. With MySQL, this can be done by using the `--skip-networking` option at server startup; the procedure differs for other database systems.

Securing Sessions

You've already seen, in Chapter 9, how PHP's built-in session management tools can be used to protect Web pages, and restrict access only to users who have successfully logged in to the system. However, this system is not foolproof: it's always possible for an attacker to "hijack" a session by gaining access to the unique session identifier and using it to recreate a user session.

The PHP Security Guide by Chris Shiflett *et al.* at www.phpsec.org/projects/guide/ recommends various methods to make such a session hijack more cumbersome to the attacker. One such suggestion involves the use of additional client-specific tokens for client identity verification. Essentially, this technique consists of recording various attributes of the client when it first requests a session-managed page—for example, the `'User-Agent'` header identifying the client's browser name—and then checking these attributes on each subsequent visit. A mismatch would imply that the original client's session has been hijacked, and access may then be appropriately denied.

Here's an illustration of how this might be used. The first step involves recording the content of the client's `'User-Agent'` header as a session variable, when the session is first initialized:

```php
<?php
// start session
// record remote client name as session variable
session_start();
$_SESSION['verif_remote_agent'] = $_SERVER['HTTP_USER_AGENT'];
echo 'Session started. Your session ID is: ' . session_id();

// processing code here //
?>
```

Now, on all subsequent accesses, in addition to checking for the presence of a valid session, the script should also check the `'User-Agent'` header sent by the client.

```php
<?php
// check session
// also check remote client name
```

```
session_start();
if (!isset($_SESSION['verif_remote_agent']) || $_SESSION['verif_
remote_agent'] != $_SERVER['HTTP_USER_AGENT']) {
  die('Session check failed.');
} else {
  echo 'Session verified.';
}

// processing code here //
?>
```

This method, though simple and quite effective, isn't completely foolproof: it's still possible for a dedicated attacker to get around it by forging the 'User-Agent' header. However, the additional test makes the task a little more difficult than it would otherwise be (because the attacker has to first guess the correct header), offering a higher level of security than otherwise.

A detailed discussion of the various techniques suggested by the PHP Security Guide to make sessions more secure is beyond the scope of this chapter; however, you'll find numerous well-documented examples online, at www.phpsec.org/projects/guide/.

Validating User Input

Web forms are not the only way a PHP script can receive user input; however, they remain the most *common* way. Before using this data, it's important to verify its validity, to cut down on instances of incorrect or incomplete data. This section discusses various techniques you can use to validate user input, received either through a Web form or in other contexts.

Working with Required Fields

One of the most common mistakes a novice programmer makes is forgetting to check for required field values in a Web form. This can result in a database with numerous empty records, and these empty records can, in turn, affect the accuracy of queries or calculations.

A simple way to test if all the required fields in a form have been filled is to test each corresponding key in $_POST or $_GET with PHP's empty() function. This function tests if the variable contains a non-empty and non-zero value. Here's an example:

```
<?php
// define array of valid data
$valid = array();
```

```php
// check for username
if (!empty($_POST['username'])) {
  $valid['username'] = trim($_POST['username']);
} else {
  die ('ERROR: Username not present.');
}

// check for password
if (!empty($_POST['password'])) {
  $valid['password'] = trim($_POST['password']);
} else {
  die ('ERROR: Password not present.');
}

// processing code here //
?>
```

In this listing, the script first tests whether data was submitted for both username and password fields. If both tests return true, then the script proceeds; if either one returns false, the script terminates immediately, without even attempting to process the form input.

Notice also the use of a $valid array in the preceding listing, which is used to store data that has passed validation. This is a good programming practice to ensure that you don't inadvertently use data that hasn't first been validated. By ensuring that your processing code only uses data from $valid, you reduce the risk of invalid values entering your database or calculations.

It should be noted that the empty() function is only suitable for use with form variables for which zero is considered an invalid value. This is because empty() returns false if the variable passed to it contains NULL, an empty string (' '), or a zero value. If zero is considered a valid value for your form variable, replace empty() with a combination of the isset() and trim() functions, as in the next listing:

```php
<?php
// define array of valid data
$valid = array();

// check for bid increment
if (isset($_POST['increment']) && trim($_POST['increment']) != '') {
  $valid['increment'] = trim($_POST['increment']);
} else {
  die ('ERROR: Increment value not present.');
}

// processing code here //
?>
```

The error check here is both simple and logical: the `trim()` function is used to trim leading and trailing spaces from the field variable, which is then compared to an empty string. If the match is true, it means the field was submitted without any data, and the script dies with an error message.

From these examples, it should be clear that a simple conditional test is all that is needed to ensure that required fields in your forms are never left empty. Failing such validation, the user's input will be processed without first checking that all required values are present. This could lead to potentially dangerous situations: for example, a user might be able to register himself or herself with the system with a blank password, a situation that might have serious ramifications for the overall security of the application.

Ask the Expert

Q: I'm already validating form input with JavaScript. Why do I need to also validate it through PHP?

A: It's common practice to use client-side scripting languages like JavaScript or VBScript for client-side form input validation. However, this type of validation is not foolproof. Two simple cases make this point:

- Web page source code can be viewed in most browsers. It is possible for a user to download the Web form, disable the client-side validation by editing the form's source code, and submit it back to the server with illegal values.

- If a user turns off JavaScript in his or her browser, client-side code will not execute. Client-side form validation routines will now be bypassed entirely, again opening the door for illegal values to enter the system.

PHP-based input validation resolves both these security issues, because PHP code executes on the server and thus cannot be modified or disabled from the client system.

Working with Numbers

As you've seen, when defining a new database table, it's also necessary to define the type of data that will be entered into each field. However, different database systems differ in how rigorously they enforce these data types. For example, SQLite allows string values to be entered into fields marked NUMERIC, while MySQL automatically "corrects" these values to 0 before inserting them into INT or FLOAT fields. Given these differences in approach, it's usually a good idea to enforce data type checking within your PHP application, to prevent incorrect or wrongly typed values from appearing in your database tables.

One easy way to test if a variable contains a numeric value is with PHP's is_ numeric() function, which returns true when called with a number as argument. The following example illustrates it in use:

```php
<?php
// define array of valid data
$valid = array();

// check if age is a number
if (is_numeric(trim($_POST['age']))) {
  $valid['age'] = trim($_POST['age']);
} else {
  die ('ERROR: Age is not a number.');
}

// processing code here //
?>
```

However, the is_numeric() function won't distinguish between integer and floating-point values. If you need this level of validation, an alternative is to first cast the questionable variable to an integer or floating-point value, and then test it with the strval() function. The following example illustrates:

```php
<?php
// define array of valid data
$valid = array();

// check if age is an integer value
if (strval($_POST['age']) == strval((int)$_POST['age'])) {
  $valid['age'] = trim($_POST['age']);
} else {
  die ('ERROR: Age is not an integer value.');
}

// check if price is a floating-point value
if (strval($_POST['price']) == strval((float)$_POST['price'])) {
  $valid['price'] = trim($_POST['price']);
} else {
  die ('ERROR: Price is not a decimal value.');
}

// processing code here //
?>
```

The logic here is quite simple: if the variable contains an integer, the string value returned by strval() after casting it to an integer will be the same as the raw string value of the variable. If, on the other hand, the variable contains a non-numeric value, the raw value of the variable will not match its post-casting value.

For an even more stringent test, use PHP's ctype_digit() function. This function checks every character of the value passed to it, and returns true only if every character is a digit between 0 and 9. Here's an example:

```php
<?php
// define array of valid data
$valid = array();

// check if age is an integer value
if (ctype_digit($_POST['age'])) {
  $valid['age'] = trim($_POST['age']);
} else {
  die ('ERROR: Age is not an integer value.');
}

// processing code here //
?>
```

CAUTION

Be aware that ctype_digit()'s rigorousness can also hinder you in some cases: the function will return false when passed decimal values, because the decimal point is not a digit between 0 and 9.

In certain cases, you may wish to enforce a range constraint on the numeric values that your application will accept. Testing this is as simple as using PHP's comparison operators, as shown here:

```php
<?php
// define array of valid data
$valid = array();

// check if day is an integer value and between 1 and 31
if ((strval($_POST['day']) == strval((int)$_POST['day'])) &&
($_POST['day'] >= 1 && $_POST['day'] <= 31)) {
  $valid['day'] = trim($_POST['day']);
} else {
  die ('ERROR: Age is not an integer value.');
}

// processing code here //
?>
```

Working with Strings

Many databases (including MySQL) will automatically truncate string values if they exceed the length specified for the corresponding field. This is disturbing, because it means that user input can easily (and silently) get corrupted without a notification being raised. So, it's usually a good idea to perform application-level input validation of string values, to alert users if their input goes above the prescribed limit and to allow them to modify it.

A good place to start for this kind of validation is the `strlen()` function, which returns the length of a string. This can come in handy to make sure that form input doesn't exceed a particular length. Consider the following example, which illustrates:

```php
<?php
// define array of valid data
$valid = array();

// check for username
if (!empty($_POST['username'])) {
  $username = trim($_POST['username']);
} else {
  die ('ERROR: Username not present.');
}

// check username length
if (strlen($username) <= 25) {
  $valid['username'] = $username;
} else {
  die ('ERROR: Username too long.');
}

// processing code here //
?>
```

If you need to be absolutely sure that a particular input field contains only alphabetic characters—for example, first and last names—PHP offers the `ctype_alpha()` function. Like the `ctype_digit()` function discussed in the preceding section, this function returns true only if every character in the string is alphabetic. Here's an example:

```php
<?php
// define array of valid data
$valid = array();

// check for first name
if (isset($_POST['firstname']) && ctype_alpha($_POST['firstname'])) {
  $valid['firstname'] = trim($_POST['firstname']);
```

```
} else {
    die ('ERROR: First name not present or invalid.');
}

// processing code here //
?>
```

TIP

PHP also offers the `ctype_alnum()` function for alphanumeric characters, the `ctype_space()` function for whitespace, and the `ctype_print()` function for printable characters. For a complete list, visit www.php.net/ctype.

Matching Patterns

For more complex string validation, PHP supports *regular expressions,* a powerful tool for matching and validating string patterns. Commonly associated with the *NIX platform, a regular expression lets you define patterns using a set of special *metacharacters.* These patterns can then be compared with text in a file, data entered into an application, or input from a Web form. Depending on whether or not the patterns match, the data can be considered valid or invalid.

A regular expression, following the Perl standard, is enclosed within forward slashes and usually looks something like this:

```
/fo+/
```

The + in this expression is a metacharacter: it means "match one or more occurrences of the preceding character." In the context of the preceding example, the regular expression translates to "a pattern containing the character *f* followed by one or more occurrences of the character *o*." Therefore, it would match the words "fool," "football," and "four-seater," but not "friar" or "flipper."

Similar to the + metacharacter are the * and ? metacharacters. These are used to match zero or more occurrences of the preceding character, and zero or one occurrence of the preceding character, respectively. So, the regular expression `/eg*/` would match "easy," "egocentric," and "egg," while the expression `/Wil?/` would match "Winnie," "Wimpy," "Wilson," and "William," though not "Wendy" or "Wolf."

You can also specify a range for the number of matches. For example, the regular expression `/jim{2,6}/` would match "jimmy" and "jimmmmmy!," but not "jim." The numbers in the curly braces represent the lower and upper values of the range to match; you can leave out the upper limit for an open-ended range match.

Metacharacter	What It Means
^	Beginning of string
$	End of string
.	Any character except a newline character
\s	A single whitespace character
\S	A single non-whitespace character
\d	A digit between 0 and 9
\w	An alphabetic or numeric character, or underscore
[A-Z]	An uppercase alphabetic character
[a-z]	A lowercase alphabetic character
[0-9]	A digit between 0 and 9
|	OR logical operator
(?=	Positive conditional test
(?!	Negative conditional test

Table 11-1   Regular Expression Metacharacters

Table 11-1 lists a few other useful metacharacters.

To see how regular expressions work, consider a Web form that requires the user to enter a username, password, and Social Security number. When validating this input, the developer needs to enforce the following constraints:

- The username must be between three and eight characters long, containing only alphabetic characters.
- The password must be between five and eight characters long, containing at least one number.
- The Social Security number must consist of nine digits, with a hyphen after the third and fifth digits.

Functions like `strlen()` and `ctype_alnum()` are typically much too simplistic for this kind of validation. Instead, a better approach is to define a pattern for each input value, and compare the actual input against the pattern to decide whether it is valid or not. Here's an illustration of how this may be done with regular expressions:

```php
<?php
// define array of valid data
$valid = array();
```

```
// check username
if (isset($_POST['username']) && preg_match('/^([a-zA-Z]){3,8}$/',
$_POST['username'])) {
  $valid['username'] = trim($_POST['username']);
} else {
  die ('ERROR: User name not present or invalid.');
}

// check password
if (isset($_POST['password']) && preg_match('/^(?=.*\d).{5,8}$/',
$_POST['password'])) {
  $valid['password'] = trim($_POST['password']);
} else {
  die ('ERROR: Password not present or invalid.');
}

// check SSN
if (isset($_POST['ssn']) && preg_match('/^([0-9]){3}-([0-9]){2}-([0-9])
{4}$/', $_POST['ssn'])) {
  $valid['ssn'] = trim($_POST['ssn']);
} else {
  die ('ERROR: SSN not present or invalid.');
}

// processing code here //
?>
```

This listing uses PHP's preg_match() function to test if the input conforms to the pattern defined for it. This preg_match() function requires two compulsory arguments: a pattern, and the value to test against the pattern. It returns true if a match is found, and false otherwise.

Coming to the regular expressions themselves, it shouldn't be too hard to decode them after reviewing the material in Table 11-1. They specify the allowed range of characters for each input value and the minimum and maximum lengths for each character subset. Only if the input matches the specified pattern will it be considered valid.

Here's another example, this one validating international telephone numbers:

```
<?php
// define array of valid data
$valid = array();

// check telephone number
if (isset($_POST['tel']) && preg_match("/^(\+|00)[1-9]{8,14}$/",
$_POST['tel'])) {
  $valid['tel'] = trim($_POST['tel']);
} else {
  die ('ERROR: Telephone number not present or invalid.');
}
?>
```

If you play with this a bit, you'll see that it'll accept the numbers *+441865123456* and *0091112345678,* even though each is formatted differently. This is because the regular expression uses the | metacharacter, which functions as logical OR and makes it possible to create a pattern that internally supports alternatives. You can, obviously, tighten or loosen the pattern, depending on the exact requirements of your application.

Thus, regular expressions provide a powerful and flexible way to validate input according to custom rules . . . even if the syntax takes a little getting used to!

Validating E-Mail Addresses and URLs

A common task when working with user input involves checking e-mail addresses and URLs to ensure that they are in the correct format. There are various ways to do this; perhaps the most common method involves regular expressions, as in the following example:

```php
<?php
// function to validate
// an e-mail address
function validateEmailAddress($str) {
    return preg_match("/^([a-z0-9_-])+([\.a-z0-9_-])*@([a-z0-9-])+(\
.[a-z0-9-]+)*\.([a-z]{2,6})$/", strtolower($str));
}

// check e-mail address
// output: 'valid'
echo validateEmailAddress("joe@some.domain.com") ? "valid" : "invalid";

// check e-mail address
// output: 'invalid'
echo validateEmailAddress("joe@dom.") ? "valid" : "invalid";
?>
```

Finding a regular expression to use for e-mail address validation isn't difficult; a large number of options can be found online, ranging from relaxed to restrictive. The preceding listing uses one of the more stringent patterns, restricting the range of characters in both the username and domain parts and requiring the length of the top-level domain to be between two and six characters.

It's possible to write a similar function to validate URLs. Here's an example:

```php
<?php
// function to validate a URL
function validateUrl($str) {
    return preg_match("/^(http|https|ftp):\/\/([a-z0-9]([a-z0-9_-]*
[a-z0-9])?\.)+[a-z]{2,6}\/?([a-z0-9\?\._-~&#=+%]*)?/", strtolower($str));
}
```

```php
// check URLs
// output: "valid"
echo validateUrl("http://www.example.com/html/index.php") ? "valid" :
"invalid";

// output: "invalid"
echo validateUrl("http://examplecom") ? "valid" : "invalid";
?>
```

URLs come in all shapes and sizes, and as with e-mail addresses, you can be generous or strict in how you choose to validate them. The regular expression used here restricts the protocol to HTTP, HTTPS, or FTP; requires the top-level domain to be between two and six characters long; and supports trailing path/filenames or anchors.

An alternative, perhaps simpler way of accomplishing the same task is to use PHP's filter_var() function, which provides built-in validation rules for common input types, including e-mail addresses and URLs. Here's a revision of the previous example for e-mail address validation:

```php
<?php
// function to validate
// an e-mail address
function validateEmailAddress($str) {
    return filter_var($str, FILTER_VALIDATE_EMAIL);
}

// check e-mail address
// output: 'valid'
echo validateEmailAddress("joe@some.domain.com") ? "valid" : "invalid";

// check e-mail address
// output: 'invalid'
echo validateEmailAddress("joe@dom.") ? "valid" : "invalid";
?>
```

Here, the filter_var() function tests the supplied variable to see if it is a valid e-mail address, returning true or false as the result. The constant FILTER_VALIDATE_EMAIL tells filter_var() to test the variable against the expected pattern for an e-mail address. Similarly, there's also FILTER_VALIDATE_URL, which can be used to test URLs for validity (although it uses a less stringent test than the regular expression shown previously):

```php
<?php
// function to validate a URL
function validateUrl($str) {
    return filter_var($str, FILTER_VALIDATE_URL);
}
```

```
// check URLs
// output: "valid"
echo validateUrl("http://www.example.com/html/index.php") ? "valid" :
"invalid";

// output: "invalid"
echo validateUrl("http:/examplecom") ? "valid" : "invalid";
?>
```

Working with Dates

Validating dates is another important aspect of input validation. It's all too easy, in the absence of proper validation, for a user to enter invalid dates like 29 February 2009 or 31 June 2008. It's important, therefore, to ensure that date values provided by the user are genuine before using them in a calculation.

In PHP, this task is significantly simpler than in other languages, because of PHP's checkdate() function. This function accepts three arguments—month, day, and year—and returns a Boolean value indicating whether or not the date is valid. The following example demonstrates it in action:

```
<?php
// define array of valid data
$valid = array();

// check for day
 if (!empty($_POST['day']) && ctype_digit($_POST['day'])) {
   $valid['day'] = trim($_POST['day']);
} else {
   die ('ERROR: Day not present.');
}

// check for month

if (!empty($_POST['month']) && ctype_digit($_POST['month'])) {
   $valid['month'] = trim($_POST['month']);
} else {
   die ('ERROR: Month not present.');
}

// check for year
 if (!empty($_POST['year']) && ctype_digit($_POST['year'])) {
   $valid['year'] = trim($_POST['year']);
} else {
   die ('ERROR: Year not present.');
}
```

```
// check for date validity
if (!checkdate($valid['month'], $valid['day'], $valid['year'])) {
  die ('ERROR: Invalid date.');
}

// processing code here //
?>
```

CAUTION

If you're storing dates in a MySQL DATE, DATETIME, or TIMESTAMP field, be aware that MySQL does *not* perform any rigorous date verification of its own. Therefore, the onus of checking a date before saving it to a MySQL table rests entirely with the application developer. The most that MySQL will do, if it encounters an obviously illegal date value, is replace it with a series of zeros . . . not necessarily the best solution! Read more about MySQL's handling of date and time values at http://dev.mysql.com/doc/mysql/en/datetime.html.

Try This 11-1   Validating Form Input

Now that you know the basics of input sanitization and validation, let's apply this learning to a practical project. This next example presents a Web form that asks users to enter various details for a book: the title, author, ISBN number, and price. It then validates this data using a mix of the techniques discussed in previous sections and, once validated, saves it to an SQLite database.

To begin, create an SQLite database and table to store the records entered by the user:

```
shell> sqlite books.db
SQLite version 3.3.17
Enter ".help" for instructions
sqlite> CREATE TABLE books (
   ...>    id INTEGER PRIMARY KEY,
   ...>    title TEXT,
   ...>    author TEXT,
   ...>    isbn INTEGER,
   ...>    price REAL
   ...> );
```

Next, write the PHP code to validate the data entered by the user through a Web form, and save it to a database. Here's the script (*books.php*):

```
<!DOCTYPE html PUBLIC "-//W3C//DTD XHTML 1.0 Transitional//EN"
   "DTD/xhtml1-transitional.dtd">
<html xmlns="http://www.w3.org/1999/xhtml" xml:lang="en" lang="en">
  <head>
    <title>Project 11-1: Validating Form Input</title>
    <style type="text/css">
    div.error {
```

```
      color:red;
      font-weight: bolder;
    }
    div.success {
      color:green;
      font-weight: bolder;
    }
    </style>
  </head>
  <body>
    <h2>Project 11-1: Validating Form Input</h2>
    <h3 style="background-color: silver">Enter Book Details</h3>
<?php
    // display input validation error
    function getInputError($key, $errArray) {
      if (in_array($key, $errArray)) {
        return "<div class=\"error\">ERROR: Invalid data for field '$key'</div>";
      } else {
        return false;
      }
    }

    $inputErrors = array();
    $submitted = false;

    // if form submitted
    // validate form input
    if (isset($_POST['submit'])) {
      $submitted = true;
      $valid = array();

      // validate title
      if (!empty($_POST['title'])) {
        $valid['title'] = htmlentities(trim($_POST['title']));
      } else {
        $inputErrors[] = 'title';
      }

      // validate author name
      if (!empty($_POST['author']) && preg_match("/^[a-zA-Z\s.\-]+$/",
$_POST['author'])) {
        $valid['author'] = htmlentities(trim($_POST['author']));
      } else {
        $inputErrors[] = 'author';
      }

      // validate ISBN
      if (!empty($_POST['isbn']) && preg_match('/^(97(8|9))?\d{9}(\d|X)$/',
$_POST['isbn'])) {
        $valid['isbn'] = htmlentities(trim($_POST['isbn']));
      } else {
        $inputErrors[] = 'isbn';
      }
```

(continued)

```php
        // validate price
        if (!empty($_POST['price']) && is_numeric($_POST['price']) && $_POST['price'] > 0)
{
            $valid['price'] = htmlentities(trim($_POST['price']));
        } else {
            $inputErrors[] = 'price';
        }
    }


    // if form not submitted
    // or if validation errors exist
    // (re)display form
    if (($submitted == true && count($inputErrors) > 0) || $submitted == false) {
?>
    <form method="post" action="books.php">
      Title: <br />
      <input type="text" size="25" name="title"
        value="<?php echo isset($_POST['title']) ? $_POST['title'] : '';?>" /><br/>
      <?php echo getInputError('title', $inputErrors); ?>
      <p>
      Author: <br />
      <input type="text" size="25" name="author"
        value="<?php echo isset($_POST['author']) ? $_POST['author'] : '';?>" /><br/>
      <?php echo getInputError('author', $inputErrors); ?>
      <p>
      ISBN: <br />
      <input type="text" size="25" name="isbn"
        value="<?php echo isset($_POST['isbn']) ? $_POST['isbn'] : '';?>" /><br/>
      <?php echo getInputError('isbn', $inputErrors); ?>
      <p>
      Price: <br />
      <input type="text" size="6" name="price"
        value="<?php echo isset($_POST['price']) ? $_POST['price'] : '';?>" /><br/>
      <?php echo getInputError('price', $inputErrors); ?>
      <p>
      <input type="submit" name="submit" value="Submit" />
    </form>
<?php
    // if form submitted with no errors
    // write the input to the database
    } else {
      // open SQLite database file
      try {
        $pdo = new PDO('sqlite:books.db');
        $pdo->setAttribute(PDO::ATTR_ERRMODE, PDO::ERRMODE_EXCEPTION);
      } catch (PDOException $e) {
        die("ERROR: Could not connect: " . $e->getMessage());
      }

      // create and execute INSERT query
```

```
    try {
      $title = $pdo->quote($valid['title']);
      $author = $pdo->quote($valid['author']);
      $isbn = $pdo->quote($valid['isbn']);
      $price = $pdo->quote($valid['price']);
      $sql = "INSERT INTO books (title, author, isbn, price) VALUES ($title, $author,
$isbn, $price)";
      $ret = $pdo->exec($sql);
      echo '<div class="success">SUCCESS: Record saved!</div>';
    } catch (Exception $e) {
      echo '<div class="error">ERROR: ' . $e->getMessage() . '</div>';
    }

    // close connection
    unset($pdo);
  }
?>
  </body>
</html>
```

Figure 11-1 illustrates what the Web form looks like.

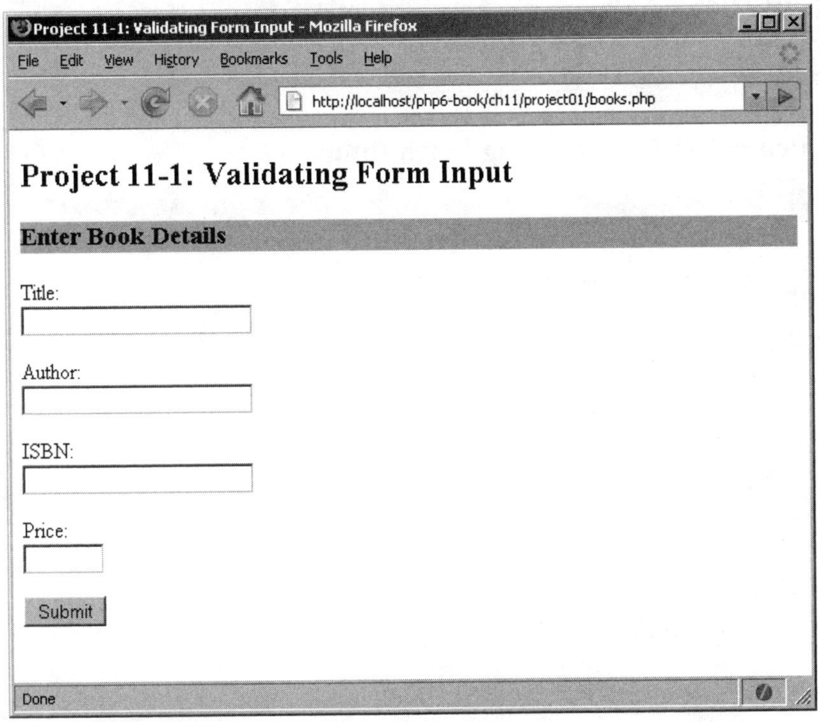

Figure 11-1   A Web form to enter book details

(continued)

When this form is submitted, the script goes to work validating the input provided by the user. In addition to checking that all the fields contain values, the script also uses regular expressions to test the author name and ISBN number, and the is_numeric() function to check that the price entered is a number. Fields that fail validation are flagged, by adding them to the $inputErrors array. Valid fields are sanitized by passing them through htmlentities() and then added to the $valid array.

Once the validation/sanitization phase is complete, the script first checks if any input validation errors occurred. Assuming no errors, a PDO connection is opened to the SQLite database, and the values from the $valid array are formulated into an INSERT query and saved to the database. If, however, one or more validation errors occurred, the form is redisplayed with prompts to correct the invalid values. Notice the user-defined function getInputError(), which checks and displays the error status of each input value, thus providing a convenient way to notify the user of all the input errors at once, instead of singly.

Figure 11-2 illustrates the output when some of the input values fail validation. And Figure 11-3 illustrates the output when the input is successfully validated and saved.

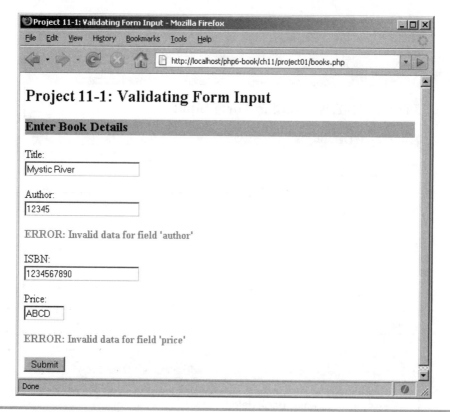

Figure 11-2 The output when form input fails validation

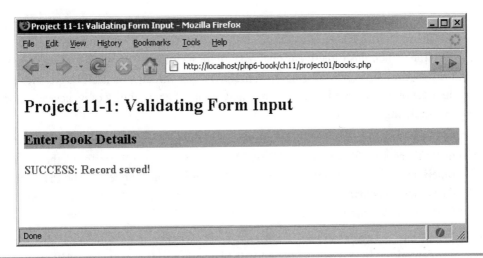

Figure 11-3 The output when form input is successfully validated and saved

Configuring PHP Security

In addition to the techniques discussed in previous sections, there are also various PHP configuration directives you can set, to reduce the risk of attackers gaining unauthorized access to your application. All these directives can be set in the PHP configuration file, *php.ini,* or at run time with PHP's `ini_set()` function. Here's a brief list:

- **'disable_functions'** The `'disable_functions'` directive allows developers to disable certain built-in PHP functions for security reasons. Examples of these are functions that allow remote execution of shell commands, like `exec()` and `passthru()`, or functions that display internal PHP or Web server information, like `phpinfo()`.

- **'disable_classes'** Like `'disable_functions'`, the `'disable_classes'` directive allows developers to disable certain PHP classes that pose a security risk.

- **'allow_url_fopen'** The `'allow_url_fopen'` directive determines whether a PHP script can read data from remote URLs as though they were files, with file functions such as `file_get_contents()`, `include()`, or `fopen()`. Unless your PHP application needs to obtain data from a remote URL over HTTP or FTP, this function should be disabled.

- **'open_basedir'** The 'open_basedir' directive allows developers to restrict all file operations taking place within a PHP script to a particular directory and its children. When this directive is enabled, a PHP script will not be able to "see" outside the top-level directory named in this directive. This directive is useful to restrict an application to a defined directory tree, and reduce the possibility of its accessing or manipulating sensitive system files.

- **'error_reporting'** You've already seen the error_reporting() function in the preceding chapter. The 'error_reporting' directive performs the same function: it allows the developer to control the error reporting level. The PHP Security Guide suggests that in most cases, this should be set to E_ALL, so that all errors (notices and warnings) are reported to the developer.

- **'display_errors'** The 'display_errors' directive controls whether the errors reported by a script are actually displayed in script output. The PHP manual recommends enabling this directive in development environments, but disabling it in production environments, as attackers can often use the diagnostic information displayed in an error message to locate and exploit vulnerabilities in your PHP code.

- **'log_errors'** Just because errors aren't displayed, that doesn't mean they should be completely ignored. The 'log_errors' directive specifies whether errors occurring in a PHP script should be written to a log file for later analysis. In most cases, this directive should be enabled, especially if 'display_errors' is turned off, so that there exists some record of the errors generated by an application.

- **'expose_php'** The 'expose_php' directive determines whether PHP adds information about itself to the Web server context. The PHP manual recommends that this directive be disabled, to avoid providing potential attackers with additional information about the server's capabilities.

- **'max_input_time'** The 'max_input_time' directive determines the maximum amount of time a PHP script has to receive and parse input data, including data passed via GET and POST. A limit on this time interval reduces the time available to an attacker attempting to interactively construct and transmit a POST or GET request.

- **'session.name'** The 'session.name' directive controls the name of the session cookie used by PHP to track user sessions. By default, this cookie is named PHPSESSID. It's a good idea to change this cookie name from the default value, again to make it more difficult for attackers to identify it and view its contents.

Table 11-2 lists where each of these directives can be set.

Directive	Can Be Set in *php.ini*	Can Be Set at Run Time with `ini_set()`
`'disable_functions'`	Yes	No
`'disable_classes'`	Yes	No
`'allow_url_fopen'`	Yes	Yes
`'open_basedir'`	Yes	Yes
`'error_reporting'`	Yes	Yes
`'display_errors'`	Yes	Yes
`'log_errors'`	Yes	Yes
`'expose_php'`	Yes	No
`'max_input_time'`	Yes	No
`'session.name'`	Yes	Yes

Table 11-2   PHP Security Directives

NOTE

It is necessary to restart the Web server in order to activate changes made to the PHP configuration file, *php.ini*.

Summary

This chapter focused specifically on security, discussing various techniques you can use to reduce the risk of damage (whether intended or accidental) to your PHP application. It showed you the basics of input and output sanitization, explained how to escape database input and defang third-party output, and offered tips on securing your application files, databases, and sessions. It also gave you a crash course in input validation, showing you how regular expressions, character type functions, and conditional tests may be used to check the validity of user input before using it in a calculation or database operation.

While this chapter covered a lot of ground, it's still only the tip of the iceberg: PHP security is a vast topic, and building a robust, attack-resistant application requires both experience and sound technical knowledge. Fortunately, acquiring expertise in this subject isn't difficult; there are numerous resources available online to help you learn about potential attacks and plug loopholes in your application code. You're encouraged to visit these to learn more about the topics discussed in this chapter:

- An overview of PHP security issues, at **www.php.net/security**

- The PHP Security Guide, at **www.phpsec.org/projects/guide/**

- Articles and discussions on PHP security by the PHP Security Consortium, at **www.phpsec.org/**

- Regular expression functions, at **www.php.net/pcre**

- Character type functions, at **www.php.net/ctype**

- A discussion of cross-site scripting attacks, at **http://en.wikipedia.org/wiki/Cross-site_scripting**

- A discussion of SQL injection attacks, at **http://en.wikipedia.org/wiki/SQL_injection**

- Examples of cross-site scripting attacks, at **http://ha.ckers.org/xss.html**

- Examples of regular expressions, at **www.regexlib.com**

- Tutorials on regular expressions, at **www.melonfire.com/community/columns/trog/article.php?id=2** and **www.regular-expressions.info/tutorial.html**

- Tutorials on client-side input validation, at **www.sitepoint.com/article/client-side-form-validation** and **http://home.cogeco.ca/~ve3ll/jstutor5.htm**

Chapter 11 Self Test

1. Name and explain any two attacks discussed in this chapter. Also indicate how to protect your application from these attacks.

2. Name and illustrate two functions you would use to escape output.

3. Demonstrate the use of a regular expression to validate U.S. postal codes, in the format *ddddd-dddd*.

4. Why should error display be disabled in production environments?

5. Explain what each of the following functions do:

- `ctype_alnum()`

- `addslashes()`

- `filter_var()`

- `htmlentities()`

- `sqlite_escape_string()`

- `preg_match()`

- `strval()`

Chapter 12

Extending PHP

Key Skills & Concepts

* Learn about the PEAR and PECL code repositories

* Understand how to install a PEAR or PECL package

* Communicate with a POP3 server using a PEAR package

* Dynamically create a Zip archive using a PECL package

As an open-source language, PHP has the support of thousands of developers across the world. This community support, coupled with the language's ease of use, has produced hundreds of widgets and extensions that can be used to add new capabilities to the core engine. These widgets and extensions form a robust, stable code base that is invaluable to developers, as it allows them to create high-quality Web applications quickly and efficiently, and with minimal "hand coding."

Two of the largest online repositories for these PHP add-ons are PEAR, the PHP Extension and Application Repository, and PECL, the PHP Extension Community Library. This chapter will introduce you to both these repositories, using practical examples to demonstrate how they can make your PHP development simpler and more effective.

Using PEAR

PEAR is the PHP Extension and Application Repository, available on the Web at http://pear.php.net/. Its purpose is to provide PHP developers with a library of reusable PHP classes (also called *packages*), that can easily be integrated into any PHP application and that follow a standard coding style and file structure. PEAR packages are distributed as compressed TAR archives and can be installed to any PHP development system using the PEAR installer (included with every PHP distribution).

PEAR packages cover a diverse array of categories. Some of these are

* User authentication (Auth, Auth_HTTP)

* Database integration (MDB, DB_DataObject, DB_QueryTool, Query2XML, and Structures_DataGrid)

* Form processing (HTML_QuickForm, Validate, and Text_CAPTCHA)

* Network protocols (Net_SMTP, Net_POP3, NET_LDAP, and Net_FTP)

* File formats (File_PDF, Archive_TAR, and Spreadsheet_Excel_Writer)

- Application localization (I18N)

- Benchmarking, logging, and unit testing (Benchmark, Log, PHPUnit)

Installing PEAR Packages

PHP comes with an automated installer for PEAR packages. This installer has the capability to automatically connect to PEAR's central server, download the requested package, and install it to your PHP development environment.

NOTE

Windows users must first configure the PEAR installer by manually executing the *go-pear* *.bat* batch file, located in their PHP installation directory. This file will configure the PEAR installer, generate the necessary registry entries, and place installer files in the correct locations on the file system. For more details, review the Windows-specific installation notes in the PEAR manual, at http://pear.php.net/manual/en/installation.getting.php.

To install a PEAR package using the installer, simply issue the following command at the shell prompt:

```
shell> pear install package-name
```

The PEAR installer will now connect to the PEAR package server, download the package, and install it to the appropriate location on your system. Figure 12-1 has an example of installing the Net_POP3 package.

```
192.168.0.9 - PuTTY
root@achilles:/tmp# pear install Net_POP3
WARNING: channel "pear.php.net" has updated its protocols, use "channel-update p
ear.php.net" to update
downloading Net_POP3-1.3.6.tar ...
Starting to download Net_POP3-1.3.6.tar (Unknown size)
.............done: 45,568 bytes
install ok: channel://pear.php.net/Net_POP3-1.3.6
root@achilles:/tmp#
```

Figure 12-1 Installing a PEAR package on UNIX

TIP

If you're not able to get the PEAR installer to work correctly, try adding the -v option to the installation command line, to display additional debugging information.

Try This 12-1 Accessing POP3 Mailboxes with PEAR

To illustrate PEAR's usefulness in real life, consider a simple application: a mailbox checker, which accepts a user's credentials and connects to his or her mail server to retrieve the corresponding mailbox data. To do this in PHP, a developer would need to either recompile PHP with support for its IMAP extension or use socket programming to directly communicate with the mail server, manually sending requests and interpreting responses. The first option is time-consuming (and often impractical on shared or production servers), while the second is both time-inefficient and resource-intensive.

PEAR, however, offers a third, much simpler option: the Net_POP3 package at http://pear.php.net/package/Net_POP3, which provides a ready-made API to connect to, and interact with, a POP3-compliant mail server. Using this package offers two important benefits: first, it can be immediately used within a PHP script, with no server-side changes necessary; and second, it provides a high-level API that already encompasses all required functionality, including error handling, significantly reducing the total development time required for the project.

Here's what the code would look like (*pop3.php*):

```
<!DOCTYPE html PUBLIC "-//W3C//DTD XHTML 1.0 Transitional//EN"
    "DTD/xhtml11-transitional.dtd">
<html xmlns="http://www.w3.org/1999/xhtml" xml:lang="en" lang="en">
  <head>
    <title>Project 12-1: Accessing POP3 Mailboxes with PEAR</title>
  </head>
  <body>
    <h2>Project 12-1: Accessing POP3 Mailboxes with PEAR</h2>
    <?php
    // if form submitted
    if (isset($_POST['submit'])) {

      // create exceptions
      class InputException extends Exception { }
      class ConnException extends Exception { }

      // get form input
      $host = $_POST['host'];
      $port = $_POST['port'];
      $user = $_POST['user'];
      $pass = $_POST['pass'];

      try {
```

```php
      // validate form input
      if (empty($host)) {
        throw new InputException('Host name missing');
      }
      if (empty($port)) {
        throw new InputException('Port missing');
      }
      if (empty($user)) {
        throw new InputException('User name missing');
      }
      if (empty($pass)) {
        throw new InputException('Password missing');
      }

      // create object
      require_once 'Net/POP3.php';
      $pop3 =& new Net_POP3();

      // connect to host
      if(PEAR::isError($ret = $pop3->connect($host, $port))){
          throw new ConnException($ret->getMessage());
      }

      // log in
      if(PEAR::isError($ret = $pop3->login($user, $pass, 'USER'))){
          throw new ConnException($ret->getMessage());
      }

      // get number of messages and mailbox size
      echo $pop3->numMsg() . ' message(s) in mailbox, ' . $pop3->getSize() . '
bytes <p/>';

      // get headers for most recent message
      if ($pop3->numMsg() > 0) {
        $msgData = $pop3->getParsedHeaders($pop3->numMsg());
        echo 'Most recent message from ' . htmlentities($msgData['From']) . ',
subject \'' . htmlentities($msgData['Subject']) . '\'';
      }

      // disconnect
      $pop3->disconnect();

    } catch(InputException $e) {
      die('Input validation error: ' . $e->getMessage());
    } catch(ConnException $e) {
      die('Connection error: Server said ' . $e->getMessage());
    } catch(Exception $e) {
      die('ERROR: ' . $e->getMessage());
    }

  } else {
  ?>
  <form method="post" action="pop3.php">
    Server name: <br />
    <input type="text" size="20" name="host" />
```

(continued)

```
    <p>
    Server port: <br />
    <input type="text" size="4" name="port" value="110" />
    <p>
    User name: <br />
    <input type="text" size="20" name="user" />
    <p>
    Password: <br />
    <input type="password" size="10" name="pass" />
    <p>
    <input type="submit" name="submit" value="Submit" />
  </form>
  <?php
  }
  ?>
 </body>
</html>
```

This script begins by generating a simple Web form for the user's mail server and access information (Figure 12-2). Once this form is submitted, the data entered into the

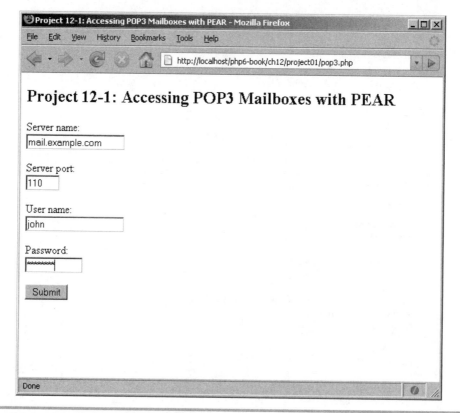

Figure 12-2 A Web form to enter mail server information

form is validated, and exceptions are thrown if any of it is found to be invalid. Next, the Net_POP3 class file is loaded, and an instance of the Net_POP3 class is initialized. The class exposes a connect() method; when passed the POP3 server name and port as arguments, this method attempts to open a connection to the specified POP3 server. Once a connection is made, the class' login() method is then used to log in to the server and access the user's mailbox, using the supplied credentials as input.

After a successful login, a number of utility methods become available to interact with the mailbox: for example, the numMsg() method returns the number of messages in the mailbox, while the getSize() method returns the mailbox size in bytes. Where possible, the subject and sender of the most recent message are also retrieved using the getParsedHeaders() method, which returns an array of message headers. Once all this information has been collected and displayed, the disconnect() method is used to cleanly terminate the connection to the server.

Figure 12-3 displays the results of a successful connection.

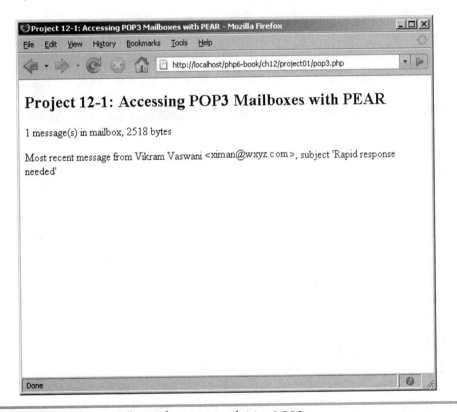

Figure 12-3 Retrieving mailbox information with Net_POP3

Using PECL

PECL is the PHP Extension Community Library, available on the Web at http://pecl.php.net/. PECL seeks to extend PHP's capabilities through low-level language modules, which are written in the C programming language and must be integrated directly into the PHP engine (usually through compilation). PECL extensions are distributed as compressed TAR archives and can be installed to any PHP development system either through a manual compile-and-install process or with the PECL installer (included with every PHP distribution).

Installing PECL Extensions

The procedure for installing a PECL extension differs on UNIX and Windows. To download, compile, and install a PECL extension on UNIX, all in one fell swoop, issue the following command at the shell prompt:

```
shell> pecl install extension-name
```

The PECL installer will now connect to the PECL server, download the source code, compile it, and install it to the appropriate location on your system. Figure 12-4 has an example of installing the Zip extension, available from http://pecl.php.net/package/zip.

```
192.168.0.9 - PuTTY
-build-root/install-zip-1.8.10
166335    4 drwxr-xr-x   3 root      root        4096 Mar 24 22:05 /var/tmp/pear
-build-root/install-zip-1.8.10/usr
166336    4 drwxr-xr-x   3 root      root        4096 Mar 24 22:05 /var/tmp/pear
-build-root/install-zip-1.8.10/usr/local
166337    4 drwxr-xr-x   3 root      root        4096 Mar 24 22:05 /var/tmp/pear
-build-root/install-zip-1.8.10/usr/local/lib
166338    4 drwxr-xr-x   3 root      root        4096 Mar 24 22:05 /var/tmp/pear
-build-root/install-zip-1.8.10/usr/local/lib/php
166339    4 drwxr-xr-x   3 root      root        4096 Mar 24 22:05 /var/tmp/pear
-build-root/install-zip-1.8.10/usr/local/lib/php/extensions
166340    4 drwxr-xr-x   2 root      root        4096 Mar 24 22:05 /var/tmp/pear
-build-root/install-zip-1.8.10/usr/local/lib/php/extensions/no-debug-non-zts-200
60613
166341  292 -rwxr-xr-x   1 root      root      291000 Mar 24 22:05 /var/tmp/pear
-build-root/install-zip-1.8.10/usr/local/lib/php/extensions/no-debug-non-zts-200
60613/zip.so

Build process completed successfully
Installing '/usr/local/lib/php/extensions/no-debug-non-zts-20060613/zip.so'
install ok: channel://pecl.php.net/zip-1.8.10
configuration option "php_ini" is not set to php.ini location
You should add "extension=zip.so" to php.ini
root@achilles:/tmp# 
```

Figure 12-4 Installing a PECL extension on UNIX

Alternatively, download the package source code and manually compile it into a loadable PHP module:

```
shell# cd zip-1.8.10
shell# phpize
shell# ./configure
shell# make
shell# make install
```

This process should generate a loadable PHP module named *zip.so* and copy it to the PHP extension directory. It will now need to be enabled in the *php.ini* configuration file.

Windows users have a much easier time of it: they need to simply download a precompiled PECL extension, copy it into PHP's extension directory, and then activate the extension in the *php.ini* configuration file. Precompiled PECL extensions for Windows are freely available on the Web, at http://pecl4win.php.net/.

Once the extension has been correctly installed and activated, restart the Web server and check the output of the phpinfo() command. If the extension has been correctly installed, phpinfo() will display an entry for the extension, as in Figure 12-5.

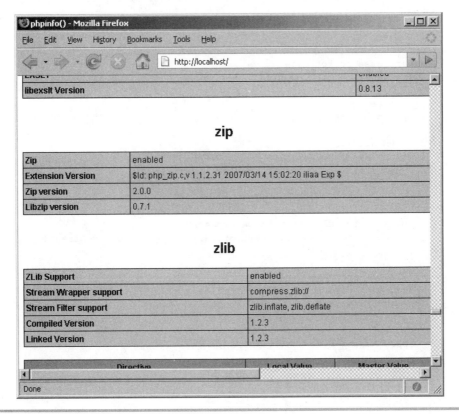

Figure 12-5 The output of the phpinfo() command, showing the new PECL extension

TIP

You can find more information on installing PECL extensions in the PHP manual, at www.php.net/manual/install.pecl.php.

Try This 12-2   Creating Zip Archives with PECL

Let's consider another example: creating a compressed Zip archive. This isn't something you can normally do with PHP, because the default PHP build doesn't include Zip file support. PECL comes to the rescue with its Zip extension, which provides a full-featured API for reading and writing Zip archives.

Here's an example of it in action (*zip.php*):

```
<!DOCTYPE html PUBLIC "-//W3C//DTD XHTML 1.0 Transitional//EN"
    "DTD/xhtml1-transitional.dtd">
<html xmlns="http://www.w3.org/1999/xhtml" xml:lang="en" lang="en">
  <head>
    <title>Project 12-2: Creating Zip Archives with PECL</title>
  </head>
  <body>
    <h2>Project 12-2: Creating Zip Archives with PECL</h2>
    <?php
      // increase script timeout value
      ini_set('max_execution_time', 300);

      // create object
      $zip = new ZipArchive();

      // open archive
      if ($zip->open('my-archive.zip', ZIPARCHIVE::CREATE) !== TRUE) {
          die ("ERROR: Could not open archive file.");
      }

      // initialize an iterator
      // pass it the directory to be processed
      $iterator = new RecursiveIteratorIterator(new RecursiveDirectoryIterator(
"app/"));

      // iterate over the directory
      // add each file found to the archive
      foreach ($iterator as $key=>$value) {
        $zip->addFile(realpath($key), $key) or die ("ERROR: Could not add file:
$key");
          echo "Adding file $key...<br/>";
      }

      // close and save archive
```

```
        $zip->close();
        echo "Archive created successfully.";
    ?>
  </body>
</html>
```

This listing illustrates how PECL's Zip extension can be used to add Zip archive support to PHP. The script begins by instantiating a ZipArchive object; this object serves as the entry point to all of the Zip extension's functions. Next, the object's open() method is used to create a new archive file, and the addFile() method is then used, in combination with a RecursiveDirectoryIterator, to iterate over the *app/* directory and its children, adding all the files found to the archive. Once all the files have been added, the object's close() method takes care of compressing and writing the final archive to disk.

Figure 12-6 demonstrates the result.

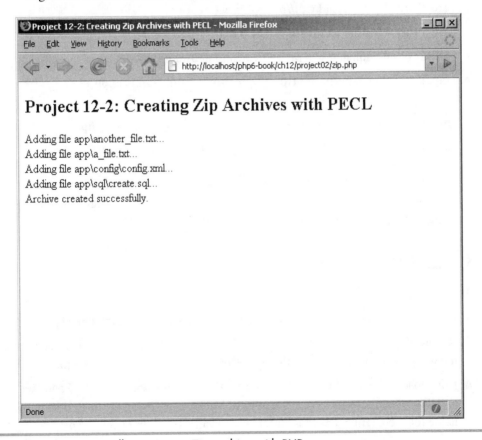

Figure 12-6 Dynamically creating a Zip archive with PHP

Summary

Although you've reached the final chapter in this book, it should be clear that your PHP journey is far from over . . . if anything, it's only just beginning! Both PEAR and PECL are popular repositories of high-quality, stable PHP add-ons and widgets, and new packages are constantly being added to them. This chapter demonstrated just two of the many hundreds of packages currently available: a POP3 client library, and a Zip format compression module.

If you ever come across a particularly knotty development problem, spare a few moments to search these repositories, and chances are high you'll find a ready-made solution that will save you hours of development time. In the meanwhile, the following links will help you learn more about the topics covered in this chapter:

- The PEAR Web site, at **http://pear.php.net**
- The PECL Web site, at **http://pecl.php.net**
- PEAR installation notes, at **http://pear.php.net/manual/en/installation.php**
- PECL installation notes, at **http://php.net/manual/install.pecl.php**
- Documentation for the Net_POP3 package, at **http://pear.php.net/manual/en/package.networking.net-pop3.php**
- Documentation for the PECL Zip extension, at **www.php.net/zip**

You've now reached the end of this book. I hope you enjoyed it and found it useful, and that you now have the grounding necessary to go out there and begin creating your own high-quality PHP applications. Good luck, and happy coding!

Chapter 12 Self Test

1. What is the difference between PEAR and PECL?

2. Describe the steps to install a PECL extension in a Windows development environment.

3. Review the documentation for the Net_POP3 package used in this chapter, and rewrite the worked example to display the complete contents of the most recent message.

4. Download and install PECL's ID3 extension for working with MP3 files, and then write a PHP application to process a directory of MP3 files, printing the track title and artist name for each. (Hint: The PECL package is available at http://pecl.php.net/package/id3, and the documentation can be found at www.php.net/id3.)

Part IV

Appendixes

Appendix A

Installing and Configuring Required Software

Key Skills & Concepts

- Learn to obtain and install MySQL, SQLite, PHP, and Apache software from the Internet

- Perform basic testing to ensure that the applications are working correctly

- Find out how to automatically activate all required components on system startup

- Take basic steps to safeguard the security of your MySQL installation

In this book, you learned about the PHP programming language and how it can be used to build sophisticated Web applications. Some of the examples in this book also involved using PHP with third-party components, such as XML, MySQL, and SQLite. This appendix shows you how to install and configure these components on your workstation, and create a development environment that can be used to run the code examples in this book.

CAUTION

This appendix is intended to provide an overview and general guide to the process of installing and configuring MySQL, SQLite, PHP, and Apache on UNIX and Windows. It is *not* intended as a replacement for the installation documentation that ships with each software package. If you encounter difficulties installing or configuring the various programs described here, visit the respective program's Web site or search the Web for detailed troubleshooting information and advice (some links are provided at the end of this chapter).

Obtaining the Software

The first step is to make sure that you have all the software you need. Here's a list:

- **PHP**   PHP provides an application development framework for both Web and console applications. It can be downloaded from www.php.net/. Here too, both source and binary versions are available for Windows, UNIX, and Mac OS X platforms. UNIX users should download the latest source archive, while Windows users should download the latest binary release. At the time of going to press, the most current version of PHP is PHP 5.3.0 alpha 1.

- **Apache**   Apache is a feature-rich Web server that works well with PHP. It can be downloaded free of charge from http://httpd.apache.org/ in both source and binary forms, for a variety of platforms. UNIX users should download the latest source archive, while Windows users should download a binary installer appropriate for their version of Windows. At the time of going to press, the most current version of the Apache server is Apache 2.2.9.

- **MySQL**   The MySQL database server provides robust and scalable data storage/ retrieval. It is available in both source and binary versions from www.mysql.com/. Binary distributions are available for Linux, Solaris, FreeBSD, Mac OS X, Windows, HP-UX, IBM AIX, SCO OpenUNIX, and SGI Irix, and source distributions are available for both Windows and UNIX platforms. The binary version is recommended, for two reasons: it is easier to install, and it is optimized for use on different platforms by the MySQL development team. At the time of going to press, the most current version of the MySQL database server is MySQL 5.0.67.

- **SQLite**   SQLite is a self-contained database library file that is significantly smaller than MySQL. It is available in both source and binary versions from www.sqlite.org/, for Windows, UNIX, and Mac OS X platforms. Windows and UNIX users should both download the binary version (a download link is available on this book's companion Web site). At the time of going to press, the most current version of SQLite is SQLite 3.6.1. However, because SQLite 3.x support in PHP 5.3 is still experimental at the time of writing, this book makes use of SQLite 2.x.

In addition to these four basic components, UNIX users may also require some supporting libraries. Here's a list:

- The `libxml2` library, available from www.xmlsoft.org/
- The `zlib` library, available from www.gzip.org/zlib/

Finally, users on both platforms will need a decompression tool capable of dealing with TAR (Tape Archive) and GZ (GNU Zip) files. On UNIX, the *tar* and *gzip* utilities are appropriate, and they are usually included with the operating system. On Windows, a good decompression tool is WinZip, available from www.winzip.com/.

NOTE
The examples in this book have been developed and tested on SQLite 2.8.17, MySQL 5.0.67, with Apache 2.2.9 and PHP 5.2.5 and 5.3.0 alpha1.

Installing and Configuring the Software

Once the required software has been obtained, the next step is to install the various pieces and get them talking to each other. The following sections outline the steps for both Windows and UNIX platforms.

NOTE

If you use an Apple workstation, you can find instructions for installing PHP on Mac OS X in the PHP manual, at www.php.net/manual/en/install.macosx.php.

Installing on UNIX

The installation process for UNIX involves a number of distinct steps: installing MySQL from a binary distribution; compiling and installing PHP from a source distribution; and compiling and configuring Apache to properly handle requests for PHP Web pages. These steps are described in greater detail in the following subsections.

Installing MySQL

To install MySQL from a binary distribution, use the following steps:

1. Ensure that you are logged in as the system's "root" user.

   ```
   [user@host]# su - root
   ```

2. Extract the content of the MySQL binary archive to an appropriate directory on your system—for example, */usr/local/*.

   ```
   [root@host]# cd /usr/local
   [root@host]# tar -xzvf /tmp/mysql-5.0.67-linux-i686.tar.gz
   ```

   The MySQL files should get extracted into a directory named according to the format *mysql-version-os-architecture*—for example, *mysql-5.0.67-linux-i686*.

3. For ease of use, set a shorter name for the directory created in the preceding step, by creating a soft link named *mysql* pointing to this directory in the same location.

   ```
   [root@host]# ln -s mysql-5.0.67-linux-i686 mysql
   ```

4. For security reasons, the MySQL database server process should never run as the system superuser. Therefore, it is necessary to create a special "mysql" user and group for this purpose. Do this with the `groupadd` and `useradd` commands, and then change the ownership of the MySQL installation directory to this user and group:

   ```
   [root@host]# groupadd mysql
   [root@host]# useradd -g mysql mysql
   [root@host]# chown -R mysql /usr/local/mysql
   [root@host]# chgrp -R mysql /usr/local/mysql
   ```

5. Initialize the MySQL tables with the *mysql_install_db* initialization script, included in the distribution.

```
[root@host]# /usr/local/mysql/scripts/mysql_install_db --user=mysql
```

Figure A-1 demonstrates what you should see when you do this.

As the preceding output suggests, this initialization script prepares and installs the various MySQL base tables, and also sets up default access permissions for MySQL.

6. Alter the ownership of the MySQL binaries so that they are owned by "root":

```
[root@host]# chown -R root /usr/local/mysql
```

and ensure that the "mysql" user created in Step 4 has read/write privileges to the MySQL data directory.

```
[root@host]# chown -R mysql /usr/local/mysql/data
```

7. Start the MySQL server by manually running the *mysqld_safe* script.

```
[root@host]# /usr/local/mysql/bin/mysqld_safe --user=mysql &
```

MySQL should now start up normally.

Once installation has been successfully completed and the server has started up, move down to the section entitled "Testing MySQL" to verify that it is functioning as it should.

```
#
# mysql_install_db
Installing all prepared tables
Fill help tables

To start mysqld at boot time you have to copy support-files/mysql.server
to the right place for your system

PLEASE REMEMBER TO SET A PASSWORD FOR THE MySQL root USER !
To do so, start the server, then issue the following commands:
/usr/bin/mysqladmin -u root password 'new-password'
/usr/bin/mysqladmin -u root -h production.securities.com password 'new-password'
See the manual for more instructions.

NOTE:  If you are upgrading from a MySQL <= 3.22.10 you should run
the /usr/bin/mysql_fix_privilege_tables. Otherwise you will not be
able to use the new GRANT command!

You can start the MySQL daemon with:
cd / ; /usr/bin/mysqld_safe &

You can test the MySQL daemon with the benchmarks in the 'sql-bench' directory:
cd sql-bench ; perl run-all-tests
```

Figure A-1   The output of the *mysql_install_db* script

Installing Apache and PHP

PHP can be integrated with the Apache Web server in one of two ways: as a dynamic module that is loaded into the Web server at run time, or as a static module that is integrated into the Apache source tree at build time. Each alternative has advantages and disadvantages:

- Installing PHP as a dynamic module makes it easier to upgrade your PHP build at a later date, as you only need to recompile the PHP module and not the rest of the Apache Web server. On the flip side, with a dynamically loaded module, performance tends to be lower than with a static module, which is more closely integrated with the server.

- Installing PHP as a static module improves performance, because the module is compiled directly into the Apache source tree. However, this close integration has an important drawback: if you ever decide to upgrade your PHP build, you will need to re-integrate the newer PHP module into the Apache source tree and recompile the Apache Web server.

This section shows you how to compile PHP as a dynamic module that is loaded into the Apache server at run time.

1. Ensure that you are logged in as the system's "root" user.

   ```
   [user@host]# su - root
   ```

2. Extract the contents of the Apache source archive to your system's temporary directory.

   ```
   [root@host]# cd /tmp
   [root@host]# tar -xzvf /tmp/httpd-2.2.9.tar.gz
   ```

3. To enable PHP to be loaded dynamically, the Apache server must be compiled with Dynamic Shared Object (DSO) support. This support is enabled by passing the `--enable- so` option to the Apache *configure* script, as shown here:

   ```
   [root@host]# cd /tmp/httpd-2.2.9
   [root@host]# ./configure --prefix=/usr/local/apache --enable-so
   ```

   You should see a few screens of output (Figure A-2 has a sample) as *configure* configures and sets up the variables needed for the compilation process.

4. Now, compile the server using make, and install it to the system using make install.

   ```
   [root@host]# make
   [root@host]# make install
   ```

   Figure A-3 illustrates what you might see during the compilation process. Apache should now have been installed to */usr/local/apache/*.

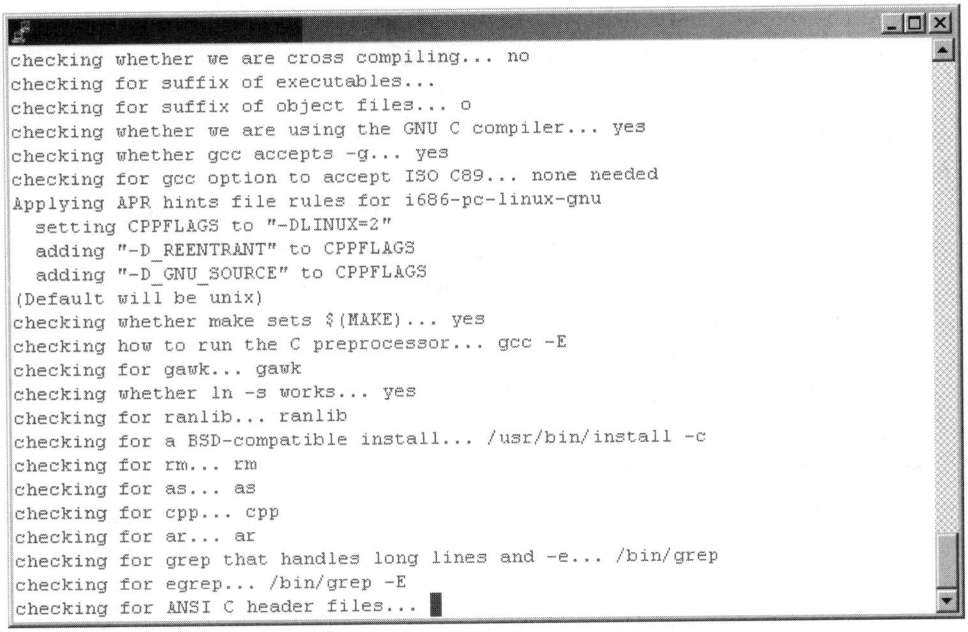

```
checking whether we are cross compiling... no
checking for suffix of executables...
checking for suffix of object files... o
checking whether we are using the GNU C compiler... yes
checking whether gcc accepts -g... yes
checking for gcc option to accept ISO C89... none needed
Applying APR hints file rules for i686-pc-linux-gnu
  setting CPPFLAGS to "-DLINUX=2"
  adding "-D_REENTRANT" to CPPFLAGS
  adding "-D_GNU_SOURCE" to CPPFLAGS
(Default will be unix)
checking whether make sets $(MAKE)... yes
checking how to run the C preprocessor... gcc -E
checking for gawk... gawk
checking whether ln -s works... yes
checking for ranlib... ranlib
checking for a BSD-compatible install... /usr/bin/install -c
checking for rm... rm
checking for as... as
checking for cpp... cpp
checking for ar... ar
checking for grep that handles long lines and -e... /bin/grep
checking for egrep... /bin/grep -E
checking for ANSI C header files...
```

Figure A-2   Configuring the Apache source tree

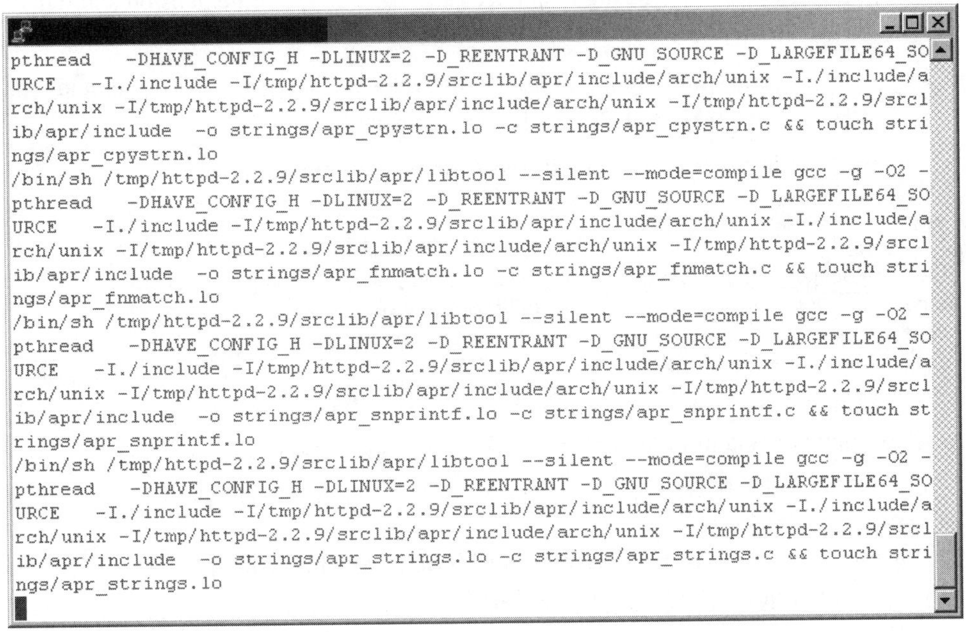

```
pthread   -DHAVE_CONFIG_H -DLINUX=2 -D_REENTRANT -D_GNU_SOURCE -D_LARGEFILE64_SO
URCE   -I./include -I/tmp/httpd-2.2.9/srclib/apr/include/arch/unix -I./include/a
rch/unix -I/tmp/httpd-2.2.9/srclib/apr/include/arch/unix -I/tmp/httpd-2.2.9/srcl
ib/apr/include  -o strings/apr_cpystrn.lo -c strings/apr_cpystrn.c && touch stri
ngs/apr_cpystrn.lo
/bin/sh /tmp/httpd-2.2.9/srclib/apr/libtool --silent --mode=compile gcc -g -O2 -
pthread   -DHAVE_CONFIG_H -DLINUX=2 -D_REENTRANT -D_GNU_SOURCE -D_LARGEFILE64_SO
URCE   -I./include -I/tmp/httpd-2.2.9/srclib/apr/include/arch/unix -I./include/a
rch/unix -I/tmp/httpd-2.2.9/srclib/apr/include/arch/unix -I/tmp/httpd-2.2.9/srcl
ib/apr/include  -o strings/apr_fnmatch.lo -c strings/apr_fnmatch.c && touch stri
ngs/apr_fnmatch.lo
/bin/sh /tmp/httpd-2.2.9/srclib/apr/libtool --silent --mode=compile gcc -g -O2 -
pthread   -DHAVE_CONFIG_H -DLINUX=2 -D_REENTRANT -D_GNU_SOURCE -D_LARGEFILE64_SO
URCE   -I./include -I/tmp/httpd-2.2.9/srclib/apr/include/arch/unix -I./include/a
rch/unix -I/tmp/httpd-2.2.9/srclib/apr/include/arch/unix -I/tmp/httpd-2.2.9/srcl
ib/apr/include  -o strings/apr_snprintf.lo -c strings/apr_snprintf.c && touch st
rings/apr_snprintf.lo
/bin/sh /tmp/httpd-2.2.9/srclib/apr/libtool --silent --mode=compile gcc -g -O2 -
pthread   -DHAVE_CONFIG_H -DLINUX=2 -D_REENTRANT -D_GNU_SOURCE -D_LARGEFILE64_SO
URCE   -I./include -I/tmp/httpd-2.2.9/srclib/apr/include/arch/unix -I./include/a
rch/unix -I/tmp/httpd-2.2.9/srclib/apr/include/arch/unix -I/tmp/httpd-2.2.9/srcl
ib/apr/include  -o strings/apr_strings.lo -c strings/apr_strings.c && touch stri
ngs/apr_strings.lo
```

Figure A-3   Compiling Apache

5. Next, proceed to compile and install PHP. Begin by extracting the contents of the PHP source archive to your system's temporary directory.

```
[root@host]# cd /tmp
[root@host]# tar -xzvf /tmp/php-5.3.0.tar.gz
```

6. This step is the most important in the PHP installation process. It involves sending arguments to the PHP *configure* script to configure the PHP module. These command-line parameters specify which PHP extensions should be activated, and also tell PHP where to find the supporting libraries needed by those extensions.

```
[root@host]# cd /tmp/php-5.3.0
[root@host]# ./configure --prefix=/usr/local/php --with-apxs2=/usr/
local/apache/bin/apxs --with-zlib --with-mysqli=mysqlnd --with-pdo-
mysql=mysqlnd
```

Here is a brief explanation of what each of these arguments does:

● The --with-apxs2 argument tells PHP where to find Apache's APXS (APache eXtenSion) script. This script simplifies the task of building and installing loadable modules for Apache.

● The --with-zlib argument tells PHP to activate compression (Zip) features, which are used by different PHP services.

● The --with-mysqli argument activates PHP's MySQLi extension and tells PHP to use the MySQL Native Driver (mysqlnd).

● The --with-pdo-mysql argument activates the MySQL PDO driver and tells PHP to use the MySQL Native Driver (mysqlnd).

Figure A-4 illustrates what you will see during the configuration process.

TIP

The PHP configuration process is extremely sophisticated, allowing you to control many aspects of PHP's behavior. To see a complete list of available options, use the command configure --help, and visit www.php.net/manual/en/configure.php for detailed explanations of what each option does.

7. Next, compile and install PHP using make and make install:

```
[root@host]# make
[root@host]# make install
```

Figure A-5 illustrates what you might see during the compilation process. PHP should now have been installed to */usr/local/php/*.

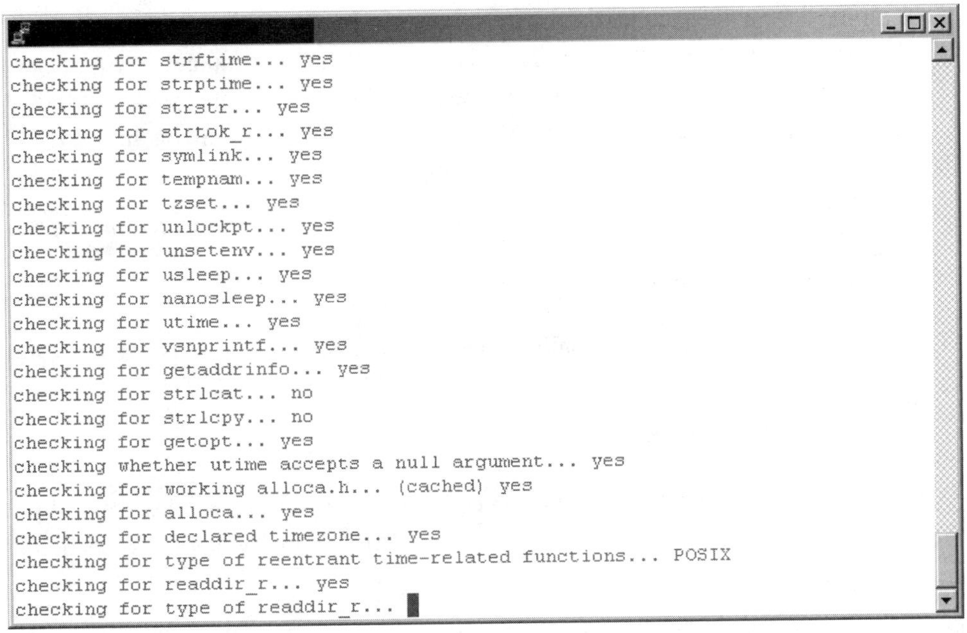

```
checking for strftime... yes
checking for strptime... yes
checking for strstr... yes
checking for strtok_r... yes
checking for symlink... yes
checking for tempnam... yes
checking for tzset... yes
checking for unlockpt... yes
checking for unsetenv... yes
checking for usleep... yes
checking for nanosleep... yes
checking for utime... yes
checking for vsnprintf... yes
checking for getaddrinfo... yes
checking for strlcat... no
checking for strlcpy... no
checking for getopt... yes
checking whether utime accepts a null argument... yes
checking for working alloca.h... (cached) yes
checking for alloca... yes
checking for declared timezone... yes
checking for type of reentrant time-related functions... POSIX
checking for readdir_r... yes
checking for type of readdir_r...
```

Figure A-4 Configuring the PHP source tree

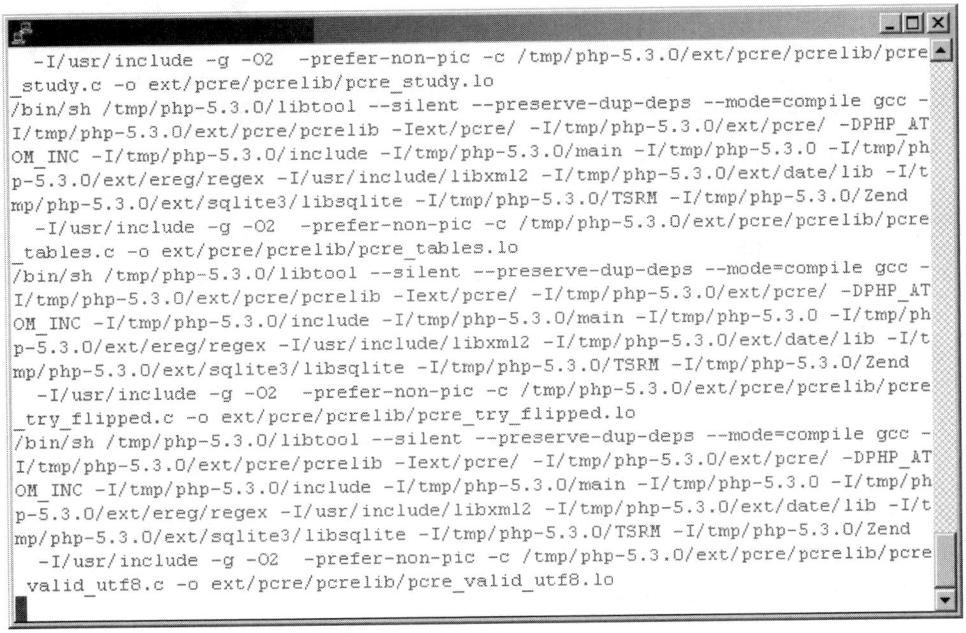

```
  -I/usr/include -g -O2  -prefer-non-pic -c /tmp/php-5.3.0/ext/pcre/pcrelib/pcre
_study.c -o ext/pcre/pcrelib/pcre_study.lo
/bin/sh /tmp/php-5.3.0/libtool --silent --preserve-dup-deps --mode=compile gcc -
I/tmp/php-5.3.0/ext/pcre/pcrelib -Iext/pcre/ -I/tmp/php-5.3.0/ext/pcre/ -DPHP_AT
OM_INC -I/tmp/php-5.3.0/include -I/tmp/php-5.3.0/main -I/tmp/php-5.3.0 -I/tmp/ph
p-5.3.0/ext/ereg/regex -I/usr/include/libxml2 -I/tmp/php-5.3.0/ext/date/lib -I/t
mp/php-5.3.0/ext/sqlite3/libsqlite -I/tmp/php-5.3.0/TSRM -I/tmp/php-5.3.0/Zend
  -I/usr/include -g -O2  -prefer-non-pic -c /tmp/php-5.3.0/ext/pcre/pcrelib/pcre
_tables.c -o ext/pcre/pcrelib/pcre_tables.lo
/bin/sh /tmp/php-5.3.0/libtool --silent --preserve-dup-deps --mode=compile gcc -
I/tmp/php-5.3.0/ext/pcre/pcrelib -Iext/pcre/ -I/tmp/php-5.3.0/ext/pcre/ -DPHP_AT
OM_INC -I/tmp/php-5.3.0/include -I/tmp/php-5.3.0/main -I/tmp/php-5.3.0 -I/tmp/ph
p-5.3.0/ext/ereg/regex -I/usr/include/libxml2 -I/tmp/php-5.3.0/ext/date/lib -I/t
mp/php-5.3.0/ext/sqlite3/libsqlite -I/tmp/php-5.3.0/TSRM -I/tmp/php-5.3.0/Zend
  -I/usr/include -g -O2  -prefer-non-pic -c /tmp/php-5.3.0/ext/pcre/pcrelib/pcre
_try_flipped.c -o ext/pcre/pcrelib/pcre_try_flipped.lo
/bin/sh /tmp/php-5.3.0/libtool --silent --preserve-dup-deps --mode=compile gcc -
I/tmp/php-5.3.0/ext/pcre/pcrelib -Iext/pcre/ -I/tmp/php-5.3.0/ext/pcre/ -DPHP_AT
OM_INC -I/tmp/php-5.3.0/include -I/tmp/php-5.3.0/main -I/tmp/php-5.3.0 -I/tmp/ph
p-5.3.0/ext/ereg/regex -I/usr/include/libxml2 -I/tmp/php-5.3.0/ext/date/lib -I/t
mp/php-5.3.0/ext/sqlite3/libsqlite -I/tmp/php-5.3.0/TSRM -I/tmp/php-5.3.0/Zend
  -I/usr/include -g -O2  -prefer-non-pic -c /tmp/php-5.3.0/ext/pcre/pcrelib/pcre
_valid_utf8.c -o ext/pcre/pcrelib/pcre_valid_utf8.lo
```

Figure A-5 Compiling PHP

8. The final step in the installation process consists of configuring Apache to correctly recognize requests for PHP pages. This is accomplished by opening up the Apache configuration file, *httpd.conf* (which can be found in the *conf/* subdirectory of the Apache installation directory), in a text editor and adding the following line to it.

```
AddType application/x-httpd-php .php
```

Save the changes to the file. Also, check to make sure that the following line appears somewhere in the file:

```
LoadModule php5_module libexec/libphp5.so
```

9. Start the Apache server by manually running the *apachectl* script.

```
[root@host]# /usr/local/apache/bin/apachectl start
```

Apache should start up normally.

Once installation has been successfully completed and the server has successfully started, move down to the section entitled "Testing PHP" to verify that all is functioning as it should.

Ask the Expert

Q: **Why do I need to manually activate the PDO MySQL driver, but not the PDO SQLite driver when configuring PHP?**

A: In PHP 5, both the SQLite extension and the PDO SQLite driver are activated by default. Therefore, there is no need to manually activate the PDO SQLite driver during the configuration process. However, all other PDO drivers, including those for MySQL, PostgreSQL, and ODBC, require manual activation.

Installing SQLite

To install SQLite from a binary distribution, use the following steps.

1. Ensure that you are logged in as the system's "root" user.

```
[user@host]# su - root
```

2. Unzip the compressed SQLite binary to an appropriate directory on your system—for example, */usr/local/bin*—and make the binary executable (Figure A-6).

```
[root@host]# cd /usr/local/bin
[root@host]# gunzip sqlite2-2.8.17.bin.gz
[root@host]# chmod +x sqlite2-2.8.17.bin
[root@host]# ln -s sqlite2-2.8.17.bin sqlite
```

```
# chmod +x sqlite2-2.8.17.bin
# ln -s sqlite2-2.8.17.bin sqlite
#
```

Figure A-6   SQLite installation

The SQLite binary is now installed and ready for use. To test it, skip ahead to the section entitled "Testing SQLite."

Installing on Windows

Compiling applications on Windows is a challenging process, especially for novice developers. With this in mind, it is advisable for Windows users to focus instead on installing and configuring prebuilt binary releases of MySQL, SQLite, PHP, and Apache, instead of attempting to compile them from source code. These releases can be downloaded from the Web sites listed in the preceding section and are to be installed one after another, as outlined in the following subsections.

Installing MySQL

The binary distribution of MySQL for Windows comes with an automated installer, which allows you to get MySQL up and running on your Windows system in just a few minutes.

1. Log in as an administrator (if you're using Windows NT/2000/XP/Vista) and unzip the distribution archive to a temporary directory on your system.

2. Double-click the *setup.exe* file to begin the installation process. You should see a welcome screen (Figure A-7).

3. Select the type of installation required (Figure A-8).

   Most often, a Typical Installation will do; however, if you're the kind who likes tweaking default settings, or if you're just short of disk space, select the Custom Installation option, and decide which components of the package should be installed.

4. MySQL should now begin installing to your system (Figure A-9).

5. Once installation is complete, you should see a success notification. At this point, you will have the option to launch the MySQL Server Instance Config Wizard, to complete configuration of the software. Select this option, and you should see the corresponding welcome screen (Figure A-10).

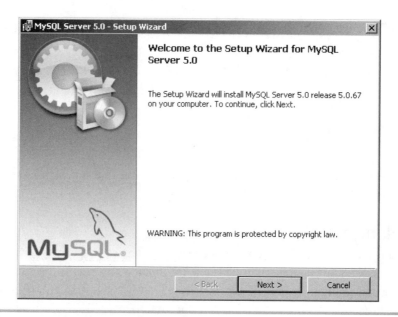

Figure A-7 Beginning MySQL installation on Windows

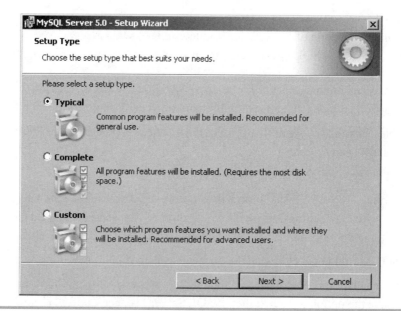

Figure A-8 Selecting the MySQL installation type

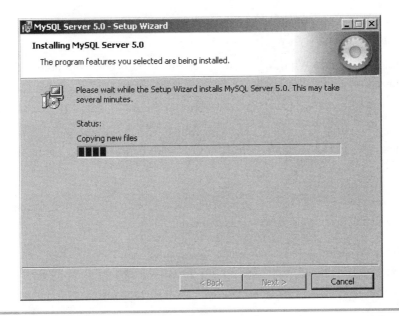

Figure A-9   MySQL installation in progress

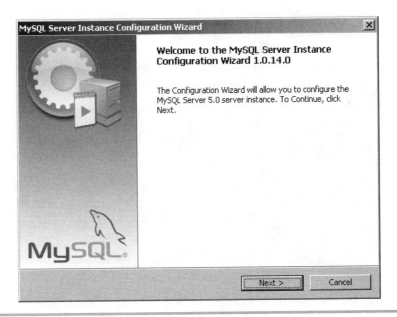

Figure A-10   Beginning MySQL configuration on Windows

6. Select the type of configuration (Figure A-11). In most cases, the Standard Configuration will suffice.

7. Install MySQL as a Windows service, such that it starts and stops automatically with Windows (Figure A-12).

8. Enter a password for the MySQL administrator ("root") account (Figure A-13).

9. The server will now be configured with your specified settings, and automatically started. You will be presented with a success notification once all required tasks are completed (Figure A-14).

You can now proceed to test the server as described in the section "Testing MySQL," to ensure that everything is working as it should.

Installing Apache

Once MySQL is installed, the next step is to install the Apache Web server. On Windows, this is a point-and-click process, similar to that used when installing MySQL.

1. Begin by double-clicking the Apache installer to begin the installation process. You should see a welcome screen (Figure A-15).

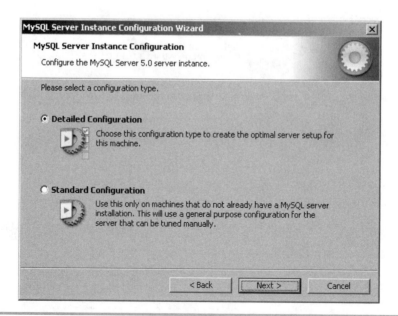

Figure A-11 Selecting the configuration time

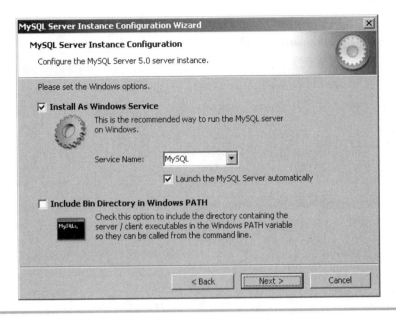

Figure A-12   Setting up the MySQL service

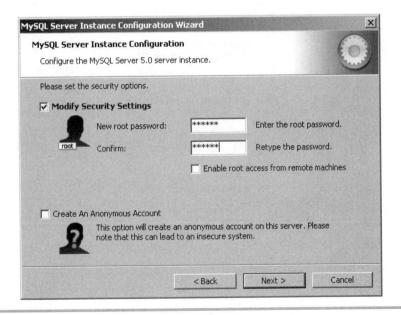

Figure A-13   Setting the administrator password

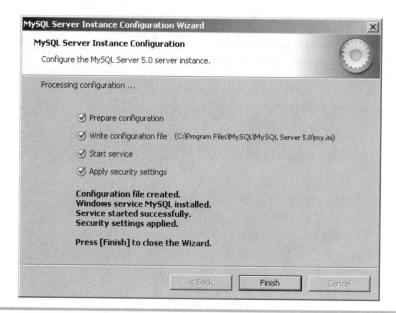

Figure A-14 MySQL configuration successfully completed

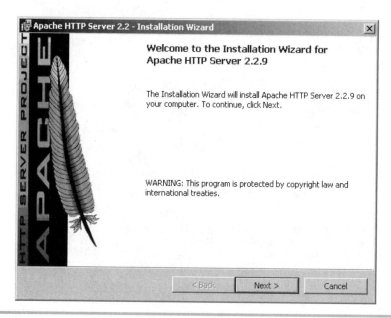

Figure A-15 Beginning Apache installation on Windows

2. Read the license agreement, and accept the terms to proceed.

3. Read the descriptive information, and proceed to enter basic server information and the e-mail address to be displayed on error pages (Figure A-16).

4. Select the type of installation required (Figure A-17).

You can select the Custom Installation option to decide which components of the package should be installed.

5. Select the location to which Apache should be installed—for example, *c:\program files\ apache group* (Figure A-18).

6. Apache should now begin installing to the specified location (Figure A-19). The installation process takes a few minutes to complete, so this is a good time to get yourself a cup of coffee.

7. Once installation is complete, the Apache installer will display a success notification and also start the Apache Web server.

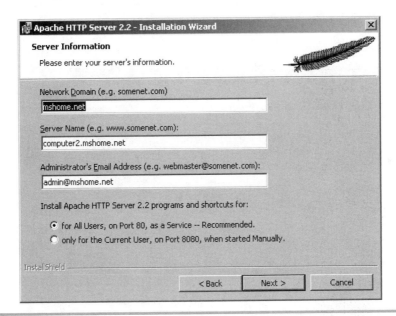

Figure A-16   Entering Apache server information

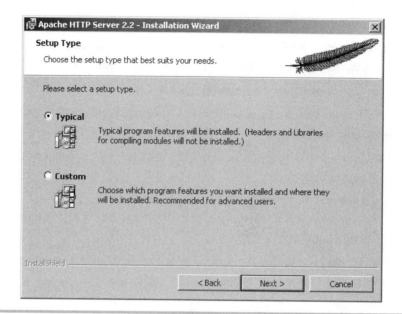

Figure A-17 Selecting the Apache installation type

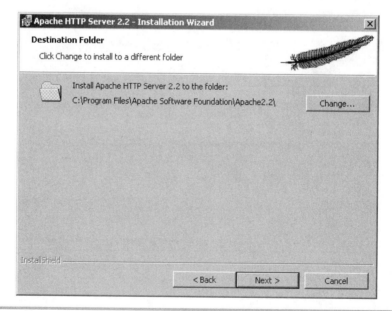

Figure A-18 Selecting the Apache installation location

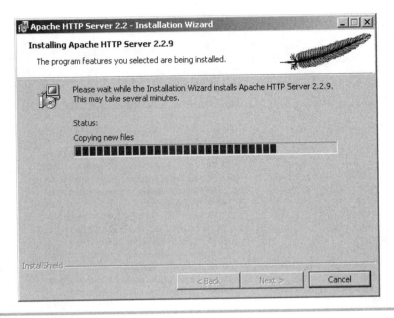

Figure A-19   Apache installation in progress

Installing PHP

There are two versions of the PHP binary release for Windows: a Zip archive that contains all the bundled PHP extensions and requires manual installation, and an automated Windows Installer version that contains only the PHP binary with no extra extensions. This section outlines the installation process for the PHP Zip archive.

1. Log in as an administrator (if you're using Windows NT/2000/XP/Vista) and unzip the distribution archive to a directory on your system—for example, *c:\php*. After extraction, this directory should look something like Figure A-20.

2. Next, rename the file *php.ini-recommended* in your PHP installation directory to *php.ini*. This file contains configuration settings for PHP, which can be used to alter the way it works. Read the comments within the file to learn more about the available settings.

3. Within the *php.ini* file, locate the line

   ```
   extension_dir = "./"
   ```

   and alter it to read

   ```
   extension_dir = "c:\php\ext\"
   ```

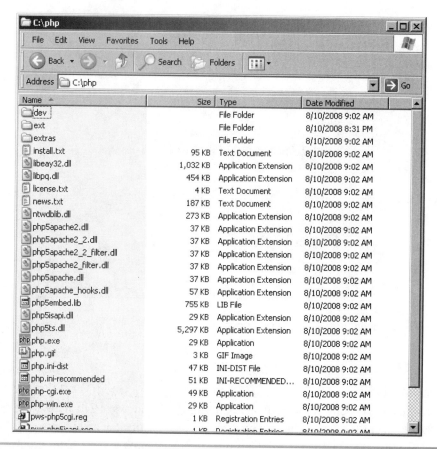

Figure A-20   The directory structure created on unpackaging a PHP binary distribution for Windows

This tells PHP where to locate the extensions supplied with the package. Remember to replace the path "c:\php\" with the actual location of your PHP installation.

4. Next, look for the following lines and remove the semicolon at the beginning of each line (if present) so that they read:

```
extension=php_pdo.dll
extension=php_sqlite.dll
extension=php_mysqli.dll
extension=php_pdo_sqlite.dll
extension=php_pdo_mysqli.dll
```

This takes care of activating PHP's MySQLi, SQLite, and PDO extensions.

5. Open the Apache configuration file, *httpd.conf* (which can be found in the *conf/* subdirectory of the Apache installation directory), in a text editor, and add the following lines to it.

```
AddType application/x-httpd-php .php
LoadModule php5_module "c:\php\php5apache2_2.dll"
SetEnv PHPRC C:\php\
```

These lines tell Apache how to deal with PHP scripts, and where to find the *php.ini* configuration file. Remember to replace the path *c:\php* with the actual location of your PHP installation.

6. When the Apache server is installed, it adds itself to the Start menu. Use this Start menu group to stop and restart the server, as in Figure A-21.

PHP is now installed and configured to work with Apache. To test it, skip down to the section entitled "Testing PHP."

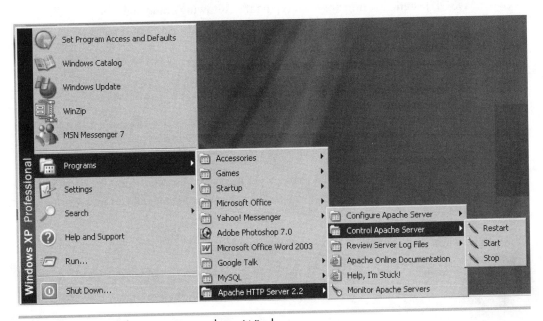

Figure A-21   Apache server controls on Windows

Installing SQLite

Because SQLite is a self-contained executable, installing it under Windows is a snap: Simply log in as an administrator (if you're using Windows NT/2000/XP/Vista) and unzip the distribution archive to a directory in your system path. For ease of use, rename the *sqlite2.exe* binary to *sqlite.exe*.

The SQLite binary is now installed and ready for use. To test it, skip ahead to the section entitled "Testing SQLite."

Testing the Software

Once the software has been successfully installed and the various servers have been started, you can verify that all is working as it should via some simple tests.

Testing MySQL

First, start up the MySQL command-line client, by changing to the *bin/* subdirectory of your MySQL installation directory and typing the following command:

```
prompt# mysql -u root
```

You should be rewarded with a prompt, as shown here:

```
Welcome to the MySQL monitor.  Commands end with ; or \g.
Your MySQL connection id is 26288
Server version: 5.0.51a-community MySQL Community Edition (GPL)
Type 'help;' or '\h' for help. Type '\c' to clear the buffer.
mysql>
```

At this point, you are connected to the MySQL server and can begin executing SQL commands or queries to test whether the server is working as it should. Here are a few examples, with their output:

```
mysql> SHOW DATABASES;
+----------+
| Database |
+----------+
| mysql    |
| test     |
+----------+
2 rows in set (0.13 sec)
mysql> USE mysql;
```

```
Database changed
mysql> SHOW TABLES;
+--------------------------+
| Tables_in_mysql          |
+--------------------------+
| columns_priv             |
| db                       |
| func                     |
| help_category            |
| help_keyword             |
| help_relation            |
| help_topic               |
| host                     |
| proc                     |
| procs_priv               |
| tables_priv              |
| time_zone                |
| time_zone_leap_second    |
| time_zone_name           |
| time_zone_transition     |
| time_zone_transition_type |
| user                     |
+--------------------------+
17 rows in set (0.01 sec)
mysql> SELECT COUNT(*) FROM user;
+----------+
| count(*) |
+----------+
|        1 |
+----------+
1 row in set (0.00 sec)
```

If you see output similar to this, your MySQL installation is working as it should. Exit the command-line client by typing the following command, and you'll be returned to your command prompt:

```
mysql> exit
```

If you don't see output like that shown, or if MySQL throws warnings and errors at you, review the installation procedure in the preceding section, as well as the documents that shipped with your version of MySQL, to see what went wrong.

Testing PHP

Once you've successfully installed PHP as an Apache module, you should test it to ensure that the Web server can recognize PHP scripts and handle them correctly.

To perform this test, create a PHP script in any text editor containing the following lines:

```
<?php
phpinfo();
?>
```

Save this file as *test.php* in your Web server document root (the *htdocs/* subdirectory of your Apache installation directory), and point your browser to http://localhost/test.php. You should see a page containing information on the PHP build, as in Figure A-22.

Eyeball the list of extensions to make sure that the SimpleXML, MySQLi, and PDO extensions are active. If they aren't, review the installation procedure, as well as the installation documents that shipped with the software, to see what went wrong.

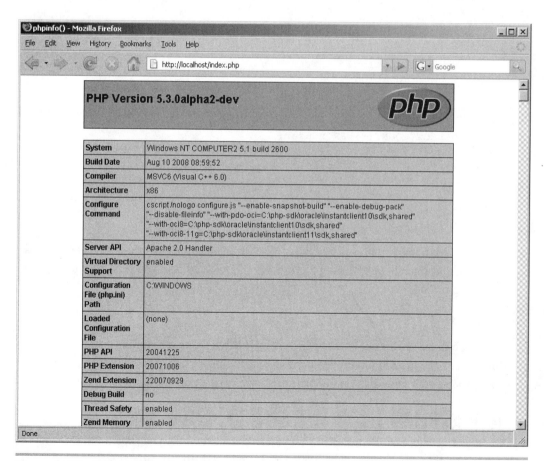

Figure A-22   Viewing the output of the `phpinfo()` command

Testing SQLite

Once you've installed SQLite, you can test it by changing to the directory it was installed into and executing the SQLite binary at the command prompt, as shown here:

```
prompt# sqlite
```

You should be rewarded with a prompt, like this:

```
SQLite version 2.8.17
Enter ".help" for instructions
sqlite>
```

At this point, you can try executing SQL commands or internal SQLite commands to test whether things are working as they should. Here are some examples:

```
sqlite> .show
     echo: off
  explain: off
  headers: off
     mode: list
nullvalue: ""
   output: stdout
separator: "|"
    width:
sqlite> CREATE TABLE test (
   ...> fld1 INTEGER PRIMARY KEY,
   ...> fld2 TEXT
   ...> );
sqlite> INSERT INTO test (fld2) VALUES ('Hello');
sqlite> SELECT * FROM test;
1|Hello
```

If you see output similar to the preceding, your SQLite installation is working as it should. Exit the command-line client by typing the following command, and you'll be returned to your command prompt.

```
sqlite> .quit
```

Performing Post-Installation Steps

Once testing is complete, you may wish to perform the following two tasks.

Setting the MySQL Super-User Password

On UNIX, when MySQL is first installed, access to the database server is restricted to the MySQL administrator, aka "root." By default, this user is initialized with a blank password, which is generally considered a Bad Thing. You should therefore rectify this as soon as possible by setting a password for this user via the included *mysqladmin* utility, using the following syntax in UNIX:

```
[root@host]# /usr/local/mysql/bin/mysqladmin -u root password 'new-password'
```

In Windows, you can use the MySQL Server Instance Config Wizard, which allows you to set or reset the MySQL administrator password (see the section entitled "Installing on Windows" for more details).

This password change goes into effect immediately, with no requirement to restart the server.

Ask the Expert

Q: Does changing the MySQL "root" password affect the UNIX system's "root" account?

A: No. The MySQL "root" user is not the same as the system superuser ("root") on UNIX. So, altering one does not affect the other.

Configuring MySQL and Apache to Start Automatically

On UNIX, both MySQL and Apache servers come with startup/shutdown scripts, which can be used to start and stop them. These scripts are located within the installation hierarchy for each program. Here's an example of how to use the MySQL server control script:

```
[root@host]# /usr/local/mysql/support-files/mysql.server start
[root@host]# /usr/local/mysql/support-files/mysql.server stop
```

And here's an example of how to use the Apache control script:

```
[root@host]# /usr/local/apache/bin/apachectl start
[root@host]# /usr/local/apache/bin/apachectl stop
```

- To have MySQL and Apache start automatically at boot time on UNIX, simply invoke their respective control scripts with appropriate parameters from your system's bootup and shutdown scripts in the `/etc/rc.d/*` hierarchy.

- To start MySQL and Apache automatically on Windows, simply add a link to the *mysqld.exe* and *apache.exe* server binaries to your Startup group. You can also start MySQL automatically by installing it as a Windows service (see the section entitled "Installing on Windows" for instructions).

Summary

As popular open-source applications, MySQL, SQLite, Apache, and PHP are available for a wide variety of platforms and architectures, in both binary and source forms. This chapter demonstrated the process of installing and configuring these software components to create a PHP development environment on the two most common platforms, UNIX and Windows. It also showed you how to configure your system to launch these components automatically every time the system starts up, and offered some tips on basic MySQL security.

To read more about the installation processes outlined in this chapter, or for detailed troubleshooting advice and assistance, consider visiting the following pages:

- MySQL installation notes, at
  http://dev.mysql.com/doc/refman/5.0/en/installing-binary.html

- General guidelines for compiling Apache on UNIX, at
  http://httpd.apache.org/docs/2.2/install.html

- Windows-specific notes for Apache binary installations, at
  http://httpd.apache.org/docs/2.2/platform/windows.html

- Installation instructions for PHP on Windows, at
  www.php.net/manual/en/install.windows.php

- Installation instructions for PHP on UNIX, at
  www.php.net/manual/en/install.unix.php

- Installation instructions for PHP on Mac OS X, at
  www.php.net/manual/en/install.macosx.php

- SQLite frequently asked questions, at **www.sqlite.org/faq.html**

Appendix B

Answers to Self Test

Chapter 1: Introducing PHP

1. The four components of the LAMP framework are the Linux operating system, the Apache Web server, the MySQL database server, and the PHP programming language.

2. PHP is superior to client-side languages such as JavaScript because all PHP code runs on the server and hence is impervious to client-side security risks as well as to browser-specific quirks.

3. The echo statement produces one or more lines of output.

4. The PHP parser ignores whitespace or blank lines in a PHP script.

5. A semicolon. However, this semicolon terminator may be omitted for the very last line of a PHP script.

6. An escape sequence is a sequence of characters that is replaced by a single "special" character. For example, \t is an escape sequence that is replaced by a tab character. Other commonly used escape sequences are \n (for line feeds) and \r (for carriage returns).

7. A. Today looks
      bright and sunny

   B. Ours not to question why;Ours but to do and die

8. A. The syntax of the comment block is incorrect.

   B. No error.

   C. The echo statement is missing the closing quotation mark.

Chapter 2: Using Variables and Operators

1. The gettype() function

2. $24 and $^b are invalid variable names. Variable names cannot begin with a numeric character, nor can they contain punctuation characters or special symbols.

3.
```
<?php
define ('FLAVOR', 'strawberry');
?>
```

4.
```
<?php
$x = 6;
$x += 3;
?>
```

5. Answers to true/false questions:

A. True

B. False

C. False

D. False

E. False

F. True

G. True

H. False

6. `$x = 179; ABC = 90`

7. As both variables are of the integer type and hold the same value, the comparison returns 1 (true).

8. The constant NUM is a string (notice the single quotes), which is then assigned to the variable $a. Therefore, $a is also a string.

9. The relevant form code is

```
<form method="post" action="convert.php">
      Exchange rate: <br />
      <input type="text" name="rate" /> <p />
      Dollar amount: <br />
      <input type="text" name="dollars" /> <p />
      <input type="submit" />
</form>
```

And the PHP processing code is

```
<?php
$dollars = $_POST['dollars'];
$rate = $_POST['rate'];
$euros = $dollars * $rate;
echo "$dollars USD is equivalent to: $euros EUR";
?>
```

10. The relevant form code is

```
<form method="post" action="convert.php">
      Temperature in Celsius: <br />
      <input type="text" name="c" /> <p />
      <input type="submit" />
</form>
```

And the PHP processing code is

```
<?php
$c = $_POST['c'];
$f = (9/5) * $c + 32;
echo "$c deg. Celsius is equivalent to: $f deg. Fahrenheit";
?>
```

11. The relevant form code is

```
<form method="post" action="display.php">
    Text input: <br />
    <input type="text" name="dsc" /> <p />
    Password input: <br />
    <input type="password" name="password" /> <p />
    Text area: <br />
    <textarea cols="10" rows="5" name="comment"></textarea> <p />
    Selection list: <br />
    <select name="color">
      <option>red</option>
      <option>yellow</option>
      <option>green</option>
    </select>     <p />
    Radio buttons: <br />
    <input type="radio" name="sex" value="male">Male</input>
    <input type="radio" name="sex" value="female">Female</input>  <p />
    Checkboxes: <br />
    <input type="checkbox" name="phone">Phone</input>
    <input type="checkbox" name="fax">Fax</input> <p />
    <input type="hidden" name="referral" value="XYZ" />
    <input type="submit" />
</form>
```

And the PHP processing code is

```
<?php
var_dump($_POST);
?>
```

Chapter 3: Controlling Program Flow

1. An `if-else` statement allows you to define actions for two possibilities: a true condition and a false condition. An `if-elseif-else` statement allows you to define actions for multiple possibilities.

2. The relevant conditional statement is

```
<?php
if ($city == 'Minneapolis') {
  echo 'Welcome to Minneapolis';
}
?>
```

3. A `while` loop checks the conditional expression at the beginning of each loop iteration, while a `do-while` loop checks the conditional expression at the end of each loop iteration. Thus, if the conditional expression evaluates to false on the first iteration, the `while` loop will never run, but the `do-while` loop will run once.

The following code illustrates the difference:

Code	Output

``php
<?php
$a = 10;
while ($a < 10) {
 echo 'Hello';
}
?>
``
	No output

``php
<?php
$a = 10;
do {
 echo 'Hello';
} while ($a < 10);
?>
``
	'Hello'

4. The relevant PHP code is

```php
<?php
$num = 1;
while ($num <= 10) {
echo "8 times $num is: " . ($num*8) . "<br/>";
$num++;
}
?>
```

5. The relevant PHP code is

```php
<?php
for ($num=1; $num<=10; $num++) {
   echo "8 times $num is: " . ($num*8) . "<br/>";
}
?>
```

6. The function matching each task is listed in the following table:

Task	Function
Decode HTML entities	`html_entity_decode()`
Uppercase a string	`strtoupper()`
Round a number down	`floor()`
Remove whitespace from a string	`trim()`
Generate a random number	`rand()`

Task	Function
Reverse a string	`strrev()`
Count words in a string	`str_word_count()`
Count characters in a string	`strlen()`
Terminate script processing with a custom message	`die()`
Compare two strings	`strcmp()`
Calculate the exponent of a number	`exp()`
Convert a decimal number to a hexadecimal value	`dechex()`

7. The output is `7402.404200`.

8. The required PHP code is

```php
<?php
$str = 'Mark had a nice day';
$newStr = substr($str,0,9) . substr($str,12,3) .
$str{13} . $str{2} . $str{14} .
$str{1} . strtolower($str{0});
echo $newStr;
?>
```

Chapter 4: Working with Arrays

1. The two types of PHP arrays are numerically indexed arrays and string-indexed arrays (also known as associative arrays). With the former, numbers are used to identify array elements; with the latter, unique string labels (keys) are used.

2. The function matching each task is listed in the following table:

Task	Function
Remove duplicate elements from an array	`array_unique()`
Add an element to the beginning of an array	`array_unshift()`
Sort an array in reverse	`rsort()`
Count the number of elements in an array	`count()`
Search for a value in an array	`in_array()`
Display the contents of an array	`print_r()` or `var_dump()`
Shuffle the contents of an array	`shuffle()`
Combine two arrays into one	`array_merge()`
Find the common elements between two arrays	`array_intersect()`
Convert a string to an array	`explode()`
Extract a segment of an array	`array_slice()`

3. The output will be

```
Array
(
    [0] => f
    [1] => g
    [2] => i
)
```

4. The relevant PHP code is

```php
<?php
$days = array(
  'Monday',
  'Tuesday',
  'Wednesday',
  'Thursday',
  'Friday',
  'Saturday',
  'Sunday'
);
foreach ($days as $day) {
  echo "$day \r\n";
}
?>
```

5. The relevant PHP code is

```php
<?php
$arr = array(23,45,2,67,17,12,5,68,14,78,192,4);
foreach ($arr as $n) {
  echo ($n < 15) ? "$n " : null;
}
?>
```

6. The relevant PHP code is

```php
<?php
$arr = array(23,45,'apple','fig',17,12,5,'fig',14,2,78,192,45);
if ($arr == array_unique($arr)) {
  echo 'Array has only unique values';
} else {
  echo 'Array has some duplicate values';
}
?>
```

Chapter 5: Using Functions and Classes

1. Functions

- Permit modularization and reusability
- Reduce duplication of program code

- Allow you to change code from a single central location

- Simplify debugging

2. An argument is an input to a function, while a return value is an output of a function.

3. The relevant PHP code is

```php
<?php
function getDistance($speed, $time) {
  return $speed * $time;
}


// time diff = 4.5 hrs
// total time in the air = 13-5 - 4.5 = 9
echo 'The distance between Bombay and London is: ' .
getDistance(910, 9) . ' km.';
?>
```

4. The relevant PHP code is

```php
<?php
// function definition
// get LCM of arbitrary set of numbers using GCF
function getLCMOfSet() {
  $nums = func_get_args();
  if (count($nums) < 2) {
    die('ERROR: You must provide at least 2 values');
  }

  $lcm = 1;
  for ($x=0; $x<count($nums); $x++) {
    $lcm = getLCM($lcm, $nums[$x]);
  }
  return $lcm;
}


// output: 160
echo getLCMOfSet(4,8,16,32,10);
?>
```

5. A constructor is a method of a class that is automatically executed when an instance of that class is created.

6. Private methods of a class are visible only within that class and are not accessible from child classes or child class instances. Attempting to access a private method of a parent class from a child class will generate a fatal error.

7. The get_class() function returns the name of the class from which it was instantiated—in this case, the Baby class.

8. The relevant class definition is

```php
<?php
class DateSelect {
  public $day;
  public $month;
  public $year;

  public function __construct() {
    // create day list
    $this->day = new Select;
    $this->day->setName('dd');
    $this->day->setLabel('Day');
    foreach (range(1,31) as $d) {
      $this->day->setOption(new Option($d,$d));
    }
    // create month list
    $this->month = new Select;
    $this->month->setName('mm');
    $this->month->setLabel('Month');
    foreach (range(1,12) as $m) {
      $mon = date('F', mktime(0,0,0,$m));
      $this->month->setOption(new Option($mon,$mon));
    }
    // create year list
    $this->year = new Select;
    $this->year->setName('yy');
    $this->year->setLabel('Year');
    foreach (range(1950,2050) as $y) {
      $this->year->setOption(new Option($y,$y));
    }
  }

  public function render() {
    $this->day->render();
    echo '<br />';
    $this->month->render();
    echo '<br />';
    $this->year->render();
  }
}
?>
```

And a usage example is

```php
<form method="post" action="date.php">
  <?php
  $datebox = new DateSelect;
  $datebox->render();
  ?>
  <p />
  <input type="submit" name="submit" value="Submit" />
</form>
```

9. Monday 17 November 2008 12:15 pm

Chapter 6: Working with Files and Directories

1. The function matching each task is listed in the following table:

Task	Function
Obtain the absolute path to a file	`realpath()`
Delete a file	`unlink()`
Retrieve the size of a file	`filesize()`
Read the contents of a file into an array	`file()`
Check if a file is writable	`is_writable()`
Check if a directory exists	`file_exists()`
Read the contents of a directory into an array	`scandir()`
Write a string to a file	`file_put_contents()`
Create a new directory	`mkdir()`
Delete a directory	`rmdir()`
Create a pointer to a directory	`opendir()`
Check if a directory entry is a file	`is_file()`

2. The `flock()` function is used to prevent multiple simultaneous processes from accessing a file, thereby reducing the risk of data corruption.

3. The relevant PHP code is

```php
<?php
echo count(file('example.txt')) . ' line(s) in file.';
?>
```

4. The relevant PHP code is

```php
<?php
file_put_contents('reversed.txt', strrev(file_get_contents('example.txt')))
?>
```

5. The relevant PHP code is

```php
<?php
// create directory pointer
$dp = opendir('.') or die ('ERROR: Cannot open directory');

// read directory contents
// print filenames found
while ($file = readdir($dp)) {
  $fileData = pathinfo($file);
```

```php
   if ($fileData['extension'] == 'txt') {
      rename($file, $fileData['filename'] . '.xtx') or die('ERROR:
Cannot rename file ' . $file);
   }
}

// destroy directory pointer
closedir($dp);
?>
```

6. The relevant PHP code is

```php
<?php
// function definition
// copy a directory and its contents
function copyTree($source, $destination) {
  if (file_exists($source)) {
    // create source pointer
    $dp = opendir($source) or die ('ERROR: Cannot open directory');

    // if destination directory does not exist
    // create it
    if (!file_exists($destination)) {
       mkdir($destination) or die('ERROR: Cannot create directory '
. $destination);
    }

    // read source contents
    // if file, copy to destination
    // if directory, call recursively
    while ($file = readdir($dp)) {
      if ($file != '.' && $file != '..') {
        if (is_file("$source/$file")) {
          copy("$source/$file", "$destination/$file")
           or die('ERROR: Cannot copy file ' . "$source/$file");
        } else if (is_dir("$source/$file")) {
          copyTree("$source/$file", "$destination/$file");
        }
      }
    }

    // close source pointer
    closedir($dp);
  }
}
?>
```

And here's a usage example:

```php
<?php
if (file_exists('mydir')) {
  copyTree('mydir', '../../../mycopy');
  echo 'File(s) copied.';
}
?>
```

7. The relevant PHP code is

```php
<?php
// create directory pointer
$dp = opendir('.') or die ('ERROR: Cannot open directory');

// read directory contents
// add files to array with mtime
while ($file = readdir($dp)) {
  if ($file != '.' && $file != '..') {
    $fileList[$file] = filemtime($file);
  }
}

// destroy directory pointer
closedir($dp);

// reverse sort by mtime
// print list
arsort($fileList);
foreach ($fileList as $file => $mtime) {
  echo $file . ' ' . date('d-M-y H:i', $mtime) . "\n";
}
?>
```

Chapter 7: Working with Databases and SQL

1. The answers are

A. False. SQL permits tables to be joined on any of their fields.

B. False. PHP has included MySQL support for many years.

C. True.

D. False. Primary keys uniquely identify table records and so cannot be empty.

E. True.

F. False. Prepared statements can be used for any SQL operation, including SELECT, UPDATE, and DELETE.

2. The relevant SQL commands are

A. DROP DATABASE

B. UPDATE

C. DELETE

D. CREATE TABLE

E. USE

3. Database normalization is the process of identifying and eliminating redundancies and unwanted dependencies between the tables of a database. This ensures that a given piece of information appears only once in the database, to avoid cross-referencing errors and to make changes easier.

4. The advantage of using a database abstraction library like PDO is that it uses generic functions that are internally translated to a database's native API; this makes it possible to switch from one database back end to another with limited impact to application code. The disadvantage is that such internal translation of API calls requires additional processing cycles and so may end up being performance-inefficient.

5. The relevant PHP code is

```php
<?php
// attempt database connection
try {
    $pdo = new PDO('mysql:dbname=music;host=localhost', 'user', 'pass');
} catch (PDOException $e) {
    die("ERROR: Could not connect: " . $e->getMessage());
}

// if form not yet submitted
// display form
if (!isset($_POST['submit'])) {

    // get artists
    $artists = array();
    $sql = "SELECT artist_id, artist_name FROM artists ORDER BY artist_name";
    if ($result = $pdo->query($sql)) {
      while($row = $result->fetchObject()) {
        $artists[$row->artist_id] = $row->artist_name;
      }
    }

    // get ratings
    $ratings = array();
    $sql = "SELECT rating_id, rating_name FROM ratings ORDER BY rating_id";
    if ($result = $pdo->query($sql)) {
```

```php
      while($row = $result->fetchObject()) {
        $ratings[$row->rating_id] = $row->rating_name;
      }
    }
  ?>

    <form method="post" action="pdo-music.php">
      Name: <br />
      <input type="text" name="name" />
      <p>
      Artist: <br />
      <select name="artist">
      <?php
      foreach ($artists as $k => $v) {
        echo "<option value=\"$k\">$v</option>\n";
      }
      ?>
      </select>
      <p>
      Rating: <br />
      <select name="rating">
      <?php
      foreach ($ratings as $k => $v) {
        echo "<option value=\"$k\">$v</option>\n";
      }
      ?>
      </select>
      <p>
      <input type="submit" name="submit" value="Save" />
    </form>

<?php
// if form submitted
// validate input and save record
} else {
  $name = $_POST['name'];
  $artist_id = (int)$_POST['artist'];
  $rating_id = (int)$_POST['rating'];

  // check input
  if (empty($name)) {
    die('ERROR: Please enter a name');
  }

  if (empty($artist_id)) {
    die('ERROR: Please select an artist');
  }

  if (empty($rating_id)) {
    die('ERROR: Please select a rating');
  }
```

```php
  // escape special characters in input
  $name = $pdo->quote($name);
  $artist_id = $pdo->quote($artist_id);
  $rating_id = $pdo->quote($rating_id);

  // insert record
  $sql = "INSERT INTO songs (song_title, fk_song_artist, fk_song_rating)
VALUES ($name, $artist_id, $rating_id)";
  $ret = $pdo->exec($sql);
  if ($ret === false) {
    echo "ERROR: Could not execute $sql. " . print_r($pdo->errorInfo());
  } else {
    echo 'New song added.';
  }
}

// close connection
unset($pdo);
?>
  </body>
</html>
```

6. The relevant PHP code for MySQL is

```php
<?php
// attempt database connection
$mysqli = new mysqli("localhost", "user", "pass", "test");
if ($mysqli === false) {
  die("ERROR: Could not connect. " . mysqli_connect_error());
}

// attempt query execution
// add a new table
$sql =
  "CREATE TABLE grades (
    id int(4) NOT NULL PRIMARY KEY AUTO_INCREMENT,
    subj_a INT(4) NOT NULL,
    subj_b INT(4) NOT NULL,
    subj_c INT(4) NOT NULL
    )";
if ($mysqli->query($sql) === true) {
  echo 'New table created.';
} else {
  echo "ERROR: Could not execute query: $sql. " . $mysqli->error;
}

// close connection
$mysqli->close();
?>
```

The relevant PHP code for SQLite is

```php
<?php
// attempt database connection
$sqlite = new SQLiteDatabase('test.db') or die ("Could not open database");

// attempt query execution
// add a new table
$sql = "CREATE TABLE grades (
            id INTEGER PRIMARY KEY,
            subj_a INTEGER NOT NULL,
            subj_b INTEGER NOT NULL,
            subj_c INTEGER NOT NULL
)";
if ($sqlite->queryExec($sql) == true) {
  echo 'New table created.';
} else {
  echo "ERROR: Could not execute $sql. " . sqlite_error_string($sqlite->lastError());
}

// close connection
unset($sqlite);
?>
```

7. The relevant PHP code is

```php
<?php
// attempt a connection
try {
    $mysql = new PDO('mysql:dbname=test;host=localhost', 'user', 'pass');
    $sqlite = new PDO('sqlite:a.db');
} catch (PDOException $e) {
    die("ERROR: Could not connect: " . $e->getMessage());
}

// prepare INSERT statement for SQLite
$sql_1 = "INSERT INTO grades (id, subj_a, subj_b, subj_c) VALUES (?, ?, ?, ?)";
if ($stmt = $sqlite->prepare($sql_1)) {

  // create and execute SELECT query for MySQL
  $sql_2 = "SELECT id, subj_a, subj_b, subj_c FROM grades";
  if ($result = $mysql->query($sql_2)) {

    // for each record
    // bind to prepared statement and insert into SQLite
    while($row = $result->fetch()) {
      $stmt->bindParam(1, $row[0]);
      $stmt->bindParam(2, $row[1]);
      $stmt->bindParam(3, $row[2]);
```

```
        $stmt->bindParam(4, $row[4]);
        $stmt->execute();
    }
    echo 'Record(s) successfully migrated.';

  } else {
    echo "ERROR: Could not execute $sql_2. " . print_r($mysql->errorInfo());
  }

} else {
  echo "ERROR: Could not prepare query: $sql_1. " . print_r($sqlite-
>errorInfo());
}

// close connection
unset($mysql);
unset($sqlite);
?>
```

Chapter 8: Working with XML

1. The two methods of parsing an XML document are the Simple API for XML (SAX)
   and the Document Object Model (DOM). SAX steps through the document, calling
   different user-defined functions to process different types of nodes. DOM reads the
   entire document into memory, generates a tree structure to represent it, and provides
   methods to move through the tree.

2. A well-formed XML document has a single root element, correctly nested elements,
   and valid element and attribute syntax.

3. The relevant PHP code is
   ```
   <?php
   // load XML file
   $xml = simplexml_load_file('email.xml') or die ("Unable to load
   XML!");

   // loop over XML <person> elements
   // get <email> child nodes and print
   foreach ($xml->person as $p) {
     echo $p->email . "\n";
   }
   ?>
   ```

4. The relevant PHP code is
   ```
   <?php
   // initialize new DOMDocument
   $doc = new DOMDocument();
   ```

```php
// disable whitespace-only text nodes
$doc->preserveWhiteSpace = false;

// read XML file
$doc->load('tree.xml');

// output: 'John'
echo $doc->firstChild->childNodes->item(2)->childNodes
 ->item(2)->childNodes->item(0)->childNodes->item(0)
 ->childNodes->item(0)->nodeValue;

// output: 'John'
echo $doc->getElementsByTagName('name')->item(0)->nodeValue;

// output: 'John'
echo $doc->getElementsByTagName('person')->item(4)
 ->childNodes->item(0)->nodeValue;
?>
```

5. The relevant PHP code is

```php
<?php
// initialize new DOMDocument
$doc = new DOMDocument();

// disable whitespace-only text nodes
$doc->preserveWhiteSpace = false;

// read XML file
$doc->load('library.xml');

// get all elements
// print size of collection
echo $doc->getElementsByTagName('*')->length . ' element(s) found.';
?>
```

6. The relevant PHP code is

```php
<?php
// load XML file
$xml = simplexml_load_file('library.xml') or die ("Unable to load XML!");

// loop over XML <book> elements
// increase each rating by 1
foreach ($xml->book as $b) {
  $b['rating'] = $b['rating'] + 1;
}

// print the revised XML
header('Content-Type: text/xml');
echo $xml->asXML();
?>
```

7. The relevant PHP code is

```php
<?php
// connect to database
try {
    $pdo = new PDO('mysql:dbname=test;host=localhost', 'user', 'pass');
} catch (PDOException $e) {
    echo "Error: Could not connect. " . $e->getMessage();
}

// set error mode
$pdo->setAttribute(PDO::ATTR_ERRMODE, PDO::ERRMODE_EXCEPTION);

try {
    // execute SELECT query
    $sql = "SELECT * FROM countries";
    $stmt = $pdo->query($sql);
    if ($stmt->rowCount() > 0) {
      // create a new DOM tree
      $doc = new DOMDocument('1.0');

      // create and attach root element <resultset>
      $root = $doc->createElement('resultset');
      $resultset = $doc->appendChild($root);

      while ($row = $stmt->fetch(PDO::FETCH_ASSOC)) {
        // loop over result set
        // set up <record> element for each row
        $record = $doc->createElement('record');
        $resultset->appendChild($record);

        foreach ($row as $name => $value) {
          // attach fields and values as <field>value</field>
          $field = $doc->createElement($name);
          $text = $doc->createTextNode($value);
          $record->appendChild($field);
          $field->appendChild($text);
        }
      }
    }
} catch (Exception $e) {
    echo "Error: Could not execute query \"$sql\". " . $e->getMessage();
    unset($pdo);
}

// close connection
// output XML string
unset($pdo);
header('Content-Type: text/xml');
echo $doc->saveXML();
?>
```

Chapter 9: Working with Cookies, Sessions, and Headers

1. With a cookie, user-specific information is stored on the user's system in a text file. With a session, this information is stored on the server in a text file or SQL database, and only a unique identifier referencing this information is stored on the user's system as a cookie.

2. To remove a previously set cookie, set the cookie's expiry date to a date in the past.

3. To register a session variable, save it as a key-value pair in the special $_SESSION associative array. This associative array is available in the global scope, so the session variable can then be accessed on any other page by referencing $_SESSION[key], after calling session_start().

4. HTTP headers must be sent before any output is generated by the script. Because the example script generates one line of output before sending the 'Location:' header, it will generate a fatal error.

5. The relevant PHP code is

A. Within the same session:

```php
<?php
session_start();
if (!isset($_SESSION['count'])) {
    $_SESSION['count'] = 0;
}
echo 'You have visited this page ' . $_SESSION['count'] . ' time(s).';
$_SESSION['count']++;
?>
```

B. Over different sessions:

```php
<?php
if (!isset($_COOKIE['count'])) {
    $count = 0;
} else {
    $count = $_COOKIE['count'];
}
setcookie('count', ($count+1), mktime()+2592000, '/');
echo 'You have visited this page ' . $count . ' time(s).';
?>
```

6. The relevant PHP code is

```php
<?php
session_start();
session_destroy();
header('Location:login.php');
?>
```

Chapter 10: Handling Errors

1. The exception-based model:

- Allows for different treatment of different error types.

- Produces cleaner, simpler code.

- Forces better analysis of error conditions.

- Allows for handling of unforeseen errors.

2. Fatal errors, startup errors, compile-time errors, and run-time parsing errors.

3. An output buffer is a temporary storage area in memory for script output. It is useful because it provides a "catchment area" for script output to be preprocessed before the user sees it. It comes in handy when working with PHP functions like setcookie(), header(), and session_start(), because it allows these functions to be invoked even after the script has generated some output.

The following example illustrates:

```php
<?php
// open output buffer
ob_start();

// send some output
// this gets stored in the buffer
echo 'Here is some output';

// send some headers
header('Content-Type: text/plain');
session_start();

// now display the output
ob_end_flush();
?>
```

4. For the first snippet, PHP's default error handler. For the second, handlerA()

5. The relevant PHP code is

```php
<?php
class Warning extends Exception { }
class Notice extends Exception { }
error_reporting(E_ALL);
set_error_handler('myHandler');

// custom error handler
function myHandler($type, $msg, $file, $line, $context) {
```

```php
    switch($type) {
      case E_NOTICE:
        throw new Notice($msg);
        break;

      case E_WARNING:
        throw new Warning($msg);
        break;

    }
  }

  try {
    echo 45/0;
  } catch (Notice $e) {
    echo 'NOTICE: ' . $e->getMessage();
  } catch (Warning $e) {
    echo 'WARNING: ' . $e->getMessage();
  } catch (Exception $e) {
    echo 'ERROR: ' . $e->getMessage();
  }
  ?>
```

6. The relevant PHP code is

```php
<?php
// define exception
class OtherException extends Exception { }
class YetAnotherException extends Exception { }

// set custom handler
set_exception_handler('myHandler');

// custom error handler
function myHandler($e) {
  $body = "Uncaught exception: " . $e->getMessage() . " at line " .
$e->getLine() . " of " . $e->getFile();
  @mail('admin@domain', 'Uncaught exception', $body, 'From:
bounce@domain');
}

try {
  throw new OtherException('Catch me if you can.');
} catch (YetAnotherException $e) {
  echo $e->getMessage();
}
?>
```

Chapter 11: Securing PHP

1. An *SQL injection attack* involves attackers manipulating your application database using input containing SQL statements. Proper input sanitization and validation can help prevent such an attack.

   A *cross-site scripting attack* involves attackers embedding rogue JavaScript or HTML code into your Web pages. Output sanitization can help prevent such an attack.

   A *session hijack* involves attackers intercepting and using a client session to gain access and privileges not normally available to them. Adding additional client-specific tokens to your session security system can help prevent such an attack.

2. The relevant PHP code is

```php
<?php
$str = '<div>
  <form action="http://www.evildomain.com/evilscript.php">
    <input type="hidden" name="op" value="add" />
    <input type="hidden" name="user" value="me" />
    <input type="hidden" name="pass" value="guessme" />
  </form>
';

// using strip_tags()
$sanitized['str'] = strip_tags($str);

// using htmlentities()
$sanitized['str'] = htmlentities($str);
?>
```

3. The relevant PHP code is

```php
<?php
// function to validate a U.S. postal code
// test if input is of the form ddddd-dddd
function validatePostalCode($str) {
    return preg_match("/^\d{5}(-\d{4})?$/" ,$str);
}
?>
```

4. Error messages can contain valuable information about your application's database schema, file naming conventions, file system structures, and data persistence mechanisms. This information could be used by attackers to find vulnerable areas in your application and craft more focused attacks. For this reason, error display in production environments should be disabled (although errors should still be logged to a separate file or database).

5. The following table lists what each function does:

Function	What It Does
ctype_alnum()	Tests if input contains only alphabetic and numeric characters
addslashes()	Escapes special characters in input with slashes
filter_var()	Tests if input matches a specified pattern
htmlentities()	Automatically converts special characters in input to the corresponding HTML entity
sqlite_escape_string()	Escapes input with quotes before inserting it into an SQLite database
preg_match()	Tests if input matches a specified regular expression
strval()	Returns the string value of input

Chapter 12: Extending PHP

1. PEAR packages consist of PHP classes that can be directly loaded and used in a PHP script. PECL packages consist of language modules that must be compiled into the PHP engine.

2. The steps to install a PECL extension in a Windows development environment are

A. Visit the PECL4WIN Web site and download a precompiled .DLL file for the extension.

B. Copy this precompiled file into PHP's extension directory.

C. Activate the extension by placing a line such as extension=ext.dll in the *php.ini* configuration file.

D. Restart the Web server to load the new extension.

3. The relevant PHP code is

```php
<?php
// create object
require_once 'Net/POP3.php';
$pop3 =& new Net_POP3();

// connect to host
if(PEAR::isError($ret = $pop3->connect($host, $port))){
    die($ret->getMessage());
}

// log in
if(PEAR::isError($ret = $pop3->login($user, $pass, 'USER'))){
    die($ret->getMessage());
}
```

```php
// get number of messages and mailbox size
echo $pop3->numMsg() . ' message(s) in mailbox, ' . $pop3->getSize() .
' bytes <p/>';

// get content of most recent message
if ($pop3->numMsg() > 0) {
  echo '<pre>' . $pop3->getMsg($pop3->numMsg()) . '</pre>';
}

// disconnect
$pop3->disconnect();
?>
```

4. The relevant PHP code is

```php
<?php
// initialize an iterator
// pass it the directory to be processed
$iterator = new RecursiveIteratorIterator(new RecursiveDirectoryIterator
("music/"));

// iterate over the directory
// get ID3 tag information for each file
foreach ($iterator as $key=>$value) {
  $tag = id3_get_tag(realpath($key));
  echo trim($tag['artist']) . ' - ' . trim($tag['title']);
  echo "<br/>";
}
?>
```

Index

D